ORIGINS OF CLASS STRUGGLE
IN LOUISIANA

Origins of Class Struggle in Louisiana

A Social History of White Farmers and Laborers
during Slavery and After, 1840-1875

By ROGER W. SHUGG

LOUISIANA STATE UNIVERSITY PRESS

ISBN 0-8071-0739-5 (cloth)
ISBN 0-8071-0136-2 (paper)
Library of Congress Catalog Card Number 39-33962
Copyright 1939 by Louisiana State University Press
Copyright renewed 1967 by Roger W. Shugg
Preface to the paperback edition copyright © 1968 by Louisiana State
University Press

TABLE OF CONTENTS

ABBREVIATIONS IN FOOTNOTES

Accts., Accounts
A.H.R., American Historical Review
Agric., Agriculture
Am., American
Annals, Annals of the American Academy of Political and Social Science
Assn., Association
Audit., Auditor
Bd., Board
Bull., Bulletin
Bur., Bureau
Cen., Census
Com., Commissioner, Committee
Cong., Congress
Const., Constitution, Constitutional
Conv., Convention
Debs., Debates
Dept., Department
Docs., Documents
Educ., Education
Emig., Emigration
Ex., Executive
Fed., Federation
G.A., [La.] General Assembly
Gen., General
H., [La.] House of Representatives
Hist., Historical
H.R., [U.S.] House of Representatives
Immig., Immigration
Inst., Institute
J., Journal
La., Louisiana
Legisl., Legislative
L.H.Q., Louisiana Historical Quarterly
Miscel., Miscellaneous
Msg., Message
M.V.H.R., Mississippi Valley Historical Review
Ofc., Official, Office
O.R., Official Records, War of the Rebellion
Prelim., Preliminary
Proc., Proceedings
Pub., Public
Q., Quarterly
R., Review
Rpt., Report

Secy., Secretary
Sen., Senate
Sess., Session
Soc., Society
Spec., Special
Suppl., Supplement
Supt., Superintendent
Svc., Service
U.S., United States

N.B. All newspapers were published in New Orleans
unless cited by the name of a town or parish.

PREFACE

In these essays an attempt is made to isolate the white farmers and laborers of Louisiana as a class in order to analyze their situation and condition in a society that passed through war from slave to free labor. The Negro is considered in his relation to the whites but excluded from the category of the masses because he always belonged to a racial caste rather than a social class. This investigation was a backward extension of research in local Populism, the agrarian crusade of the nineties, which appeared to be a class struggle without any roots except the current economic depression unless some continuity could be established with earlier decades. My study, briefly stated, shows that the structure and relation of classes had long been in conflict, but it failed to come to any issue, except for the Civil War and abolition of slavery, because of the bondage of one race, the military rule of another, and the institutions and conditions of the day.

It is my hope that these essays may suggest the value of examining local history in terms of classes. I have deliberately avoided treating them from a purely Marxian point of view because there was not sufficient evidence to justify it. Readers who regard classes as fictions and disagree with my interpretation of them may nevertheless find some interesting facts of a general nature in these pages. It is information of this kind that I have tried to add to our knowledge of the history of Louisiana. The Historical Records Survey has recently uncovered rich stores of material, and from these sources the deficiencies of my investigation are bound to be repaired by other students.

All the chapters in this book except the last were originally presented to Princeton University in a different form in partial fulfillment of the requirements for the degree of Doctor of Philosophy.

Although no one but myself is responsible for this work, I have incurred many obligations in the course of it. Especially to be thanked are Professor T. J. Wertenbaker of Princeton, who supervised the research with much patience; Dean John Pomfret of Vanderbilt, who gave me helpful advice; Professor Walter Prichard of Louisiana State University, who kindly read the manuscript and saved me from at least a few errors; and Mr. M. M. Wilkerson, Director of the Louisiana State University Press, who took great interest in the production of this volume and kindly attended to the proofs in my absence.

To Professor Clifton R. Hall of Princeton I owe most, and much more than this book indicates. Likewise, to Mr. C. H. Bowden, my parents, and my wife, I am grateful for what cannot be easily acknowledged.

R. S.

PREFACE TO PAPERBACK EDITION

"It is impossible," says Golo Mann, "to hide when—in the intellectual climate of which decade—a book was written." [1] Any reader of this study of Louisiana in the nineteenth century will recognize it as a product of the Depression of the 1930's and of the historical philosophy of Charles and Mary Beard. Intellectual fashions and concerns change so fast, with almost every successive decade bringing forth a new kind of revisionism in historical thinking, that the evidence and interpretations in this book would probably be quite different if I were to do my research and writing anew today.

The title would certainly be changed, because its present phrasing has misled so many readers into expecting the book to be a neo-Marxian study of local history, even though I warned them in my original preface that I had no such purpose or intention. My first choice of title for this book was "The Plain People of Louisiana," but a librarian who read the manuscript told the publisher that he would classify it as sociology, not history, because it dealt with class struggle. With the brashness of youth, I adopted the librarian's phrase as my title. Much better would have been simply "Class Conflict in Louisiana," because the elements of a Marxian struggle between classes were never to be found in any Southern state.

Strangely, this study of Louisiana's social history in terms of classes, and of conflict between them, proves to be more in accord with the thinking of these late 1960's than with that of the 1930's or, certainly, with that of the period about which I wrote. In those earlier times the prevailing concept of American democracy was one of a classless society; we are now

[1] *The History of Germany Since 1789* (New York, 1968), ix.

xi

coming to see that whether we choose to recognize or to
ignore the class divisions among us, they do exist and are of
crucial importance in explaining how our government and
our economy work.

A serious shortcoming of this study, which no reviewer, to
my knowledge, has ever pointed out, is its exclusion of the
Negro "from the category of the masses because," as I claimed
in my preface, "he always belonged to a racial caste rather
than a social class." I fell into this error because I drew from
reading Du Bois, Risley, and Senart a false analogy to the element of *varna*, or color, in the caste system of India. The
Negro, both as slave and as freedman, should have been a direct concern of my investigation if I hoped to explain adequately the economic and social class conflict in Louisiana,
because it was the Negro who was the proletarian performing
the most profitable agricultural labor of the State. He does
bulk large in this study, of course, especially during Reconstruction, and that is why the late Howard K. Beale recognized the book as one of the first "revisionist" histories of Reconstruction.[2]

Among his criticisms of the book, Beale emphasized my
failure to carry the analysis through the Bourbon restoration
into the flowering of Populism so as to compare Bourbon conservatism with Reconstruction radicalism. He was right, and
others have since made good this deficiency, notably C. Vann
Woodward in his several books, especially in his *Reunion and
Reaction* (1951) and *Origins of the New South* (1951).

Nevertheless, in respect to the span of time this book covers, I can claim that it was among the first to break away
from the rigid periodization of *ante-bellum* and *post-bellum*
established by the Civil War with effects as arbitrary and un-
historical as the classic B.C. and A.D. I sought to demonstrate

---

[2]"On Rewriting Reconstruction History," *American Historical Review*,
XLV (July, 1940), 807–27.

that nothing could be understood about an American state before the Civil War unless it was also studied after the war —and, because of the dangers of "present-mindedness" in history, vice versa.

It is only fair to remind the reader that the most serious criticism of this book was made by the late Frank L. Owsley when he reviewed it in the *Journal of Southern History*.[3] He contended that my analysis of the nonslaveholding yeomanry was distorted because in the three chapters on social and economic conditions before the Civil War, as well as in the statistical appendixes, I made "little distinction between the landed and the landless" and lumped together "all nonslaveholders as proletarians . . . ." Using the unpublished Federal Census records of 1850 and 1860, as I had not done, Owsley developed this argument in his book, *Plain Folk of the Old South* (1949).

I confess that I remain unconvinced even though a majority of historians appear to have adopted Owsley's views. The fact that yeomen farmers owned small tracts of land and cultivated them without slave labor has never seemed very significant to me, because land is only one of the three classic factors in production; labor and capital, both of which the farmer lacked, are equally important. Owsley, at one time a Southern Agrarian, was inclined, in my opinion, to draw too idyllic a picture of the prospering Southern farmer in the 1850's and to assign him too large a role in the region's economy. I tend to stand rather with M. I. Finley: "What counts in evaluating the place of slavery in any society is . . . not absolute totals or proportions, but rather *location* and *function*. If the economic and political elite depended primarily on slave labor for basic production, then one may speak of a slave society. It does not matter, in such situations, whether

[3]Vol. VI (February, 1940), 116–17.

as many as three-fourths were not slaveholders." [4] Or were small landowning farmers, I would add.

For an economic historian's appraisal of the thesis of Owsley and his followers, and a better defense of my analysis than I could make, the reader should consult Fabien Linden's long article on "Economic Democracy in the Slave South" in the *Journal of Negro History*.[5] It has been too often overlooked; at least I have never found or read a refutation of Linden's views and of both the theoretical and the factual evidence he marshals to support them.

Yet many important studies on every aspect of slavery and Reconstruction have been published since my book first came out in 1939, and an entire generation of working historians have enlarged and refined my interpretations. I hope that this earlier study of mine is still worth reading because so many of these historians have found it of some value and stimulus for their own endeavors.

Roger W. Shugg

Albuquerque, New Mexico
June, 1968

---

[4] "Slavery," *International Encyclopedia of the Social Sciences* (New York, 1968), Vol. XIV.
[5] Vol. XXXI (April, 1946), 140–89.

ORIGINS OF CLASS STRUGGLE
IN LOUISIANA

CHAPTER I

THE TRAVELERS' VIEW RECONSIDERED

> Throughout this country, the region of planta-
> tions is the region of wealth and sickness, and of
> the pine woods, of health and poverty.
> —TIMOTHY FLINT [1]

Among the host of travelers attracted to the Old South by a
curiosity in slavery and the picturesque plantation agriculture,[2]
there were few who could resist the temptation to visit Louisiana. It appeared to be the most colorful and romantic of
Southern states.[3] What gave it glamour was the Creole heritage
derived from French colonization early in the eighteenth century, followed by a brief spell of Spanish rule, and the subtropical cultivation of sugar cane which had been introduced
from Santo Domingo. In the lower parishes were to be found
the sugar plantations of a people descended from French and
Acadian settlers, devoted like their ancestors to the Catholic
faith, fluent in a foreign tongue, and tenacious of peculiar folk-
ways.[4] The metropolis of this alien culture was New Orleans,
largest city of the Old South. Long after its Creole population

[1] *Recollections of the Last Ten Years, etc.* (Boston, 1826), 329.

[2] See F. R. Brink, "Literary Travellers in Louisiana between 1803 and 1860"
(unpublished master's thesis, Louisiana State University, 1929), and works
cited in the following pages. For a good bibliography of travels published
between 1763 and 1846, see W. P. Trent *et al.*, eds., *The Cambridge History
of American Literature* (New York, 1917), I, 468–90; and for French travelers, F. Monaghan, *French Travellers in the United States 1765–1932* (New
York, 1932).

[3] D. A. Dondore, *The Prairie and the Making of Middle America: Four
Centuries of Description* (Cedar Rapids, Iowa, 1926), 364.

[4] For an interesting popular account, see L. Saxon, *Old Louisiana* (New
York, 1929), *passim.*

was outnumbered by the immigration of Americans, Irish, and Germans, New Orleans retained the appearance of "a provincial town in France, badly paved, badly drained, badly kept," but alive with Gallic gaiety.[5]

Visitors who gazed upon this strange panorama early in the last century had reason to doubt if lower Louisiana belonged to the South, or even to the United States, so marked was the contrast in their cultural landscapes. Timothy Flint, the far-wandering New England schoolmaster, observed these differences in 1823, when they were fast vanishing under the influence of American domination.[6] Not until a traveler journeyed northward, up the Red River beyond Alexandria or up the Mississippi above Baton Rouge, did he find the landmarks which characterized the South as a section, the pine-clad uplands and broad fields of cotton, owned by inhabitants of English and Scotch-Irish stock, Protestant in faith.[7] Louisiana was one state only in name and government; in other respects it comprised two regions and peoples of dissimilar culture.

Every traveler, as is the habit of his kind, described Louisiana in the bright colors of what appeared strangest to him. Since the majority of travelers were Englishmen or Americans, acquainted with slavery and cotton planting in other Southern states, it followed that in Louisiana their attention was drawn chiefly to the unfamiliar features of Creole life, the busy traffic and high levees along the Mississippi River, the splendid mansions of sugar planters and their peculiar ways of growing this staple. Of equal interest was New Orleans, for it was also anomalous in the rural South. Because travelers were fascinated chiefly by these aspects of Louisiana, they recorded in their writings a picture of the life of planters, merchants, and slaves,

[5] Francis and Theresa Pulszky, *White, Red, Black, Sketches of American Society, etc.* (New York, 1853), II, 93.

[6] *Op. cit.,* 300.

[7] Cf. R. B. Vance, *Human Factors in Cotton Culture* (Chapel Hill, N. C., 1929), chap. I.

with the Creole in the foreground. It remains an excellent if incomplete picture of ante-bellum society, not the whole truth but true within its limits, and especially significant because it reveals the fact that the Mississippi River fed the low-lying river bottoms, which gave rise to rich plantatio⅂ agriculture, which in turn enhanced the prosperity of New Orleans—all of which, like the house that Jack built, made Louisiana a wealthy and important state.

The geography of the region was partly responsible for what the traveler saw and confirmed the truth of what he reported. What altitude there is makes a land which in geological formation was once a submarine deposit, then a prehistoric swamp, and finally an American kind of Netherlands.[8] From an elevation of nearly 500 feet on its Arkansas border, Louisiana slopes gently southward to desolate coast marshes that dissolve into the Gulf of Mexico.[9] The entire area has an average altitude of only 100 feet; one-third of the surface is hardly half as high, and actually lies below the banks of rivers running through it. This immense lowland is saved from flood by levees from ten to fifty feet in height, which extend over 1,700 miles in length.[10] The eastern part of the state belongs to the flood delta of the Mississippi, "an immense plain, intersected by rivers and chequered with lakes." [11] These waters cover a twenty-fifth portion of the entire state.[12]

[8] E. King, *The Great South* (Hartford, Conn., 1875), 67.

[9] E. W. Hilgard, "Report on the Cotton Production of the State of Louisiana, with a Discussion of the General Agricultural Features of the State," *U. S. Cen., 1880, Rpt. on Cotton Production*, I, 113, 123. (Cited hereafter as Hilgard *Rpt.*)

[10] *Ibid.*, 119; *U. S. Cen., 1910, Suppl. on La.*, 607; J. H. Foster, "Forest Conditions in Louisiana," U. S. Dept. Agric., *Forest Svc. Bull. no. 114* (Washington, 1912), 6.

[11] W. Darby, *Geographical Description of the State of Louisiana*, 2nd ed. (New York, 1817), 49.

[12] W. H. Harris, *Louisiana* (New Orleans, 1885), 4. According to J. D. B. De Bow, following Forshey, "about *one eighth* of the state is constantly

Rivers were the chief architects of Louisiana.[13] They flooded the country with fertile mud before levees held them to their channels. As their banks were raised high enough to contain all but the worst spring freshets, they were tamed into carriers of commerce. These streams have made rich with alluvium and trade the land which they once threatened to submerge in swamps.[14] The greatest river, of course, is the far-reaching Mississippi, which drains from a vast hinterland between the Allegheny and Rocky Mountains the soil and produce that have made Louisiana equally prosperous in agriculture and commerce.[15] Flowing down through the northwestern part of the state into the Mississippi is the Red River; together these muddy watercourses form a meandering, Y-shaped drainage basin which has always been the alluvial seat of the most profitable agriculture.[16] From the north also comes the Ouachita; to the south run the Atchafalaya and Lafourche, which serve as outlets of the Mississippi.

In few parts of the world has there been deposited so much alluvial soil as in Louisiana, where it makes up one-third of the land.[17] These so-called river bottoms expand to a width of thirty miles along the banks of the Mississippi from the Tensas cotton belt in the northeast to the spreading "Sugar Bowl" of the delta, which extends seventy miles beyond the coast line

---

under water, and . . . more than *two fifths* of it are subject to inundation." De Bow, *Encyclopaedia of the Trade and Commerce of the United States, more particularly of the Southern and Western States: etc.*, 2nd ed. (London, 1854), II, 149.

[13] S. H. Lockett, "Louisiana As It Is" (Baton Rouge, 1873), 143. [An unpublished MS, Howard Memorial Library.]

[14] R. B. Vance, *Human Geography of the South* (Chapel Hill, N. C., 1932), chap. XI.

[15] *Ibid.*, 263–68; Lockett MS, 144; *U. S. Cen., 1880, Rpt. on Cities*, 270; De Bow, *op. cit.*, II, 143, for New Orleans imports from the interior between 1841 and 1851.

[16] Foster, *op. cit.*, 5.   [17] *U. S. Cen., 1910, loc. cit.*

to the southeast.[18] Alluvial soil is also to be found for about five miles on either side of the Red River, and along the banks of the Black, Ouachita, Atchafalaya, and Lafourche. This region is a "land of low ridges, flats, cypress swamps, canebrakes, sloughs, and bayous, covered everywhere with great hardwood forests."[19] The black and brown clay is so prodigally fertile that it yields more cotton and sugar than other Southern soil.[20] It is so deep, moreover, as to be almost inexhaustible,[21] and through fifty years of unvaried cultivation produces crops which finally diminish to only half the size of the first.[22]

Such rich land could be profitably exploited only by rich planters. It early brought prices beyond the reach of newcomers without plenty of capital. Indeed, none but the wealthy could afford to cultivate, much less to buy, these river bottoms.[23] The danger of floods made it necessary to protect them with great earthworks, and the cost of constructing these levees at first fell directly on riparian proprietors.[24] Nor was this the chief expense of river bottom agriculture. Sugar plantations required machinery to grind the cane,[25] and cotton plantations a large number of workers to clear and drain the

[18] Hilgard *Rpt.*, 111, 149, 156; Isaiah Bowman, *Forest Physiography* (New York, 1911), 526.

[19] F. E. Dorriss, "The Yazoo Basin in Mississippi," *Journal of Geography*, XXVIII (February, 1929), 72–81. These words also apply to Louisiana; see Bowman, *op. cit.*, 526.

[20] *U. S. Cen., 1860, Prelim. Rpt.*, 200–1. After 1870 the black, waxy prairie of Texas rivaled Mississippi alluvium; since 1900 the boll weevil has hurt both regions.

[21] *De Bow's Review*, IX (July, 1850), 290.

[22] *The American Farmer*, X (1828), 236; Hilgard *Rpt.*, 115, 150.

[23] U. B. Phillips, "Plantations with Slave Labor and Free," *A. H. R.*, XXX (July, 1925), 746.

[24] E. g., J. H. Rills, ed., *A New Digest of the Laws of the Parish of Iberville* (Plaquemine, La., 1859), Art. 136.

[25] F. L. Olmsted, *A Journey in the Seaboard Slave States* (New York, 1856), 669.

land, for the heavy alluvial clay demanded more labor than other soils.[26] This labor was recruited by the purchase of slaves, because the lowlands were so malarial that only the Negro was thought to be capable of working here.[27]

Since agriculture in the river bottoms called for so much capital and Negro labor,[28] this region became the seat of slave plantations, "the big business of colonial and ante-bellum times." [29] From the concentration of slaves on plantations developed a black belt, over three-fourths of which was alluvial.[30] It was a clear example of the fact that good soil was prerequisite to the growth of a slave plantation economy. Only four alluvial parishes lay outside the black belt: Jefferson and Orleans were urban, Lafourche was marshy, and Caldwell, thinly settled. But eight of the thirty-one black belt parishes in 1860 were not completely alluvial : three, East Baton Rouge, East and West Feliciana, were covered by a loess of equal fertility; four, Bossier, Caddo, De Soto, and Natchitoches, embraced large tracts of Red River bottoms. Finally, ten alluvial parishes, Carroll, Concordia, Madison, Rapides, Tensas, Ascension, Assumption, St. James, St. Mary, and Terrebonne, were the heart of the black belt: the first five produced the most cotton, the second five, the most sugar; together they raised half the cotton and sugar grown in Louisiana. Inhabited by hardly one-tenth of the free people, these parishes contained one-third of the slaves, one-fifth of all plantations over

[26] Ibid., 663; The Southern Planter, XII (1852), 28.

[27] This common ante-bellum notion was a superstition, a rationalization of slavery, or both; white mortality, omitting cholera from which slaves suffered most, was less than black in the swamp parishes in 1850. See E. D. Fenner, ed., Southern Medical Reports, II (1850), 152.

[28] Phillips, "Origin and Growth of the Southern Black Belts," A. H. R., XI (July, 1906), 798.

[29] Phillips, op. cit., A. H. R., XXX (July, 1925), 745; F. V. Emerson, "Geographic Influences in American Slavery," Bulletin of the American Geographical Society, XLIII (1911), 175.

[30] Appendix, Table 2.

fifty acres in size, and two-fifths of the assessed wealth outside New Orleans.[31] The entire black belt was wonderfully rich in 1860. It produced the largest part of the two staples, sugar and cotton.[32] Only a quarter of the free people lived here,[33] but this minority owned half the wealth, two-thirds of the slaves, and nearly half the plantations in Louisiana.[34] No other region could compare with this black belt.[35] Here the average planter boasted of more slaves than elsewhere in the South,[36] and the size of his estate was surpassed only in Texas.[37]

The wealth and importance of the planting interest in Louisiana impressed all travelers. They rarely spared adjectives, however shy of dull statistics, to describe it. But few travelers realized that the plantation system [38] was not in exclusive possession of the lowlands. Large parts of the river bottoms, swampy,[39] densely timbered,[40] or remote from transportation,[41] were ill adapted to extensive agriculture. One observant foreigner remarked of the Mississippi River Coast in 1857, "I could but notice how little of this rich country was cultivated, and how thin a belt of land made profitable by the plough extended between the dark river and the darker forest which

[31] Cf. Appendix, Tables 1, 2, 3.   [32] Appendix, Table 2.

[33] Unlike some Southern states before 1860, Louisiana had little absentee ownership; only in Carroll, Livingston, and Morehouse was as much as a fifth of the real estate owned by nonresidents. See *Rpt. La. Audit. Pub. Accts., 1861,* 3–106.

[34] Appendix, Table 2.   [35] *U. S. Cen., 1860, Agric.,* 202.

[36] In 1860 the median slaveholding was 23 in the entire South, 32.5 in the lower South, and 49.3 in Louisiana. L. C. Gray, *History of Agriculture in the Southern United States to 1860* (Washington, 1933), I, 530. Cf. Appendix, Table 6.

[37] *U. S. Cen., 1910,* V, 75.

[38] Hereafter the term "plantation" is used to designate farms of more than 50 acres before 1860, and farms of more than 100 acres after 1860; the former were generally worked by slaves, and the latter rented to Negroes and whites. See chaps. IV, VIII.

[39] Hilgard *Rpt.,* 157; Bowman, *Forest Physiography,* 526.

[40] *Ibid.,* 149; Foster, *op. cit.,* 14–17.   [41] See below, 106–7.

bounded the view on every side." [42] Where the planter could not take his slaves—into the forest and swamps—the humble farmer found a happy refuge. Small farms were especially numerous along bayous which cut the land up into such narrow tracts that it could be cultivated only in patches.[43] The French custom of dividing paternal acres among all male children restricted poor Creoles and Acadians to small plots.[44] In the alluvial region, therefore, over half the landholdings were farms under fifty acres in size, and over half the white inhabitants owned no slaves. Even among the planters a large majority were yeomen with less than six Negroes.[45]

Travelers were correct in their report that large plantations dominated the river bottoms, because these estates produced the bulk of staples like cotton and sugar.[46] But it was the size and wealth of plantations, not their number, which gave the lowlands a feudal appearance. Slave estates were most conspicuous, but small farms more numerous.[47]

The principal deficiency in travelers' writings arose from their failure to journey beyond the river bottoms. They naturally went where it was comfortable, interesting, or profitable to go, along the Mississippi and in New Orleans, and seldom penetrated the interior. The larger part of Louisiana,

---

[42] C. Mackay, *Life and Liberty in America* (London, 1859), I, 259–60.

[43] Olmsted, *The Cotton Kingdom* (New York, 1861), II, 44–45. In one part of Assumption, for example, land was so broken that forty-six farms were located within a radius of one mile, according to A. Henry and V. Gerodias, eds., *The Louisiana Coast Directory* (New Orleans, 1857), 41–43.

[44] Olmsted, *op. cit.*, II, 46; W. H. Russell, *My Diary North and South* (London, 1863), I, 403. Innumerable cases of small sugar and rice patches cultivated by individuals with the same family name can be found in Henry and Gerodias, *op. cit.*, *passim*. Not all these people were Acadians; in Lafourche and Terrebonne were groups of poor Creole farmers. *Ibid.*, 46–47; *The American Farmer*, X (1828), 236.

[45] Appendix, Tables 1, 3.   [46] Gray, *op. cit.*, II, 896–98.

[47] *De Bow's Review*, VI, 457; and see below, 77–78.

with its swamps, bayous, lakes, prairies, sandy pine flats, and forested hills, was inaccessible.[48] Of the travelers who published accounts of their journeys, none except Olmsted and a few others traversed the back country where plantations gave way to farms, and farms to the frontier and wilderness.[49] The geography of these regions will serve to reveal their importance and the forgotten but humble folk who inhabited them.

Oak and pine uplands were exclusively "the poor man's paradise." [50] They cover the northwestern parishes, the upper part of the "Florida parishes," [51] and altogether, about half the state.[52] Although the soil is considerably varied, it is like that of the Atlantic coastal tablelands stretching from Maine to Texas.[53] Except for ferruginous red and brown loam on the oak-clad ridges, fertile enough to withstand exhaustive tillage, the upland is light and sandy, and yields but half the cotton of the river bottoms.[54] Other natural features rendered these hills unattractive to plantation agriculture.[55] Forests of

[48] As late as 1855, during an epidemic of yellow fever, there was "scarcely any communication at all" between Shreveport and New Orleans; transportation was intermittent and expensive along the Red River. Isabel B. Williamson to her father, E. G. W. Butler, Sept. 9, 1855, *Butler* MS [Duke University Library].

[49] One-third of Louisiana, estimated at ten and a half million acres, had not even been surveyed by the public land office in 1850. De Bow, *Encyclopaedia of the Trade and Commerce . . .* , I, 443.

[50] J. B. Robertson, *Memorials and Explorations* (New Orleans, 1867), 7.

[51] The five northeastern parishes of Louisiana, between the Mississippi and Pearl rivers, were called the Florida parishes because Spain retained them as part of (West) Florida when retroceding Louisiana to France in 1800. They became part of the United States by insurrection in 1810.

[52] Harris, *Louisiana*, 4.

[53] Hilgard *Rpt.*, 128. The Louisiana uplands belong to this interior coastal plain, which also embraces parts of Texas and Arkansas. See Vance, *Human Geography of the South*, 88.

[54] Hilgard *Rpt.*, 105–6, 127, 132–33. The alluvial lowlands averaged three-fourths of a bale of cotton per acre, the uplands, two-fifths of a bale.

[55] Appendix, Table 1.

oak and pine covered the rolling country and made it hard to penetrate;[56] slowly at first the pioneer's axe, then swiftly after the Civil War the lumber syndicate's sawmill, opened these dense woods.[57] Where the land lay thinly timbered, it was often situated miles from any bayou plied by steamboats, and in places so remote from commercial markets, staple crops were as useless as self-sufficient agriculture was necessary.[58] Consequently, the uplands were never as much sought after nor as well settled as the lowlands. Where they were not open to pre-emption, and later to homestead entry, their price ranged from fifty cents to three and six dollars an acre throughout the last century.[59] Small wonder that poor men settled them.

The uplands were actively sought by men with little or no capital, yeomen farmers, pioneers, and squatters, in preference to other regions. If the soil produced less cotton, it also sprouted fewer weeds than the wet river bottoms, and it required neither drainage nor deep plowing.[60] In the hills could be found timber for fuel and log cabins, and a family could live on game from the forest and fish from the bayou, while their cattle and swine rooted the woods for mast even in winter.[61] Another attraction was the climate, which was generally thought to be superior to the miasmic and malarial lowlands.[62] These advantages combined to draw the poorer elements of the population to the pine and oak hills. Here

[56] In Winn Parish, for example, but 10 per cent of the land was cleared as late as 1907. *Rpt. U. S. Bur. Soils, 1907,* 599.

[57] *Idem;* Lockett MS, 223; F. V. Emerson, "The Southern Long-Leaf Pine Belt," *Geographical Review,* VII (February, 1919), 82.

[58] *Crescent,* Aug. 6, 11, 1860.   [59] See below, chaps. IV, VIII.

[60] *Crescent,* July 18, 1860; *The Southern Planter,* XII (1852), 28.

[61] D. R. Hundley, *Social Relations in Our Southern States* (New York, 1860), 261-62; *Rpt. U. S. Bur. Soils, 1904,* 376.

[62] This was the common belief, whatever doctors might assert on the basis of mortality statistics in *Southern Medical Rpts., loc. cit.*

lived one-third of the white people outside New Orleans in 1860. This minority owned nearly half of all the farms in the state under fifty acres in size.[63] With a fifth of the slaves divided among them in very small holdings, they produced but an equal proportion of the cotton, and were assessed for scarcely a ninth part of the state's wealth.[64] These proportions did not change materially after the Civil War.[65]

There is no longer any need to distinguish the oak uplands from the pine hills because much of the oak was cut long ago and most of the land is now in pine.[66] But a word is necessary lest their original difference be overlooked. As the oak tree is everywhere a sign of fertile soil, the land upon which it stood was superior to piney woods.[67] Yeomen slaveholders naturally preferred boundaries of oak, where they settled and prospered, leaving the pine forests chiefly to those without slaves. The result was that by 1860 the area defined by oak trees merged into the black belt, produced almost all the cotton and had the larger share of wealth in the uplands. The piney woods were sparsely inhabited by white people of little means. Small farms were predominant in both regions, however, with at least three out of five agrarian holdings under fifty acres.[68]

Altogether different from the rolling, timbered uplands were the level and comparatively treeless prairies to the south.[69] They form about one-tenth of the area of Louisiana and extend along the Gulf into Texas.[70] This region comprised three types of soil, good, bad, and indifferent. Black calcareous loam of considerable fertility bordered the coast marsh, but as late as 1880 attracted few settlers; the Calcasieu prairie of silt pine land was valuable chiefly for timber; and

[63] U. S. Cen., 1860, Agric., 202.   [64] Appendix, Table 1.
[65] Cf. Rpt. La. Audit. Pub. Accts., 1880, passim.   [66] Foster, op. cit., 9.
[67] Hilgard Rpt., 105–6.   [68] Appendix, Table 1.
[69] Hilgard Rpt., 124.   [70] Harris, Louisiana, 4.

the Attakapas prairie of brown clay grew a coarse grass excellent for pasturage.[71] Before the Civil War the inhabitants were mainly of French or Acadian stock.[72] The richest owned but a few slaves, and the majority had none; but their landholdings were large because of the extensive pastures required for foraging cattle.[73] The thrifty Creoles of this vicinity raised some cotton, sugar cane, and rice,[74] and supplied modest wants with cattle and corn, the basis of their livestock and self-sufficing agriculture.[75] The prairies were so isolated before the Civil War that they contained relatively few inhabitants.[76] Thirty years later, when railroads brought in thousands of Northern immigrants to transform the land into thriving fields of rice,[77] this region embraced only 10 per cent of the state's population.[78]

Pine barrens were the characteristic home of poor whites throughout the Old South.[79] This white, "crawfishy" soil of sand and clay covers but 8 per cent of the area of Louisiana.[80] Pine flats extend along the Pearl River, which is the lower boundary of Mississippi to the east, and along the Sabine River, which cuts off Texas in the west. A small proportion of people lived in either district before 1860.[81] But they did not escape notice by the two travelers who went farthest into the back country, Flint and Olmsted. The former observed many families respectably engaged in felling timber and herding cattle on the flats of the Florida parishes as early as 1824.[82]

[71] Hilgard Rpt., 124–27.
[72] Olmsted, A Journey through Texas (New York, 1857), 394–97.
[73] Rpt. U. S. Bur. Soils, 1901, 622.
[74] Rpt. La. Audit. Pub. Accts., 1855, 33–51.
[75] R. Taylor, Destruction and Reconstruction (New York, 1879), 105–6.
[76] U. S. Cen., 1860, Prelim. Rpt., 262.
[77] M. K. Ginn, "History of Rice Production in Louisiana to 1896" (unpublished master's thesis, Louisiana State University, 1930), 32–35.
[78] U. S. Cen., 1890, I, 490.   [79] De Bow's Review, XXXI, 361–63.
[80] Harris, op. cit., 4; Hilgard Rpt., 128.   [81] See above, n. 76.
[82] Recollections of the Last Ten Years, 317.

The latter saw a less respectable variety of outlaws, "clay-eaters," and half-breeds who ranged stolen cattle on the banks of the Sabine in the fifties.[83] These poor whites were few in number and peculiar to Louisiana.[84]

In addition to uplands, prairies, and pine flats, the other thinly settled regions of the state were the Mississippi River bluffs and Gulf Coast marshes. The bluffs lie east of Baton Rouge and join a silt loam highland which stretches northward to Canada.[85] It is a narrow plateau of loess gullied by wind and rain.[86] The soil was so fertile before erosion set in that it supported plantations and became part of the black belt.[87] Tidal marshes extend along the Gulf of Mexico in strips from ten to forty miles wide, beginning with low, grassy prairies or moss-curtained cypress swamps and ending in salt flats flooded by the ocean.[88] What land there was, and what manner of people lived upon it, remained a mystery during the last century. The marshes are not fit for human habitation and have always been the natural haunt of lonely hunters and fishermen.[89]

From this brief review of regions which few travelers visited, it becomes apparent that Louisiana had a greater variety of life than they thought. The plantation black belt was only one region, the Creole planters and their slaves only a minority of the population; there were also poorer soils, prairies, and forests, where humble farmers tilled their acres without slaves. As the South was never a single section but contiguous geo-economic provinces, even in the crisis of secession, so Louisiana was not simply one state but several physiographic regions.

If the nature of the soil influenced the life of every region

---

[83] Olmsted, *A Journey through Texas*, 382–86. [84] See below, 20–22, 45–46.
[85] Vance, *Human Geography of the South*, 88. [86] Hilgard *Rpt.*, 123–24.
[87] Appendix, Tables 1, 2.   [88] Hilgard *Rpt.*, 156–58; Foster, *op. cit.*, 18.
[89] J. H. Matthews, "Fisheries of the South Atlantic and Gulf States," *Economic Geography*, IV (October, 1928), 323–48.

in more ways than the average traveler could conceive, local variations of climate were no less important, especially in agriculture. Differences of temperature and humidity adapted the chemical resources of the soil to different staples.[90] What travelers failed to observe in this respect may be explained geographically.

Louisiana is divided between a humid subtropical region south of thirty-one degrees latitude, where the Red River empties into the Mississippi, and a temperate region to the north.[91] The latter section, where autumn rainfall drops to ten inches, is the natural home of cotton. These parishes have higher temperatures, a longer growing season, and generally better soil than the rest of the South; otherwise, they are not very different from the cotton counties of Mississippi, Alabama, and Georgia.[92] It is impossible to grow cotton successfully in the lower parishes because the heavy autumn rainfall —over fourteen inches—damages the lint and interferes with picking.[93] But sugar cane, rice, and citrus fruits flourish in the subtropical heat and rainfall.[94] Sugar cane, of course, is at best an exotic plant in the United States: nothing but a severely protective tariff enabled it to survive in Louisiana, where a frostless growing season of 250 days could not compare with the full year of Cuba and other tropical countries.[95] Although Louisiana produced nearly equal amounts of sugar and cotton in 1860,[96] by the end of the century not half as much sugar cane was grown.[97] Rice, once the exclusive product of South

[90] O. E. Baker, "Agricultural Regions of North America," *Economic Geography*, III (January, 1927), 71.

[91] Hilgard *Rpt.*, 111; *U. S. D. A. Yearbook, 1921*, 416.

[92] Baker, *op. cit.*, 65-67.   [93] *Ibid.*, 67.

[94] *Ibid.*, 59-64; for some interesting facts on the orange orchards along the lower Mississippi, which did not bear fruit for ten years after planting, see C. Nordhoff, *The Cotton States in the Spring and Summer of 1875* (New York, 1876), 68-69.

[95] Vance, *op. cit.*, 219-20.   [96] *U. S. Cen., 1860, Prelim. Rpt.*, 201, 208.

[97] *U. S. Cen., 1900*, VI, 432.

Carolina, was transferred to the prairies of Louisiana after the Civil War by Northern wheat farmers equipped with harvesting machinery.[98] The firm and level prairies supported these machines, which helped the white farmer to cultivate rice in successful competition with the cheap manual labor of the Orient.[99] Artificial irrigation was facilitated by an annual rainfall of more than fifty inches which came with prevailing winds from the Gulf of Mexico.[100] Citrus fruits, particularly the sour orange, and many vegetables were grown on the delta for New Orleans markets before the Civil War;[101] new vegetables and fruits, notably the strawberry, have since been brought into cultivation in the humid southeast.[102] Thus lower Louisiana is a distinct agricultural region, unique for its sugar cane and rice, and not without truck and fruits similar to those raised in subtropical Florida.[103]

The eastern and western parishes, with sufficient rainfall but poor soil, have specialized in livestock or lumber.[104] Small farms were cultivated for a supply of corn and potatoes.[105] Over the forest ranges, which no man owned, roamed thousands of cattle.[106] Neither subsistence farming nor stock-raising could stand in the way of railroads, which later went through this poor country on direct routes to distant markets. With the railroads came portable sawmills.[107] Within fifty years after the Civil War about twelve million acres of timber were cut to the ground in Louisiana.[108] Where cutover lands

---

[98] Ginn, *op. cit.*, 32–35.   [99] Vance, *op. cit.*, 215–17.

[100] Baker, *op. cit.*, 62–63.

[101] Flint, *Recollections of the Last Ten Years*, 326; U. S. Cen., *1850, Comp.*, 253.

[102] Baker, *op. cit.*, 52, 56, 59.   [103] Vance, *op. cit.*, 225–36.

[104] Hilgard *Rpt.*, 136.   [105] U. S. Cen., *1850, Comp.*, 250–53.

[106] Flint, *op. cit.*, 328–29.

[107] *Rpt. U. S. Bur. Soils, 1905*, 494, 512–13; Emerson, "The Southern Long-Leaf Pine Belt," *Geographical Review*, VII (February, 1919), 82.

[108] Vance, *op. cit.*, 124–25; Foster, *op. cit.*, 9–21.

were not restocked, they remained a desolate waste or were put without profit to the cultivation of staple crops.[109]

Nothing more clearly reveals man's adaptation to the physiographic features of Louisiana than the composition and distribution of population, which travelers were generally wont to ignore except for their notice of Creoles and slaves. Since rivers, particularly the Mississippi and Red, provided natural access to the best land, their banks were most thickly settled by 1860.[110] Flint remarked the suburban appearance of the Mississippi Coast where plantations fronted the river at intervals of a quarter mile from Baton Rouge down to New Orleans.[111] Behind the mansion houses, as far as the swamps, stretched fertile fields of cotton and sugar cane which drew southward gangs of slaves and transformed the river bottoms into a land of colored people.[112] Down the Mississippi flowed the trade of the Middle West to make New Orleans, where exports were transferred to ocean-going vessels, the great commercial metropolis of the valley.[113] A curious result of this urban congestion was that more free people were engaged in commerce in 1850 than in agriculture.[114] New Orleans attracted the immigration which attends foreign trade in a young nation: to the original French settlers were added successive waves of Acadians, Germans, Irish, Italians, and Mexicans, until the city was the largest "melting pot" in the South.[115]

It was this polyglot white majority in New Orleans which alone saved Louisiana from being predominantly black. Of the total population in 1860, 51 per cent were white; but outside

---

[109] Vance, *op. cit.*, 131–32, 143–44.   [110] Appendix, Table 1.

[111] E. g., Flint, *op. cit.*, 300; *Crescent*, Apr. 30, 1860.

[112] Appendix, Table 2.

[113] Vance, *op. cit.*, 262–66; E. F. Campbell, "New Orleans at the Time of the Louisiana Purchase," *Geographical Review*, XI (July, 1921), 423–25.

[114] *U. S. Cen., 1850, Comp.*, 128.   [115] *Ibid.*, 53–54.

the city this proportion was reduced to 39 per cent. Exclusive of Orleans, only fourteen of the remaining forty-seven parishes had a white majority.[116] These parishes were situated either in the north or at a distance from the river bottoms. Wherever good upland or alluvial soil was to be found, there were more colored than white people.[117] In the black belt the slave population grew rapidly after 1830,[118] according to a tendency natural throughout the South for established plantation areas to attract more planters and slaves.[119] In the country, therefore, slaves increased faster than freemen.[120] In New Orleans, on the other hand, the white population trebled during the two decades before 1860 as the colored decreased by one half.[121]

Although before the Civil War Louisiana continued to grow in numbers faster than the South as a whole, it was not the focus of southwestern immigration after 1840.[122] Rich, unplowed land diverted planters to Arkansas and Texas. By 1850, the population of Louisiana was relatively more stable than in other central southern states.[123] Over half the white inhabitants were native-born, a fifth had come from other parts of the country, especially Mississippi, Alabama, Georgia, South

[116] *U. S. Cen., 1860, Prelim. Rpt.*, 262; *Journal of the American Geographical and Statistical Society*, I (February, 1859), 62.

[117] Appendix, Table 1.

[118] A. A. Taylor, "The Movement of Negroes from the East to the Gulf States from 1830 to 1850," *Journal of Negro History*, VIII (October, 1923), 381.

[119] Phillips, *American Negro Slavery* (New York, 1918), 333.

[120] *U. S. Cen., 1850*, 473; *ibid., 1860, Prelim. Rpt.*, 262.

[121] Phillips, *Life and Labor in the Old South* (Boston, 1929), 151 *n*.

[122] *U. S. Cen., 1890*, I, xxxviii. Emigration to Louisiana was heaviest from 1810 to 1820.

[123] *U. S. Cen., 1850, Comp.*, 114. The excess received from other states was 31 per cent of the population born and residing in Louisiana, 42 per cent in Alabama, 83 in Mississippi, 136 in Arkansas, and 173 in Texas.

Carolina, Tennessee, and Virginia,[124] and the remainder from foreign lands, particularly Ireland, the German states, and France.[125] American immigrants tended to be yeomen slaveholders who settled in the northern parishes; [126] foreigners either stayed in New Orleans or went up the Mississippi to farm in the Middle West. A larger number of immigrants entered the United States through New Orleans before 1860 than by any other port except New York.[127] So many of these foreign-born, chiefly Irish, remained in New Orleans that they constituted almost half the local population on the eve of the Civil War.[128]

Louisiana was originally settled, of course, by the French; their descendants were Creoles who tried to maintain purity of blood and a hybrid foreign culture in the face of an American invasion.[129] Even before Louisiana was joined to the United States, Americans swarmed there in search of trade and virgin land.[130] In 1830 there were two French residents for each American; [131] but by 1850 this foreign stock was submerged, numerically and economically, beneath the tide of Americans flooding the Southwest.[132] As the Creole had entered Louisiana by the Mississippi, he was to be found in

[124] Thirty-four states sent emigrants to Louisiana, but Mississippi, Alabama, Georgia, South Carolina, and New York each furnished more than 5,000 settlers. J. K. Greer, "Louisiana Politics, 1845–1861," *L.H.Q.*, XII (July, 1929), 387.

[125] A. W. Bell, comp., *Louisiana State Register* (Baton Rouge, 1855), 130–31.

[126] See below, 80–81.

[127] *U.S. Cen.*, *1850*, xc, 473.

[128] *U.S. Cen.*, *1860*, I, 58.

[129] L. W. Newton, "Creoles and Anglo-Americans in Old Louisiana," *Southwestern Social Science Quarterly*, XIV, 31–48.

[130] M. A. Hatcher, *The Opening of Texas to Foreign Settlement* (Austin, Tex., 1927), 7–40.

[131] Newton, *op. cit.*, 33.

[132] *U.S. Cen.*, *1850*, 473.

possession of the lower river banks; [133] Americans who came downstream or overland settled in either the northern parishes or New Orleans.[134] In 1840 the French were preponderant in fifteen parishes to the south and Americans in twenty-one parishes to the north and east.[135] But the economic and social life of the generation before the Civil War was typically American; French influence was weak,[136] and travelers described it as an archaic curiosity.

There is perhaps no better way to grasp the vivid reality of life in ante-bellum Louisiana than to read the accounts which travelers have left us in many old books. It has been impossible, of course, to recapitulate them in these few pages. Rather was it necessary to supplement them by reference to the physical and social geography of the state in order to reveal the regional and economic basis of living for thousands of poor people whom travelers generally ignored or neglected. It next becomes essential to analyze the skeleton of this society, and then to restore to it the flesh and blood of social, economic, and political life.

[133] Of 1,700 families living along the Mississippi from its mouth to Baton Rouge in 1857, 83 per cent had French names. Henry and Gerodias, *The Louisiana Coast Directory*, index.

[134] E. C. Semple, *American History and Its Geographic Conditions* (Boston, 1903), 109.

[135] *Biographical and Historical Memoirs of Louisiana*, The Southern Publishing Co., comp. (Chicago, 1890), I, 220.

[136] Cf. Newton, *loc. cit.*

Chapter II

CHARACTERISTICS OF THE SEVERAL CLASSES

> The interest of the poor man and the rich man
> are the same in this country, one and indivisible.
> We have but two classes here, the white man and
> the negro.
>
> —Alexandria Constitutional [1]

Society in the Old South, according to a lingering romantic tradition, consisted of three classes, the planting aristocracy, slaves, and "poor whites." [2] This view, as plausible as any legend, does violence to the facts. [3] A majority of the free people were neither poor whites, in the odious sense of the term, nor slaveholding planters. [4] But so persistent are ideas to the contrary that it is essential to examine them at some length.

"All whites who were poor," it has been truly said, "were not poor whites." [5] The most popular variation of this epithet, "po' white trash," was probably coined by slaves who felt themselves superior to white people of the lowest social and economic position. [6] It came to be applied as an expression of contempt to the so-called "hillbillies" in Arkansas, Ken-

---

[1] Jan. 5, 1861.

[2] The pretensions which clustered around the plantation and slavery are exposed by F. P. Gaines, *The Southern Plantation* (New York, 1925).

[3] *Ibid.*, 144, 152; A. N. J. Den Hollander, "The Tradition of 'Poor Whites,'" in W. T. Couch, ed., *Culture in the South* (Chapel Hill, N. C., 1934), 403-4.

[4] Cf. Hundley, *Social Relations in Our Southern States*, esp. chap. V; E. B. Seabrook, "The Poor Whites of the South," *The Galaxy*, IV, 681-90; Edw. Ingle, *Southern Sidelights* (New York, 1896), 20-21.

[5] Ingle, *op. cit.*, 22. Quotation marks are omitted.

[6] Cf. J. R. Gilmore (pseud. Edmund Kirke), *Among the Pines: or, the South in Secession-Time*, 5th ed. (New York, 1862), 83.

tucky, and Tennessee, "Tarheels" and "sand-hillers" in the
Carolinas, "crackers" in Georgia, "red-necks," "wool hats,"
or "swamp-dwellers" in Alabama, Mississippi, and Louisiana,
and in scattered parts of the South the "clay-" or "dirt-eaters"
who suffered from hookworm, and "piney woods folks." [7]
    All these poor whites might be reduced to two types, "mean
whites" and the "deserving poor." [8] The former were described as incredibly ignorant and poverty-stricken, lazy,
bibulous, filthy, promiscuous, violent, and "sunk into a depth
of depravity." [9] Their wretched condition was ascribed to
their evil character, the product of a degenerate ancestry
which supposedly could be traced to the ne'er-do-well in-
dentured servants, vagabonds, and criminals dumped on American shores in colonial times.[10] Seldom has biological heredity
been falsely invoked to explain social consequences so disastrous and so remote.[11] The "deserving poor," on the other
hand, were regarded as victims of environment, because if
their poverty and ignorance were occasionally as woeful as
among the much contemned "mean whites," at least it was
not aggravated by similar vices.[12] They were thrifty but poor,

[7] L. C. Gray, *History of Agriculture in the Southern United States to 1860*
(Washington, 1933), II, 484; W. B. Hesseltine, *A History of the South* (New
York, 1936), 324-25. For the best studies of these people, see P. H. Buck, "The
Poor Whites of the Ante-Bellum South," *A. H. R.*, XXXI, 41-54; A. O. Cra-
ven, "Poor Whites and Negroes in the Ante-Bellum South," *Journal of Negro
History*, XV, 14-25; W. M. Brewer, "Poor Whites and Negroes in the South
since the Civil War," *Journal of Negro History*, XV, 26-37; and Den Hol-
lander, *op. cit.*, 403-31.

[8] B. W. Arnold, "Virginia Women and the Civil War," *Southern History
Assn. Publications*, II, 256-58.

[9] Seabrook, *op. cit.*, 688.

[10] Hundley, *op. cit.*, 250-58; Ingle, *op. cit.*, 23-24; S. A. Hamilton, "The
New Race Question in the South," *The Arena*, XXVII, 352-58.

[11] Den Hollander, *op. cit.*, 427-28. Cf. T. J. Wertenbaker, *Patrician and
Plebeian in Colonial Virginia* (Charlottesville, Va., 1910), in which the argument from descent, in this case the Cavaliers, was first refuted.

[12] Arnold, *loc. cit.*

industrious but illiterate. Some owned land; others simply occupied it without title or lease. Every family cultivated a self-sufficient farm on inferior soil, which was partly responsible for its low standard of living.[13] These plain people are now admitted to have been the larger as well as the better portion of the poor whites.[14]

But nothing is gained by continuing to call them by this name.[15] Any appellation like "poor whites," compounded of snobbish prejudice and used without discrimination, has little value to the presumably impartial historian.[16] It explains nothing about the people it slanders, and even fails to classify them precisely. Poor they were, and white, but the two words together mean something different to each one who uses them. To Olmsted the "poor whites" embraced all "who bring nothing to market to exchange for money but their labor." [17] This is a sound economic definition. It designates, to use a term more acceptable to European than American scholars, the proletariat; [18] or to follow American usage, the small farmers and squatters in the country and the artisans and laborers in the city. For want of a better name, they might well be called the common people. Where they are mentioned in this study as "poor whites," it is because they really were—with a comma—poor, white people.

This large group was originally distinguished from others by the fact that it never owned any Negroes. Contrary to the popular belief of later times, in which the imagination of every Southerner was prone to endow his ancestors with many black servants, these nonslaveholders constituted a majority

[13] Craven, op. cit., 15; T. P. Abernethy, "Social Relations and Political Control in the Old Southwest," M. V. H. R., XVI, 534.

[14] Den Hollander, op. cit., 404.

[15] Phillips, Life and Labor in the Old South, 340.

[16] Abernethy, loc. cit.

[17] A Journey in the Seaboard Slave States, II, 84.

[18] Cf. Paul Lewinson, Race, Class, and Party (New York, 1932), 3, 5-7.

of the free population.[19] Their numerical predominance was
first brought to national attention by Hinton Rowan Helper.[20]
He regarded them as poor whites, oppressed from above by
the planters, from below by the slaves, and injured by the
indirect competition of servile labor.[21] The way out of their
sorry plight, he thought, was to wage class war on the plantation "lords of the lash" and race war on their enslaved "black
and bi-colored caitiffs." [22] No one gave heed to his appeal.
People in the North, interested in abolition or free soil, either
failed to realize that the nonslaveholders were potential allies
or else confused them with helpless poor whites.[23] As for
the nonslaveholders themselves, there were few who knew of
Helper's book; and even if many could have read it, they
would not have sympathized with his views.[24] Because they
were inarticulate and powerless in a slaveholding society, they
became the forgotten men of the South.

   Their former existence was not generally remembered until the closing decades of the last century, when economic and
political changes brought poor people out of their traditional
obscurity. The industrialization of the South depended in
part on an adequate supply of cheap white labor,[25] and the
agrarian revolt against the conservative Democracy revealed
their number and power.[26] Curiosity over the probable ante-

[19] *U. S. Cen., 1860, Agric.,* 247.

[20] *The Impending Crisis of the South: How to Meet It* (New York, 1857).

[21] *Ibid.,* 42–44, 120.

[22] *Ibid.,* 156–57. Cf. U. B. Phillips, "The Central Theme of Southern History," *A. H. R.,* XXXIV, 33.

[23] E. g., H. B. Stowe, *Key to Uncle Tom's Cabin* (Boston, 1853), 184–87;
G. M. Weston, *The Progress of Slavery in the United States* (Washington,
1858), *passim.*

[24] See below, chap. V.

[25] Holland Thompson, *From Cotton Field to Cotton Mill* (New York,
1906).

[26] C. E. Cason, "Middle Class and Bourbon," in W. T. Couch, ed., *Culture
in the South,* 482 ff.

cedents of these people in the prewar South led to a study of old census records which did much to destroy the fictions that had grown up about slavery and the plantation.[27] It was realized anew that in 1860 nearly three of every four white people had no proprietary interest in slavery.[28]

As nonslaveholders were numerically preponderant in the South as a whole, they likewise constituted a majority of the free population in Louisiana. Here, in 1860, 71 per cent of the people did not own Negroes.[29] A little more than half these nonslaveholders were landless laborers, artisans, clerks, and petty shopkeepers in New Orleans. The rest, living in the country, were small farmers, plantation overseers, and the landless squatters, hunters, and fishermen known as poor whites.[30]

The nonslaveholding proportion of the free population varied in different parts of Louisiana.[31] In New Orleans, a commercial center where few people would have any use for bondservants, nearly nine out of ten residents lacked them. But in the country, where agriculture made slave labor profitable, four out of ten inhabitants belonged to slaveholding families. In the black belt, where slavery was most extensive because of the predominance of Negroes, half the free people were slaveholders. In the rural white belt only three in every ten inhabitants were connected with slavery.

There was a great difference in the proportion of nonslaveholders to be found in regions devoted to sugar and cotton. Indicative of the concentration of wealth and slaves in

[27] The growing recognition of these people may be traced in the following literature of the times: Arnold, *op. cit.*; J. L. M. Curry, "The South in Olden Times," *Southern History Assn. Publications*, V, 35–48; Hamilton, *op. cit.*; G. K. Holmes, "The Peons of the South," *Annals*, IV, 265–74; Ingle, *op. cit.*

[28] Phillips, *Life and Labor in the Old South*, 339.

[29] See Appendix, Table 3.   [30] See below, chap. IV.

[31] See Appendix, Table 3.

the expensive process of sugar manufacture was the fact that three out of five people lacked Negroes in the leading cane parishes. This is worthy of remark because it has been commonly thought that the Sugar Bowl was almost exclusively occupied by slaveholders. They were much more numerous in the principal region devoted to cotton, where half the free people owned Negroes, since this staple might be cultivated with less capital and smaller slaveholdings than sugar.[32]

All rural nonslaveholders may be regarded as the poorer or common people, because they did not possess the colored human labor which was capitalized as the most productive property in the agricultural society of the Old South.

But in commercial New Orleans, where slavery was relatively unprofitable, the ownership of Negroes could not be considered a reliable index of economic position. A local business directory of 1857 enumerates 5,704 people, each probably the head of a family, who were engaged in occupations of considerable capital and affluence.[33] They belonged to the upper or middle classes, and doubtless included in their ranks all the urban slaveholders, who numbered 4,169.[34] To judge from occupations, there were also 1,535 nonslaveholding families of upper or middle class standing. In other words, about one in every eight families in New Orleans owned slaves, but one in every six enjoyed a position of social respect and economic power. This disparity can be more readily understood if it is remembered that in the city to own even one slave, usually for personal or household service, was a luxury and a badge of social esteem. The great majority of nonslaveholders in New Orleans, like those in the country,

---

[32] *Ibid., nn.* 6–9.

[33] See Appendix, Table 4, *nn.* 3, 5, 7. W. H. Rainey, comp., *A. Mygatt & Company's New Orleans Business Directory* (New Orleans, 1857), 1–240.

[34] *U. S. Cen., 1860, Agric.*, 230.

were poor people. To this lower class belonged about three in every five residents of the city, almost equally divided between skilled and unskilled occupations.[35] Among the former were thrifty people of some means. A detailed report of the New Orleans Savings Institution in 1859 shows that 2,496 depositors had an average account of $390, and three out of five depositors were shop clerks, domestic servants, mechanics, or laborers.[36]

Over half the slaveholders in the country probably lived in less comfort. They were yeomen farmers who owned from one to nine Negroes, besides their land, and might well be called common people "on the make." [37] With a family of five slaves, according to Olmsted, a yeoman was lucky to earn $150 a year from the cotton he could raise.[38] The proportion of small yeomen who owned less than six slaves varied in different regions of the state. In the black belt, where the larger plantations were concentrated, only two in five slaveholders belonged to this group. But in the white belt, where the absence of a Negro majority indicated smaller properties, three out of five slaveholders were in this category. In the leading sugar parishes, despite their great plantations, nearly half the planters held less than six slaves. This shows again how many poor people lived on humble farms along the bayous of the Sugar Bowl.[39] In the parishes which produced the most cotton, two out of three planters owned more than five bondsmen, which contradicts the popular belief that slavery was less attached to cotton than sugar.[40]

Everywhere in the Old South the yeomanry is generally

[35] See Appendix, Table 4, *nn.* 16, 17.
[36] *La. Legisl. Docs., 1859,* 42–43; *La. H. J., 1859,* 95.
[37] See Appendix, Table 4, *n.* 8.
[38] *The Cotton Kingdom* (New York, 1861), I, 18.
[39] Cf. *Southern Medical Reports,* I, 234.
[40] Computed from *U. S. Cen., 1860, Agric.,* 230.

thought to have been the backbone of slaveholding society.[41] In Louisiana, where about three in five slaveholders had less than ten Negroes, it is obvious that these yeomen were the mainstay of the institution of human bondage. Although they included hardly one in seven free people, it was this small group which held a numerical balance of power between the nonslaveholding masses and the minority of merchants and large planters.[42]

The latter belonged to the upper and middle classes. Almost as numerous as the yeomanry but much higher in economic and social position was the middle class. It embraced one in every seven free families, of whom a scant majority lived in the country. They owned plantations of less than five hundred acres and from ten to forty-nine Negroes. Their number included nearly a third of the rural slaveholders, their holdings about two-fifths of all the slaves.[43] Urban members of the middle class pursued a wide variety of occupations and ranged from those who dwelt in very prosperous circumstances to those who enjoyed the barest comfort. However their work might differ, it commonly required some capital, but almost no manual labor, and constant discretion in management, negotiation, and exchange. The detailed supervision of the business of New Orleans, with its hundreds of retail shops and extensive agencies of transportation, was in the hands of the middle class.[44]

But the largest part of the wealth of Louisiana and the control of its commerce and plantation agriculture belonged chiefly to a small upper class. About one in thirty-seven families was a member of this powerful group. The sons and

[41] Hundley, *op. cit.*, 193, 219; J. S. Bassett, *Slavery in the State of North Carolina* [Johns Hopkins Univ., Studies in Hist. and Pol. Sc. (Baltimore, 1899), XVII, nos. 7–8], chap. III; Abernethy, *op. cit.*, 532.

[42] See Appendix, Table 4.   [43] *Ibid., n. 6.*   [44] *Ibid., n. 7.*

daughters of fifty families were each said to be worth more than $100,000, and of nearly a hundred more, over $50,000.[45] Their parents owned the great estates in the country, produced most of the sugar, and much of the cotton. The rural slaveholders possessed over half of all the slaves, although hardly one in ten was a large planter.[46] Allied to these planters were the bankers, brokers, factors, and lawyers in New Orleans who dominated the business of the city. Upon them depended the credit, legal negotiations, and facilities for export and import so essential to the economic life of a slave plantation system.[47]

Despite this concentration of wealth, slaves, and power in the hands of a few, little resentment was expressed by the less fortunate majority. The rich planters in the black belt did not excite great envy among the overseers, woodcutters, and poor farmers who surrounded them. To the contrary, a West Feliciana overseer boasted that all the land was "owned by big bugs," among whom his employer was "one of the biggest sort." [48] Middle class planters felt their relative inferiority more keenly; one of them dubbed the large slaveholders on the Mississippi Coast "swell-heads . . . nothing but swell-heads." [49] In the hill country, unlike the black belt, people were everywhere so poor that they shared the leveling democracy of backwoods poverty.[50] Well-born Creoles in New Orleans held aloof from rich American *parvenus*,[51] and looked upon good blood as "a hygienic virtue." [52] Their

---

[45] S. S. Hall, *The Bliss of Marriage; or How to Get a Rich Wife* (New Orleans, 1858), app., 1–8. Here are to be found the initials of young ladies and the names of eligible gentlemen, with an estimate of their marriageable wealth!

[46] See Appendix, Table 4, *n.* 4.   [47] *Ibid., n.* 5.

[48] Olmsted, *A Journey in the Back Country,* 21.   [49] *Ibid.,* 25.

[50] C. Lyell, *A Second Visit to the United States of North America* (New York, 1849), II, 69–70.

[51] Newton, *op. cit., Southwestern Social Science Quarterly,* XIV, 31–48.

[52] A. Rhodes, "The Louisiana Creoles," *The Galaxy,* XVI, 259.

pride earned the contempt of Americans, who thought it a sorry consolation for Creole indolence and want of material success.[53] Whatever the nationality of a merchant, he had no social relations with the mass of poor immigrants and natives who performed the manual labor essential to his shipping and trade. The contemporary press used a nomenclature familiar all over the nation to distinguish "the solid, the wealthy and the fashionable" from "the honest, hard-working and hard-fisted men of the humbler classes," [54] who were expected to work out their lives as "hewers of wood and drawers of water." [55] Class distinctions were in the air: to accept them unconsciously was as natural as to breathe, because they were implicit in the economic and social order of the Old South.[56]

Whenever politicians among the small farmers of northern Louisiana pointed to the economic gulf which separated them from rich slaveholders, the press was quick to heal the breach by reminding all whites of their common superiority to the Negro. "Unblushing demagogues will tell you," admitted a rural editor,[57] that "there are two classes in this country; that there is a conflict between the poor man in the pine woods and the rich planter. Such is not the case." Race or caste, not class, was the only recognized fissure in society. To escape the cry of white supremacy, by which all classes were united against the Negro, one must search newspapers back to the days when Jacksonian Democracy raised its head, and conflict among white people was as unconcealed as in this letter from a Donaldsonville resident who protested the removal of the capital from his town: "For many years the aristocrats of New Orleans have given law to the State. Composed principally of men suddenly grown rich . . . [the Whigs] cannot bear the idea of sharing the government

---

[53] Lyell, *op. cit.*, II, 157. [54] *Crescent*, Sept. 4, 1860.
[55] *Weekly Mirror*, Mar. 12, 1859. [56] See below, chaps. III, IV, V.
[57] Alexandria *Constitutional*, Jan. 5, 1861; see above, *n.* 1.

with honest farmers and mechanics of the country. They are aware that if the seat of Government be permanently fixed out of the vortex of their intrigues, the good sense of the country members of the Legislature will enable them to introduce reform into the State, check the influence of foreign capital working through New Orleans Banks, and above all, eradicate from our social system the remnants yet of Spanish feodality. This may be emphatically termed the time for asserting the rights of the people—for laughing into scorn machinations of those knots of Aristocrats who regard the Working Man as nothing. And it will be disgraceful to the people of Louisiana at a time when the popular cause is so nobly progressing in France and the Netherlands, it should cower to a band of Aristocrats on the banks of the Mississippi." [58] These romantic Jacksonian epithets for the struggle between Whig and Democrat, city and country, rich and poor, disappeared from the political vocabulary of the next generation.[59]

The absence of overt class hostility was at bottom the result of slavery and the plantation system.[60] The former put the burden of labor on the Negro and made his race as odious as its bondage. A white man might be as poor as a slave, but at least he was free, and did not have to work beyond the elementary needs of subsistence. From this privileged position he could look down upon one lower than himself, the enslaved black, with the contempt which might otherwise have been directed against those who were his equal or superior. Race prejudice, in other words, filled the void of class hatred.[61] Whatever jealousy or resentment the poor felt toward the rich was mitigated by the plantation system. It prevented friction

[58] *Baton Rouge Gazette*, Jan. 29, 1831. I am indebted to Mr. L. M. Norton of Louisiana State University for calling my attention to this letter.

[59] Cf. below, chap. V.   [60] Seabrook, *op. cit.*, 685–87.

[61] Cf. Buck, *loc. cit.*

by a partial geographical segregation of different groups: [62] the majority of small farmers lived up in the hills or along the bayous, and all large slaveholders down in the river bottoms.[63] Since only the wealthy could afford to travel far beyond their native parish, and they went either to New Orleans or the North, the backwoods farmer rarely came into contact with a planter.[64] In the city, of course, rich and poor rubbed shoulders, and there were frequent election riots and an almost continuous crime wave.[65] But here, as in the country, slavery and the plantation system operated to soften class animosity. There was no political party to serve the interests of the poor: to attack slavery would have been revolutionary. Nor could a plantation economy support efficient free public schools to enlighten the masses and equip them with the mental ability to help themselves. The "system which degraded them, tended also to create . . . ignorance" of the injury it inflicted.[66] Finally, slavery and the plantation system endowed the upper class with the "power which intelligence of the highest order must always have over the grossest ignorance, and unbounded wealth over abject poverty." [67] Class struggle was not to be expected in a society where only one class was articulate and conscious of its interests.

Social distinctions had not been established long enough to be translated into political and economic conflict. Many planters looked back scarcely a generation to the beginning of their estates; the bulk of their wealth had been accumulated in the boom years following 1830.[68] Then the specula-

[62] Phillips, *American Negro Slavery*, 333.

[63] The latter held the former in low esteem, according to Nordhoff, *The Cotton States*, 73.

[64] Interview with H. L. Brian of Shreveport, May 2, 1933.

[65] See below, chaps. III, V.   [66] Seabrook, *op. cit.*, 685.   [67] *Ibid.*, 686.

[68] E. g., K. M. Rowland and M. L. Croxall, eds., *The Journal of Julia LeGrand* (Richmond, Va., 1911), 17–21, C. F. LeGrand to Thos. Croxall, Apr. 9, 1836.

tive fluctuations of cotton, sugar, and slave prices,[69] the failure or success of overseers, the intermittent disasters of flood and yellow fever, and the constant pressure of credit charges upon net profits [70] made the rich poor and the poor rich in a single lifetime.[71] It was a society of *"novi homines"* [72] in which, except among the Creoles, group relations were determined by money rather than birth, and the upper class was more of a plutocracy than an aristocracy.[73]

Hence all classes were somewhat mobile, and transition from one to another not impossible. Many names could be mentioned to prove the dynamic character of this society. John Burnside, an Ulster emigrant, started life as a grocer's clerk in upland Virginia, moved to New Orleans in the fifties, accumulated capital as a merchant, and invested his profits in sugar plantations. On the eve of the Civil War he owned six thousand acres of land and more than a thousand slaves, and was accounted one of the richest men in the South, worth two million dollars.[74] Duncan Kenner was a slave trader who became a respectable sugar planter, a leading Whig and state senator, and one of the largest slaveholders in the South.[75] Governor Paul Hébert, a descendant of poor Cajuns, won for himself a magnificent plantation and political honors.[76] Another governor, Joseph Walker, was a trader in Texas cattle, with no more than a rudimentary education.[77] Names of the men who were humbly born but eminently successful

[69] Gray, *op. cit.*, II, 715, 1033; Phillips, *American Negro Slavery*, 370.

[70] "There are many planters in the State whose whole property is covered by mortgages," remarked one. *La. Sen. Debs.*, 1853, 67.

[71] Gray, *op. cit.*, II, 898–900.   [72] Flint, *op. cit.*, 298.

[73] A. O. Hall, *The Manhattaner in New Orleans* (New York, 1851), 30–33.

[74] *Le Courrier des Opelousas*, 4 Fev. 1860; W. H. Russell, *My Diary North and South*, I, 268–79.

[75] S. C. Arthur and G. C. H. deKernion, *Old Families of Louisiana* (New Orleans, 1931), 160. Cf. Phillips, *American Negro Slavery*, 246.

[76] A. Fortier, *A History of Louisiana* (New York, 1904), III, 197.

[77] *The Louisiana Almanac for 1867* (New Orleans, 1866), 39.

would fill many pages.[78] Even in a slaveholding society it was sometimes possible for poor, white people, if not poor whites, to gain wealth and power. But their success was exceptional, not the lot of the majority. Class lines remained, and only a few managed to cross them.[79]

Admission to the aristocracy became next to impossible in the decade before secession because of the increasing stratification of classes.[80] As plantations and slaveholdings grew larger in size, their total number diminished.[81] The ranks of the yeomen and middle class were thinned out, the proportion of common people enlarged; and the aristocracy, into whose hands this wealth flowed, became more select and more class-conscious. They began to develop a culture appropriate to their newly won fortunes by attending the Creole opera and building magnificent houses.[82] But they were hardly settled in their new mansions when the North attacked their whole social system. To parry the thrusts of Abolitionists, Free Soilers, and Republicans, the Southern planters consolidated support at home by spreading their mantle over all classes and denying the existence of any class except the white and black races.[83]

The social philosophy of the planters was a rationalization of their desire to preserve slavery, the stratified society to which it had given rise, and the dominant position it afforded them.[84] The major premise in the proslavery argument was

[78] See Christian Roselius and Pierre Soulé, *D. A. B.*, Judge Whitaker, *Sketches of the Life and Character in Louisiana* (New Orleans, 1847), 1–85; A. Meynier, Jr., *Louisiana Biographies* (New Orleans, 1882), pt. I.

[79] Cf. Seabrook, *op. cit.*, 682.   [80] See below, chaps. IV, V.

[81] Gray, *op. cit.*, I, 529–31; see Appendix, Table 6.

[82] A. O. Hall, *op. cit.*, 91–100; Saxon, *Old Louisiana*, 142–50; N. Scott and W. P. Spratling, *Old Plantation Houses in Louisiana* (New York, 1927), *passim*.

[83] See W. E. Dodd, "Social Philosophy of the Old South," *American Journal of Sociology*, XXIII, 735–46.

[84] *Ibid.*, 736.

the view, for which there was considerable historical evidence, that classes arose in every society according to the division of labor.[85] The minor premise, that in the status economy of the South "the bondsmen are the lower class . . . , and all white men are the upper class," [86] was false, because it identified race with class in spite of the fact that the majority of white people were not slaveholders. Only in theory was every white man an actual or potential slaveholder. Hence the conclusion to the proslavery syllogism, that all whites prospered by colored labor, was equally untrue.[87] "Slave labor, by its unequal competition," as a planter observed, "thrust the poor white man completely out of all possibility of employment in those occupations which normally belong to his condition. . . . Instead of being an active, vital member of the organism of society, [he] was merely an excrescence upon its body. Useless to others, he became helpless to himself." [88]

From the belief that white civilization depended on Negro bondage issued the mistaken corollary that slavery not only made possible, but had already developed, a high type of culture. Louisiana and the Old South, it was said over and again, stood for "the good old patriarchal notions of the sanctity of the family—of the chivalry required from individuals, of the superiority of intellect to wealth, and the right of Thought to govern Gold instead of Gold becoming the overseer of Thought." [89] The culture of Southern planters, like that of all aristocracies, was supposed to justify their wealth and power and to vindicate the subordination of the common people.[90]

The way of life associated with the great plantations has

[85] E. g., *Delta*, Oct. 8, 1856.   [86] *Crescent*, Oct. 11, 1859.
[87] E. g., *Weekly Delta*, Dec. 14, 1856; *Crescent*, Oct. 27, 1859.
[88] Seabrook, *op. cit.*, 683, 685.   [89] *Delta*, Sept. 4, 1856.
[90] Dodd, *op. cit.*, 736.

left a glorious tradition but few tangible memorials.[91] The rare country houses in Louisiana which have survived the ravages of weather, flood, war, and reconstruction testify to the gracious amenities of a comfortable existence.[92] But it pales in comparison to the urban culture of the New Orleans Creoles. Their finest institution was the French Opera, doubtless the best and certainly the first of its kind in the United States.[93] The enthusiastic patronage of Creole society attracted Calvé and other European artists for repertoires of French and Italian opera.[94] Not only were the best families in attendance, but also "unwashed patrons . . . for a dollar a head." [95] "The Neapolitan and the Spaniard, . . . in the person of the lowest laborer, [would] give their last dollar to the character of their native airs." [96]

The civilization of Louisiana, like its opera, was French at heart. In the American St. Charles Theatre, as a Creole complained, the audience applauded vociferously the singing of "one petite baby catch some sleep," but showed no "gusto for de bon music." [97] The better-educated Creoles read the novels current in Paris,[98] and kept the French language alive in the southern parishes.[99] But music, language, literature, the Old World architecture of their city houses, and their cere-

[91] See F. P. Gaines, *The Southern Plantation* (New York, 1925), *passim*. In a study of the common people little space can be devoted to the culture of the aristocracy; what comments are made here have reference to its social and class implications, not its aesthetic content and value.

[92] See above, *n*. 82.

[93] Probably established in 1809. R. L. Rusk, *The Literature of the Middle Western Frontier* (New York, 1926), I, 361 *n*.; B. M. Norman, *New Orleans and Environs* (New Orleans, 1845), 176–78.

[94] A. O. Hall, *op. cit.*, 91–95.   [95] *Ibid.*, 93.

[96] *Weekly Picayune*, Dec. 17, 1838, quoted by Newton, *op. cit.*, 46.

[97] *Ibid.*   [98] Notices occur in *L'Abeille* . . . , *passim*.

[99] The law required all public documents to be printed in French as well as English.

monious Catholicism were all but the vehicles of Creole culture. Its essence was a peculiar manner of family life and the grace, pride, and loquacious gaiety which animated their domestic circles.[100] Observers of Anglo-American background and prejudice criticized them severely for their indolence, provincialism, vanity, and reckless living. In their opinion the Creoles were chiefly remarkable for fine clothes and feminine beauty, for dancing, drinking, gambling, and duels, and for the peculiar *placée* system of colored concubinage.[101] Creole culture was by definition colonial. It flowered briefly in the eighteenth century, and quickly passed into a lingering, sterile decadence, noteworthy for its tradition and manner, but without creative understanding or vitality.[102]

If French culture in Louisiana was decadent, that of the newcomers, American and foreign, was unborn. The latter was "rugged and ugly, the other pretty and feeble." [103] Getting and spending absorbed the Americans. "You may search the world over to find the science of money-making reduced to such perfection, and become of such all-engrossing influence as in New Orleans," remarked a visitor, and he knew whereof he spoke because he came from New York.[104] An Exchange erected by New Orleans merchants for the discussion of literary and commercial matters was limited within a year to nothing but business; [105] everywhere "stocks, cotton, sugar, and money [were] the liveliest topics." [106]

To refute "the charge . . . that the 'Crescent City' . . . is nothing more or less than a kind of half-way house between civilization and California," [107] an anthology of local litera-

---

[100] Rhodes, *op. cit.,* 252–53, 257–58.

[101] A. O. Hall, *op. cit., passim;* Lyell, *op. cit.,* II, 157–58; Newton, *op. cit.,* 31–48; Pulszky, *White, Red, Black,* II, 93 ff.

[102] This subject, needless to remark, is in great need of serious study.

[103] Rhodes, *op. cit.,* 257.   [104] A. O. Hall, *op. cit.,* 32–33.

[105] *Ibid.,* 19.   [106] *Ibid.,* 24.

[107] R. G. Barnwell, ed., *The New-Orleans Book* (New Orleans, 1851), x.

ture, consisting of sermons, verse, and lawyers' briefs, was published.[108] It proved, confessed the editor, that despite the colonial heritage of France and Spain, and the advantages of considerable wealth and leisure, there was no literature and little literary taste in Louisiana.[109] "It is not sugar plantations," he protested, "nor cotton bales, nor pork barrels which constitute a State."[110] But his protest fell on deaf ears, because sugar, cotton, pork, and a hundred other commodities were the occupation, preoccupation, and wealth of every citizen. When a visiting geologist asked a French shopkeeper for a local museum, he was mournfully informed: "Monsieur, on n'est pas ici pour la littérature et les sciences, mais pour accrocher quelque chose, et puis filer le camp avant de mourir."[111]

Life in this flourishing metropolis was divided between pleasure and business;[112] and life in the country, even on great plantations, could not be very different. One was governed by the daily fluctuations of the market, the other by the seasonal routine of making crops.[113] New Orleans belied its age, and was more like a boom town than a city over a century old. The well-settled Mississippi Coast was a region of capitalistic agriculture, not the seat of a leisurely society. Except for the accident of earlier settlement, Louisiana was as raw and young as the whole Southwest. The avocations of all but a

[108] See also Thomas M'Caleb, ed., *The Louisiana Book: . . .* (New Orleans, 1849), *passim.*

[109] Barnwell, *op. cit.,* v, vii.   [110] *Ibid.,* vii.

[111] G. W. Featherstonhaugh, *Excursion through the Slave States* (New York, 1844), I, 140.

[112] Rev. Theo. Clapp, *Autobiographical Sketches and Recollections* (Boston, 1857), 253.

[113] Cf. P. L. Prudhomme, "A Record of the State of the Weather, the Daily News, and My Occupations and Amusements," printed in Saxon, *Old Louisiana,* 170–229, with E. J. Capell, MS *Record and Account Books,* Pleasant Hill Plantation [La. State Univ. Library], and *Plantation Diary of the late Mr. Valcour Aime* (New Orleans, 1878), *passim.*

few planters were necessarily limited by the prevailing il-
literacy or the continuing struggle with the soil. A commercial
traveler told Olmsted that he would "travel several days, and
call on a hundred planters, and hardly see in their houses more
than a single newspaper a-piece, in most cases; perhaps none
at all: nor any books except a Bible, and some Government
publications that had been franked to them through the post-
office, and perhaps a few religious tracts or school-books." [114]
Louisiana, in short, was too young to have either an aristocratic
culture or a genuine aristocracy. But there was a plutocracy
of *nouveaux riches* who aspired to become an aristocracy—
and only succeeded in the legend of later years.[115]

The common people, in city and country, did not enjoy
the relative comfort of the minority, and lacked all their cultural pretensions. Let us consider the city and its tide of immigration.

New Orleans, richest [116] and largest [117] metropolis of the
Old South, was three cities in all but name.[118] There was the
original French town below Canal Street, where Creoles lived
in houses of white and yellow stucco along the narrow streets;
adjoining it was the more prosperous American section of red
brick buildings which grew up with the Mississippi River
trade; [119] and on the marshy outskirts was a district, "half
village, half city," inhabited by Irish and German immi-

[114] Olmsted, *A Journey in the Seaboard Slave States,* 652. Cf. Flint, *op. cit.,*
335–39.

[115] This whole subject awaits careful study and research, which may prove
the comments above to be particular rather than general, and consequently
false. See R. P. McCutcheon, "Books and Booksellers in New Orleans, 1730–
1830," *L. H. Q.,* XX, 606–18.

[116] *U. S. Cen., 1850, Comp.,* 189.

[117] Except Baltimore and St. Louis. *U. S. Cen., 1860, Prelim. Rpt.,* 242–43.

[118] A. O. Hall, *op. cit.,* 34.

[119] Symbolic is the fact that the only access to the first American theatre
in this district was over "flat-boat gunwales." Norman, *op. cit.,* 67. See also
Flint, *op. cit.,* 302–3.

grants.[120] Of these three sections the American was wealthiest,[121] the French most populous, and the Irish-German poorest in both numbers and money.[122]

During the fifties New Orleans grew faster by immigration than any other Southern city. The population almost doubled, and by 1860 passed 170,000, of whom only eight in a hundred were slaves, and six, free people of color.[123] The winter season generally attracted 35,000 transients.[124] But permanent increase came from foreign immigration: almost half the residents of New Orleans had been born abroad—28,207 in Ireland, 26,614 in the German states, and 14,938 in France.[125]

Next to New York, New Orleans was the largest antebellum port of entry in the United States.[126] There arrived 120,000 immigrants between 1852 and 1855, more than a fourth of all those reaching the country in this period.[127] They came because of the cheap rates afforded them as return ballast on transatlantic cotton vessels.[128] The absence of low-priced land [129] and the competition of cheap slave labor [130] moved three out of every four immigrants to continue their journey up the Mississippi River.[131] They also fled New Orleans because of yellow fever, which carried off one-fourth of the Germans who arrived in 1853,[132] and sought more healthful

[120] A. O. Hall, op. cit., 35–36.

[121] Its nonresident wealth was immense because so many citizens made their homes up the River at "Carroltown" (now Carrollton) or left the city for northern resorts in the hot and sickly months. J. W. Oldmixon, *Transatlantic Wanderings* (London, 1855), 146.

[122] *Rpt. La. Audit. Pub. Accts., 1861,* 3–106.   [123] See above, *n.* 117.

[124] Helper, *op. cit.,* 338, report of Mayor's secretary.

[125] *U. S. Cen., 1860, Mortality & Miscel. Statistics,* 58; *Population,* 196.

[126] *U. S. Cen., 1850, Comp.,* xc.   [127] *Rpt. La. Com. Emig., 1870,* 32.

[128] J. H. Deiler, *Germany's Contribution to the Present Population of New Orleans* (reprinted from *Louisiana Journal of Education,* May, 1886), 3–4.

[129] *Crescent,* June 15, 1860; also see below, chap. IV.

[130] Cf. Phillips, *American Negro Slavery,* 396.   [131] Deiler, *op. cit.,* 4.

[132] L. Voss, *History of the German Society of New Orleans* (New Orleans, 1927), 80.

regions with the climate and latitude of their European homes.[133] Those who remained, frequently for want of the means to leave,[134] settled among their compatriots in the French or Irish-German sections.

Here they lived with many natives in "rotten rows, hidden from the streets by buildings of some pretensions, yet populous as bee hives," and on "blind alleys which lead into lots absolutely crowded with . . . tenements, where whole families occupy a single room." The floors were below street level and quickly went to pieces on the damp, undrained earth. Stagnant cesspools filled the yards with foul odors. There were "hundreds of old shanties, tottering with decay, admitting the rain and the winds, unsightly and never repaired, filled with dirt and vermin," where "the avarice of some landlords will never suffer improvements as long as people will occupy, pay rent, and die in their . . . hovels." "These miserable rookeries, which the avarice of landlords consecrate by the name of houses for the poor," [135] were a natural home for sickness and disease.[136] Such slums were no more fit for human habitation, in the opinion of one editor, than the meanest slave cabins on a run-down plantation.[137] Yet they sheltered thousands of free laborers who moved the cotton and sugar which made New Orleans prosperous.

The sailor from the vessels which carried this rich freight was no better off.[138] He was reported to be "entirely in the

[133] *Crescent,* June 15, 1860.
[134] Voss, *op. cit.,* 76–77, 81.
[135] *Creole,* Jan. 29, 1857.
[136] *Southern Medical Reports,* II, 232.
[137] *Creole,* Jan. 29, 1857.
[138] According to Norman, *New Orleans and Environs,* 75, there were about 10,000 men working on the Mississippi River steamboats in 1845. De Bow reports 2,778 river steamboat arrivals at New Orleans in 1851–52, and 2,351 ocean-going ship arrivals; in addition, 1,318 flatboats reached the Crescent City. *Encyclopaedia of the Trade and Commerce . . . ,* III, 566. There were 4,263 free males employed in sea and river navigation in Louisiana in 1850; from this number are excluded such large groups as stevedores and flatboatmen. *U. S. Cen., 1850, Comp.,* 128.

power of the 'Crimp,' whose interest is in drugging his body and getting the money he works for. He is taken, on arrival here, from the vessel to the liquor shop, and is shipped when the landlord wants his advance." [139]

On the levee, where a "forest of masts and chimneys tower[ed] over the river," [140] the whole business of the city appeared to be transacted. Here were piled, row on row for over a mile, bales of cotton, hogsheads of sugar, and barrels of molasses, pork, and flour. Milling around the levee, shouting, swearing, were crowds of sailors, stevedores, and clerks; and in their midst, groups of merchants and planters who bargained over the tops of bales and hogsheads.[141] There was "a melee of all classes and costumes—French, Spaniards, Americans, Creoles, Quadroons, Mulattoes, Mexicans, Negroes," and consequently a "Babel of languages." [142]

Walt Whitman saw this colorful throng as he strolled down the levee: [143] stevedores coming to work at dawn with tin lunch kettles; longshoremen in red shirts, blue cottonade pantaloons, coarse brogans, and stockingless; Irish draymen in "quaintly cut blue coats and tarnished brass buttons"; [144] and clerks, aping their employers, in glazed boots, snowy pantaloons, black coats, and gay vests adorned with big, gold watch chains.[145] But while he worked on a New Orleans newspaper, Walt Whitman never reported the presence of "an amphibious race of human beings, whose mode of living is much like that of the alligator, with whom they ironically claim relationship."

---

[139] Memorial to the General Assembly from the Trustees of the Seamen's Home, *La. Legisl. Docs., 1857,* 2–3.

[140] Pulszky, *op. cit.,* II, 93.   [141] A. O. Hall, *op. cit.,* 26–27.

[142] C. J. Latrobe, *The Rambler in North America* (London, 1836), II, 332–33.

[143] W. K. Dart, "Walt Whitman in New Orleans," *La. Hist. Soc. Publications,* VII, 97–112.

[144] *Crescent,* May 15, 1848, signed "W."

[145] *Crescent,* Apr. 26, 1848, signed "W."

They came with the flatboats and were "the children of the Mississippi . . . combining all the most striking peculiarities of the common sailor, the whaleman, the backwoodsman, and the Yankee." [146] There were thousands of these hardy backwoodsmen who floated down the river in their flatboats and scows; the strain of their labor encouraged equally intense dissipation, and drinking, fighting, and gambling were common diversions.[147]

City dwellers took to flatboats like "children of the Mississippi" whenever it broke through the levee above New Orleans. Flood brought disaster not only to immigrant families who cultivated market gardens near the city,[148] but also to those in the slums. A crevasse in 1849 submerged two thousand tenements and left twelve thousand people homeless.[149] They were "mostly of the humble classes of laboring men, to whom small losses are heavy burdens." [150]

Besides New Orleans there were only seven towns in Louisiana which boasted a population of over a thousand.[151] Most important was Baton Rouge, the capital, where more than 4,000 inhabitants were classified by the local press as divided into 2,450 "office holders and seekers' and gentlemen of leisure," 700 merchants, 500 professional men (chiefly in law), and 200 clerks, all of whom were said to live by credit on the labor of 250 mechanics.[152] Up the Red River were found Alexandria, with a population of 1,600,[153] Natchitoches, with an equal number of Creoles and "several large and finely appointed barrooms," [154] and Shreveport, metropolis of the

[146] Norman, *op. cit.,* 75.
[147] Dondore, *The Prairie and the Making of Middle America,* 181.
[148] *De Bow's Review,* I (February, 1866), 172.
[149] *U. S. Cen., 1880, Rpt. Cities,* 262.   [150] *Crescent,* June 9, 1849.
[151] *U. S. Cen., 1850, Comp.,* 474.
[152] *Baton Rouge Daily Comet,* Sept. 15, 1852.
[153] *Crescent,* June 12, 1860.   [154] *Ibid.,* July 11, 1860.

northwestern parishes, with 3,500 people and "more stores than residences."[155] Natchitoches,[156] established as a Spanish outpost, was the oldest town in Louisiana. Its population was notoriously mixed: besides a majority of Creoles, there were many Spaniards, Indians, Mexicans, Italians, Germans, half-breeds known as "red-bones,"[157] and "Yankees, of course." It was not uncommon to hear children and slaves speak a patois of English, French, and Spanish.[158]

At all these towns could be found fairly well-to-do Yankee merchants and mechanics. Trade in a few villages was monopolized by Jewish storekeepers who stood their guard, ready to undersell bold interlopers and peddlers.[159] The ubiquitous peddler sometimes stopped at the village hotels and discovered that the food was more like that of the surrounding farms than legendary Southern cooking. "At few country stopping-places do I find milk, eggs, butter, fresh meat or vegetables," observed a traveler;[160] "the fare . . . is bacon and bread for breakfast, bread and bacon for dinner, and some bacon and bread for supper. We have bacon on the table and bacon under the table—the latter very much alive and uncured, the former very salt and rusty."[161]

Although Louisiana was completely rural outside New Orleans, it had an unusual number of small villages for a plant-

[155] *Ibid.*, July 21, 1860. Donaldsonville in the Sugar Bowl and Opelousas on the central prairie were also important towns. *U. S. Cen., 1860, Population*, 195.

[156] Pronounced "nak-itosh," the name of an Indian tribe.

[157] A local name for people of Indian, Negro, and French or Spanish blood to be found in Natchitoches and Calcasieu.

[158] Olmsted, *A Journey in the Seaboard Slave States*, 632.

[159] *Crescent*, Aug. 27, 1860.

[160] The newspaper correspondent, Dorr, who wrote a series of twenty-eight articles on northern Louisiana which were published in the *Crescent* from April to August, 1860, under the title, "Louisiana in Slices," and signed, "Tourist."

[161] *Crescent*, July 30, 1860.

ing state. This is illustrated by the publication of forty-five rural newspapers, or nearly one for every parish in 1855.[162] There were also more merchants than could usually be found in the Old South. Upland farming parishes like Caldwell and De Soto boasted ten or more apiece, and Carroll, Madison, and St. Mary in the plantation black belt, over a dozen each.[163] New Orleans was not Louisiana.

The country as a whole was divided among large planters in the river bottoms, small planters in the second bottoms, yeomen slaveholders on the oak uplands and prairies, and non-slaveholding farmers and poor whites on the pine hills and flats.[164] Since many parishes embraced both alluvial lowlands and hilly back country, large slave plantations could be found in one section and small farms without slaves in another.[165] But the farms of yeomen and nonslaveholders were most conspicuous in the northern uplands of Jackson, Bienville, Claiborne, and Bossier.[166] Here the inhabitants raised a little cotton and devoted "much attention to making other crops, rearing stock, etc., and thus [were] enabled to live luxuriously." [167] Secluded on sandy, timbered ridges in the back country, which provided wood for fuel and shelter, and a free range for cattle and swine, were the cabins of poor squatters from the southeastern states.[168] Remote from navigable rivers and civilization, they grew patches of corn and pastured livestock in the woods, but lived more by the gun than the plow, shooting deer, wild fowl, and fur-bearing animals by the thousands.[169] "Nothing

---

[162] *La. State Register, 1855*, 127, names and locates each one.

[163] Rev. John P. Campbell, ed., *The Southern Business Directory and General Commercial Advertiser* (Charleston, 1854), 180–83.

[164] *Crescent*, May 7, June 13, 1860.

[165] E. g., Ouachita. *Rpt. U. S. Bur. Soils, 1903*, 436–37.

[166] *Crescent*, July 30, Aug. 6, 11, 14, 1860.   [167] *Ibid.*, Aug. 6, 1860.

[168] J. G. Belisle, *History of Sabine Parish* (Many, La., 1912), 71, 77; *Rpt. U. S. Bur. Soils, 1904*, 376.

[169] *Picayune*, Dec. 15, 1860.

can be easier than subsistence in the pine woods," remarked Flint. "There being little call for labour, the inhabitants labour little, and are content with indolence, health, and poverty." [170]

Through Natchitoches, eastern terminus of the Spanish colonial trail to Santa Fe, and through Shreveport passed caravans of emigrants from the East bound for the virgin land of Texas.[171] In 1850, according to an exuberant railway promoter, 63,000 immigrants came this way.[172] The barren piney woods along these trails were spotted by the deserted cabins of families who had "gone to Texas," and in more fertile clearings at intervals of four miles, the small plantations of those who remained in Louisiana. Many emigrants, stricken by sickness or stopping to plant a crop, never left this region. Some appeared to till patches of ground, declared a planter, but actually "derived their whole lazy subsistence from their richer neighbors' hog droves." Others settled in shanties along the trail and furnished travelers with corn, spirits, and lodging. A countless number retired into the forest, built log cabins, and supported themselves by hunting, fishing, and occasionally herding cattle for the Texas drovers. Constantly riding back and forth along the trails were these picturesque cowboys, "ranchero-looking fellows, with their wide hats, rough attire, bearded faces, and belted ornaments of long bowie knives and army revolvers . . . savagely anti-Comanche and anti-Greaser —not to say particularly dirty and dusty." [173]

In the southwest on both sides of the Sabine River, which separates Louisiana from Texas, lived a motley population of mulattoes, red-bones, and poor white Creoles. Some had once

[170] *Recollections of the Last Ten Years,* 329.

[171] E. C. Barker, "Notes on the Colonization of Texas," *M. V. H. R.,* X, 147, 149.

[172] B. H. Payne, *Report on the Algiers and Opelousas Railroad* (New Orleans, 1851), 18.

[173] Olmsted, *A Journey through Texas,* 43, 53, 62–63, 66, 391; *Crescent,* June 13, 1860.

set out for Texas and stopped just short of it; others had married mulattoes and returned to Louisiana because of the severe Texas law against miscegenation. Many free people of color in this region owned slaves, but most whites were too poor to own either land or slaves. They kept herds of gaunt, half-starved cattle and lean, goatish swine. Patches of corn and a few rows of cotton made up their farms; jerked beef cooked in Creole style was their chief food. These people were rough, dirty, and profane: the women dipped snuff and smoked pipes, and the men, often drunk, quarreled murderously with knives and pistols.[174]

On the pine flats of the Florida parishes, in eastern Louisiana, lived French and Spanish families of " 'petits paysans,' small planters, engaged in the lumber trade, in making tar and charcoal, or . . . in raising cattle. The wealth of a young lady about to be married [was] measured by the number of her cows, as in the planting part of the State, . . . by her negroes. Some [had] two thousand cattle; and the swamps afford[ed] ample winter range, while the pine woods furnish[ed] grass in the summer." [175] When the New Orleans, Jackson, and Great Northern Railroad opened this region to immigrants in 1854, the natives resented the curtailment of their free cattle range and fought an unrecorded campaign against railroad and immigrants alike.[176]

Along the fringes of the Gulf Coast were poor German families who tilled the marshy, unwanted land.[177] Near by lived Cajun and Creole fishermen who dredged oysters in the bogs and bayous for the New Orleans market; nearly two hundred luggers and small sloops, of five to ten tons, were engaged in this trade.[178] Along the banks of the Mississippi, wherever the forest came close to the river, stood the "plank

[174] Olmsted, *A Journey through Texas*, 381–86.

[175] Flint, *op. cit.*, 317.

[176] *Rpt. U. S. Bur. Soils, 1905*, 512.

[177] *Crescent*, Nov. 8, 1859.

[178] *De Bow's Review*, III, 309.

shanties" of woodsmen who chopped the trees into fuel for passing steamboats. "They do not own the woods," observed a traveler, "but cut and sell it for some rough planter." [179] Among them were emigrants from Michigan intent on saving enough money to buy farms in the free West.[180] But other lumberjacks, like the fishermen, were part of the backwash of the frontier, or frontiersmen who had never moved on.

The most picturesque folk in the country were those contemptuously called Cadians or Cajuns, a vulgarization of Acadia, the land from which their forebears had been expelled in the eighteenth century.[181] About five thousand of these exiles ended their wanderings in Louisiana; [182] so prolific was their stock that it increased to about forty thousand in the course of a century.[183] They were especially numerous on the central Attakapas prairies, up in Pointe Coupee and Avoyelles, down Bayou Lafourche, and along other bayous and swamps in the Sugar Bowl.[184] They have been described in a highly contradictory light as people of Acadian virtues and as good-for-nothing peasants. The extremes are represented by Longfellow's idealization of Gabriel and Evangeline,[185] and by travelers who thought them indolent and ignorant.[186] Each view has some truth, distorted by considerable exaggeration,

[179] Oldmixon, *Transatlantic Wanderings*, 135–36; *Crescent*, Apr. 30, 1860.

[180] Tyrone Power, *Impressions of America* (Philadelphia, 1836), II, 118–19.

[181] Among the other variant spellings were " 'Cadiens," "Cadgens," and "Cajens." Cf. Rhodes, *op. cit., The Galaxy*, XVI, 254; Nordhoff, *op. cit.*, 73.

[182] F. X. Martin, *The History of Louisiana* (New Orleans, 1827; enl. ed., 1882), 25; Gray, *op. cit.*, I, 338.

[183] J. S. Zacharie, *The New Orleans Guide* (New Orleans, 1885), 166.

[184] H. M. Brackenridge, *Views of Louisiana* (Pittsburgh, 1814), 178; [anonymous], *An Account of Louisiana* (Washington, 1803), 7; *Crescent*, June 4, 1860.

[185] Cf. Dondore, *op. cit.*, 265, 266 n.

[186] E. g., "Journal of Capt. Harry Gordon's Journey . . . to New Orleans, etc., 1776," N. D. Mereness, ed., *Travels in the American Colonies* (New York, 1916), 481; Brackenridge, *loc. cit.*

for there were good people and bad, and the majority were doubtless a mixture. Cajuns might be divided into three kinds: the thrifty and comfortable, who owned their farms, sent their children to school, and had contact with the towns; the ignorant, whose main reliance was on truck gardening, and whose children went without schooling; and those who were lazy and improvident as well as ignorant, and consequently suffered all the privations of poverty.[187]

The lowest type of Cajun resembled the traditional picture of a poor white. With long, unkempt hair, a dirty, patched shirt, and faded cottonade pants, he went about barefoot, always scratching himself. His wife might be seen sniffling from a cold and wiping her nose on the hem of a bedraggled skirt. They lived with a brood of dirty children in a "dilapidated" cabin which had wide gaps between the boards and a roof covered with green or gray moss. A "broken down rail fence" surrounded the hut and enclosed a few stray brindle cattle and Creole ponies. A patch of ground might be planted in corn, rice, and a little cane. A family in this squalid condition seldom ate anything but the proverbial salt pork and corn pone, with milk or molasses on rare occasions.[188]

A better and more numerous class of Cajuns was depicted by the Confederate General, "Dick" Taylor, who described them as simple and virtuous peasants. "Isolated . . . , they spoke no language but their own *patois;* and, reading and writing not having come to them by nature, they were dependent for news on their curés and occasional peddlers. . . . Their little *cabanes* dotted the broad prairie in all directions, and it was pleasant to see the smoke curling from their chimneys, while herds of cattle and ponies grazed at will. Here, unchanged, was the French peasant . . . of Louis le

---

[187] G. A. Coulon, *350 Miles in a Skiff through the Louisiana Swamps* (New Orleans, 1888), 34–35.

[188] *Ibid,* 35–36.

Grand." [189] "They have chickens, pigs, cows and ponies in abundance," reported another observer; "their gardens yield them vegetables, the woods game and the river fish, and the small crops they raise furnish the little money they require; and so they live on comfortably and sleepily, undisturbed by ambitious dreams of wealth. . . . They are now very much what they were a century ago." [190] The philosophy of Cajuns was to "digest well by day and sleep well of nights." For them, life was "a great fair." [191]

No traveler recorded in detail the life of Louisiana poor whites,[192] whose degrading poverty repulsed everyone. But Olmsted has left us a good picture of a prosperous nonslaveholding family. At sunset one day, on the prairie road west of Opelousas, he approached a small low cottage which was built of timber and plastered with mud; the roof sloped sharply on all sides, and the chimney appeared to be made of sticks and clay. There was a stalwart man, who looked like a German, hoeing in the field with five slaves, three men and two women, whom he hired every Sunday from a local planter for fifty cents each. His wife, a Frenchwoman, was milking some bony cows at the cottage door. When Olmsted asked for lodging, the man and his wife replied in a *patois* of French and English, but their two young boys greeted him only in French. They showed Olmsted into the cottage, which consisted of three rooms, a long one in the center for living quarters, and one on either side for sleeping and cooking. The middle room had a plank floor, the others no floor but the ground, and all the walls were plastered with mud. On the living room mantel reposed a Connecticut clock, two mirrors,

[189] R. Taylor, *Destruction and Reconstruction*, 105-6. Cf. Alcée Fortier, *Louisiana Studies* (New Orleans [1894]), 162–81.

[190] *Crescent*, May 25, 1860.

[191] Rhodes, *op. cit., The Galaxy*, XVI, 254.

[192] Olmsted stopped overnight with them in Mississippi, but not in Louisiana.

and a few cups and saucers, luxuries bought of some Yankee peddler. There was no furniture to be seen except chairs with deerhide seats from which sprang "an atrocious number of fresh fleas." Sitting uneasily on one of these chairs, Olmsted was served a supper of fried eggs, bacon, sweet potatoes, milk, and bread dipped in molasses, and, after spending the night as a guest of mosquitoes, a breakfast of bacon and potatoes. All the food, and some cotton besides, was raised on a farm of twenty acres, where fences kept hungry cattle and razor-backed hogs out of the corn. What little money the family saw each year came from selling a few bales of cotton to the nearest plantation gin, ten miles away, and livestock "on the hoof" to drovers bound for New Orleans. As far as Opelousas, the prairie road was lined with small farms like this one [193]— typical of the yeomen in Louisiana.

[193] Olmsted, *A Journey through Texas,* 402–5.

CHAPTER III

SOCIAL CONDITIONS IN THE OLD REGIME

> Permanent prosperity . . . mainly depends upon
> the degree of salubrity that is to be attained and
> enjoyed by the *mass* of the inhabitants,—not the
> wealthy portion.
>
> —DR. E. H. BARTON [1]

Poor people in the country, contrary to a popular belief,[2] did not enjoy good health to compensate for their poverty. While the country as a whole was much more healthful than the city, the rural western parishes had twice the death rate of those in the east.[3] This climatic anomaly, generally unrecognized at the time and long since forgotten, may be ascribed to several causes. Fundamental was the fact that river-bottom planters, situated chiefly in the eastern parishes, were more careful of sanitation and were closer to the medical facilities of New Orleans than the farmers who lived in the western uplands. For example, the planters kept clean their cistern drinking water, which fell with the rain, but farmers carelessly drew water from any river or well and consequently suffered epidemics of typhoid fever.[4] The thinly settled country outside the plantation belt could not afford to organize parish sanitation and good medical service.[5] When people who lived near New Orleans were ravaged by yellow fever, they could find doctors and hospitals in the city; but farmers, fishermen, woodcutters, and peddlers

[1] "Report upon the Meteorology, Vital Statistics and Hygiene of . . . Louisiana," *Southern Medical Reports* (New Orleans, 1850–51), II, 122.

[2] Flint, *Recollections of the Last Ten Years*, 329.

[3] *Southern Medical Rpts.*, II, 151–52. New Orleans was omitted in calculating the death rate of the eastern lowlands.

[4] *Rpt. U. S. Bur. Soils, 1903*, 421.   [5] *Southern Medical Rpts.*, II, 121.

in remote western parishes frequently died of fever or disease long before they could reach a doctor.[6] They lived beyond the pale of medical science. Infant mortality was so great in one rural parish that not more than half the children survived their tenth birthday.[7] Hookworm, diagnosed as "intestinal worms" or "acid stomach," led to the eating of clay wherever poor whites lived.[8] Men and women on the frontier, it should be remembered, were constantly exposed to physical hardships unknown in the city or on large plantations, and therefore met death more often by accident or neglect. Even wet feet, strange to say, were the beginning of the end of many frontiersmen.[9]

But what chiefly made the country so unhealthful was the poverty of its inhabitants and the ignorance which everywhere attends poverty. This was the reason that, notwithstanding the superior climate they enjoyed, only one in three white farmers in the hills had a better chance of reaching old age than had slaves in the swamps.[10] Negroes on the large plantations were so valuable that masters supervised their health with the aid of physicians whom the poor hill farmer could neither afford nor obtain.[11] Hence colored mortality was only a third greater than white in the lowlands, but almost equal in the uplands.[12] That farmers in the cool hills should suffer greater

[6] E. D. Fenner, *Report on the Epidemics of Louisiana, . . . for 1854 and 1855* (Philadelphia, 1856), 1–55.

[7] *Southern Medical Rpts.*, II, 161, 184. Hookworm was held responsible for the heavy death rate of children in the country.

[8] *Ibid.*, I, 194–95; II, 184. Dr. J. B. Duncan reported the eating of dirt to be common in St. Mary among poor white women and slaves. He attributed the habit to a scurvy condition which resulted from a poor diet, deficient in fresh meat and vegetables; but he also thought that the eating of dirt might be a cause as well as a symptom of disordered digestion. Some planters tried to cure slaves of the habit by chaining them to plank floors and putting tin masks and iron gags on their faces.

[9] *Ibid.*, II, 157–85.   [10] *Ibid.*, II, 152–53.   [11] Fenner, *op. cit.*, 46–48.
[12] *Southern Medical Rpts.*, II, 152–53.

mortality than planters and slaves in the hot lowlands shows that poverty shortened more lives than did climate.

Louisiana, to be sure, had the largest death rate of any state, and New Orleans of any city, in the United States.[13] Yellow fever, the worst scourge, took a toll of over fifty thousand lives in New Orleans alone during the twenty years before the Civil War.[14] The most fatal epidemic, in 1853, accounted for twelve thousand of these casualties.[15] Although the plague broke out in tenements along the levee,[16] it spread to more prosperous sections and prostrated rich and poor alike.[17] The rich soon fled from the city in terror.[18] But people too poor to follow were stricken in their beds, in stores, on the streets, and frequently died in carriages and carts on the way to hospitals. Funeral processions crowded the streets and cemeteries. Some were buried with pomp, others in long, anonymous rows with a few shovels of dirt, which the rain soon uncovered, leaving corpses to rot under the hot sun. In an effort to purify the mephitic air, and perhaps to drive the plague away, four hundred shots were fired from cannon; but not until cold weather did the epidemic abate—only to return the following summer.[19]

Although the stegomyia mosquito had not yet been identified as the agent of yellow fever, there was good reason for physicians of the day to suspect that the disease was introduced by ships from the West Indies, where the stegomyia was later found to be endemic. Certainly this pest was not wanting in New Orleans. As a local Irishman said, "there is one set of

[13] U. S. Cen., 1850, Comp., 105, 107, 111; Southern Medical Rpts., II, 215.
[14] U. S. Cen., 1880, Rpt. Cities, 264–65. Cf. Rpt. La. Bd. Health, 1880, 9.
[15] Fenner, op. cit., passim; La. State Register, 127.
[16] New Orleans Medical and Surgical Journal, X, 275.
[17] Ibid.; Flint, op. cit., 302.   [18] Southern Medical Rpts., II, 122.
[19] U. S. Cen., 1880, Rpt. Cities, 265–66. For a detailed account of this epidemic, see J. F. Rhodes, History of the United States (New York, 1895–1906), I, 400–13.

musquitoes who sting you all day, and when they go in toward dusk, another kind comes out and bites you all night." [20] Doctors were quick to observe that the open sewer gutters and uncovered cisterns gave rise to "myriads of mosquitoes," [21] and that the filthy, unpaved streets, shallow-ground privies, swampy yards, and slums of New Orleans invited plagues.[22] After the epidemic of 1853 a few enlightened physicians demanded that sewers be laid underground,[23] streets paved,[24] sanitary laws enforced,[25] tenements torn down, and vessels quarantined.[26]

Except for a lax ship quarantine, however, nothing was done.[27] Wealthy taxpayers, who could afford to escape yellow fever by leaving the city in summer, were loath to underwrite an expensive civic house cleaning. Instead, they joined shop- and hotelkeepers in a conspiracy of silence and warned all who valued the prosperity of the city not to admit that it was unhealthful. Newspapers, following their advice, denied the existence of yellow fever whenever it broke out, and minimized its ravages after it had disappeared for a season.[28] To

[20] Lyell, *A Second Visit to the United States*, II, 121.

[21] *Southern Medical Rpts.*, I, 23.

[22] *Rpt. New Orleans and Lafayette Bd. Health, 1850*, 77–99; *New Orleans Medical and Surgical Journal*, X, 275; *Southern Medical Rpts.*, II, 139–41; W. M. Carpenter, *Sketches from the History of Yellow Fever, etc.* (New Orleans, 1844), 43.

[23] Because of the marshy subsoil, underground sewers were not laid until the eighties. *U. S. Cen., 1880, Rpt. Cities*, 265.

[24] Only half the streets, chiefly in the wealthy and commercial sections, were paved in 1849. *Southern Medical Rpts.*, I, 21–22.

[25] A city ordinance required the contents of privies, which could be only four feet deep, to be emptied into the Mississippi every night by private contractors; but anyone with a nose could tell how little this regulation was observed. *Ibid.*, 26.

[26] *Ibid.*, II, 208; *Creole*, Jan. 29, 1857.

[27] *U. S. Cen., 1880, Rpt. Cities*, 266; V. Parsons, "A Study of the Activities of the Louisiana Board of Health from 1855 to 1896 in Reference to Quarantine" (unpublished master's thesis, Tulane University, 1932), chaps. I, II.

[28] *Southern Medical Rpts.*, II, 122, 206–7.

their support came some members of the Board of Health, who held unacclimatized "floaters" responsible for the plague.[29] A majority of the victims at Charity Hospital, it was pointed out, were recent immigrants from Ireland and the German states.[30] But this comforting theory, which smacked of medical Know-Nothingism, was discredited by the fact that native Americans comprised the majority of all who died in New Orleans.[31]

Even when the agitation for preventive measures shifted from humanitarian to economic grounds,[32] the well-to-do were not aroused to act in their own self-interest. It came to be realized that yellow fever not only caused absenteeism, "retarding, like a curse from God, the population and progress" of the city,[33] but also discouraged railway investment [34] and immigration.[35] Yet the only remedy adopted was to enforce the ship quarantine with greater efficiency.[36]

Such apathy on the part of its most influential citizens made New Orleans a pesthole in the first half of the nineteenth century. Yellow fever, sometimes sporadic, at other times epidemic, broke out every summer from 1812 to 1861. Not as common but almost as fatal was cholera, which took the lives of two thousand people in 1849.[37] Heavy infant mortality was caused by ignorant midwives and diphtheria, the former more deadly than the latter.[38] Typhus, dysentery, tuberculosis, and malaria, each contributed its share of victims to the local cemeteries.[39] Of all who died from every cause, it was estimated that at least a half were men, women, and chil-

[29] Ibid., 207, 229.
[30] La. Sen. J., 1850, app.
[31] Rpt. La. Bd. Health, 1859, 28.
[32] Creole, loc. cit.
[33] Southern Medical Rpts., II, 122.
[34] See below, chap. IV.
[35] Southern Medical Rpts., II, 142–43.
[36] Parsons, op. cit., chaps. II, III.
[37] U. S. Cen., 1880, Rpt. Cities, 264.
[38] New Orleans Medical and Surgical Journal, VII, 49; Rpt. La. Bd. Health, 1860, 9, 14–17.
[39] Rpt. La. Bd. Health, loc. cit.

dren of the working classes.[40] Their deaths, like those of the
more prosperous half, were attributed by some physicians to
the ignorant and selfish well-to-do who would not tax themselves in order to clean up the city.[41] These fearless doctors,
among whom Barton, Dowler, Fenner, and Simonds should
not be forgotten by posterity, [42] were conspicuous for their
humanitarian crusade. But the medical science of their day
was powerless to heal the sick in a place as sickly as New
Orleans.

To the credit of state and city, however, were many benevolent institutions, of which the largest and most famous was
Charity Hospital in New Orleans.[43] Here competent physicians and the Sisters of Charity cared for more than fifteen
thousand patients every year; and in spite of receiving many
desperate cases in the last stage of a disease, they kept the death
rate down to 10 per cent.[44] From 1830 to 1850 Charity Hospital treated 100,000 patients at an average cost of five dollars
each.[45] Even this small expense was not all charity, for half
of it was defrayed by a head tax of two dollars [46] on the immigrants who filled the hospital beds.[47]

[40] *Southern Medical Rpts.*, II, 232.   [41] *Ibid.*, 107–53.

[42] See especially the presidential address of Dr. E. H. Barton to the Medical
Society of Louisiana in 1851. *Southern Medical Rpts.*, II, 107–53.

[43] Established privately in the eighteenth century, and taken over by the
city in 1811, the hospital was located in brick buildings, containing five hundred beds, supplied by the state at a cost of $150,000. Norman, *New Orleans
and Environs*, 117–19.

[44] *Ibid.*; *New Orleans Medical and Surgical Journal*, VII, 817.

[45] *Southern Medical Rpts.*, I, 253.

[46] *Delta*, Aug. 8, 1852. Other revenues accrued to the hospital from the
municipal license fees of gambling parlors and houses of ill fame. Flint,
op. cit., 309–10.

[47] The roster of nationalities found at Charity Hospital is an index to the
sources of immigration. Among the 11,000 foreign-born patients treated in
1860 were 6,400 Irish, 2,200 German, over 1,000 French and English, and
nearly 1,000 Prussian, Swiss, Swedish, Scottish, and Canadian people. *Rpt.*

Orphanages sheltered the children who were left destitute when their parents succumbed to yellow fever.[48] Half a dozen of these institutions, housed in brick buildings, provided better care for five hundred children than most orphanages of this period. At the Poydras Female Asylum,[49] for example, children slept two in a bed, forty in a room, and had three meals a day, consisting of bread and milk for breakfast and supper, and soup, meat, a vegetable, and pudding for dinner. At the New Orleans Female Asylum the children rose at half past five, attended classes taught by Sisters of Charity, studying English in the morning, French and sewing in the afternoon, said their prayers in the evening, and retired at eight.[50]

Other public charitable institutions for which Louisiana was justly famous before the Civil War were the State Insane Asylum established at Jackson in 1847 to care for one hundred patients,[51] the Deaf and Dumb Institute founded in 1852 at Baton Rouge,[52] and the New Orleans House of Refuge, a reformatory for the industrial education and apprenticeship of juvenile delinquents and vagrants.[53] The state was so liberal in its charities that in 1859 it expended nearly $100,000, a twelfth part of its entire budget, to support benevolent institutions.[54]

Nor did private purses leave all charity to the state. Relief associations, for example, helped immigrants on their arrival

---

Charity Hospital, 1860, 12. Of 1,700 American patients in 1849, 400 came from New York, 300 from New England, 200 from Pennsylvania, and only 147 from Louisiana. *La. Sen. J., 1850*, app.

[48] Zacharie, *The New Orleans Guide*, 55.

[49] One of the oldest and best, the benefaction of Julien Poydras (1746–1824). See *D. A. B.* Flint observed that the children here were all neatly clad and industrious. *Op. cit.*, 305.

[50] *Southern Medical Rpts.*, I, 237–44.

[51] *La. Sess. Laws, 1847*, 56–58 [no. 69]; *Rpt. Secy. State, 1902*, 479–81.

[52] *Rpt. Secy. State, 1902*, 470.   [53] *La. Sess. Laws, 1847*, 203 [no. 245].

[54] *Ibid., 1859*, 235–40 [no. 283].

at New Orleans.[55] The best known was the German Society, established by immigrants of this nationality in 1847, which expended thousands of dollars and built an orphanage to aid fellow countrymen.[56] That immigrants could help themselves to this extent measures the prosperity of some and the poverty of others. New Englanders, who generally fared well in New Orleans,[57] formed a society in 1842 to assist the poorer emigrants and sailors from their home ports.[58] The age-old charity of the poor looking after the poor was to be witnessed in such mutual penny and dollar relief associations as the United Laborers' Benevolent Society.[59]

But all these charities did nothing to diminish crime, which troubled Louisiana more than other Southern states.[60] In New Orleans, notorious for being the most lawless city in the country,[61] were to be found a majority of the criminals: [62] it was not uncommon to see them walking the streets with the handle of a bowie knife, or an "Arkansas toothpick," protruding from their pockets.[63] The French custom of settling *affaires d'honneur* with pistol or sword, although constitutionally outlawed,[64] kept alive a tradition of violent individualism not to be matched elsewhere unless on the frontier. Characters like Whitman's "Daggerdraw Bowieknife" lurked about the gambling saloons.[65] A police force of less than four hundred af-

[55] Their dire need of assistance was described in the novel by Friedrich Gerstäcker, *Nach Amerika*, cited by Dondore, *The Prairie and the Making of Middle America: . . .* , 302–5.

[56] Voss, *History of the German Society of New Orleans*, 75 f.

[57] *Courier*, Aug. 11, 1852.   [58] *New Orleans Directory, 1857*, app., 25.

[59] *La. Sess. Laws, 1855*, 57 [no. 60].   [60] *U. S. Cen., 1850, Comp.*, 166.

[61] *Creole*, June 4, 1857. Although New Orleans was known as the wickedest city in America, a boy was arrested in 1856 for hawking about the streets a scandalous paper entitled "Life in Boston," which "only prostitutes and Thugs would or could read." *Delta*, Aug. 1, 1856.

[62] *Rpt. Audit. Pub. Accts., La. H. J.*, 1852, app.

[63] A. Mackay, *The Western World* (Philadelphia, 1849), II, 89, 97.

[64] *Const. 1845*, Art. 89.   [65] *Crescent*, Mar. 23, 1848.

forded little protection to 170,000 citizens. Timid strangers were escorted by policemen from beat to beat and warned against "pick-pockets, droppers, mock-auctioneers, and all other vicious persons." [66] Murderers were not always apprehended; and when they were arrested, it was difficult to convict them because witnesses feared that unfavorable testimony would bring horrible retribution. The processes of justice moved slowly in a city with only one criminal court, where it was not easy to form juries.[67] Nevertheless, the police frequently acted in a wholesale manner to make or meet the crime "waves" which were annual phenomena. In two years of extraordinary activity, partly of a political nature, the police arrested 44,000 people, or nearly one in four of the urban population; but all except eight thousand of the arrests were among the foreign-born.[68]

For neither the native whites nor the free persons of color but rather the floaters and immigrants gave the city its criminal reputation.[69] Because New Orleans was the metropolis of the Southwest, all the vagabonds and desperadoes visited the city at one season or another.[70] With hundreds of footloose immigrants, they made fraud and gambling a profession, larceny a paying occupation, and battery and assault a prerequisite to the franchise.[71]

A large proportion of these criminals, however, were simply vagrants—drunkards, prostitutes, beggars, and what we would now call the unemployed.[72] Despite the fact that the South boasted of its freedom from pauperism, because slavery was supposed to provide all white men with cheap labor and all colored men with subsistence,[73] there were nevertheless many

[66] *Rules and Regulations of the Police Department of New Orleans* (New Orleans, 1852), 3, 14–15.
[67] *Rpt. Atty. Gen., 1857*, 7–9.   [68] *Creole*, June 27, 1857.
[69] *Ibid.*, June 4, 1857.   [70] A. Mackay, *loc. cit.*   [71] See below, chap. V.
[72] *Rules and Regulations of the Police Dept. etc.*, 44.
[73] *Commercial Bulletin*, Jan. 22, 1867.

paupers, as well as the poor whites who constituted as a class the slum element of the South.[74] Even in the country provision had to be made for relieving the indigent by public funds.[75] In 1850 the state supported over four hundred paupers at a cost of nearly $40,000,[76] and there were almost as many people in the almshouse before as after the Civil War.[77]

But the great majority of paupers, commonly mistaken for vagrants,[78] could be found in the New Orleans workhouses, where they were confined for three to six months.[79] In one district of the city during 1860 nearly four hundred men and women were sentenced for vagrancy. Not all of them, as the press alleged, had Irish or German names.[80] Along with petty criminals, serving short terms, the men worked at blacksmithing, cobbling shoes, or picking oakum, the women at sewing, and the slaves, shackled in gangs, at paving and draining the streets. Their prisons were not like other nineteenth-century pesthouses, and there was less cholera and yellow fever there than in the rest of the city, owing possibly to the fact that all inmates except slaves were isolated.[81]

Criminals sentenced to long terms were sent to the state penitentiary,[82] which was really a cotton bagging factory leased to private contractors.[83] Here labored three hundred convicts, of whom two-thirds were white, and only one-third foreign-born. Murder was the crime for which a third of the prisoners had been convicted; larceny and burglary were charged against the rest. Their sentences, no more severe than

[74] Buck, *op. cit., A. H. R.,* XXXI, 46–47.
[75] Rills, *A New Digest of the Laws of the Parish of Iberville,* 43.
[76] *U. S. Cen., 1850, Comp.,* 163.
[77] *U. S. Cen., 1890, Rpt. Crime, Pauperism, and Benevolence,* pt. II, 655.
[78] *Rules and Regulations of the Police Dept. etc., loc. cit.*
[79] *La. Sess. Laws, 1852,* 219–20 [no. 321].
[80] *Vagrant Record Book* (1859–61), 3rd District Recorder's Office [MS in City Hall Archives].
[81] *Southern Medical Rpts.,* I, 24–25.
[82] *La. Sess. Laws, 1850,* 244 [no. 247].   [83] *De Bow's Review,* XII, 22–30.

those of today, ran from one to five years for larceny, twenty years for manslaughter, and life for murder.[84]

Although there was naturally less crime in the country than in the city, law and order were not always maintained in sparsely settled regions along the frontier. On the Attakapas prairies, for example, organized bands of thieves preyed upon the settlers, stealing cattle, robbing stores, burning cabins, and often killing whoever resisted them.[85] If apprehended and brought before local courts, these bandits were acquitted by juries which they bribed or intimidated. Since the state seemed incapable of punishing them, the citizens took the law into their own hands. In 1859 over three thousand vigilantes besieged 150 alleged bandits in a fortified house and took half of them prisoners. After drumhead trials they were lashed, some with three hundred stripes, and banished under threat of hanging.[86] Neighboring parishes immediately formed posses to track down the brigands fleeing across their borders.[87] In six months of bitter strife hundreds suffered death or exile at the hands of vigilantes, who were exonerated and disbanded by the grand jury.[88]

Perhaps this was not as simple an affair of frontier justice as it at first appeared, for there was much murmuring that it had become a private war between rich and poor. "The Vigilance Committee," charged a local newspaper, "have poured their wrath upon none but poor men. Are the rich men of those . . . parishes all honest? . . . Are there not some rich men connected with these late extraordinary pro-

[84] La. H. J., 1854, 2–14, 16, 18.

[85] H. L. Griffin, "The Vigilance Committees of the Attakapas Country, etc.," Mississippi Valley Hist. Assn. Proceedings, VIII, 146–59.

[86] Plaquemine [Iberville] Magnolia, Sept. 17, quoted in Crescent, Sept. 20, 1859.

[87] Marksville [Avoyelles]Organ, Oct. 8, quoted in ibid., Oct. 15, 1859.

[88] Griffin, op. cit., 159; Opelousas [St. Landry] Courier, quoted in Crescent, Oct. 25, 1859.

ceedings who are anxious to obtain divers little patches of land, and some Creole horses and cows, at half price? Is not cunning avarice already at work in many a bosom, and many a piece of property already half sold at an immense sacrifice to the original owner? We do not think this was the object at first, but believe it is fast running into a speculation." [89] There can be found no evidence to confirm or deny these insinuations, but suspicion of their truth attaches to the fact that Governor Wickliffe and some New Orleans newspapers denounced the vigilantes.[90]

Louisianians were not much more concerned with the judgments of Heaven than with those of the state. Roman Catholicism was the faith of the French colonists and remained supreme for over a century until the advent of American immigration.[91] Not one Protestant church steeple was seen by Flint, in 1823, along the entire Mississippi Coast from St. Francisville to New Orleans; at regular intervals of six miles the landscape was marked by the cross of Catholic churches.[92] In 1850 there were fifty-five of these buildings, valued at a million dollars, with 37,000 communicants; [93] ten years later, these figures had doubled, and 15 per cent of the free people were accounted Catholics.[94] The Church was strongest in lower Louisiana among the Creoles, Cajuns, and Irish. In seven southern parishes there was not a single Protestant church, and only one in each of seven others.[95] Catholicism was most firmly entrenched in New Orleans, seat of the diocese, where half its members and the more valuable part of its property were

---

[89] *Franklin* [St. Mary] *Banner*, Sept. 17, quoted in *ibid.*, Sept. 20, 1859.

[90] Griffin, *op. cit.*, 157–58, overlooks this interpretation of the affair.

[91] V. A. Moody, "Early Religious Efforts in the Lower Mississippi Valley," *M.V.H.R.*, XXII, 163–64. Toward the end of the Spanish regime, there were estimated to be 43,087 Catholic souls in Louisiana and Florida.

[92] *Recollections of the Last Ten Years,* 300.

[93] *U.S. Cen. 1850, Comp.*, 133–36.

[94] *U.S. Cen., 1860, Mortality & Miscel. Statistics*, 401–3.   [95] *Ibid.*

located.[96] Here the Church dispensed many social services, especially to the poor Irish and German immigrants; [97] Sisters of Charity nursed the sick and reared the orphans, and Carmelite and Ursuline nuns educated white and colored children.[98] Among Creole and Cajun farmers in the country, and to a lesser degree among the Irish in the city, the Catholic Church was a French state within the American state. The Cathedral of St. Louis meant more to Creoles in New Orleans and affected their lives in many more ways than the Capitol at Baton Rouge.

New Orleans was transformed into a Protestant stronghold by the horde of Americans who came to Louisiana in later years. By 1860 there were half again as many Protestants as Catholics in the city.[99] The first Protestant church to be established in the Southwest was an Episcopal parish which was organized in New Orleans in 1805.[100] After several years of missionary work a Methodist church was finally erected in 1819,[101] and held its ground among "a pleasure-loving dissolute, heterogeneous people" that "was divided between superstition and infidelity." [102] The large transient population and commercial character of the city made it a comparatively irreligious community for the nineteenth century,[103] with never more than three in twenty-five people attending any church.[104] A majority of the faithful were Presbyterians, Methodists, and Episcopalians, the denominations which next

[96] *La. H. Debs., 1864*, app., 58.

[97] See the tribute of the Unitarian minister, Rev. Theo. Clapp, in his *Autobiographical Sketches* . . . , 231–34, 248–49.

[98] Norman, *New Orleans and Environs*, 103–5, 119.

[99] *La. H. Debs., 1864, loc. cit.*

[100] Zacharie, *op. cit.*, 75–76; J. Koch, "Origins of New England Protestantism in New Orleans," *South Atlantic Quarterly*, XXIX, 60–76.

[101] W. B. Posey, *The Development of Methodism in the Old Southwest 1783–1824* (Nashville, 1933), 125–26.

[102] H. N. McTyeire, *A History of Methodism* (Nashville, 1884), 548.

[103] Clapp, *op. cit.*, 253.   [104] *U. S. Cen., 1860, Prelim. Rpt.*, 130–31.

to the Catholics were the best organized in the city. An influx
of Germans gave birth to eleven Lutheran churches, and Jews
came in sufficient numbers to support three synagogues.[105]

The great strength of Protestantism lay in northern Louisiana, where no Catholic church was ever established in thirteen
parishes. Here the people were almost equally divided between
Methodists and Baptists. The former were more numerous
in the northeastern parishes, East and West Feliciana, Livingston, Morehouse, Rapides, St. Helena, and Tensas; the
latter in the northwestern parishes, Bienville, Bossier, Caldwell, Claiborne, Jackson, Sabine, and Union. In this region,
by 1860, there were nearly 200 Methodist churches with a
seating capacity of 58,000, and over 150 Baptist congregations
of 47,000. In the state as a whole one in five free people belonged to these denominations. Either faith was superior to
Catholicism in numbers, but not in wealth.[106]

The Methodist and Baptist churches were slow to take root
but quick to grow in upper Louisiana, because this region was
not settled until late, and then by emigrants from the southeastern states who brought with them their native evangelical
faiths. In 1841, before the flood tide of their arrival, Bishop
Polk could not find "a single church west of the Mississippi
River"; and he met "few or no Presbyterians, and only now
and then a wandering Methodist." [107] The spread of Wesley's
faith showed how churches, like schools and other social institutions, waited on settlement.[108] Methodism was first trans-
planted to Louisiana in 1805 by a young Kentuckian under
the charge of Bishop Asbury.[109] There were apparently few
people to be converted on the thinly inhabited frontier, and

[105] *La. H. Debs., 1864, loc. cit.*

[106] *U. S. Cen., 1860, Mortality & Miscel. Statistics,* 401–3; D. W. Harris and
B. M. Hulse, *History of Claiborne Parish* (New Orleans, 1886), 65.

[107] W. M. Polk, *Leonidas Polk, Bishop and General* (New York, 1915),
I, 169.

[108] Cf. Moody, *op. cit.,* 171–72.   [109] Harris and Hulse, *op. cit.,* 116–17.

they were not easily organized into circuits or districts, for as late as 1836 only eleven Methodist preachers were assigned to Louisiana by the newly formed Arkansas Conference.[110] But with the increasing Methodist immigration of the next ten years, Louisiana was recognized as a Conference.[111] Soon it was partitioned into six districts, equally divided between the northern parishes and the towns of New Orleans, Baton Rouge, and Opelousas, with sixty-two ministers stationed at regular churches.[112] The development of the Baptist Church was similar but never as extensive.[113] It was organized west of the Mississippi River in 1819,[114] and grew with the settlement of the region. The Baptists, like the Methodists, doubled their numbers in a decade of heavy immigration after 1850.[115]

These evangelical faiths suited the character and needs of the settlers of upper Louisiana. They "responded especially to the democratic circuit-riding ministry of the Methodists and to the ministrations of Baptist preachers who toiled as did the people for six days a week and preached as best they might on the Sabbath."[116] True to their Protestant heritage, the settlers believed in religion as a power for law and order, and built churches to develop the country and break up the wilderness into communities.[117] Periodic revivals converted the ignorant and renewed the zeal of the faithful. To these gatherings came the country people, white and black, from miles around. Since they commonly lived far apart in the hills,[118] where there was little to feed their imagination and no group in which to express their emotions, they found the camp meeting an exhilarating experience. It was a social as well as religious festival.

[110] Moody, op. cit., 164. [111] Harris and Hulse, op. cit., 117.
[112] Baton Rouge Democratic Advocate, Jan. 19, 1848.
[113] J. T. Christian, A History of the Baptists of Louisiana (Nashville, 1923).
[114] Moody, op. cit., 164. [115] U. S. Cen., 1860, loc. cit.
[116] Moody, op. cit., 171. [117] Ibid., 171–72. [118] Crescent, Aug. 20, 1860.

Even the Presbyterians tried to match the colorful appeal of other faiths by holding revivals. At one of their meetings in 1858, a year noted for revivalism, the preaching continued from morning until night. Men were frightened by predictions of fire and brimstone; the women were more gently aroused by the slogan, "Every *Lady* is a Christian." [119] Presbyterian theology, of course, proved difficult for simple country folk to understand. It was not until 1854 that a presbytery was organized in northern Louisiana, with churches in Shreveport and five villages.[120]

Of the rough piety of these rural Protestants, commonly Methodist or Baptist, more rarely Presbyterian or Episcopalian, there can be little doubt. Not content with strenuous proselytism in their own parishes, they put a Bible in every cell at the state penitentiary.[121] They thought New Orleans a den of wickedness, French planters an immoral lot, and Catholicism an unholy and gaudy form of worship.[122] But their piety did not reform the habits of the frontier. A traveler observed that the Methodists and Baptists in one place were "good, sober folks, albeit there are one or two more whiskey restaurants than seem necessary." [123] In another evangelical community he discovered that "some of the bar-rooms close when the church-bell rings in the evening, that the bar-keepers may follow their customers to the place of meeting." [124] Hard drinking and hard praying seemed to go with hard labor on the farms of upper Louisiana.

The economic complexion of religion could be clearly discerned. A great disparity in wealth separated Catholicism from Protestantism, the former being richer, chiefly because

[119] [Baton Rouge] *Weekly Gazette and Comet*, May 16, 1858.

[120] *Red River Presbyterian*, Nov. 5, 1929.   [121] *La. Sen. Debs., 1853*, 76.

[122] Flint, *op. cit.*, 300; interview with H. L. Brian, whose father was an evangelical clergyman, May 2, 1933.

[123] *Crescent*, Aug. 14, 1860.   [124] *Ibid.*, Aug. 20, 1860.

it was established in Louisiana a century before the latter and had so much more time in which to accumulate property. Among the Catholics were to be found all classes of people from the humblest Cajun and free man of color to the proudest Creole. Protestant denominations were less inclusive. The poorer rural people joined Baptist or Methodist churches, which were generally situated in their neighborhoods. More prosperous and urban families were inclined to be Presbyterians or Episcopalians. Their small number, filling but one church in every ten, may be regarded in part as a sign of the concentration of wealth in Louisiana.[125] The Episcopal Church penetrated the lower ranks of society with two missions among the poor Germans and mechanics of New Orleans, but these outposts disappeared in the unemployment which followed the Panic of 1857.[126]

Because all the Protestant denominations were comparatively poor and loosely organized, but without extremes of wealth and poverty, they could not support as many charities and social services as the Catholics. Nevertheless they figured as good Samaritans in New Orleans during epidemics of yellow fever. Typical was the visit of their Y. M. C. A. relief committee to a German widow whose husband had died of the plague. "We tried to lead her to place her dependence upon God," was the report. "She said she had but 50 cents in the world and a few potatoes, and three children dependent upon her for support." [127] So the committee promised her admission to St. Anna's Asylum, "a retreat for poor gentlewomen." [128]

What money the evangelical churches could raise, they devoted to education. In the northern parishes they built academies in every large town. In Claiborne, for example, Baptists

[125] U. S. Cen., 1850, Comp., lvii, 134–36; cf. De Bow's Review, XIV, 435.
[126] Journal of the Proceedings of the 21st Convention of the Protestant Episcopal Church, Diocese of Louisiana (New Orleans, 1859), 41–42.
[127] The True Witness, Sept. 18, 1858.   [128] Zacharie, op. cit., 58.

and Methodists conducted two male and two female "colleges" with an attendance of nearly four hundred pupils.[129] There were a dozen or more denominational institutions in other parishes.[130] Hardly superior to common schools, these academies offered the only secondary training available to country children before the Civil War.

Free public education in Louisiana, as elsewhere in the Old South,[131] suffered for want of civic support. There was neither the will nor the means to educate the masses. It did "not pay in plowing and ditching" Southern fields "as in the mechanical arts" of Northern towns.[132] The population was too scattered and the majority too poor for the multiplication of schools.[133] To the richer slaveholders, who could provide their children with tutors and private schooling, the cost of educating the poor seemed prohibitive. If defrayed by taxation, it would necessarily fall on slaveholders through increased assessments on their slaves,[134] who constituted over half the wealth of the state.[135] There was no more profitable source of revenue where land was relatively cheap, thinly settled, and in wide areas still a wilderness.[136] "Large estate[s] . . . exclude population," observed a parish official; and "where the private fence is far, the public school, of course, cannot be near, nor the church nor the court-house nor any other public establish-

[129] *Crescent*, Aug. 6, 1860.
[130] Fortier, *Louisiana Studies*, 302; cf. *Rpt. State Supt. Pub. Educ., 1854*, 47.
[131] See C. W. Dabney, *Universal Education in the South* (Chapel Hill, N. C., 1936), I, *passim*.
[132] *Rpt. State Supt. Pub. Educ., 1854*, 35–36.
[133] *De Bow's Review*, V (December, 1868), 1107; in 1850, with only eleven inhabitants per square mile, including slaves, Louisiana could hardly support schools like those of Massachusetts, which had 126 inhabitants to every square mile. De Bow, *Encyclopaedia of the Trade and Commerce . . .* , III, 425.
[134] *Ibid.*, 1108.   [135] *Rpt. La. Audit. Pub. Accts., 1861*, 3–106.
[136] In 1860 there were fifteen persons per square mile in Louisiana, of whom half were slaves. If New Orleans is excluded from these figures, the density of rural population would be much less. *U. S. Cen., 1860, Prelim. Rpt.*, 262.

ment." [137] Unless the black belt financed the white belt, slavery and the plantation system formed an economy which was by nature hostile to the free education of poor, white people. This was the predicament of the entire South, and it was aggravated in Louisiana by the peculiar opposition of the French population to any kind of secular instruction that would usurp what they regarded as the prerogative of church and family.[138]

In spite of this antagonism the advent of American control marked the beginning of brave but futile efforts to diffuse knowledge among the people. The early governors were emphatic in recommending schools to the legislature,[139] and from 1812 to 1843 over one and a half million dollars were appropriated for education.[140] No state in the union was more liberal in proportion to its population.[141] But over half the money was used to subsidize academies and colleges, and the "primary school [was] lost sight of." [142] Insufficient sums were subscribed annually for schools in each parish and for the instruction of pupils too poor to pay tuition. Under these conditions parents would not permit children to attend schools which branded them as paupers; parish officials administered the state money indifferently; and taxpayers were averse to supplementing it with local funds.[143] The result was almost the same as if there had been no schools. It was estimated by Governor Roman that from 1818 to 1830 only 354 poor children obtained any benefit from state appropriations amounting to over a third of a million dollars. While four hundred Louisianians were attending college in Europe and the North,

[137] *La. H. J., 1852,* 12.
[138] J. R. Ficklen, "The Origin and Development of the Public School System in Louisiana," *Rpt. U. S. Com. Educ., 1895,* 1300.
[139] Especially Governors Claiborne, Robertson, and Roman. See *Rpt. State Supt. Pub. Educ., 1854,* 25, 30, 35.
[140] *Ibid.,* 47.
[141] *Ibid.,* 42; Flint, *op. cit.,* 324.
[142] *Rpt. State Supt. Pub. Educ., loc. cit.*
[143] *Ibid.,* 27, 36, 43; Flint, *loc. cit.*

more than five thousand children at home "receive[d] no education whatever." The Governor vainly urged the legislature to create free day schools in populous districts and boarding schools in every parish, to be taught by the Lancastrian method, with special provision for the poor. "Louisiana will never reach the station to which she is entitled amongst her sister States," he declared, until "none of her electors shall need the aid of his neighbor to prepare his ballot." [144]

It was the adoption of white manhood suffrage that finally brought the establishment of a state system of free public schools. These democratic reforms, each essential to the other and achieved together, were the work of the Constitutional Convention of 1845.[145] Provision was made for the permanent endowment of free schools from the interest on government land funds, a dollar poll on white males, and an assessment of one mill on all taxable property. Local interests were geared to state planning by the provision that a superintendent was to be appointed by the governor, and parish supervisors were to be elected by their constituencies.[146] Conservative Whigs joined progressive Democrats in support of this educational system, and not a single vote was cast against it.[147] The convention recognized free education as a natural corollary of manhood suffrage.[148] "Without you enlighten the sources of political power," remarked Eustis, a leading delegate, "we shall have no government. . . . You have adopted the principle of universal suffrage, but the basis is public education." [149]

This was the note struck throughout the United States by reformers who argued that free education was the best safeguard of democracy. In Louisiana this universal maxim—educate your rulers—was explored beyond its political connotations to the economic self-interest from which it sprang. "We

---

[144] *Rpt. State Supt. Pub. Educ.*, 35–40.
[146] *Const. 1845*, Title VII.
[148] *Ibid.*, 906.
[145] Cf. Ficklen, *op. cit.*, 1301.
[147] *Const. Conv. Debs., 1845*, 907.
[149] *Ibid.*, 909.

want public schools," declared Judah Benjamin, "for those who cannot afford to pay, as well as for those who can," because "the only safety for our liberties . . . is public education. Imbue the minors of the rising generation with knowledge, and they will understand the acts of scheming demagogues" and "secure our institutions." [150] This was an indirect plea for educating voters, while still children at school, to respect property and the *status quo;* and it was often admitted in subsequent years to be among the principal aims of free public education. "The system [was] based on the just and sacred principle that the rich . . . are bound to contribute . . . for the education . . . [of] those not so fortunately situated," announced one senator. "It is their interest as well as their duty to do so. The perpetuity of free institutions depend[s] upon it. The protection of their very property requires it." [151] Educate the poor man, argued another, because he "fights the battles of the country . . . performs the manual labor that contributes to the luxury of the rich . . . protect[s] the property of the rich, and a pittance from that property should be religiously applied to further [his] moral and intellectual advancement." [152] Again it was said that "property and liberty can be protected by no other than a well governed, orderly, well trained people, who has to defend . . . [it] in war, and out of war . . . [and] the less educated is the people[,] . . . the less safe is your property and liberty." The perennial complaint that school taxes fell on the rich for the benefit of the poor was answered by this epigrammatic summary of the case for free education: "The rich parishes have property and no men, the poor parishes have men and no property. The rich parishes pay for the poor; what is that? Property pays for protection." [153]

Apparently education was never intended to inform poor,

[150] *Ibid.,* 905-6.
[152] *Ibid.,* 69-70.

[151] *La. Sen. Rpts., 1850,* 66.
[153] *La. H. J., 1852,* 12.

white people how slavery affected them.[154] But at least one veteran advocate of free schools had believed that education might increase and diffuse as well as protect property. Governor Robertson had observed in 1823 that "countries that boast of their Universities, like most of those in Europe, and are destitute of primary schools, may also exhibit their palaces, and a land covered with miserable hovels; they are, indeed, cause and effect." [155]

Whatever the reasons for inaugurating public education in Louisiana, there is no question of its rapid development after 1845. The first superintendent, Alex Dimitry, was father of the state school system. Within five years of its constitutional authorization, he built or rented over six hundred log cabins and frame houses in the rural parishes and enrolled half the white children in elementary classes for annual terms of six months.[156] In New Orleans, where state funds were tripled by municipal school taxes, there were commodious buildings and an active corps of teachers to train half the white children of the city.[157]

The realities of country schooling were later recalled by a professor of mathematics at Louisiana State University.[158] Before the war he attended classes in a cabin which served as both church and school near Cane Ridge. It was built of round pine logs, the floor of heavy slabs hewn with a broadax, and seats of half logs. The course of study consisted of "spelling, reading, writing, ciphering, and flogging." Among the familiar textbooks were Webster's blue-back speller and Smiley's arithmetic. No less important, since the school was as much interested in character as in knowledge, were chinquapin switches for girls and hickory for boys. Whippings occurred

[154] Cf. Gilmore, *Among the Pines*, 174–75.
[155] *Rpt. State Supt. Pub. Educ.*, 1854, 30.
[156] *Ibid.*, 1850, *passim.*   [157] *Ibid.*, 1866, *passim.*
[158] J. W. Nicholson, *Stories of Dixie* (New York, 1915).

daily, and parents heartily approved of them as necessary to good discipline. This was the "old-fashioned" education of rural America.[159]

Advanced study, "for . . . the men who are to administer your government," always enlisted more interest in the Old South than the three "R's." [160] From the attempt in 1804 to create a university in New Orleans to the successful establishment of Louisiana College at Jackson in 1827, continuous efforts were made to organize institutions of higher education.[161] As a result of this prolonged campaign colleges were to be found in 1841 at Baton Rouge, Jackson, Opelousas, and in St. James, each receiving small contributions from the state. The aggregate attendance was over four hundred, with one in every seven an indigent scholar who enjoyed free tuition. All these colleges except Jefferson, in St. James, and Louisiana, at Jackson, collapsed the following year, when the legislature would not renew the annual subsidies because of embarrassed public finances.[162] A proposal in the Constitutional Convention of 1845 to establish a full-fledged state university in New Orleans was opposed by the sectional jealousy of country delegates.[163] Provision for establishing the University of Louisiana,[164] without any guarantee of government aid, was all that could be secured.[165] A law department was soon added to the existing Medical College in New Orleans, and with state assistance the doors of both branches were opened to a few poor students from each parish.[166] On the eve of the

[159] Ibid., 30–32.   [160] Const. Conv. Debs., 1845, 909, 911.

[161] Rpt. State Supt. Pub. Educ., 1854, 25–43. Cf. M. L. Riley, "The Development of Education in Louisiana Prior to Statehood," L. H. Q., XVIX, 629–31.

[162] Ibid., 47.   [163] Const. Conv. Debs., 1845, 910.

[164] Organized in 1834 as the Medical College of Louisiana and granted $100,000 by the state, this institution later became Tulane University. Rpt. Secy. State, 1902, 438–39.

[165] Const. 1845, Arts. 137–39; Const. 1852, Arts. 139–40.

[166] La. Sen. Debs., 1853, 151.

Civil War a state university and military academy was finally established near Alexandria from the proceeds of Federal land grants.[167] Like the normal school [168] and other institutions of higher learning, it was temporarily closed by the war.[169]

But the rural public school system began to decline seven years before war broke out. It was undermined in a fit of economy by the substitution of unsalaried directors for parish supervisors.[170] Generally incompetent and indifferent, the new officials appointed ignorant teachers, paid them little,[171] and seldom reported the progressive deterioration of schools in their districts.[172] Where half the educable children had once gone to school, scarcely one in three attended classes in 1858.[173] New Orleans suffered less than the country because its funds were more efficiently distributed among an urban population: there were 20,000 children in municipal classes in 1858, almost as many as in all the rural parishes put together.[174] In the country the school system became a plum of political patronage.[175] The few buildings were inconveniently located, the teachers poor, and supervision inefficient.[176]

Nothing was done to remedy these conditions because of the indifference of wealthy planters and Creoles toward popular education. Their apathy was chiefly responsible for the failure of free schools in Louisiana before the Civil War.[177] Planters rebelled at sending their children to what were known as pauper institutions.[178] But they did not scruple to appropri-

---

[167] Rpt. Secy. State, 1902, 446.   [168] La. Sess. Laws, 1861, 76 [no. 102].

[169] Walter L. Fleming, Louisiana State University, 1860–1896 (Baton Rouge, 1936), chap. VII.

[170] La. Sen. Debs., 1853, 35; La. Sess. Laws, 1855, 422–27 [no. 321]; Rpt. State Supt. Pub. Educ., 1857, 4.

[171] Rpt. State Supt. Pub. Educ., 1857, 8–9.   [172] Ibid., 1853, passim.

[173] Opelousas [St. Landry] Patriot, Feb. 12, 1859.

[174] Ficklen, op. cit., 1303.   [175] Opelousas Patriot, loc. cit.

[176] Rpt. State Supt. Pub. Educ., 1854, 3, 8, 1857–59, passim.

[177] Ficklen, op. cit., 1302.   [178] Ibid., 1864, 157–58.

ate public money for private instruction at their own planta-tions.[179] The result was that the poorer sections of a parish lacked any educational facilities.[180] In one district of Cata-houla, for example, there were 250 children of school age, but only one building with forty pupils; for fifteen years the district money was expended on this lone school by a neigh-boring planter who dominated the local directors.[181] Although planters frequently added money of their own to that which they took from the state, the increased sum was devoted to but few schools.[182] The real difficulty of rural instruction con-tinued to be the absence of facilities for its dispensation, owing in part to this diversion of public money to private hands. "See-ing that the rich planters were satisfied, the legislature simply did nothing but appropriate ample funds, which often never reached the [public] schools for which they were destined." [183]

The parents of poor children little realized what their off-spring were missing. Their indifference arose from their own lack of education and a grim preoccupation with earning the "means of subsistence." [184] They were sometimes incredibly ignorant, and generally devoid of any incentive to light up the darkness of their minds. "It is impossible to elevate in the scale of mental improvement a people who are at the same time barred from material progress." [185]

[179] *Ibid., 1859, passim.*
[180] Ficklen, *loc. cit.*
[181] *La. H. Debs., 1864, 203.*
[182] Because a private tutor charged monthly what the state allowed a public school teacher annually. *Rpt. State Supt. Pub. Educ., 1857, 7.*
[183] Ficklen, *loc. cit.*
[184] *Rpt. State Supt. Pub. Educ., 1854, 8.*
[185] Seabrook, *op. cit., The Galaxy,* IV, 687.

Chapter IV

FREE LABOR AND SLAVERY

The niggers are worth too much to be risked below and if the paddies are knocked overboard or
get their backs broke nobody loses anything.
— A Steamboat Mate [1]

The non-slaveholders possess generally but very
small means, and the land which they possess is
almost universally poor and so sterile that a scanty
subsistence is all that can be derived from its
cultivation, and the more fertile soil being in
the hands of the slaveholders, must ever remain
out of the power of those who have none.
— J. D. B. De Bow [2]

Historians have paid so much attention to the plantation
system and slavery that the poor white laborers and small
farmers have been almost forgotten.[3] Nothing should reveal
their importance in the Old South so clearly as a study of how
the majority of free people in Louisiana obtained a livelihood.

This remains a problem scarcely less difficult for us to
solve than for the poor people of long ago to whom its solution brought "corn 'n taters." It puzzled a Donaldsonville
policeman who was vexed by a shrewish wife and her hungry
family. "How did the friends, relatives, and tribe of his wife
live? No one could say. They reared chickens, and they
caught fish; when there was a pressure on the planters, they

[1] Quoted by Olmsted, *A Journey in the Seaboard Slave States*, II, 193.

[2] *The Industrial Resources, etc. of the Southern and Western States* (New Orleans, 1853), II, 106.

[3] See the studies by U. B. Phillips and A. H. Stone, which have lately been amplified by L. C. Gray to include the frontier and farming economy of regions outside the plantation belt.

turned out to work . . . but those were rare occasions. The policeman had become quite grey with excogitating the matter, and he had 'nary notion how they did it.' " [4] If he had consulted the census reports, he might have learned much without becoming wiser.

From this source it appears that few Louisianians earned their living directly from the plantation system. Over two-thirds of the free people owned no slaves, and consequently lacked the labor necessary to operate plantations.[5]

So it is hardly surprising to find that Louisiana was apparently a greater farming than planting state before the Civil War. The farm may be conveniently distinguished from the plantation both as to size and crop: the former seldom extended beyond a hundred acres, often falling short of fifty, which were cultivated by the owner's family chiefly in subsistence crops like potatoes and corn; the plantation was much larger, worked by slaves, and devoted principally to such staples as cotton and cane.[6] In 1850, only about two in five agricultural holdings could be called plantations; of 13,422 properties, 4,205 raised over five bales of cotton and 1,558 had sugarhouses.[7] In the score of parishes that made up the Sugar Bowl, especially notable for large estates, about three out of four landholdings were farms, which produced little cane and had no machinery to reduce it to molasses and raw brown sugar.[8] Even in the heart of the plantation black belt one in every twenty-two free families tilled patches smaller than ten acres, and almost one-third of all the cultivated land belonged to farms of less than a hundred acres.[9] In 1860 nearly half the agricultural properties enumerated by the census were

[4] Russell, *My Diary North and South*, I, 415–16. [5] See Appendix, Table 3.
[6] See Appendix, Table 5. [7] *U. S. Cen., 1850, Comp.*, 169, 178.
[8] P. A. Champomier, *Statement of the Sugar Crop Made in La., 1849–50*, *passim;* Olmsted, *A Journey in the Seaboard Slave States*, 670–73.
[9] *U. S. Cen., 1850, Comp.*, 175. The parishes tabulated in this survey were East Feliciana, Ouachita, Plaquemines, Pointe Coupee, and Rapides.

farms under fifty acres, and about two in every three did not exceed one hundred acres.[10] To judge by the size and product of all landholdings, Louisiana had more farms than plantations before the Civil War.[11]

This seems at first thought to be a historical heresy, for Louisiana has always been regarded as pre-eminently a state of large plantations. But the contradiction is more apparent than real, and easily resolved. Although there were more farms than plantations, the former could hardly be compared to the latter in total acreage and value, and in the amount and value of all products. Plantations embraced in area nearly seven times the land used in farming;[12] the value of plantations, exclusive of slaves, greatly exceeded that of farms; and plantation staples such as cotton and sugar, which were sold to a world market, were worth much more than the food crops raised and consumed at home.[13] Hence, plantations surpassed farms in value and extent, but not in number; and ante-bellum Louisiana may be regarded as both a planting and a farming state.

To the social historian the fact that the smaller landholdings outnumbered the larger is of the greatest importance. It conclusively proves what the distribution of slavery indicated,[14] that a majority of free people in the country were nonslaveholding farmers and not planters with Negroes. It also calls into question the relation of slavery and the plantation system to the economic welfare of the bulk of the population. An examination of this complex subject will show that the prevailing agricultural regime did not benefit them. Farmers were actually hurt by slavery and the plantation economy, which gradually deprived them of all opportunity to acquire

---

[10] *U. S. Cen., 1860, Agric.,* 202. [11] See Appendix, Table 5.
[12] *U. S. Cen., 1860, Agric.,* 221.
[13] *Rpt. La. Audit. Pub. Accts., 1855,* 33–51; *1861,* 3–106.
[14] Cf. Appendix, Tables 3, 4.

Negroes and fertile land, or to participate on a large scale in the production of profitable staples such as cotton and sugar cane.[15]

During the earlier decades, when the lower South was being settled, farmers stood every chance of becoming planters. Until late in the fifties most planters or their fathers before them started life as yeomen, occasionally with a few slaves, but generally without any hands except their own.[16] The heyday of these poor people lasted as long as land and slaves were cheap, enabling them to realize their ambition to be planters and slaveholders, as so many succeeded in doing while Louisiana remained largely an unsettled frontier.

The region first offered happy prospects to farmers toward the end of the eighteenth century. Spain desired to make it a buffer against American expansion, and accordingly granted free land and tools for several years to discontented Americans and colonies of Acadian, French, Irish, and Dutch settlers.[17] After Jefferson purchased Louisiana the American invasion commenced in full force. Farmers from the southeastern states trooped in to take advantage of the cheap but fertile land, where the profits of bumper crops soon dowered them with slaves, more land, and yet more slaves. The Attakapas and Opelousas prairies, which were settled after 1810, yielded

[15] This was the opinion of Olmsted (e. g., *A Journey in the Back Country*, 33, 306–7), which has been confirmed and elaborated by Phillips, "Origin and Growth of the Southern Black Belts," *A. H. R.*, XI, 798, "The Decadence of the Plantation System," *Annals*, XXXV, 39, *American Negro Slavery*, 337, 398; Buck, "The Poor Whites of the Ante-Bellum South," *A. H. R.*, XXXI, 41–54; and, to mention only one other, Brewer, "Poor Whites and Negroes in the South Since the Civil War," *Journal of Negro History*, XV, 26. Cf. L. C. Gray, "Economic Efficiency and Competitive Advantages of Slavery under the Plantation System," *Agricultural History*, IV, 41.

[16] See above, chap. II.

[17] M. A. Hatcher, *The Opening of Texas to Foreign Settlement*, 7–40; *Rpt. U. S. Com. Gen. Land Ofc.* [on Bastrop Grant], 32 Cong., 2 sess., *Sen. Ex. Doc.* no. 4.

the handsome annual profit of $500 a hand in cotton and $800 in sugar.[18] Rich alluvial land in southern and western Louisiana could be bought at this time for as little as two to four dollars an acre.[19] But the swelling tide of immigration put a premium on good sites, and prices advanced rapidly in the face of new settlers who sought virgin soil. As early as 1818 the alluvium along the lower Mississippi was selling at fifty dollars an acre, and at twenty-five to fifty on the lower Red River.[20] Consequently, the better land soon fell into the possession of slaveholders with capital, and nonslaveholders had to seek or squat elsewhere.

Prosperous yeomen pushed up the Red River in quest of fertile bottoms which brought forty and fifty dollars an acre. When Jackson and Van Buren removed the Indians from this region, cleared away the jam of fallen timber and debris in the Red River, and opened it to navigation as far as Shreveport, the whole valley was quickly transformed into a plantation black belt.[21] With the occupation of the banks along the Mississippi and Red rivers, immigrants pursued the Ouachita and other bayous to the second bottoms and oak uplands of northern Louisiana. So relentless was the pressure of settlement during the forties and fifties, under the new

[18] *Niles' Weekly Register*, XIII, 38.

[19] Gray, *History of Agriculture in the Southern United States to 1860*, II, 688.

[20] Judge F. X. Martin to a Georgia correspondent, July 22, 1818, MS first printed in the *Picayune*, Dec. 2, 1860. These prices obtained at the height of the boom preceding the Panic of 1819. Cf. Gray, *History of Agriculture . . .* , II, 642, 688, 898.

[21] *De Bow's Review*, X, 103; XIX, 439; Gray, *History of Agriculture . . .* , II, 898; A. A. Taylor, "The Movement of Negroes from the East to the Gulf States from 1830 to 1850," *Journal of Negro History*, VIII, 367–83. The receipts from sale of public lands in Louisiana rose with the speculative boom of the decade from $111,809 in 1833 to $822,080 in 1839, and then fell sharply to $189,875 the following year; from 1833 to 1840 the total receipts amounted to $3,240,369. De Bow, *Encyclopaedia of the Trade and Commerce . . .* , I, 439.

policy of graduated prices, that public land offices at Monroe and Natchitoches did a thriving business in tracts which had once gone begging and were now eagerly purchased for less than a dollar the acre.[22]

At this rate it was not long before upper Louisiana was settled. Bossier Parish, for example, was organized in 1843, and within seven years recruited a population of 2,500 white people and almost twice as many slaves. This was a period of great prosperity for the planters who came in large numbers from Mississippi, Alabama, Georgia, and the Carolinas. Not exceptional was the case of an immigrant from Alabama who arrived in 1848 with four slaves and about $2,000 to his name; in 1860 he sold the property which he had accumulated for $30,000.[23] Pioneering farmers pushed beyond the river bottoms and rich oak uplands into the piney woods, where they improved modest tracts of twenty acres, as in Claiborne, and rarely claimed as much as a hundred.[24]

But the day of the farmer began to wane rapidly after 1850. If he had not already obtained good land, it became doubtful that he could ever improve his fortunes. All the fertile soil that was not under cultivation was generally held by speculators at mounting prices. In northern Louisiana they demanded from five to ten dollars the acre for unimproved uplands, from twenty to seventy-five dollars for uncleared alluvial lowlands,[25] and one hundred dollars or more for each acre of improved plantations.[26] Tracts "from which a tree has

[22] E. g., *Rpt. U. S. Secy. Int., 1855*, 34 Cong., 1 sess., *H. R. Ex. Docs.*, I, no. 1, 168–69, 174–75.

[23] *Biographical and Historical Memoirs of Northwest La.*, 109–10, 227; Harris and Hulse, *History of Claiborne Parish*, 21; *Crescent*, July 18, 1860.

[24] MS *Returns, U. S. Cen., 1860, La. Agric.*

[25] *Crescent*, July 11, 18, 21, 30, Aug. 6, 14, 20, 27, 1860. Cf. Gray, *History of Agriculture* . . . , II, 642.

[26] *Picayune*, Jan. 8, 1860, and T. C. Dunn, *Morehouse Parish* (New Orleans, 1885), 8.

never been cut" were held at fifty dollars the acre in Avoyelles. It was reported from Morehouse that "only a moiety
of [the] lands are under cultivation, but every inch of them
is in the hands of those who thoroughly understand their
value and are willing to wait to get it." "The rise in lands
on [Red River]," observed a traveler, "has been, and con-
tinues to be, most extravagant, notwithstanding its reputation
for sickness and overflows. Places which sold two years ago
[1857] at seventeen dollars per acre, now command forty
and fifty dollars, and last week a farm sold on the river at
seventy-five dollars per acre. In my steamboat travel, the
sole topic of general conversation seemed to consist in land.
. . . Men from Georgia, Alabama, Florida, Mississippi, and
everywhere else, seemed bent on purchasing soil on that
stream." [27] These land-hungry men, it need hardly be remarked, were not humble farmers, but planters touched with
the fever of speculation.

It may well be wondered why the poor farmer could not
afford to buy land when there was constant complaint
throughout the South that it was grossly undervalued.[28] River
bottoms were sometimes sold on the Mississippi Coast for
thirty dollars an acre, to yield sugar worth a hundred dollars.[29]
But these apparent bargains failed to attract nonslaveholders,
who had neither the capital nor labor necessary to exploit
them. Any kind of soil at thirty dollars an acre was too expensive for their scant purses.

With inferior public land available at only twenty-five
cents, however, the poorest nonslaveholder could obtain a
small tract. He was driven to this type of soil as the price of

[27] *Crescent*, Nov. 17, 1859, June 5, Aug. 23, 1860.
[28] But land was valued more highly in Louisiana than elsewhere in the
South. See *De Bow's Review*, I (February, 1866), 212.
[29] *Delta*, Oct. 15, 1852; *Affleck's Southern Rural Almanac for 1855* (New
Orleans, 1854), 63.

better grades soared. From 1855 to 1860 government sales of cheap land increased twofold and exceeded the acreage of all tracts selling above a dollar.[30] But the cheaper land was generally unsuited to agriculture because it lay in dense forests or undrained swamps, which accounted for its low price.[31] What land the nonslaveholder could buy, therefore, he was unable to use profitably.

Speculators grabbed the most fertile land. As early as 1818 they had engrossed large tracts along the upper Mississippi in Ouachita and Concordia.[32] In succeeding years their operations spread to every part of Louisiana, and they followed close on the heels of government surveyors who were opening new districts.[33] "There is a good deal of land in the upper part of [Bossier]," observed a traveler in 1860, "on which the surveyors are yet at work, closely watched by speculators and others who have 'spotted' the best tracts, and are in waiting to secure them as soon as brought into the market." [34] With shrewd eyes and ready cash, or the credit and political influence which were as negotiable as cash, they stood between the government and the poor settler, taking title to the public domain upon which none could thenceforth trespass without their leave.[35] On the piney woods frontier of De Soto, for example, two men were each reported to possess twenty thousand acres.[36] While some speculators did nothing but traffic in the public domain, the majority were planters, and they frequently gained more from buying and selling

[30] *Rpt. U. S. Secy. Int.*, *1855*, loc. cit.; ibid., *1860*, 36 Cong., 2 sess., *Sen. Ex. Docs.*, I, no. 1, 88–89, 94–95. Cf. *ibid.*, *1850*, 31 Cong., 2 sess., *Sen. Ex. Docs.*, II, no. 2, 26, 31.

[31] *La. H. J.*, *1850*, *Rpt. Com. Pub. Lands*, app., 1, 3.

[32] Judge F. X. Martin to a Georgia correspondent, July 22, 1818, MS letter printed in the *Picayune*, Dec. 2, 1860.

[33] *Crescent*, July 11, 18, 21, 1860.   [34] *Ibid.*, July 30, 1860.

[35] For an excellent account of speculative operations, see Featherstonhaugh, *Excursion through the Slave States*, I, 170–74.

[36] *Crescent*, July 18, 1860.

than from cultivating land. One planter "multiplied his fortune a hundred fold by his investments in land." [37]

It was the speculator who thwarted the government's intention to settle the country rapidly and cheaply because he did not perform the economic function of an entrepreneur, absorbing financial risks at commensurate profits, but preferred to engross land until its unearned increment, accruing from the development of transportation and the influx of immigrants, satisfied his ambition for easy profits. The consequences were to be seen along Red River in 1860. "Settlements and plantations are few and far between," observed a traveler. "Land speculators are holding almost all the best lands and demanding such prices as at present deter purchasers." [38] When the national government granted Louisiana more than eight million acres of rich swamp land to be reclaimed by levees,[39] speculation became so rife that in self-defense the state stopped all sales until the construction of levees could be assured. Despite this short-lived precaution a minority report to the General Assembly in 1856 claimed that nearly one million acres had been engrossed by speculators at a dollar and a quarter, to be sold when leveed at eight dollars.[40] "When a levee is built, . . . the lands in the rear become more valuable," explained a senator, "and speculators, with that sharp, keen eye for the main chance, which generally characterizes them, would go and enter these lands, and thus reap the benefit of the labors of the State to its own injury." [41]

[37] M. A. Ross, MS acct. of her family, the Glovers, written at Mobile, Mar. 22, 1908, and now in private hands at New Orleans.

[38] *Crescent*, July 3, 1860.

[39] *Rpt. U. S. Secy. Int., 1855*, 34 Cong., 1 sess., *H. R. Ex. Docs.*, I, no. 1, 144; *Picayune*, Feb. 29, 1852; *Rpt. La. Com. Pub. Lands and Levees* (New Orleans, 1859), 26.

[40] *Rpt. La. Com. Pub. Lands and Levees* (New Orleans, 1856), *passim*.

[41] *La. Sen. Debs., 1853*, 83.

Wherever the soil was fertile, speculative pre-emption tended to exclude the nonslaveholder. It was the absence of good, cheap land and not slavery that drove the poor immigrant from Louisiana, according to one newspaper: "Doubtless Mr. Sumner will argue that it is slavery that keeps them from the South. But this is not true. . . . These immigrants can go [North], and buy rich and productive Government lands for a mere trifle—never over one dollar and a quarter an acre. They can buy no such lands in the South at that price." [42] This is revealing testimony of the way in which land prices alone operated in the fifties to prevent the farmer from becoming a planter.

Thousands of poor nonslaveholders never owned any land, but squatted on the public domain, in some places to have their homes sold over their heads.[43] Physical possession of the land, far from being a reprehensible seizure of what did not belong to them, was the only way in which many farmers could obtain a few acres to work. But legal possession, too expensive for them to acquire, gave others the right to oust them. This may be illustrated by the dispute over the Houmas Grant of several hundred thousand acres in Ascension.[44] The boundaries of this tract, when ceded by the Houmas Indians, had been vaguely defined; and after dubious surveys, passed into the hands of the Wade Hampton family and other speculators. Meanwhile, land-hungry settlers poured into the region, which was sold among speculators as if it were a small principality without reference to the occupation of squatters.[45]

[42] *Crescent*, June 15, 1860.

[43] Under the pre-emption law the squatter could exchange his claim for a title at the minimum price; but long after the Civil War, with free homesteads available, there were many untitled squatters. See Belisle, *History of Sabine Parish*, 71, 77–78.

[44] *American State Papers*, II, 297.

[45] *Crescent*, May 7, 1860; S. A. Marchand, *The Story of Ascension Parish, Louisiana*, 105.

When they applied for relief to the Louisiana courts, the Houmas patent was declared void. John Slidell, the Democratic boss who had purchased a large share of the grant, thereupon sought to have it confirmed by Congress.[46] It was alleged that this action "legislated into the pocket of Mr. Slidell a half million dollars, . . . and turned out of their homes about five hundred families." [47] The lot of the squatter was not a happy one.

It is impossible to discover how many people were squatters, occupying land without title or lease, because the census never counted them, but their number must have been very large. If it is assumed that every agrarian property in rural Louisiana was either operated or supervised by one free family,[48] then three out of five families owned no land in 1860.[49] Not all these people, of course, were squatters. Probably the majority were overseers, mechanics, hired laborers, boatmen, fishermen, and woodcutters.[50] But a surprising minority could hardly have been anything but squatters. So far as the law of property prevailed, the landless proletariat must have been numerous indeed.

Nonslaveholders were depressed and excluded from the plantation system not only because they failed to secure good land, but also because they gradually lost the ability to buy Negroes. In 1830 when prime field hands were selling at New Orleans for $850, equivalent to twenty-one bales of cotton at current prices, the yeomen could purchase slaves.[51] As late

[46] L. M. Sears, *John Slidell* (Durham, N. C., 1925), 165–67. For Slidell's defense of his action, see his speech, *Congressional Globe*, 36 Cong., 1 sess., May 29, 1860.

[47] *True Delta*, March 15, 1859. Slidell declared that his land was assessed at only $15,000. *Cong. Globe, loc. cit.*

[48] Cf. Gray, *History of Agriculture* . . . , I, 501.

[49] See Appendix, Tables 3, 5.

[50] In 1850 there were about nineteen thousand free males engaged in these pursuits. *U.S. Cen., 1850, Comp.*, 128–29.

[51] Phillips, *American Negro Slavery*, opp. 370.

as 1850, because of low cotton prices in previous years, Negroes cost only a few more bales.[52] But during the fifties, slave prices rose out of all proportion to cotton prices,[53] which rarely went above twelve cents,[54] because an increasing number of planters flocked to the Southwest [55] and sharpened the competition of selling cotton and buying slaves.[56] Characteristic was the report in 1853 that planters "are now investing the proceeds of their crops in the purchase of negroes . . . at prices so high as to excite general astonishment." [57] By 1860 a field hand at New Orleans cost $1,800 or forty-one bales of cotton,[58] double the rates of 1830, and as high as $2,200 in the country up Red River.[59] At these prices it required three years for a good Negro to "pay for himself." [60]

Slaves were now worth more money than the average farmer possessed or could afford to borrow. When cotton sold at low levels, even the small planters lost their Negroes. "The number of slaveholders is constantly decreasing," it was remarked, "while the price of negroes has risen to such a figure as to substantially put it out of the power of the masses to become pecuniarily interested in the institution profitably." [61] The hiring of slaves, to which many yeomen had previously resorted,[62] was also growing more expensive because their annual charge was generally equal to one-fifth of their purchase price.[63] In northern Louisiana, where field

[52] Ibid., 371–73. [53] Olmsted, A Journey in the Seaboard Slave States, 652.
[54] Phillips, American Negro Slavery, opp. 370. [55] Crescent, Jan. 30, 1860.
[56] Phillips, "The Economic Cost of Slave-holding in the Cotton Belt," Political Science Quarterly, XX, 268.
[57] La. Sen. Debs., 1853, 120; Olmsted, A Journey in the Seaboard Slave States, 652–53.
[58] Phillips, American Negro Slavery, loc. cit.
[59] Crescent, Nov. 17, 1859.   [60] Ibid.
[61] Ibid., Sept. 17, 1859. Cf. Delta, Sept. 25, 1856; De Bow's Review, XXVI, 654.
[62] E. g., see above, 49.
[63] F. Bancroft, Slave-Trading in the Old South (Baltimore, 1931), 160.

hands could ordinarily be hired at $170,[64] they brought $300 in 1860, the highest yearly wage for slaves in the entire South.[65]

Consequently, the occasional assistance of a hired slave, as well as his lifelong service when purchased, was no longer available to yeomen and nonslaveholders. Small wonder that one of their rural newspapers announced, as the fifties drew to a close, that "the slave trade will have to be opened in time, to prevent the slaves from getting into the hands of a few, thereby forming a monopoly. That minute you put it out of the power of common farmers to purchase a negro man or woman to help him in his farm, or his wife in the house, you make him an abolitionist at once." [66] Although the common people had generally lost the ability to become slaveholders by 1860, they did not turn to abolition. If slaves were emancipated, white farmers and laborers would face the competition of free Negroes. This prospective degradation was more abhorrent than any want of slaves.[67]

Even while the Negro was in bondage the common people unwittingly suffered from his indirect competition because the chief advantage of slavery lay in the fact that it was cheaper than free labor.[68] Nearly everyone admitted that this held true for unskilled field work.[69] It was no less true, concluded planters in the legislature after prolonged debate, for relatively skilled labor. Slave mechanics and carpenters could be hired at one-fourth the wages of whites, reported the State Engineer, and this saving offset the greater efficiency with which the latter were reputed to work.[70] The following balance sheet in favor of slavery, after the initial investment

[64] *Rpt. U. S. Com. Agric., 1866*, 416.   [65] *De Bow's Review*, XXIX, 374.
[66] Sparta [Bienville] *Jeffersonian*, Sept. 7, quoted in *Crescent*, Sept. 17, 1859.
[67] See below, 175.   [68] Russell, *My Diary North and South*, I, 394.
[69] Olmsted, *A Journey in the Seaboard Slave States*, 687–88; Phillips, "Origin and Growth of the Southern Black Belts," *A. H. R.*, XI, 803.
[70] *La. Sen. Debs., 1853*, 140.

of purchase, was calculated by a senate committee for the construction of levees, canals, and plank roads: [71]

Free Labor

300 whites, hired at $30 a month, per year	$108,000
Provisions	18,000
6 superintendents, at $1,000	6,000
Total cost of free labor per year	$132,000

Slave Labor

[300 slaves, bought at $1,000 each	$300,000]
Interest on investment, at 5%	$ 15,000
Provisions and clothes	16,500
Loss of slaves by death, etc.	15,000
6 superintendents, at $1,000	6,000
Extra food for superintendents	360
Total cost of slave labor per year	$ 52,860
Balance in favor of slave labor	$ 79,140

The annual saving on slaves, according to these figures, would pay for them within four years. The state was thus persuaded by experienced slaveholding accountants to abandon its system of hiring free labor in 1853 and to purchase one hundred Negroes. When these slaves were finally sold in 1860, after many had grown old working on internal improvements, it was found that they had reaped the state a handsome profit.[72]

Aside from highly skilled crafts in which free mechanics were superior,[73] there was one kind of work where whites

[71] *Ibid.,* 73.
[72] *Rpt. La. State Engineer, 1856,* 7; *Rpt. La. Bd. Pub. Wks., 1860,* 7.
[73] Olmsted, *A Journey in the Seaboard Slave States,* 589.

cost less than blacks, and that was labor dangerous to life or limb. Because the services of a slave were bought for life, planters could ill afford to lose him. The general practice, therefore, was to employ gangs of Irish immigrants to ditch and drain plantations at five dollars an acre, or to build levees at a dollar a day.[74] "It was much better," explained an overseer, "to have Irish to do it, who cost nothing to the planter if they died, than to use up good field-hands in such severe employment." The cutting of timber to clear arable land on a plantation was likewise left to poor whites, because it was "death on niggers and mules." [75] Free laborers were generally engaged as steamboat roustabouts for the same reason.[76] "I have seen white men," testified a veteran who had journeyed up and down the rivers for twenty years, "laboring under the sun day after day, in the mud and water of the canals, where a negro could not have stood it for twelve hours." [77] This was an ironic comment on the Southern contention that slavery was necessary in a climate too warm for white people to work.[78] In the hottest fields and at the most brutal tasks, they were actually preferred to slaves because they cost less, and not a penny was lost if they dropped in their tracks from exhaustion or disease.

Outside these occupations, however, slavery was unquestionably cheaper than free labor. An important reason for its greater economy was the inability of bondsmen to stop work and strike for better treatment. "The real foundation of slavery in the Southern States," observed a correspondent of the London *Times*, "lies in the power of obtaining labor at will at a rate which cannot be controlled by any combina-

---

[74] *La. Sen. Debs., 1853,* 67; *Crescent,* Dec. 5, 1859; May 26, 1860. "The pay attracted those whose labor was their life; the risk repelled those whose labor was their capital," observed Phillips, *American Negro Slavery,* 302–3.

[75] Russell, *op. cit.,* I, 395, 408.   [76] See above, *n.* 1.

[77] *La. Const. Conv. Debs., 1864,* 218.   [78] *De Bow's Review,* XXX, 67–77.

tion of labourers." [79] A sugar planter discovered this advantage of slavery when he experimented with free labor. He replaced his inefficient Negroes with a hundred Irish and German immigrants. In the middle of the grinding season, when the whole crop was at stake, they struck for double pay. He could not find other workmen or purchase slaves quickly enough to avert the loss of sugar worth $10,000, which spoiled in the refining vats.[80] This episode illustrates why slaveholders boasted that the " 'dragon of democracy,' the productive laboring element, having its teeth drawn, [is] robbed of its ability to do harm by being in a state of bondage." [81]

But the main reason for the cheapness of slave labor, in spite of its heavy capitalization,[82] lay in the fact that a master had tenure for life in the services of his bondsman, whom he could force to work as much as a human being was able, and all the fruits of whose labor he could appropriate to himself—beyond whatever was necessary to keep the slave efficient and alive.[83] No employer could earn such exorbitant profits with free labor because it would not endure discipline or conditions of living which resembled slavery. Nor could the freeman who worked on his own account make as much for himself as the slave for a master because of the divergence of their standards of living. The difference between cost and production in slave labor was greater than in free labor. "It was this appropriable surplus," as Gray has observed, "that gave slave labor under plantation organization an irresistible ability to displace free labor, whether hired or engaged in production

[79] Russell, op. cit., I, 393.

[80] Lyell, A Second Visit to the United States . . . , II, 162–63.

[81] Crescent, Oct. 27, 1859.

[82] Phillips, "The Economic Cost of Slave-holding in the Cotton Belt," Political Science Quarterly, XX, 275.

[83] E. J. Capell, MS Record & Account Books of Pleasant Hill Plantation [La. State Univ. Library], passim; Olmsted, A Journey in the Seaboard Slave States, 687–88.

on family-sized farms. . . . The planter was able, if necessary, to produce at price levels which left little more than
the expense of maintaining the slave. White labor could bid
no lower." [84]

It was consequently excluded from the plantation economy,
except where it might supervise or supplement slave labor.[85]
Chief among freemen on the plantation was the overseer, pivot
of the whole system of large estates. In Louisiana his tribe
numbered nearly three thousand in 1860. These men, the
sons of yeomen slaveholders or of poor farmers, were engaged
by planters at salaries which ranged from $400 to $1,500.
Some saved the money or secured the credit necessary to buy
a few Negroes and establish themselves as planters. Many
more, changing from plantation to plantation every year,
never rose beyond their station.[86] In parishes such as Tensas
and Concordia in the upper Mississippi black belt, where
planters dwelt in mansions across the river in Natchez, nearly
all the white residents formed "a population of employes,
not of owners [but of] overseers." [87]

Less numerous than overseers were the artisans, carpenters,
bricklayers, coopers, and mechanics, who lived in the country villages and worked at surrounding plantations or traveled
from place to place wherever a job was to be found.[88] Since

[84] Gray, "'Economic Efficiency and Competitive Advantages of Slavery . . . ,'" *Agricultural History*, IV, 41. "As a matter of fact," adds Gray,
"the basis of competition rarely reached so low a level. There were extensive
areas of fertile land where white labor could find an outlet for its energies
without coming into acute competition with slave labor." For a discussion
of this point, with which I cannot agree so far as Louisiana is concerned, see
below, 95–97.

[85] Cf. Phillips, *American Negro Slavery*, 337.

[86] Olmsted, *A Journey in the Seaboard Slave States, loc. cit.*; Craven, "Poor
Whites and Negroes in the Ante-Bellum South," *Journal of Negro History*,
XV, 22.

[87] *Crescent*, Sept. 8, 1860; *De Bow's Review*, XIV, 431–36. Cf. Phillips,
American Negro Slavery, 333.

[88] *La. Sen. Rpts., 1850*, 31.

they were skilled craftsmen and very scarce, their customary wages varied from a dollar or two a day to thirty-five or fifty dollars a month.[89] A Dutch carpenter frequently employed at one plantation received besides his food and lodging, $100 for three months of work in 1840, but only $75 for five months in 1856. In the meantime this plantation, like many others, discontinued the practice of engaging itinerant craftsmen; their tasks were gradually assumed by slaves, in this case by a carpenter and brickmason.[90] Even skilled labor was displaced by slavery as it became profitable for large planters to own a corps of artisans.[91]

Whenever extra help was required for the harvest or for severe tasks such as the ditching and draining of plantations, slaveholders had recourse to poor whites. Cajuns were commonly hired to cut sugar cane. To pick cotton, white labor could be obtained at fifteen to thirty dollars a month, and slaves at ten.[92]

Conspicuous throughout the lowlands were gangs of Irishmen who built levees and drained the marshes. They were immigrants, strong, ignorant, and credulous, victims of their work and the contractors who battened upon it. One employer was described by a plantation overseer as having "made plenty of money out of his countrymen, whose bones are lying up and down the Mississippi." His ways were characteristic of his kind. He did not provide his laborers with "half the rations we give our negroes, but he can always manage them with whiskey, and when he wants them to do a job he gives them plenty of 'forty rod,' and they have their fight out —regular free fight, I can tell you, while it lasts. Next morn-

[89] *Rpt. U. S. Com. Patents, 1850*, 1151.

[90] Capell, MS *Record*, entries of May 3, 25, June 8, 15, 1850; *Record of Negroes, 1853, passim, 1856*, flyleaf.

[91] Olmsted, *A Journey in the Back Country*, 180–81, 376.

[92] *De Bow's Review*, XI, 62, 606. The average wage for farm labor in 1850 was $12.80 a month with board. *U. S. Cen., 1850, Comp.*, 164.

ing they will sign anything and go anywhere with him." [93] The Irish actor, Tyrone Power, was moved to compassion when he saw his countrymen digging a canal between New Orleans and Lake Pontchartrain in 1835. "Hundreds of fine fellows [were] wading amongst stumps of trees, mid-deep in black mud, clearing the spaces pumped out by powerful steam-engines; wheeling, digging, hewing, or bearing burdens it made one's shoulders ache to look upon." They lived, many with their families, in open log shelters half submerged in the swamps, "worse lodged than the cattle of the field . . . the only thought bestowed upon them appears to be, by what expedient the greatest quantity of labour may be extracted from them at the cheapest rate to the contractor." They ate the coarsest food and were plied with alcohol to excite them to rivalry in their tasks. Mortality was terrific. The Catholic priest was "the only stay and comfort of these men." [94] "Heaven knows," remarked a correspondent of the London *Times*, "how many poor Hibernians have been consumed and buried in these Louisianian swamps, leaving their earnings to the dramshop keeper and the contractor, and the results of their toil to the planter." [95]

Beyond such casual and accessory labor, the plantation economy offered no direct means of livelihood to the majority of free whites. "Like other capitalistic systems," in the opinion of Phillips, "it sadly restricted the opportunity of such men as were of better industrial quality than was required for the field gangs, yet could not control the capital required to make themselves captains of industry," or masters of slave plantations.[96] Since nonslaveholding farmers were unable to operate on a large scale and with cheap labor, they could not special-

[93] Russell, *My Diary North and South*, I, 402; *Crescent*, Dec. 5, 1859; May 26, 1860.
[94] Power, *Impressions of America*, II, 149–53.　　[95] Russell, *op. cit.*, I, 395.
[96] Phillips, "The Decadence of the Plantation System," *Annals*, XXXV, 39.

ize in profitable staples such as cotton and sugar, nor cultivate land especially valuable for their production. A host of farmers were therefore expelled from fertile regions by the expanding plantation system.[97] The best soil was needed for commercial agriculture, and planters were able to command it at a premium because of the profit derived from slavery.[98] Yeomen and nonslaveholders had no choice but to move westward or retreat to sandy patches in the woods and narrow margins along the swamps and bayous.[99] Wherever their small properties could be consolidated or added to a large estate, slaveholders were quick to buy them.[100] In Concordia a planter purchased "three small settlements from white men who owned no negroes" and installed twenty-five slaves.[101] Worthless land was frequently acquired at ridiculously high prices in order to get rid of poor white neighbors who traded or tampered with slaves, encouraged them to steal from their masters, plied them with whiskey, or simply set them the bad example of a lazy life.[102] "A certain class of white men," complained a country paper, ". . . have been suffered to remain in our midst too long, and [their] intercourse with the slave population is altogether too intimate. So long as their presence is tolerated it will be found a difficult matter to preserve that decorum so essential among slaves." [103] The plantation and farm, like slave and free labor, were in-

[97] Cf. Olmsted, *A Journey in the Back Country*, 306–7.

[98] Gray, *op. cit.*, *Agricultural History*, IV, 41.

[99] Olmsted, *A Journey in the Back Country*, 310; *The Cotton Kingdom*, II, 44; F. Lieber, *Slavery, Plantations and the Yeomanry* (New York, 1863), 5.

[100] Olmsted, *A Journey in the Back Country*, 33; *De Bow's Review*, I (February, 1866), 172.

[101] *De Bow's Review*, XI, 59–60.

[102] Olmsted, *A Journey in the Back Country*, 75, 449–50; *A Journey in the Seaboard Slave States*, 674–75.

[103] Pointe Coupee *Echo*, Dec. 13, quoted in *Crescent*, Dec. 19, 1856, with the ominous comment, "There must be . . . new white laws as well as new black laws." See below, chap. V.

compatible. As time went on, a growing number of farmers left the black belt. Typical was the evacuation predicted of hundreds of yeomen in west Carroll when the Vicksburg and Shreveport Railroad connected their land with the world cotton market in 1860: "These small properties will soon be bought up by large owners, in the progress of that inevitable system of the concentration of wealth which is now going on throughout the country, and which promises to root out of all the most productive regions . . . the great body of small agriculturalists." [104]

These changes in the agrarian pattern of Louisiana had early segregated large plantations and slaveholdings in an alluvial black belt.[105] This section expanded in the decade before 1860 to embrace three additional parishes.[106] Because of increasing migration and rising prices in cotton and sugar, the plantation system grew rapidly at the expense of the farming economy.[107] Small properties were consolidated and slaveholdings enlarged. While the average slaveholding increased 20 per cent between 1850 and 1860, the number of owners multiplied only 5 per cent.[108] Meanwhile the average acreage of all agricultural holdings expanded 41 per cent, but the number of farms under a hundred acres only 29 per cent.[109] Slaveholdings and plantations did not grow at this rate in another Southern state; in Georgia, South Carolina, and Texas the average size of landholdings was actually diminished.[110] In Louisiana alone, during the decade before the Civil War, the slaveholding plantation system encroached upon the nonslave-

---

[104] *Crescent*, Sept. 10, 1860.   [105] See Appendix, Table 2.

[106] Catahoula, Franklin, and St. Helena.   [107] See Appendix, Table 6.

[108] *U. S. Cen., 1850, Comp.*, 95; *La. State Register, 1855,* 131; *U. S. Cen., 1860, Agric.,* 230. Cf. Gray, *History of Agriculture in the Southern United States to 1860,* I, 530. Cf. Jefferson County, Miss., which adjoined the Louisiana parishes of Feliciana, in Phillips, "Origin and Growth of the Southern Black Belts," *A. H. R.,* XI, 811–14.

[109] *U. S. Cen., 1860, Agric.,* 222.   [110] *Rpt. U. S. Com. Agric., 1865,* 111.

holding farm economy. By 1860, in consequence of such changes, the poor and the rich on their farms and plantations, raising subsistence and staple crops, were to be found chiefly in different regions of the state. Notwithstanding the fact that a multitude of poor farmers remained in the canebrakes and along the narrow banks of rivers and swamps, where the configuration of land and water left no space for large estates, the alluvial country came to be dominated by slaveholders. The poorer people were confined to less desirable sections—cattle herdsmen to the southern and western prairies, "corn 'n tater" farmers to the sandy north, lumbermen and cattlemen to the piney woods of the Florida parishes, and fishermen and hunters to the Gulf Coast.[111]

In these pursuits, and not by the staple agriculture of slave plantations, the common people obtained their livelihood. Excluded from the plantation economy for want of Negro labor and fertile land, they were unable to compete with the planter in the production of staples: 85 per cent of the cotton and sugar came from the black belt plantation parishes.[112] Sugar was the special monopoly of the richer planters because its production entailed machine manufacture as well as slave

[111] See Appendix, Table 1. It should be emphasized again, however, that plantations never gained exclusive possession of any region. The true picture of the agrarian pattern is much more confused than the truisms into which a multitude of facts are condensed. The census marshals in 1860, for example, reported many small farms of from 10 to 70 acres in a rich sugar parish like Iberville; likewise in Ascension, of 171 families enumerated around New River, 120 Creoles did not own over 20 improved acres each; in Ward 5 of Carroll, a leading cotton parish, there were farms of 10, 30, and 40 acres which raised less than 10 bales; and in the Western District of St. Mary there were so many small Creole farms that the acreage of separate properties was enumerated in this order: 40, 40, 40, 180, 56, 40, 380, 120, 180, 260, 60, 160, 200, 60, 60, 240, 50, 80, 40, 20, 20, and so on to the great sugar plantations of W. T. Weeks & Co., embracing 5,300 acres and worth $140,000, of G. S. Fuselier, 6,490 acres valued at $250,000, and of Duncan & McWilliams, 3,930 acres estimated to be worth $200,000. MS *Returns, U. S. Cen., 1860, La. Agric.*

[112] See Appendix, Table 2.

agriculture. It was a highly capitalized industry that required an investment on the larger and more profitable estates of over $50,000.[113] Small planters made less than a hundred hogsheads with twelve slaves, "lived in most wretched tumbledown wooden houses not much larger than ox sheds," [114] and depended on open evaporation pans or horsepowered mills to extract the saccharine from the cane. Since they could not survive the competition of steam-driven mills, which cost $6,000 for the engine alone,[115] the number of small planters was cut in half during the decade before 1860.[116] It was impossible for farmers to manufacture sugar without at least evaporation pans. Central mills, surrounded by farms, might have developed if there had been railways to transport the perishable and bulky stalks.[117] In their absence, farmers generally limited production to their own needs.

Since three out of five free people in the sugar parishes were nonslaveholders,[118] it may be wondered who they were, and how they gained a living if they did not raise sugar cane. The majority were poor Creole and Cajun farmers, content to grow corn and potatoes for their families, and other vegetables and rice for the New Orleans market. Of 286 families reported by the census marshal in one district of Lafourche, 118 owned less than twenty acres each. Typical was Louis Cheriot, who had thirty-seven acres, valued at $800, of which five were devoted to the production of two hundred bushels of corn and thirty of sweet potatoes; he also owned four horses, one cow, and sixteen pigs, worth $100, and cut a ton of hay. In St. Bernard, around Bienvu, there were many French and

[113] *Picayune*, Jan. 10, 1860; Olmsted, *A Journey in the Seaboard Slave States*, 669–70, 686.

[114] Russell, *My Diary North and South*, I, 386.

[115] Phillips, *Life and Labor in the Old South*, 125.

[116] Champomier, *Statement of the Sugar Crop Made in La., 1849–50*, 51; *ibid., 1858–59*, 39.

[117] Phillips, *American Negro Slavery*, 241–42.   [118] See Appendix, Table 3.

Spanish families who cultivated truck gardens of less than twenty acres. A man like Pedro Rodriguez earned $100 annually from marketing his vegetables; but others made four and five times this amount on truck patches of seventeen to thirty acres. St. James Parish was noted for the cultivation and cure of perique tobacco: the farms were very small, from two to twenty acres being improved as in the case of the Roussels, but exceedingly valuable for their product.[119] Small farmers and humbler folk were especially numerous in Ascension, Assumption, Lafourche, Plaquemines, St. John, St. Landry, Terrebonne, and Vermilion parishes.[120] Those along the Mississippi appeared "to rely principally on . . . catfishing and wood-chopping," [121] and lived "without enterprise and without care" in cabins and cottages nested among the great plantations.[122] Dividing the land among their children until all were at last reduced to pauperism, they nevertheless resisted every effort of the sugar planters to eject them. When they went too deeply into debt, frequently for gambling, they did not go west, but fell back to patches of low ground near the swamps.[123]

Humble Creoles and Cajuns were also conspicuous along the Bayou Lafourche, on the Attakapas prairies, and wherever a narrow ridge between swamp and bayou permitted the cultivation of farms no larger than ten acres. Here were "the poorest, most ignorant, set of beings you ever saw," wrote the famous Mississippian, S. S. Prentiss. "They raise

[119] De Bow's Review, I (February, 1866), 172; Picayune, Oct. 7, 1866; E. F. Campbell, "New Orleans at the Time of the Louisiana Purchase," Geographical Review, XI, 415, 417; MS Returns, U. S. Cen., 1860, La. Agric.

[120] Idem; Rpt. La. Audit. Pub. Accts., 1855, 33–51.

[121] Crescent, Apr. 30, 1860.

[122] Russell, My Diary North and South, I, 403; Henry and Gerodias, The La. Coast Directory, 41, 43, 46–47.

[123] Lyell, A Second Visit to the United States, II, 157; Olmsted, The Cotton Kingdom, II, 46.

only a little corn and a few sweet potatoes—merely sufficient
to support life; yet they seem perfectly contented and happy,
and have balls almost every day." [124] "As soon as the young
man attains the age of puberty," reported a Terrebonne
planter, "his paternal share is meted out to him, usually consisting of a gun and a few pounds of powder, and he is left
to shift for himself. He can, however, always find a living.
Free labor here is worth $1.25 per day, and during the [sugar]
rolling season, he is employed in taking off the crops, by
which means he is enabled to furnish his family with provisions. They generally till a few acres of land—raise corn,
potatoes and rice, though few of them have slaves. During
the winter they kill vast numbers of duck and other game,
both for use and market." [125] The inhabitants of the prairies
were generally much better off, more prosperous and ambitious; [126] but a traveler declared that everywhere poverty
made it difficult to procure food at their cabins.[127] The poor
Cajuns and Creoles who occupied the lowlands in their humble dwellings were much more alike than posterity cares to
believe.

Rice was their most enterprising crop. It was not grown on
plantations, as in South Carolina,[128] but on small Creole farms
of twelve to fifty arpents.[129] From unselected seed the rice
was sown on land flooded by crude ditches, cultivated without help from slaves, and threshed by the ancient practice of
flailing it with sticks, or having horses trample it under hoof.
Hulled by hand in wooden mortars and half-cleaned, surplus
rice was sent to New Orleans, where it sold for less than the

[124] G. L. Prentiss, ed., *A Memoir of S. S. Prentiss* (New York, 1899), I, 95.
[125] *De Bow's Review*, XI, 606.   [126] See above, chap. II.
[127] Olmsted, *A Journey in the Seaboard Slave States*, 648.
[128] Phillips, *Life and Labor in the Old South*, 126.
[129] The French arpent was about five-sixths of an American acre, to which
it compared as 512 to 605. *Nuttall's Journal*, R. G. Thwaites, ed., *Early Western Travels* . . . . (Cleveland, 1904-7), XIII, 313 *n*.

superior Carolina product, although the former was preferred by many Creoles for its sweetness. When Carolina methods of rice culture were recommended to a poor Creole farmer, he would shrug his shoulders and make the characteristic reply, "Je fais comme mon père." [130]
Livestock was the principal means of subsistence in poor parishes to the extreme west and east. Of 239 families enumerated by the census marshal in Calcasieu in 1850, half of whom had Creole names, fifty-seven owned over one hundred acres, and seventy-six less than twenty-one acres of improved land; a few bales of cotton were grown by thirty-one families, a little sugar cane by thirteen, and rice by forty. Although every family followed the self-sufficient rule of farming by growing its own sweet potatoes and corn, each was much more interested in livestock, for this parish was a great range. Each family boasted many horses and ponies; nineteen had over one hundred, and one over one thousand. The pasturage for these animals was the public land. Only a very rich stockbreeder like Alex. Hebert, who had twelve hundred horses and three thousand cattle, owned his range land, which amounted in this case to five thousand acres. Of 251 families in Washington Parish, where land was cheap, 150 owned over a hundred acres each, but 75 had less than twenty acres of improved land; 140 raised cotton, and only 41 of these over five bales each. Much rice was cultivated, generally over a thousand pounds apiece, by eighty-eight families. Self-sufficiency prevailed: corn, sweet potatoes, and some oats were grown everywhere. Livestock was plentiful, and each family kept swine, and horses or cattle, or both in small numbers. Such was the

---

[130] *Picayune*, Oct. 7, 1866, July 11, 1874, Aug. 30, 1877; *Price Current Yearly Report, 1875–76*, xxxii; Olmsted, *A Journey in the Seaboard Slave States*, 682; *Proc. La. State Agric. Soc., 1887*, 70–74. Primitive methods persisted long after the war: Nordhoff reported in 1875 that rice was still cut by sickle and threshed by driving horses over it in a large circle. *The Cotton States*, 69.

way of life in regions of infertile soil like the Florida parishes and southwestern prairies.[131]

Cotton was the chief staple cultivated to any extent by non-slaveholding farmers, but it is impossible to calculate the proportion of this crop that came from farms rather than plantations. It was estimated that in the entire South a quarter of a million white men worked in cotton fields before the war.[132] In Louisiana the majority of these people lived on the uplands, where there were "many small planters . . . , working little more force than their own two hands, strong and willing, who make in the aggregate a good deal of cotton." [133] It is a mistake to imagine that farmers did not enter the cotton economy until after the Civil War, though it is true that a large proportion had nothing to do with the staple, and that specialization in it was not general or harmful until later years. The situation before the war may be seen in upland parishes such as Winn and Claiborne in 1860. In the former, all but 57 out of 344 farmers raised some cotton, and 133 produced over five bales apiece; in the latter, however, only 160 of 284 farmers cultivated cotton, and of these only 61 more than five bales each.

The agrarian pattern of Claiborne reveals the frontier in transition to agriculture. One-third of the farmers had settled public land, and of this particular group less than half made any cotton, and then only a bale or two. All the farmers, with an eye for the need of self-sufficiency, raised several hundred bushels of Indian corn and almost as many of sweet potatoes. Nearly everybody owned some cattle, but the number was never large. Swine were common and numerous; fifty-three families each laid claim to over a hundred pigs, though it may be doubted whether they could always make good

[131] MS *Returns, U. S. Cen., 1850, La. Agric.*
[132] *Opelousas Courier*, May 5, 1866, letter of J. W. B[urwell].
[133] *Crescent*, July 30, 1860.

their claim when swine generally ran wild in the forest. Martin Wood of Claiborne was an example of the prosperous planter who followed the farmer's diversified economy. He held over 3,000 acres of land, of which 660 were improved, and his whole plantation was valued at $16,000. In 1860 he raised 50 bales of cotton, 4,000 bushels of corn, 1,000 of sweet potatoes, 100 of peas and beans, and 50 of oats. In addition, he sheared 140 pounds of wool from his seventy sheep, and made 300 pounds of butter from the milk of thirty cows. But Martin Wood was among the fortunate few. There were many more like Caleb Goodson, who owned forty acres of public land, two horses, two cows, and twenty swine, valued altogether at $437; in 1860 he raised two hundred bushels of corn and twenty-five of sweet potatoes. He was typical of the men who were getting a start.[134]

Their life, as recalled by one farmer, was typical of the frontier. He came with his father in 1830 to establish a plantation in a part of Avoyelles known as "Shinbone Alley." The country was then a wilderness of gigantic trees and wild cane, which had to be cleared away slowly, season after season. At first cotton and corn were planted by chopping the ground with axes and dropping seed into the holes. After three years of farming like Indians, they noted the decaying girdled cane and tree roots, and they used their Cary plow. This was a clumsy, wooden moldboard, covered with pieces of sheet iron an eighth of an inch thick. It was so heavy, owing to friction in the ground, that a horse could hardly pull it. With rich soil and high cotton prices, these pioneers prospered. But in 1841 caterpillars destroyed their standing cotton and forced them to turn to sugar cane, grain, and vegetables.[135]

Another farmer, who planted sixteen acres of cotton and ten of corn, was described by Olmsted. He had a horse and

[134] MS *Returns, U. S. Cen., 1860, La. Agric.*
[135] *Bull. La. Farmers' Inst., 1898*, no. 2, 77–78.

wagon, but no slaves, and his wife worked in the fields. Apparently lazy and none too efficient, he was despondent when Olmsted met him. "Grass and bushes were all overgrowing him; he had to work just like a nigger; this durnation rain would just make the weeds jump, and he didn't expect he should have any cotton at all. There warn't much use in a man's trying to get along by himself; every thing seemed to set in agin him." [136]

Natural misfortunes mocked the most industrious farmers. The caterpillar, or army worm, often made disastrous forages through fields of cotton.[137] Rare, but terrible when it occurred, was drought. In the summer of 1860, the corn and cotton in the northern uplands wilted beneath a hot and rainless sky. "Thousands of acres in grain," it was reported, "have not yielded the seed planted. The forest crop of acorns and nuts are blasted and gone. The grass is dried and wilted, and there is no hope for grain or meat, for the year's supply, being raised by our farmers. . . . All the upland cotton is a failure, so the . . . means to purchase corn and meat is lost to hundreds." [138] Corn became so scarce that it sold at three dollars a bushel wherever it could be obtained. Swine and cattle showed their ribs. Several thousand farmers were reduced to want, unable to buy fodder or food; and to avert famine, the legislature appropriated money to supply them with provisions at public corn depots.[139] This disaster revealed the complete dependence of every farmer on seasonal crops, and the slight margin that separated him from destitution. Land and livestock were his capital, cotton his only income, and corn, salted meat, and vegetables his daily food.

[136] Olmsted, *A Journey in the Back Country*, 197, 204.

[137] E. g., *Concordia Intelligencer*, Aug. 2, quoted in *St. Landry Whig*, Aug. 28, 1845.

[138] *Crescent*, Aug. 28, 1860.

[139] *North Louisiana Baptist*, Aug. 16, quoted in *Crescent*, Aug. 24, 1860; *Rapides National Democrat*, Oct. 13, quoted in *ibid.*, Oct. 20, 1860.

Farmers as a rule were more self-sufficient than planters. Besides corn, they raised sweet potatoes, peas, pumpkins, and other vegetables, and had fish and game at hand as well.[140] This was always true of Creoles, but less frequently of Americans. They would "rather raise fifty dollars worth of cotton than five hundred dollars worth of anything else," observed a traveler. "At few country stopping-places do I find milk, eggs, butter, fresh meat or vegetables. Occasionally one of [these] articles . . . , seldom more than one . . . , and ordinarily not any of them." [141]

From the yeoman to the greatest slaveholder, planters were chiefly to blame for specializing in staples at the expense of their land and pocketbook. Prone to exhaust the soil and glut the cotton market, they literally mined the rich alluvium and sold it "in the form of lint." [142] There appeared to be no need of spending twenty dollars an acre, simply in labor, to replenish with manure ground that was so prodigally fertile.[143] The river bottoms could withstand this exhaustive cultivation, but not the uplands, and farmers later paid dearly for their spendthrift folly as pioneers.[144]

The evil of undiversified agriculture became apparent as early as the forties, when cotton prices touched a prewar bottom of four and a half cents.[145] This was ruinous to farmers without resources to carry them through an unprofitable season, and hardly less harmful to planters with high overhead costs. Complaints were heard of overproduction in cotton. "It would be even better . . . to burn a portion of the crop," in the opinion of a country paper, than to continue producing

[140] De Bow's Review, III, 305; XXVI, 601; Crescent, Aug. 6, 1860.
[141] Crescent, July 30, 1860.
[142] Phillips, "Plantations with Slave Labor and Free," A. H. R., XXX, 746.
[143] Olmsted, A Journey in the Back Country, 374.
[144] Ibid., 20.
[145] Bayou Sara [W. Feliciana] Ledger, quoted in St. Landry Whig, Mar. 6, 1845. Cf. Phillips, American Negro Slavery, opp. 370.

too much.[146] "*Plant less!*" urged another editor, "and turn the labor of a portion of the plantation to other sources of revenue." [147] "If the crop could be thus reduced by the diversion of lands and labor to the production of bacon, corn, negro clothing, horses, mules, &c., which are now principally procured from the north and west, it would not only put an additional ten millions and a half into the pockets of the planters, but would reduce their expenses nearly the same amount." [148] Yet nothing was done to diversify agriculture, and as cotton prices recovered, production expanded as never before.[149]

To the increasing amount of cotton Louisiana farmers added but little because they cultivated less productive land which was remote from markets. On the Attakapas prairies and the pine flats of the Florida parishes, the ground was better for cattle than cotton.[150] In many parts of the uplands it was lack of transportation and not of fertile soil which made cotton culture unprofitable. Sparta, the parish seat of Bienville, was located in the woods eighteen miles from the nearest steamboats on Lake Bisteneau; and in the drought of 1860, corn was hauled over bad country roads from the Ouachita River eighty miles away.[151] During the summer season of low water, when rivers grew dry, northern Louisiana was almost cut off from the rest of the world.[152] The Ouachita was one of its principal water routes, but it often receded to the dimensions of a creek, which prevented steamboats from approaching within 150 miles of a market town such as Monroe. The

---

[146] *Bayou Sara* [W. Feliciana] *Ledger, loc. cit.*

[147] *St. Landry Whig*, Mar. 6, 1845.

[148] *Bayou Sara* [W. Feliciana] *Ledger, loc. cit.*

[149] *De Bow's Review*, XXXII, 283; *Picayune*, Sept. 1, 1866. Between 1850 and 1860, cotton production increased 153 per cent in the Southwest, but only 44 per cent in the Southeast. *U. S. Cen., 1860, Prelim. Rpt.*, 201.

[150] E. g., *De Bow's Review*, VIII, 148; Olmsted, *A Journey through Texas*, 393; *Rpt. U. S. Bur. Soils, 1901*, 622.

[151] *Crescent*, Aug. 11, 1860.   [152] *La. Sen. Debs., 1853*, 192.

only way to travel across this region above Red River before the war was by the Vicksburg and Shreveport stage line.[153] Everywhere the roads were notoriously poor. In thickly settled plantation parishes, wagon paths lay deep in mud from winter to spring, and were seldom repaired by the inhabitants, or connected with bridges across the many small bayous that intersected them.[154] Rivers and steamboats took the place of roads in the plantation belt, which was generally accessible to water. In the back country, where roads were most necessary, the people were too few, poor, and scattered to build them. Farmers in the interior were consequently isolated, forced to be more or less self-sufficient, and to carry on a subsistence agriculture from which they could never escape so long as there was no means to transport their produce to market. The great demand for foodstuffs at New Orleans made truck gardening and livestock profitable as far away as St. Landry Parish, in spite of the fact that it cost fifty cents a dozen to send eggs to the city.[155] But in the overland provisions trade the northern parishes could not compete with more distant places along the Mississippi River which enjoyed the advantage of low steamboat freight rates. This was extremely unfortunate because it prevented local farms from developing a profitable commerce with the plantations and New Orleans.

The advent of railroads promised to connect the back country with the rivers, and in this way to create a diversified but balanced intrastate economy. It was the idea which dominated

[153] *Crescent*, Aug. 14, 20, 1860. A railroad was projected along this route, but its tracks were twenty-eight miles short of the distance between Vicksburg and Monroe in 1860. *Ibid.*, Aug. 20, 1860.

[154] *De Bow's Review*, IX, 238; XI, 60.

[155] *Proceedings of the Adjourned Meeting of the New Orleans* [etc.] *Railroad Convention* (New Orleans, 1852), 10. The country was also hurt by lack of transportation; in northern Louisiana, Western flour sold at $15 a barrel, or three times its price in New Orleans. *La. Sen. Debs., 1853*, 192.

the thought of leading railway promoters such as James Robb. "We should look to something more than sugar and cotton planting," he declared. "We should invite and foster every species of industry that tends to make a commonwealth permanently great and prosperous." [156] In proportion to its wealth and population, however, Louisiana built fewer miles of railroad before 1860 than any other state in the South. New forms of transportation appeared superfluous where there were so many miles of navigable waterways and a great river to tap the commerce of the Middle West.[157]

But early in the fifties, Louisiana merchants began to realize that steamboats were not enough. Every year New Orleans had been losing more of the Mississippi Valley trade, not only to the railroads running east but also to other Southern cities.[158] So large and enthusiastic conventions were held in 1851 and 1852 to concert a remedy.[159] Even some northern parishes awoke to the need of better transportation and staged their own convention.[160] This campaign of education led to a sudden burst of railroad activity. Large grants of land, amounting to over a million and a half acres, were obtained from Congress and the legislature; [161] and several millions of dollars were raised by selling bonds to the state, certain par-

[156] *On Extending the Commerce of the South, etc.* [Railway pamphlet] (New Orleans, 1852), 8.

[157] *De Bow's Review*, I (March, 1866), 318.

[158] *Address of the Board of Directors of the New Orleans, Opelousas, and Great Western Railroad to the Property Holders of the City of New Orleans* (New Orleans, 1852), 5–6, 10. For the best contemporary account of this railroad movement, of which he was a leading advocate, see De Bow, *Encyclopaedia of the Trade and Commerce* . . . , II, 434–63, 478–86, 523–26.

[159] For a full account, see R. S. Cotterill, "The Beginnings of Railroads in the Southwest," *M. V. H. R.*, VIII, 318–26; "Southern Railroads, 1850–1860," *ibid.*, X, 396–405.

[160] *Delta*, Aug. 13, 1852.

[161] *Hunt's Merchants' Magazine and Commercial Review*, LVII, 283–84.

ishes, wealthy planters, and London banking houses.[162] A few enterprising men like Robb projected three lines. The New Orleans, Jackson and Great Northern to Chicago, later incorporated in the Illinois Central system, was actually built from New Orleans into Mississippi before 1860.[163] The New Orleans, Opelousas and Great Western, which afterward became part of the Southern Pacific network, was to open southern Louisiana and Texas.[164] The Vicksburg, Shreveport and Texas Railway would connect northern Louisiana and Texas with the Mississippi River.[165] These routes were all designed primarily to strengthen the grip of New Orleans on the plantation trade of the Mississippi Valley and Texas. But they were so ambitious in scope and costly in execution that before construction was well under way the Civil War broke out.[166]

Country people were divided in their attitude toward railroads. The more prosperous and enterprising planters realized that they would provide access to new markets and land.[167] Rich and poor alike in some parishes remained cool to the prospect of heavy taxation for purposes of construction.[168] Farmers and squatters who lived within the railway land grants faced dispossession unless they could pay the com-

162 *La. Sess. Laws, 1853*, 195–97 [no. 231]; *ibid., 1860*, 9–10 [no. 8]; *Rpt. of the President and Board of Directors of the New Orleans, Opelousas, and Great Western Rail Road Company to the Stockholders* (New Orleans, 1853), 10–12. *De Bow's Review*, XXXII (June, 1861), advertisements.

163 *Picayune*, Jan. 21, 1860; *Hunt's Merchants' Magazine and Commercial Review*, LVI, 134.

164 *Rpt. of . . . the New Orleans, Opelousas, and Great Western Rail Road, passim; Picayune*, Dec. 25, 1867.

165 *Delta*, Aug. 13, 1852.

166 *De Bow's Review*, I (March, 1866), 318. Tracks laid before 1860 ran to only 334 miles.

167 *Delta, loc. cit.*

168 *Crescent*, Feb. 23, 1857.

panies from five to twenty dollars an acre.[169] Although the
roads ousted no one before the war, because little progress was
made in laying tracks, these enormous land grants constituted
dangerous mortgages on the farmer's future.[170]

What already impaired his security more seriously than
the threatened encroachment of railways was the crop-lien.
It is a mistake to think that this credit device, originally known
as a crop privilege, was not invented until after the Civil
War.[171] In Louisiana, as early as 1843, factors and merchants
accepted stored or standing crops as collateral for advances
in money, slaves, land, or goods.[172] This practice was sanc-
tioned by the legislature, recognized in the civil code, and enforced on numerous occasions by the courts.[173] Planters generally borrowed money by mortgaging land, slaves, and
houses, or simply giving their note or *parole d'honneur*.[174]
But if extremely hard pressed, they would actually pledge
their cotton and sugar. The extent of these financial operations was indicated in 1861 by the current indebtedness of
Louisiana planters for eight million dollars to about forty
factors, who had obtained the money from New Orleans
banks on the collateral of plantation mortgages, crop privileges, and notes.[175]

Whereas the planter had many assets, the farmer had but

[169] *De Bow's Review*, XXXII (June, 1861), *loc. cit.* The terms called for
one-fourth of the purchase price to be paid in cash and the remainder in
notes running two to three years at 8 per cent interest.

[170] "Report on the New Orleans, Baton Rouge & Vicksburg R. R.," *H. R.
Rpts.*, 45 Cong., 2 sess., II, no. 1018.

[171] Cf. A. H. Stone, "Cotton Factorage System of the Southern States,"
A. H. R., XX, 557–65; M. B. Hammond, *The Cotton Industry* [Publs. Am.
Econ. Assn., no. 1, 1897], 109–12, 141–42, 145–46.

[172] *La. Sen. Debs., 1853*, 116; *Picayune*, Sept. 21, 1867.

[173] T. G. Morgan, comp., *Civil Code of the State of Louisiana* (New Orleans, 1853), 71, 406, 410–11, 418, Arts. 456, 3153, 3184–85, 3226, and cases
cited; *La. Sess. Laws, 1861*, 77 [no. 104].

[174] *La. Sen. Debs., 1853*, 114–15.

[175] *La. H. Debs., 1864–65*, app. "B," 103, 109.

two—cheap land and valuable cotton. The result was the crop-lien. Among small planters, yeomen, and nonslaveholding farmers, especially in the northern parishes, it was customary to buy supplies from country merchants "on a credit of six or ten months, at a considerable advance in cash prices." [176] It was reported from Winn Parish in 1860 that "most of our farmers have paid out, for the last one or two years, all the money they could possibly get hold of for their lands, and went in debt to their merchants for their dry goods and groceries, trusting to the incoming crops to pay their debts." When drought destroyed these crops, there remained no "means of redeeming their last year's pledges, nor anything wherewith to live on till another crop can be raised." [177] The early crop-lien foreshadowed the later development of high interest rates and constant pressure toward specialization in a negotiable product, such as cotton. These evils were not apparent before the war because farmers then had less occasion to go into debt. "Neither rich nor very poor," they were opening a frontier where the bounty of Nature, the timber, fish, game, and furs, provided an alternative to commercial agriculture which could be freely enjoyed. [178]

Upon the prosperity of agriculture in the Mississippi Valley, and especially in the plantation belt, depended the prosperity of its commercial metropolis, New Orleans. [179] Because of the rapid settlement of this region and the spread of

[176] *Crescent*, Nov. 17, 1859.
[177] *Winn Sentinel*, July 25, quoted in *Crescent*, Aug. 2, 1860.
[178] Cf. *Picayune*, Dec. 15, 1860; *De Bow's Review*, XXXI, 361–69.
[179] *Crescent*, Oct. 8, 1860. "Pork without end, as if Ohio had emptied its lap at the door of New-Orleans," exclaimed the lively writer quoted by De Bow, *Encyclopaedia of the Trade and Commerce* . . . , II, 138. But the cotton exports were even more valuable: during 1850–51 New Orleans received over 10,000,000 pounds of pork in bulk from the interior, 618,156 bales of cotton from the plantations of Louisiana and Mississippi, and 236,821 bales from those of Arkansas. *Ibid.*, 143.

cotton over the Southwest, the population and wealth of the Crescent City multiplied several times during the first half of the century.[180] Its growth might well have been greater if local handicaps and the commercial competition of other states had not interfered. The advantages which first accrued to New Orleans from the Mississippi River steamboat trade were later cut in half by the development of canal and railway transportation to the East. These new rail and water routes diverted the commerce of the upper Mississippi Valley to the Atlantic seaboard and left New Orleans only the business of the lower valley. During the forties the city advanced less rapidly in population and wealth and fell in rank from fourth to fifth place in the nation.[181] Many local handicaps contributed to this relative decline. New Orleans was primarily a depot of one-way trade, chiefly in exports, for she lacked the manufactures and urban population which require large imports. The long river approach to the harbor, across mud bars at the mouths of the Mississippi, kept away ocean vessels as they increased in size. To dredge these passes, deepen the harbor, set up manufactures, and build railways— all essential to the continued growth of the city—was beyond the ability of a society with little liquid capital and less commercial enterprise among its dominant planters. In spite of these obstacles, which promised sooner or later to dwarf her, New Orleans enjoyed a final burst of prosperity in the fifties because of the great boom in cotton and sugar production.[182]

It was this tremendous volume of commerce passing through the Crescent City that made Louisiana, unlike other Southern

[180] *U. S. Cen., 1880, Rpt. Cities*, 251–64.

[181] *Ibid.*, 252, 255; see De Bow, *op. cit.*, II, 450.

[182] *Ibid.*, 257–58, 263; *U. S. Cen., 1850, Comp.*, 191. The capital, deposits, and circulation of New Orleans banks doubled in this decade. *U. S. Cen., 1860, Prelim. Rpt.*, 192–93.

states, more commercial than agricultural in its interests. In 1850 two out of three freemen were engaged in trade and transportation around New Orleans.[183] Here were to be found, as might be expected, over half of all the nonslaveholders, and three-fifths of the people who belonged to the lower ranks of society.[184]

This class was divided almost equally in New Orleans between skilled and unskilled labor. Especially numerous among the former were carpenters, shoemakers, tailors, coopers, blacksmiths, and painters; and among the latter, laborers of all kinds, carters, drivers, and boatmen.[185] Prevailing wages were higher than elsewhere in the South and compared favorably to the rates in Northern cities. The average unskilled laborer received seventy-three cents a day with board, and a dollar or so without board.[186] Steamboat firemen and deck hands were paid from thirty to sixty dollars a month, according to the number available for these occupations.[187] Skilled laborers, such as carpenters or mechanics, earned over two dollars a day.[188] Although these rates appear munificent for the times, the high cost of living in New Orleans greatly reduced their purchasing power.[189] "Goods selling at northern prices" was a sign commonly found in shop windows; and Irish hotel servants complained that they could not save enough from their high wages to pay doctors' bills.[190] Decent

[183] In every other Southern state agriculture engaged at least double the number of free people in commerce. *U. S. Cen., 1850, Comp.,* 128.

[184] See Appendix, Tables 3, 4.   [185] See Appendix, Table 4.

[186] *De Bow's Review,* VI, 296; *U. S. Cen., 1850, Comp.,* 164.

[187] *Baton Rouge Daily Comet,* Nov. 14, 1852; Olmsted, *A Journey in the Seaboard Slave States,* 616.

[188] *De Bow's Review,* VI, 296; *U. S. Cen., 1850, loc. cit.*

[189] See the table of wholesale food prices at New Orleans, which reached a prewar peak in 1857, *Sen. Rpts.,* 52 Cong., 2 sess., III, pt. 4, 1654–1767, 1806–9.

[190] Lyell, *A Second Visit to the United States* . . . , II, 121.

board and lodging, comfortable but by no means luxurious, cost a dollar a day or four dollars a week, even in the small city of Baton Rouge.[191]

Skilled labor nevertheless enjoyed a favorable position in the South because of its relative scarcity. It occasionally capitalized this advantage by organizing trade unions. The first in Louisiana to leave any record was the New Orleans Typographical Society, established by the printers in 1835 to enforce uniform wages and prices. Owing to differences among its members, the society was disbanded in 1844, reorganized the next year, and then dissolved again. Gerard Stith, later to become mayor of New Orleans, put the society on a permanent basis in 1852; and delegates were sent to Pittsburgh the following year to meet representatives from other printing unions. This convention organized the International Typographical Union and chartered the New Orleans Society as Local no. 17.[192] Its existence has continued without interruption to the present day.

Strongest of the nineteenth-century labor unions in Louisiana was the Screwmen's Benevolent Association, established in 1850 by a hundred stevedores who stowed or "screwed" cotton aboard ocean-going vessels. They were highly skilled laborers, worked in gangs of five, and earned a daily group wage of $13.50. The union initiation fee and weekly sick benefit of three dollars showed them to be aristocrats of labor. Their membership tripled by 1853 and came to include nearly all white screwmen by 1860. Although the association was primarily a mutual benefit society which administered sickness and death funds, its wage rates were advanced without a

[191] Baton Rouge Democratic Advocate, Jan. 26, 1848; Olmsted, A Journey in the Seaboard Slave States, 588.

[192] Times-Democrat, Nov. 26, 1887. The existence of this union is not noticed until 1836, a year after its establishment, in J. R. Commons et al., Documentary History of American Industrial Society (Cleveland, 1910), VI, 348.

single strike because of its practical monopoly of the labor supply in this occupation. They reached a prewar peak in 1858, when gangs were paid $21 a day. Two companies of Screwmen's Guards, mustering 350 soldiers, fought for the Confederacy, and only twelve members stayed at home to care for the widowed and destitute. The war almost destroyed the union. Membership fell from 500 to 100, the benefit funds dwindled to $160, and the 1861 wage rate of three dollars a day was shattered by general unemployment.[193] In a brief decade, however, the screwmen had made an exceptional record in the annals of Southern labor, stranger for having been entirely forgotten, and all the more remarkable because trade unions were rare in the slaveholding South.

Screwmen and printers were the only workingmen to form real unions in Louisiana before 1860. Even the skilled building and clothing trades, heavily represented in New Orleans and well organized in Northern cities, remained without the semblance of a mutual benefit society. There were other general labor organizations. A short-lived United Laborers' Benevolent Association sprang up among unskilled workers in New Orleans.[194] Baton Rouge had social groups, such as the Agricultural and Mechanics Association and the Mechanics' Society.[195] The latter was especially active. It registered a vain protest with the General Assembly against leasing the state penitentiary to private manufacturers.[196] Once before, in 1845, mechanics had successfully coerced the lawmakers by deserting Baton Rouge, and twice threatened to leave

---

[193] *Picayune*, Nov. 25, 1887; *Times-Democrat*, Nov. 26, 1887, Nov. 26, 1892, Feb. 11, 1895. This historic union was organized as the "Independent Screwmen's Benevolent Society," Nov. 18, 1850. The first regular meeting was held in the Eagle Fire Company House, Jan. 6, 1851, and it was incorporated by the legislature, Apr. 23, 1851.

[194] *Weekly Mirror*, Mar. 12, 1859.

[195] *Baton Rouge Democratic Advocate*, Jan. 5, 12, 1848.

[196] *Baton Rouge Gazette*, Mar. 6, 1852.

again if the competition of convict labor was renewed.[197] In both New Orleans and Baton Rouge could be found struggling Mechanics' Institutes which offered special opportunities for education to the ambitious artisan.[198] It is obvious that the workingmen were becoming class-conscious on the eve of the Civil War and were groping their way toward some kind of protective solidarity.

It is not hard to understand why labor in Louisiana made little progress toward organization. It was composed of jealous elements, white and colored, native and foreign, slave and free, divided among themselves and isolated from the Northern trade union movement. Above all, it was completely submerged in a slaveholding society which regarded status rather than contract as the normal basis of its labor supply.[199]

The South was hardly of a mind to bargain with workers of one race when it owned so many of another. This was revealed by what happened to white deck hands on the steamboats. Horribly exploited, they were said to be "more of a slave than the lowest African on the plantation of the most cruel master." [200] Although confronted by the competition of thousands of immigrants ready to take their sorry places, these deck hands desperately resorted to frequent strikes.[201] The exasperated steamboat owners induced the legislature to outlaw all stopping of work on ships or freight wharves.[202] Henceforth strike leaders were arrested for "tampering" with the crew—as if they were all slaves.[203] Bond or free, labor suf-

---

[197] Ibid., Mar. 13, 1852; Baton Rouge Advocate, July 27, 1857; Crescent, Mar. 4, July 30, 1857.

[198] Commercial Bulletin, Nov. 13, 1856.

[199] Baton Rouge Gazette, Apr. 10, 1852.

[200] [Baton Rouge] Weekly Gazette and Comet, July 25, 1858.

[201] Louisiana Democrat, Apr. 4, 1860.

[202] La. Sess. Laws, 1858, 142–43 [no. 198].

[203] Weekly Mirror, Oct. 30, 1858. Although slaves and free Negroes were also employed on steamboats, these strikes occurred only among whites, and the law applied to them.

fered from the feudal outlook of slaveholders and could not easily organize for self-defense. The free worker in New Orleans was in danger of losing his freedom and being pulled into the orbit of slavery. There might have been more labor unions if New Orleans had developed industrially. Following the establishment of a textile mill in South Carolina by William Gregg, there was a growing sentiment for manufactures to employ poor whites and make the South independent of Northern goods.[204] De Bow proposed a textile plant for the Crescent City on the model of the Lowell mills to absorb the large number of white female domestics who were reduced to competing at twelve dollars a month with slave menials.[205] But such factories were not established in Louisiana until after the war.[206] Whether the absence of industry should be attributed to inertia, want of capital, preoccupation with trade and agriculture, or all three obstacles, is hard to say. The only manufactures Louisiana had before 1860, located principally in New Orleans, were very small iron, flour, and lumber mills, brick-making shops, a tannery, and a sugar refinery.[207] Although the number of these places increased during the fifties by more than half, they never employed over nine thousand workingmen, and they represented a total investment of but seven million dollars.[208] Manufacturers could hardly be expected to attract the capital which more essential railway projects were unable to obtain. Louisiana therefore remained a commercial and agricultural state, where the absence of industry further restricted the employment and livelihood of poor white people.

In trade and transportation, as in farming and planting, free labor came into conflict with slavery. But the result of this

[204] De Bow's Review, VIII, 24–29. Cf. Olmsted, A Journey in the Back Country, 303–5.
[205] De Bow's Review, VIII, 1–20.   [206] E. g., Picayune, Apr. 22, 1869.
[207] U.S. Cen., 1850, Comp., lxxix.   [208] U.S. Cen., 1890, VIII, pt. ii, 297.

competition in the city was quite different from that in the country. Because skill was at a premium in many urban trades, slave prices were high, and a cheap supply of immigrants was always available, free labor won in New Orleans.[209] Draymen, for example, were colored in the thirties; they were white ten years later.[210] But the general replacement of Negro labor by immigrants had unpleasant connotations, for it simply meant that free labor was cheaper, and slaves worth more than freemen.[211] "Of all species of property," remarked the *Crescent*, "[slavery] is the most aristocratic, the most odious to poor men. We see here on the levee the practical operation of the contest between free and slave labor. The slaves are being rapidly withdrawn from the competition." [212]

It was not the supposedly greater skill of the white man that led to his substitution for the Negro. Immigrants drove slaves out of the most unskilled employments, such as carting, hauling, and every form of rough manual labor.[213] Especially in dangerous work, as we have already noticed, poor Irishmen were preferred to Negroes. But trained slaves and colored men were not *always* replaced by white artisans. There were slaveholding boss mechanics, and Olmsted observed Irish immigrants along Canal Street carrying bricks on mortarboards to Negro masons.[214] The freemen of color in New Orleans, who might erroneously be thought less capable than whites, retained a large share of the good jobs in skilled trades.[215]

---

[209] Olmsted, *A Journey in the Seaboard Slave States*, 590.

[210] Lyell, *A Second Visit to the United States . . .* , II, 160–61.

[211] Cf. Phillips, "The Economic Cost of Slave-Holding in the Cotton Belt," *Political Science Quarterly*, XX, 271 *n*.

[212] Feb. 27, 1850. Cf. *Caddo Gazette*, Sept. 11, quoted in *True Delta*, Sept. 21, 1852.

[213] Olmsted, *A Journey in the Seaboard Slave States*, 590.   [214] *Ibid.*, 588.

[215] Cf. *ibid.*, 589. Here I take exception to Olmsted, who had a natural bias against the Negro as well as slavery, because of the large number of free Negroes in skilled trades. Cf. J. R. Creecy, *Scenes in the South* (Washington, 1860), 25.

Half of them were engaged in 1850 in pursuits which involved education or skill—a proportion much greater than among whites. The free Negro, in fact, was much better off at this time in New Orleans than in New York.[216] He gradually lost remunerative work to white men, as the fifties wore on, partly because of the growing belief that his prosperity jeopardized the discipline of slavery.[217] But many freemen of color remained in skilled trades, along with white artisans, since both classes of labor were cheaper than slaves.

There was consequently a great deal of jealousy and ill feeling between white and colored workers. Slaveholding boss mechanics could seldom persuade white men to work with the Negroes.[218] And white mechanics bitterly opposed slave artisans who took bread out of their mouths and stung their pride by doing the skilled work of a freeman.[219] The poor Irish, especially, resented the presence of so many Negroes, bond and free, in occupations superior to their own.[220] Had these immigrants been less ignorant, admitted a rural newspaper, or better able to organize, they would have fought to abolish slavery. "The great mass of foreigners who come to our shores are laborers, and consequently come in competition with slave labor. It is to their interest to abolish Slavery.

[216] *U. S. Cen., 1850, Comp.* 80–81. Four-fifths of the freemen of color in Louisiana were mulattoes, of whom a large proportion were quadroons and octoroons. Among the 1,792 free colored males over fifteen years of age employed in New Orleans in 1850, listing in numerical order all occupations at which more than 50 men worked, there were 355 carpenters, 278 masons, 179 laborers, 156 cigar makers, 92 shoemakers, 82 tailors, 64 merchants, 61 clerks, and 52 mechanics. In the country parishes there were 244 planters and 158 farmers who were freemen of color.

[217] *Opelousas* [St. Landry] *Patriot,* Feb. 5, 1859. "We lay it down as an incontrovertible proposition, that slave labor and free negro labor are incompatible and can not exist together without serious and constant collisions of the most deleterious character upon society."

[218] Olmsted, *A Journey in the Seaboard Slave States,* 588.

[219] Olmsted, *A Journey in the Back Country,* 300.

[220] Lyell, *A Second Visit to the United States,* II, 161.

These men come from nations where Slavery is not allowed, and they drink in abolition sentiments from their mothers' breasts; they entertain an utter abhorrence of being put on a level with blacks, whether in the field or in the work-shop. Could Slavery be abolished, there would be a greater demand for laborers, and the prices of labor must be greatly enhanced." [221] Why the poor farmers and laborers of Louisiana did not struggle to abolish colored bondage, which threatened to enslave them as well, is to be considered in the next chapter.

[221] *Morehouse Advocate,* quoted by Olmsted, *A Journey in the Seaboard Slave States,* 590.

CHAPTER V

GOVERNMENT BY GENTLEMEN [1]

There never was a people so enslaved by stupid
laws, so degraded by class legislation. Everything
heretofore in Louisiana tended to one end, the
aggrandizement of a small, narrow minded, selfish,
ignorant and domineering class.
—TRUE DELTA [2]

Gosh, nigger, we's equal to them poor white folks
in Catahoula. They vote, but they don't elect nobody, and our masters vote for us, and elects
a member of the legislator.
—HARRISONBURG ADVOCATE [3]

If it is true that "in democracies, the majority alone gives
law," [4] slaveholding Louisiana never pretended to be a democratic state. Suffrage or representation, and sometimes both,
were arranged to exclude a majority of the people, white or
black, from effective control of their government. They were
ruled by a minority made up of planters, merchants, and lawyers. To understand how this commercial and planting aristocracy came to dominate Louisiana before 1860, it is necessary to examine the ostensible source of political power,
suffrage, and the division of legislative power, representation.

The original constitution, under which Louisiana was governed from 1812 to 1845, conferred the franchise on all free

[1] The first part of this chapter, on suffrage and representation, has been rewritten from my "Suffrage and Representation in Ante-Bellum Louisiana,"
L.H.Q., XIX, 390–406, with the kind permission of the editor, Walter
Prichard.
[2] Aug. 3, 1852.   [3] Quoted in *ibid.*, Sept. 10, 1852.
[4] *The Education of Henry Adams* (Boston, 1927), 336.

white males who had purchased public land or paid state taxes.[5] Insignificant as this property test may appear, it served to keep the ballot chiefly in the hands of landowners and shopkeepers,[6] and to bar from the polls two-thirds of the adult freemen.[7] Voters were restricted in the election of legislative and executive officials to candidates whose landed estates ranged in value from $500 to $5,000.[8] The right to vote and to stand for office depended on the possession of property.

It was stipulated in the first constitution that representation should be "equal and uniform" according to the number of registered electors.[9] Yet little effort was made to put this principle into practice. In the lower chamber of the General Assembly, each district was granted its proportionate share of seats, to be adjusted every four years to the increase of the electorate. But the Senate, with power to veto all legislation and constitutional amendments, was drawn from fourteen districts, "forever . . . indivisible," whose permanent boundaries favored planters in the black belt at the expense of white people in New Orleans and on the frontier. The city contained a quarter of the state's population, but had only two senators, while black belt districts with an equal proportion of people boasted of seven senators, or half the entire upper chamber.[10]

It was perhaps natural that the southeastern black belt should control early legislatures because this region was the

[5] *Const. 1812*, Art. II, sec. 8. This constitution was printed in *Niles' Weekly Register*, IV, 428–31. Together with later constitutions, it may be conveniently found in the *Rept. Secy. State, 1902*, 55–309, and B. W. Dart, ed., *Constitutions of the State of Louisiana* (Indianapolis, 1932).

[6] Cf. M. Evans, *A Study in the State Government of Louisiana* (Baton Rouge, 1932), 29.

[7] E. g., the presidential election of 1844, *U. S. Cen., 1850, Comp.*, 45, 50.

[8] *Const. 1812*, Art. II, secs. 4, 12; Art. III, sec. 4.   [9] *Ibid.*, Art. II, sec. 6.

[10] *Ibid.*, Art. II, sec. 10; Schedule, sec. 8. Cf. *Niles' Weekly Register*, I, 388; VI, 393.

oldest and most thickly settled, and its plantation agriculture was the main interest of Louisiana. An unequal apportionment of legislative seats and a propertied franchise were all that could be expected of a constitutional convention in which half the delegates were conservative, well-to-do Creoles, and less than a fifth from the frontier north of Red River.[11]

But it was inevitable that this constitution would prove a strait jacket to a state growing as fast as Louisiana. When population doubled between 1810 and 1820, and again by 1840,[12] the newcomers did not find themselves adequately represented in the General Assembly. In 1843 the northern piney woods parishes were outvoted three to one in the lower house by the southeastern rural black belt, although the latter exceeded the former in white population by only two to one.[13] The wealthy, slaveholding, sugar parishes had a preponderance in legislation that was no longer justified by their numbers. What gave them even greater political weight and caused more discontent on the frontier was the propertied franchise.

A government so aristocratic in principle and practice was hardly to the liking of a generation that put Andrew Jackson in the White House. What appeared proper to people in 1812 came to seem grossly unjust as early as 1830. Because of its apportionment and property qualifications, the legislature had always been "virtually an Aristocracy";[14] and because of exclusive suffrage, elections had at last "become a sort of monopoly."[15] The Jacksonian farmers who settled in Louisi-

---

[11] *Niles' Weekly Register*, IV, 431.   [12] *U. S. Cen., 1890*, pt. I, xxxviii.

[13] *La. H. J., 1843*, 5, and *Journal of the Proceedings of the Convention of . . . 1845* (New Orleans, 1845), opp. 56.

[14] J. W. Windship to Wm. Plumer, Jr., Apr. 2, 1814, in E. S. Brown, ed., "Letters from Louisiana, 1813–1814," *M. V. H. R.*, XI, 575. These letters present an excellent picture of early Louisiana politics.

[15] Bernard Marigny, speaking in the *Proceedings and Debates of the Convention of . . . 1845* (New Orleans, 1845), 105.

ana [16] hated all monopolies, and none so bitterly as a monopoly
of government. Manhood suffrage and equal representation
were the primary articles in a civic creed that enlisted their
faith as fervently as religion.[17] To obtain these democratic
rights, men of their way of thinking had already revised state
constitutions in the conservative East; [18] now in Louisiana
they demanded that the charter of 1812 be brought into accord with the spirit of the times. This movement was led by
Solomon W. Downs of Ouachita, a lawyer and planter from
Tennessee and Kentucky, who built up the "Red River Democracy" as a spearhead of reform.[19]

Every defeat suffered by the Democratic advocates of
electoral revision only postponed it. Twice in the thirties, a
Whig Senate rejected the calls of the House for a constitutional convention, and when at last the upper chamber was
won over, the Governor interposed his veto.[20] Although
Whigs feared that any political change would lead to revolution,[21] they conceded the necessity of banking amendments
after the Panic of 1837,[22] and climbed on the bandwagon of
reform lest it run away without them.[23] In 1841 Governor
Roman signed a resolution for a convention to modify the

[16] *Biographical and Historical Memoirs of Northwest Louisiana*, 109-10;
Harris and Hulse, *History of Claiborne Parish*, 21.

[17] Lyell, *A Second Visit to the United States* . . . , II, 125-26; C. R. Fish,
The Rise of the Common Man, 1830-1850 (New York, 1927), *passim*; F. J.
Turner, *The United States, 1830-1850* (New York, 1935), 20, 24-26.

[18] J. B. McMaster, *A History of the People of the United States* (New
York, 1910), V, chap. I; VII, chap. LXXIV.

[19] *Weekly Delta*, Aug. 27, 1854; C. Lanman, *Dictionary of the United
States Congress* (Philadelphia, 1859), q. v.; M. M. Ruffin and L. McLure,
"General Solomon Weathersbee Downs," *L. H. Q.*, XVII, 10-11, 14.

[20] J. K. Greer, "Louisiana Politics, 1845-1861," *L. H. Q.*, XII, 409.

[21] *Bee*, Nov. 20, 1844, quoted by Greer, *op. cit.*, 410.

[22] J. S. Kendall, *History of New Orleans* (Chicago, 1922), I, 143.

[23] *St. Landry Whig*, July 17, 24, 1845.

organic law in the direction of greater democracy.²⁴ The proposed extension of popular government was beyond question the main reason why Whigs had opposed and Democrats favored revision.²⁵ It accounted for the overwhelming endorsement of the belated convention at the polls. Twice, according to law, the people breached the dikes of Whiggery and voted to reform the property holders' government that had ruled them since 1812.²⁶ In many northern parishes not ten ballots were cast in favor of the old order. The common people rose up in revolt wherever they were numerous. It was natural that they should elect to convention seats twice as many Democrats as Whigs: ²⁷ the party which had always befriended reform was preferred to the party that had so long opposed it.

The Convention of 1845 threw aside the old constitution and wrote a new one,²⁸ which became the fundamental law that all later conventions took as the basis for their work of revision.²⁹ In many ways it was a remarkably democratic document. Some provisions, like the abridgment of legislative power, the multiplication of local elective offices, and the prohibition of monopolies, special charters, and incorporated banks,³⁰ reflected the temper of Jacksonian Democracy.³¹ Such

²⁴ *La. Sen. J., 1841–43,* 10–16, 22, 31–32. The proposed amendments called for changing suffrage qualifications, without saying how, adjusting legislative representation to population, allowing the election of governors without legislative choice between the highest candidates, and enlarging the jurisdiction and membership of the Supreme Court.

²⁵ *Southern* [Jefferson] *Traveller,* June 19, 1844.

²⁶ In 1842, 13,396–4,030, *La. Sen. J., 1843,* 10; and 11,229–2,767 in 1843, *Journal de la Chambre des Représentans, 1844,* 12–13.

²⁷ *Southern* [Jefferson] *Traveller,* July 20, 1844.

²⁸ *Const. Conv. J., 1845,* 16.

²⁹ Except the Reconstruction Convention of 1868. See Evans, *op. cit.,* 33.

³⁰ *Const. 1845,* Arts. 5, 25–26, 82–83, 117–18, 122–25.

³¹ Cf. C. E. Merriam, *A History of American Political Theories* . . . (New York, 1924), chap. V.

safeguards as the limitation of state debts revealed the lessons taught by the Panic of 1837.[32] Other measures for the establishment of free public education and the protection of civil liberties [33] revived the spirit of Jeffersonian Democracy.[34]

But the signal achievement of the convention was the abolition of all property tests for voters and public officials.[35] These restrictions were swept away by Democrats from the northern and central parishes, who voted down the Whigs from New Orleans and the southern parishes, and rescinded the requirement that gubernatorial candidates should own estates worth at least $5,000.[36] If no property qualification was to be demanded of the governor, it followed as a matter of course that none should be asked of legislators.

Both parties agreed to abolish the propertied franchise, but not for the same reasons. Democrats opposed taxpaying qualifications as bad in principle, "measuring mind by dollars and cents," and declared that "if man can *think* without property, he can *vote* without property." [37] "Place all citizens upon a footing of perfect equality as to their political rights," said one, "and you will promote the well-being and happiness of all." [38] Others agreed that this was the philosophy of the Declaration of Independence and the genius of American institutions.[39] Property should not remain the basis of suffrage, according to the Democrats, because human rights and liberties were para-

---

[32] *Const. 1845*, Arts. 113-14, 121.

[33] *Ibid.*, Arts. 105-11, 133-39. See also *Debs.*, 96-97, 111-12.

[34] Cf. G. Chinard, *Thomas Jefferson* (Boston, 1933), 82-83, 95-97.

[35] *Const. 1845*, Arts. 6, 10, 12, 18, 39.

[36] *Const. Conv. J., 1845*, 63. The vote was 38-28. Party affiliations of the convention delegates are given in the *Southern* [Jefferson] *Traveller*, July 20, 1844.

[37] *Const. Conv. Debs., 1845*, 106-7.　　　　[38] *Ibid.*, 99.

[39] *Ibid.*, 96-97, 111-12.

mount. To timid Whigs their retort was that property could always take care of itself.[40]

This growing belief, that economic power was also political, persuaded many Whigs to abandon their traditional insistence upon a propertied electorate. They came to agree with the Democrats that white manhood suffrage would not upset existing institutions. "There is no danger from the poorer classes," the Democratic leader, General Downs, assured members of the convention. The poor "have always been the defenders and protectors of the property of the rich, and will ever be so. . . . Property and money are power, and will always exercise a sufficient control over the poor, without denying to them a voice in the administration under the plea that they are the rabble—poor devils. . . . There is no necessity, no true wisdom, in degrading the poorer classes and placing them on an equality with slaves, by denying them the most important privilege of freemen." Downs repeatedly argued that "property . . . is an element of power, and will and can defend itself. . . . [It] will not only be safe, by leaving suffrage unrestricted, but it will become safer. . . . In none of the States, where suffrage is free, have property holders suffered." [41]

Not every Whig subscribed to this sort of "Bunkum"; [42] many still adhered to their ancient faith that only those who paid taxes should levy them.[43] But the majority conceded that property qualifications had degenerated into a farce because of widespread fraud and were no longer effective in restricting suffrage.[44] It was well known that in recent elections both parties had circumvented the taxpaying test of the old constitution. Judah P. Benjamin had converted the cabdrivers of New Orleans into Whig voters by issuing 1,500 licenses in

[40] *Ibid.*, 110, 112.   [41] *Ibid.*, 116, 118. See also Miles Taylor, *ibid.*, 125.
[42] *Ibid.*, 100.   [43] *Ibid.*, 123.   [44] *Ibid.*, 105, 108, 886.

1842, and John Slidell had turned the tide for the Democrats in 1844 by shipping down the river to Plaquemines, to vote a second time, two steamboats full of Irishmen.[45] Remembering these evasions of a property test, and mindful that "social progress" and the people demanded its abolition,[46] the convention voted almost unanimously against the substitution of a poll tax.[47]

Instead, to safeguard the suffrage, the requirement for residence was extended from one to two years.[48] In this way both parties sought to avoid being submerged by the thousands of foreigners who were pouring into New Orleans.[49] Planters were afraid that agriculture would suffer if immigrants could be herded to the polls by city merchants.[50] The merchants were no less afraid that the many foreign-born voters would come to hold the balance of power between their own rival factions.[51]

The Whigs were already stricken by the plague of Native Americanism that was to prove their mortal disease.[52] They distrusted all foreigners not only because they generally became Democrats,[53] but also because they were a propertyless

[45] *Journal of the Special Committee of the* [Louisiana] *House of Representatives to Investigate the Frauds Perpetrated in the Late Presidential Election* (New Orleans, 1845), *passim;* P. Butler, *Judah P. Benjamin* (Philadelphia, 1907), 66–68.

[46] *Const. Conv. Debs., 1845,* 106, 109.

[47] *Const. Conv. J., 1845,* 152. The vote was 49–12. See also *Debs.,* 886.

[48] *Const. Conv. Debs., 1845,* 95; *Const. Conv. J.,* 343; *Const. 1845,* Art. 10. The vote was 44–23.

[49] *Const. Conv. Debs., 1845,* 99, 127.

[50] *Ibid.,* 108–9.

[51] *Ibid.,* 105. The city delegation favored longer residence, 10–1. *Ibid.,* 127.

[52] G. M. Stephenson, "Nativism in the Forties and Fifties, with Special Reference to the Mississippi Valley," *M. V. H. R.,* IX, 185–202; W. D. Overdyke, "History of the American Party in Louisiana," *L. H. Q.,* XV, XVI, *passim.*

[53] A. O. Hall, *The Manhattaner in New Orleans,* 35–36; Greer, *op. cit., L. H. Q.,* XII, 387 n.

"rabble, the dissolute and the vicious: the pauper and the ignorant," [54] suspected of covert Free Soil sympathies.[55] Foreigners fill the Charity Hospital, declared one Whig, and threaten to "take our bed, and eat up our dinner!" cried another.[56] Whether immigrants to Louisiana were foreign or American, they were thought to have little understanding of local institutions, no stake in the country, and yet to be capable of turning "the scale at the ballot box." [57] Any stipulation as to residence, however long, would fail to keep them from the polls, warned a clairvoyant Whig, because they could swear as falsely to having lived in Louisiana two years as one.[58] It was nevertheless agreed by a coalition of Whigs and Democrats from New Orleans and the southern parishes that the best precaution was to bar all immigrants from voting for two years after their arrival.[59]

This innovation was fought in vain by a solid phalanx of Democrats from the northern parishes, where numerous farmers who had migrated from the southeastern states would suffer temporary disfranchisement.[60] Their delegates claimed that it was revolutionary to double the term of residence required by the old constitution, under which the members of this convention had been elected. Immigrants had made Louisiana what it was, they said, and therefore had as much right as natives to a voice in its government.[61] But no Whig, were he Creole or American, listened to these arguments. Together with wealthy Democrats they had a foreboding sense of what poor foreigners and immigrant farmers might vote to do. And they had gone far enough on the democratic tide of liberalism,

[54] *Const. Conv. Debs., 1845,* 124.
[55] J. F. Jameson, ed., *Correspondence of John C. Calhoun* [American Hist. Assn. Rpt., *1899*], II, 1188–90.
[56] *Const. Conv. Debs., 1845,* 100, 105.   [57] *Ibid.,* 99, 112.
[58] *Ibid.,* 112. Cf. *Bee,* Nov. 5, 7, 1855, for charges of wholesale illegal naturalizations.
[59] *Ibid.,* 103–4, 127.   [60] *Ibid.,* 127.   [61] *Ibid.,* 98, 112–13, 127.

so they thought, when they consented to the abolition of a propertied franchise.[62]

The suffrage reform of 1845 worked little change. It enlarged the electorate by only a third of the number voting under the old constitution, and left the franchise in the hands of two-fifths of the adult freemen.[63] Probably half these voters were slaveholders, because this class seldom failed to attend elections, and the total number of slaveholders in the state was equal to over half the ballots cast in every contest before 1860.[64] Louisiana, in other words, was controlled at the polls by a slaveholding minority of its population.

The majority of nonslaveholders were either unable or unwilling to vote.[65] In the country, "mechanics, artizans and overseers" frequently failed to qualify for the franchise, even by a year of residence, because they moved from place to place in search of employment.[66] Hunters, fishermen, and a multitude of poor farmers in the backwoods either lived too far from the polls or were too indifferent to attend them.[67] In New Orleans hardly 7 per cent of the white people were registered voters,[68] and one-third of this fragmentary electorate was sometimes kept from voting by violence and intimida-

[62] *Ibid.*, 104, 853, 855.

[63] Cf. the vote in the presidential elections of 1844 and 1848 with estimates of free adult population, *U. S. Cen., 1850, Comp.*, 45, 48, 50.

[64] If all slaveholders voted, for example, they cast 58 per cent of the ballots in the presidential election of 1848, 57 per cent in 1852, and—the lowest proportion at any time—44 per cent in 1860. Computed from *U. S. Cen., 1850, Comp.*, 50, 95; *U. S. Cen., 1860, Agric.*, 230; *Crescent*, Dec. 4, 1860.

[65] Cf. *Crescent*, Dec. 22, 1856.   [66] *La. Sen. Rpts., 1850*, 31.

[67] Lafourche, for example, with a white population of 1,857 men over twenty years of age, cast 1,047 votes in 1860. *U. S. Cen., 1860, Popul.*, 188–89; *Crescent*, Dec. 4, 1860. Cf. Assumption, Ascension, St. Mary, Tensas, and Winn.

[68] Computed from data for the apportionment of 1859 in the *Rpt. Secy. State, 1859, passim*, and *La. Sess. Laws, 1859*, 7–9 [no. 7].

tion [69]—generally directed against those who were immigrants.[70] In spite of white manhood suffrage, therefore, Louisiana was not a democracy because an active slaveholding minority outvoted the majority of free people.[71]

As if this plurality was not enough to secure their interests, the slaveholders, merchants, and lawyers arranged representation in the legislature to increase the preponderance which they enjoyed at elections. On this question, as on so many others, they shared a common objective but disagreed as to the means by which it could be attained. Delegates were divided by the natural opposition between city and country, commerce and agriculture.[72] Each group wanted a greater voice in legislation than the other; and to obtain it, each desired representation to be based on what the other fell short of—the country on slaves, the city on voters.[73] In an effort to reconcile them General Downs abandoned the electoral basis of the old constitution and proposed the Federal ratio, by which three-fifths of the slaves would be counted in addition to the free population.[74]

This proposition was bitterly attacked by Christian Roselius and the New Orleans Whigs. They charged that it would enable the country to gain control of the legislature at the expense of the city which paid two-thirds of the state's taxes.[75] From their point of view the country had already been given too many seats by the guarantee that each parish, regardless of population, should have at least one representative.[76] To count three-fifths of the slaves was not only to confirm the

[69] *Msg. Gov. Wickliffe to G. A., 1857,* 16. Half the citizens of New Orleans had always abstained from voting, admitted the *Picayune,* Dec. 3, 1862.

[70] E. g., *Bee,* Nov. 5, 7, 1855. See Greer, *op. cit., L. H. Q.,* XIII, 81–82, 87, 277 *n.*

[71] See Appendix, Table 7.

[72] *Const. Conv. Debs., 1845,* 109.

[73] *Picayune,* Feb. 1, 1845.

[74] *Const. Conv. Debs., 1845,* 313.

[75] *Picayune, loc. cit.; Bee,* Feb. 18, 1845.

[76] *Const. 1845,* Art. 8.

predominance of rural parishes but also to favor their slaves above other kinds of property to be found in the city.[77] Urban delegates preferred representation on the basis of all taxable property, and failing that, the qualified electorate.[78] In reply to their charges Downs argued that New Orleans had ruled the state too long, and that under his Federal ratio it would still choose half the lawmakers.[79]

Downs had no answer for Democratic colleagues who attacked his proposal as vehemently as the New Orleans Whigs, but on very different grounds. The Federal ratio, they declared —impugning the famous compromise of the national Constitution—was "unjust . . . unequal, and operated exclusively in favor of the rich. . . . It would be repugnant to the true principle of democracy to say, that a farmer without slaves, working on his own farm, should have less weight in the government than the rich proprietor adjoining his little farm, who had a hundred negroes [and would be entitled to representation for sixty of them]. They are all citizens alike [farmers and planters], whether rich or poor." "I never imagined," exclaimed the most eloquent of the delegates opposing the Federal ratio, "that the poor would be placed upon an equality with negroes—and that representation would be claimed for the latter upon the same principle that it is accorded to freemen, to wit: that poor white people performed the menial services required of our slaves! That may be true, . . . but I think there is a vast difference between the one and the other." [80] There were not many delegates to defend the poor whites, but there were enough to help the Whigs defeat Downs' proposal of a Federal ratio.[81]

In its place the convention adopted a compromise which

---

[77] Cf. Greer, op. cit., L. H. Q., XII, 412–13.   [78] Const. Conv. J., 1845, 139.
[79] Picayune, Feb. 1, 2, 1845.   [80] Const. Conv. Debs., 1845, 315–16.
[81] Const. Conv. J., 1845, 112. The vote, with many delegates judiciously absent, was 29–22.

satisfied the planters by apportioning senatorial seats on the basis of total population, limiting New Orleans to one-eighth of the membership, and placated merchants and lawyers by continuing to apportion the lower chamber according to the qualified electorate.[82] It was charged at the time, and borne out in convention roll calls,[83] that this compromise was made by a coalition between the black belt and the city.[84] It was not what either most desired, but rather the best that both could get. New Orleans and the southern parishes lost many seats to the northern parishes; but the Federal ratio was defeated, and also the old electoral basis for *both* chambers. The result gave New Orleans the balance of power in the House, where it had a quarter of the seats,[85] and the conservative black belt a majority in the Senate sufficient to veto hostile legislation.

Comparison of representation in both chambers shows that a majority of white people ruled the lower, and a minority, most of whom were planters, the upper. The black belt of twenty-eight parishes, inhabited by a third of the free population, elected over two-fifths of the House. The white belt of eighteen parishes, with two-thirds of the free people and 56 per cent of the voters, elected over half the representatives.[86] The distribution of seats in the lower chamber exactly reflected the number of voters in each section, as was to be expected from the electoral apportionment of this body. While

[82] *Const. 1845*, Arts. 8, 15, 16.

[83] The representatives of New Orleans voted with the black belt. They stood unanimously for making property the basis of senatorial representation, and against striking out total population in the mode finally adopted. They also voted, 8–3, for apportioning the lower chamber according to electors, and 10–1 against doing likewise with the upper chamber. See *Const. Conv. J.*, *1845*, 83, 139, 155, 167.

[84] *Const. Conv. Debs.*, *1845*, 568. Downs evaded this charge, *ibid.*, 579.

[85] *Const. 1845*, Art. 143.

[86] Computed from data for the apportionment of 1848 in the *La. Sen. J.*, *1848*, 81, 88–89.

it was responsible to the free people, they did not have the full representation to which they were entitled on a democratic basis. In the Senate the disproportion was even more striking. The black belt elected three-fifths of this body, and also influenced members from other districts where two of these parishes were grouped with one from the white belt.[87]

With the conservative black belt overrepresented, and the active electorate dominated by slaveholders and men of property, not much can be said for the democratic reforms of the Convention of 1845. Suffrage and representation determine what republican government can do: in Louisiana it could do nothing against the will of the slaveholding minority of the population. Yet the Constitution of 1845 was so much more liberal than the one it replaced that the people gave it their overwhelming approval.[88]

Only the mercantile interests of New Orleans remained dissatisfied. Their delegates had voted against adoption of the constitution.[89] Although the city ratified it, the vote was surprisingly small—one of resignation rather than approval,[90] for Democrats had defeated Whigs, and realty had beaten personalty interests in the convention.[91] However conservative the Democrats had proved themselves to be in political reform, there was no question of their sympathy for Jacksonian agrarianism. The Panic of 1837 bred in them a lasting distrust of the ways of finance: it left a heavy state debt and ruined many banks.[92] So they limited the legislative right to borrow money, prohibited public loans to internal improvement companies, banned the charter of banks, and restricted the life of

---

[87] E. g., Caddo and De Soto with Sabine; Ouachita and Morehouse with Union.

[88] *Weekly Delta*, Dec. 1, 1845. The state vote was 12,277–1,395.

[89] *Const. Conv. J., 1845*, 325.

[90] The vote was 1,760–401. *Jeffersonian*, Dec. 1, 6, 1845. The city vote in the preceding presidential election totaled 8,638.

[91] *Const. Conv. J., 1845*, 242, 266.   [92] *Const. Conv. Debs., 1845*, 125.

all corporations to twenty-five years.[93] Against these agrarian taboos the New Orleans Whigs, who were ambitious business-men, fought in vain.[94]

The commercial interests now found themselves in a constitutional strait jacket. They could not attract capital or build railroads.[95] "What instance is there in the history of the Anglo-Saxon race of an inhibition to embark in an enterprize requiring over five hundred thousand dollars capital?" exclaimed the railway promoter, James Robb. Such was "the anomalous situation of Louisiana." [96] With the mounting prosperity of the fifties and the increasing need of railways, New Orleans Whigs moved swiftly toward emancipation from the agrarian restrictions of 1845.[97] Having made revision of the organic law their platform, the Whigs carried the state election of 1851.[98] They at once submitted to the people a resolution for another convention,[99] which met with great popular approval.[100]

The voters desired constitutional changes not so much to help personalty interests, however, as to extend democratic political reforms. They were not satisfied with the progress made by the last convention and demanded that the judiciary and all executive officers be elected rather than appointed, and that the residence required for voting be reduced to one year.[101] All these reforms had been proposed as constitutional

[93] *Const. 1845*, Arts. 113–14, 121–25.   [94] *Const. Conv. J., 1845*, 242, 266.

[95] *On Extending the Commerce of the South, etc.* [letters and speeches of the New Orleans Railway Convention, 1852], 51–52; *Address of the Board of Directors of the New Orleans, Opelousas and Great Western Railroad to the Property Holders of . . . New Orleans* (New Orleans, 1852), 11.

[96] *Proceedings of the Adjourned Meeting of the New Orleans, Algiers, Attakapas and Opelousas Railroad Convention* (New Orleans, 1852), 8.

[97] *True Delta*, May 12, 1852. See also the opinion of the Supreme Court in *Police Jury v. McDonough*, quoted by Evans, *op. cit.*, 33–34.

[98] *Weekly Delta*, Oct. 27; Nov. 24, 1851.   [99] *La. Sess. Laws, 1852* [no. 73].

[100] *True Delta*, Apr. 13, 1852. The vote in New Orleans was 5,490–171.

[101] *Crescent*, Dec. 8, 1851. Cf. newspapers quoted by Greer, *op. cit.*, *L. H. Q.*, XII, 595.

amendments by the Democratic legislature,[102] only to be stolen by the Whigs as a popular cloak for their own designs. The result was that the people expected democratic reforms of a convention promoted by the Whigs primarily for capitalistic reform.[103] Because the latter called the convention and fought for its membership on straight party lines,[104] while the Democrats were content with the slow process of amendment and took no stand on economic issues,[105] the people filled two-thirds of the seats with Whigs.[106]

The Whig majority leaped to the opportunity of undoing the Democratic work of 1845. "We now have it in our power to place Louisiana beyond the reach of Locofocoism and to retain its government in our hands for years to come," they declared as the Convention of 1852 opened.[107] Under the efficient leadership of Judah P. Benjamin they proceeded first to grant the commercial interests everything they wanted, and then to make changes in representation that might perpetuate the power of Whiggery.

In many of the economic reforms which they carried against the opposition of the northern parishes,[108] Whig delegates were simply voting themselves favors. Among the members were directors and large stockholders of the two leading railroads,[109] seeking state aid,[110] and equally large stockholders

[102] *La. Sen. J., 1852*, 24; *La. Sess. Laws, 1852*, 14–15 [no. 24].

[103] *True Delta*, May 12, 1852; *Crescent*, Nov. 15, 1852; *Southern Democrat*, quoted in *Baton Rouge Daily Comet*, Sept. 8, 1852.

[104] Butler, *op. cit.*, 103.

[105] *Picayune*, Nov. 2, 1851; Sears, *John Slidell*, 85.

[106] *Baton Rouge Gazette*, June 26, 1852; *Picayune*, July 10, 1852. There were eighty-five Whigs and forty-five Democrats.

[107] *Baton Rouge Gazette*, July 10, 1852.

[108] *Const. Conv. J., 1852* (New Orleans, 1852), 70, 73, 78–80.

[109] Cf. *ibid.*, 3; *List of Stockholders of the New Orleans, Opelousas and Great Western Railroad Company* (New Orleans, 1852), 1–31; *Southern and Western Rail-Road Convention* (New Orleans, 1852), 2–3.

[110] *Const. Conv. J., 1845*, 72.

in the Citizens' Bank,[111] who sought to save what opponents dubbed their "shin plaster mill."[112] It was, one newspaper said, a speculators' convention.[113] They knew what they wanted, and by changing the constitution they were able later to procure it from the legislature.[114] Limitation of the state's capacity to borrow money was wiped out; public subscriptions to internal improvement companies were authorized; and the General Assembly was empowered to charter conservative, specie-paying banks by special or general laws.[115] The convention repealed by omission the articles of 1845 which had limited the life of corporations to twenty-five years and prohibited monopolies.[116] Most amazing of all constitutional provisions was one that salvaged the Citizens' Bank, confirmed previous acts in its behalf which were thought to have been unconstitutional, and exempted it from the safeguards of note registry and specie redemption to be required of all other banks.[117] Small wonder that farmers believed the Whig merchants wanted "banks to steal the money of the people, and . . . railroads to run away with it."[118]

It was strange, and did not escape notice at the time, that the same delegates who saved the Citizens' Bank also led in changing the basis of legislative representation to one of total population.[119] Their black belt parishes stood to gain by both measures, for they held over half the Citizens' Bank shares and would now elect a majority of the lawmakers. This was

111 *Ibid.*, 46, 80; *True Delta*, Sept. 12, 1852.   112 *Jeffersonian*, Feb. 12, 1847.
113 *Southern Democrat*, quoted in the *Baton Rouge Daily Comet*, Sept. 8, 1852.
114 E. g., *La. Sess. Laws, 1853*, 141–43, 195–97 [nos. 176–77, 231]; *La. Sen. Debs., 1853*, 37.
115 *Const. 1852*, Arts. 109–11, 118.   116 *Const. 1845*, Arts. 123–25.
117 *True Delta*, Sept. 12, 1852; *Const. 1852*, Art. 121.
118 *Delta*, Oct. 24, 1852.
119 *True Delta*, Sept. 12, 1852. Benjamin and Roman were the authors of both provisions. See *Const. Conv. J., 1852*, 46; Butler, *op. cit.*, 110.

not an accident, claimed the *True Delta*, because legislative control was essential to the future safety of the bank.[120]

The connection between this bank and the new basis of representation was slight, however, compared to the perfect community of interest that existed between planters from the black belt and merchants and lawyers from New Orleans.[121] They struck an alliance because they had surplus funds to invest, in land and slaves or banks and railroads.[122] Their mutual welfare consequently depended on sufficient capital and sound enough banks to finance the expansion of plantations and the building of railways.[123] Each group needed the other's assistance if they were to hold off the flood of paper money or stop the agrarian legislation which had threatened them since 1845.[124] "I am a believer in the sacred and inalienable rights of property," asserted James Robb, whose sentiments were echoed by all Whigs, "[and I believe] that the practical character of every government is the result of a state of property."[125] Therefore, the object of the Whigs in changing legislative representation was not to make secure a single bank but to strengthen their party and erect a bulwark for all property, personal no less than real.[126] They were not alone, of course, in their ambition to safeguard capital by this device, for many Democrats followed their leadership.[127]

Although the new scheme of representation failed to re-

[120] See table of parishes, their population and bank shares, in *True Delta*, Sept. 12, 1852.

[121] *Const. Conv. J., 1852*, 67–68, 79, 82. This combination, dominated by the sugar planters, controlled the Second Congressional District.

[122] *La. Sen. Debs., 1853*, 120.   [123] *Picayune*, Dec. 26, 1852.

[124] *La. Sen. Debs., 1853*, 121–23.

[125] *On Extending the Commerce of the South*, etc., 72.

[126] *Baton Rouge Gazette*, July 10, Nov. 6, 1852; Butler, *op. cit.*, 110. On a basis of total population, Whigs boasted that they could control the legislature and rule the state for thirty years to come. See Greer, *op. cit.*, *L. H. Q.*, XII, 598–99.

[127] *True Delta*, Aug. 17, 27; Sept. 2, 1852.

store the Whigs to their former ascendancy,[128] largely because the national party was already moribund,[129] it transferred control of the legislature from the people to property.
To award seats on the basis of total population was to count
all slaves, and consequently to allocate the greatest representation to large slaveholders. This undemocratic principle had
been applied first to the Senate in 1845 and was now extended
to the House, where it replaced the apportionment by voters.[130]
This system of representation, according to the *True Delta*,
conferred political power on one-third of the people,[131] and
put the planters firmly in the saddle.[132]

This was no exaggeration. The black belt in 1854, with three
more parishes and 2 per cent more voters than in 1848, added
to its seats in the lower chamber by 6 per cent, and thus won
control of both branches of the legislature by a scant majority.[133] Its plurality was increased to a comfortable margin in
the apportionment of 1859. Although the white belt was
inhabited by two-thirds of the free people and half the voters,
its representation was reduced to less than half of the lawmakers.[134] If this disparity of representation should appear
slight in view of the almost equal division of the active electorate between white and black belts, it would be well to remember that in the latter twice as many electors went to the
polls.[135] Hence the injustice of the black belt's legislative
preponderance should be weighed according to its small free
population, and not its numerous voters. Moreover, if black

---

[128] *Baton Rouge Gazette,* Dec. 11, 1852. Over half the parishes failed to
send delegates to the Whig State Convention four months later.

[129] Butler, *loc. cit.*   [130] *Const. 1845,* Art. 15; *Const. 1852,* Art. 8.

[131] Nov. 8, 1852.   [132] Aug. 17, 1852.

[133] Computed from data for the apportionment of 1854 in the *La. H. J.,*
1854, 25–26, and the *La. Sen. J., 1854,* 26.

[134] Computed from data for the apportionment of 1859 in the *Rpt. Secy.
State, 1859, passim,* and *La. Sess. Laws,* 1859, 7–9 [no. 7].

[135] *Ibid.*

and white belts are compared in similar parts rather than as a whole, the legislative advantage of large slaveholders is seen in its true disproportion. For example, thirteen black parishes elected nearly three times as many representatives as six white parishes, although there was a difference of but five hundred in their free population;[136] and twelve colored parishes chose as many legislators as twenty white parishes with double the number of free inhabitants.[137] Other invidious comparisons were drawn by the press of the day.[138] But no more illustrations seem necessary to establish the fact that through representation according to total population a slaveholding minority ruled Louisiana before the Civil War. Other states in the Old South were also governed by this class, but nowhere else were slaveholders able to shape legislation through the representation of their slaves.[139]

It required sharp parliamentary tactics to write so unpopular a device into the constitution. The way was opened for it by a conflict of sectional ambitions which confused the Convention of 1852 more than that of 1845. While black belt parishes always desired to count their slaves,[140] the city and rural white belt still wished to count only voters.[141] But on the electoral basis, all country parishes, white and black alike, realized that New Orleans would eventually run the legislature;[142] so they moved that no parish should be entitled to more than a quarter of the seats in the House.[143] A majority of the city delegates,

---

[136] Cf. *La. Sess. Laws, 1859,* 7–9, *U. S. Cen., 1860, Prelim. Rpt.,* 262. The black belt parishes cited above are Bossier, Carroll, Concordia, East and West Feliciana, Iberville, Madison, Pointe Coupee, St. Charles, St. James, St. Mary, Tensas, and West Baton Rouge; the white belt parishes are Bienville, Claiborne, Jackson, Sabine, Union, and Winn.

[137] *True Delta,* Sept. 2, 1852.   [138] *Ibid.,* Aug. 15, 22, 1852.

[139] *Ibid.,* Aug. 17, 1852. *La. H. J., 1853,* 64.   [140] *Const. Conv. J., 1852,* 46.

[141] *Ibid.,* 64. The vote was 59–51, and then 56–55.

[142] *True Delta,* June 9, 1852.

[143] *Const. Conv. J., 1852,* 63. The vote was 75–34.

alarmed by this blow at their future power,[144] deserted the rural white belt, abandoned the electoral plan, and cast their votes with the black belt for total population without parish restrictions.[145] Although some city members realized that by counting slaves the black belt would win legislative ascendancy, the majority were confident that the time was not far off when even on this basis New Orleans would outnumber the black belt because of its heavy immigration.[146]

This parliamentary deal, in which city merchants and lawyers joined hands with black belt planters to force slave representation upon the poorer white parishes, may on first thought appear to be the familiar story of sectional controversy. But it was more than a conflict between city and country, or commercial and agricultural interests, for the country itself was divided,[147] and in the nature of its division was to be found the economic motive which inspired so much sectional politics. "The wealthy class of planters" from the black belt had nothing in common with "settlers in the remote frontier parishes." [148] But they were bound by every tie of self-interest to their factors and lawyers in New Orleans.[149] Thus arose the conservative alliance of wealth, personal and real, urban and rural, that dominated Louisiana through the legislative representation of slave property.[150]

Such domination, and the device by which it was secured,

[144] *Ibid.*, 66; *Crescent*, Nov. 8, 1852.

[145] *Ibid.*, 65–66. Of twenty-eight city delegates, eighteen voted for total population, and upon their ballots depended its adoption. *True Delta*, Aug. 15, 1852.

[146] *Ibid.*, 66; *True Delta*, Aug. 15, 1852; *Crescent*, Nov. 8, 1852.

[147] *Delta*, Aug. 7, 1852.

[148] *True Delta*, Aug. 15, 17, 1852; *Delta*, Aug. 7, 1852.

[149] *Baton Rouge Gazette*, May 22, 1852; *Weekly Gazette and Comet*, Dec. 6, 1858.

[150] Observe the vote for exempting homesteads from taxation, *La. H. J.*, *1852*, 147, *La. Sen. J.*, *1852*, 175–76, and for public aid to railways, *Crescent*, Feb. 23, 1857.

aroused fierce protests in the poorer parishes.[151] Dissenting members of the Convention of 1852 declared that slave representation destroyed "the essence of republicanism," which was the political equality of all freemen, because it placed "the African and the white man on a level," based representation on property rather than numbers, and transferred all power "into the hands of the large slaveholders, thereby stamping upon this Government the odious principles and character of an aristocratic Government."[152] Slave representation was attacked as "a deliberate conspiracy to confer upon property [political] rights." It was said that the freemen of Louisiana would never "be reconciled to any system by which political power is to be transferred from their hands to those of men owning large gangs of slaves."[153]

The campaign against slave representation as government by slaveholders was soon translated into a popular but groundless denunciation of "nigger rule." The economic issue, for the first but not the last time, was beclouded by race prejudice. It would fan the flames of class conflict to condemn the new constitution as the bulwark of realty and personalty; safer, then, to attack the slave than the slaveholder.[154] So the *True Delta* led the rural press in lampooning the "negro-good-as-a-white-man Constitution,"[155] and country editors in the white belt whipped up racial antagonism between nonslaveholders and slaves.[156] "Anti-nigger Constitution meetings" were held

---

[151] *Picayune*, Oct. 24, 1852.   [152] *Const. Conv. J., 1852*, 53, 66, 99–100.

[153] *True Delta*, Aug. 13, 1852. See also *ibid.*, Nov. 26, 1852, and *Crescent*, Nov. 8, 1852.

[154] *Picayune*, Oct. 24, 1852. Cf. for an illustration of this change, the *True Delta*, Aug. 3, 15, 19, 1852.

[155] *Ibid.*, Oct. 15, Nov. 7, 8, 1852.

[156] See the *Ouachita Register, Minden* [Claiborne] *Herald, Baton Rouge Advocate*, and [Morehouse] *North Louisianian*, quoted in *True Delta*, Sept. 10, 1852. Also see above, *n.* 3.

all over northern Louisiana; [157] and with few exceptions, the parishes in this section voted against the adoption of the new constitution.[158]

The state as a whole, however, ratified the document by a small majority.[159] Most black belt parishes liked the prospect of slave representation,[160] and New Orleans looked forward to increased prosperity from the promotion of banks and railways.[161] Sectional and economic alignments did not always hold, of course, for a few white belt parishes were converted to the constitution by its reduction of voting residence to one year,[162] and several black belt parishes, traditionally Democratic, opposed the constitution as the phoenix of the Whig party.[163]

Opposition to slave representation never died out. Vain attempts were made to amend it in the next session of the legislature,[164] and an intermittent struggle was waged to mitigate its worst evils.[165] Yet nothing could be done to rid the state of slave representation so long as slavery existed, because planters and merchants feared that without it they would be plunged "toward the Vortex of Agrarianism, taxation without representation would at once be re-enacted . . . and the French doctrine that 'property is robbery' . . . formally inaugurated in the State House." [166]

Suffrage and representation, the anatomy of a republican

[157] *Baton Rouge Comet*, Oct. 29, 1852.

[158] *Baton Rouge Gazette*, Nov. 27, 1852.

[159] *Ibid*. The vote was 19,383–14,989.

[160] *Concordia Intelligencer*, quoted in the *Delta*, Sept. 1, 1852.

[161] *Crescent*, Nov. 15, Dec. 27, 1852.

[162] *Baton Rouge Comet*, Sept. 8, 1852.

[163] *Crescent*, Dec. 27, 1852. See also the letter of John Slidell, *Louisiana Courier*, Oct. 14, 1852.

[164] *La. H. J., 1853*, 64–65; *La. Legisl. Docs. & Debs., 1853*, app. 3–4.

[165] *La. H. J., 1854*, 28–29, 34–35; *Picayune*, Mar. 5, 6, 1857.

[166] *Crescent*, Mar. 6, 1857.

government, have been described at some length.[167] There remain two interesting and novel illustrations of how the franchise worked on critical occasions.

Although suffrage was constitutionally restricted to white freemen, local elections were sometimes so closely contested that rival candidates enlisted the aid of free people of color. The most notorious cases in the Old South, long since forgotten, occurred in Rapides. Here in the so-called "Ten-Mile Precinct" lived a hundred or more mulatto families, reputed to be the offspring of North Carolina slaves who had migrated to Louisiana in 1804, after their emancipation, and settled on the frontier. Far removed from any courts of law, they won an evil reputation for unpunished crimes, and were said to be the terror of their poor white neighbors. But relations were not so unfriendly as to prevent considerable miscegenation, for the color of their progeny was admitted to be no clue to their race. Whig politicians first marched these Negroes to the polls in 1838 and entered public land in their names so that they might qualify to vote as if they were white men. "Some of the Democratic boys . . . changed them over to their side" in 1841. The astonished Whigs were outraged and haled their rivals into court. But the trial decided nothing, and henceforth these free people of color voted the Democratic ticket. The scandal was aired by the American party in a desperate effort to defeat Colonel Robert A. Hunter, Democratic candidate for State Treasurer in 1857. He was charged with being "the voter of free negroes, this African suffragate [sic]," and many affidavits were sworn against him. But "Ten-Mile Bob," as his opponents dubbed him, carried Rapides by sixty-eight ballots—presumably colored, and the state by several thousand—unquestionably white. The incident revealed through the confession of both parties that white

[167] This subject has been thoroughly examined in the Atlantic states but totally neglected in Louisiana.

politicians had already learned the value of colored votes in an emergency.[168] Although Louisiana was never affected by anti-slavery propaganda, her immigrants were suspected of being born Abolitionists. "New Orleans is almost Free Soil in their opinions. The populations [*sic*] is one half Northern agents; another ¼ or ⅓ are Foreigners. The remnent [*sic*] are Creoles who cannot be made to comprehend their danger until the negroes are being taken out of the fields," wrote one of Calhoun's correspondents in 1849.[169] His alarm was groundless. The year before, in a suburban district adjoining New Orleans, a meeting of the "Lafayette Van Buren Free Soil Club" took place. A score of people passed resolutions in favor of the Wilmot Proviso, Van Buren, and the sale of public lands at cost to actual settlers. Apprehensive of a sharp warning from the mayor, they subordinated their belief in Free Soil to loyalty for Louisiana, and resolved "so to use our political rights as not to incur the penalty of either the penitentiary or gallows." [170] Ridiculed by the press, "Free Dirt [got] nowhere in Louisiana." [171] But concern over the attitude of propertyless immigrants toward the peculiar institution of slavery never abated. As the crucial election of 1860 approached, Democratic leaders in New Orleans came to mistrust their Irish followers, whose secret sympathies were suspected to be with Lincoln. [172] "In the city," John Slidell informed President Buchanan, "seven eighths at least of the

---

[168] For a full treatment of this episode, and the sources from which it is taken, see my "Negro Voting in the Ante-Bellum South," *Journal of Negro History*, XXI, esp. 359–63. See below, chap. VII.

[169] H. W. Connor to Calhoun, Jan. 12, 1849, Jameson, ed., *Correspondence of John C. Calhoun*, II, 1189. Local planters assured him, however, "that the country was sound."

[170] *Weekly Delta*, Aug. 21, 1848.

[171] *Crescent*, Sept. 16, 1848; cf. *ibid.*, Sept. 13, 23, 1848.

[172] John Slidell, in the *Weekly Delta*, Oct. 6, 1860.

votes for Douglas were cast by the Irish & Germans, who are at heart abolitionists." He was nevertheless confident that "they can easily be taken care of." [173] Where heresy was more easily detected, in the country, a few men were thrust into jail because "they hurrahed for Lincoln" or revealed "the darkest Abolitionist proclivities." [174] Nonslaveholders obviously could never vote to abolish slavery even if they so desired. It was all very well for the press to observe that "right here, in the State of Louisiana, a majority of voters are non-slaveholders, and . . . can, according to universally admitted precepts, whenever so disposed, abolish slavery." [175] But economic and political coercion could always be used to protect the peculiar institution of a slave state.[176] Repression was unnecessary in Louisiana until the crisis of secession because public opinion was almost exclusively the opinion of the ruling planters and merchants.[177]

The majority of poor, white people in New Orleans, who might have been expected to swing elections to their own interest, were practically destitute of real political power.[178] There were few who voted, and the suffrage of the city was in the hands of about six thousand citizens.[179] In one sense the foreign-born population determined the temper of urban politics in so far as they provoked or suffered violence, aroused the fear of conservative people, set the tone of elections, and aggravated party strife. The Irish became Democrats and made

[173] Quoted by Sears, *John Slidell*, 174. New Orleans had voted for Bell and left Breckinridge trailing Douglas. *Crescent*, Dec. 4, 1860.

[174] *Franklin* [St. Mary] *Banner*, Sept. 1, quoted in *Crescent*, Sept. 3, 1860; and *Picayune*, Dec. 16, 1860.

[175] *Crescent*, Dec. 22, 1856. Cf. Appendix, Table 7.

[176] *Ibid.*, Sept. 16, 1848; Sept. 3, Dec. 16, 1860.   [177] See below, chap. VI.

[178] *Msg. Gov. Wickliffe to G. A., 1857*, 16; *Creole*, June 27, 1857.

[179] In the riotous local election of 1856, for example, it was estimated that less than half of 13,000 registered voters—in a population of about 150,000—attended the polls. *True Delta*, June 5, 1856.

up the machine which first took New Orleans from the Whigs.[180] When the Whigs turned into Know-Nothings and then local "Americans," they vented their spleen on immigrants.[181] New Orleans was an armed camp at several elections in the fifties, and bloodshed frequently attended Know-Nothing victories at the polls.[182] Political contests were "a farce and fraud; the knife, the sling-shot, the brass knuckles determining, while the shame is being enacted, who shall occupy and administer the [public] offices." [183] While violence was generally returned for violence, there can hardly be any doubt that the foreign-born bore the brunt of it.[184] They had desperate reason to take up arms upon hearing wild rumors that Know-Nothings planned to slaughter them and fire their churches.[185] But there was no reasonable excuse for the lawless conduct of Native Americans, however great their fear of ignorant Irish Democrats gaining control of the city.[186] Immigrants were simply the pawns of factional party politics, the Irish voting Democratic, and the Germans, Whig.[187]

Within these parties the workingmen of New Orleans exerted some influence. They secured abolition of imprisonment for debt and an ineffectual mechanics' lien law.[188] Their leaders generally drifted into city politics and occasionally attained office. Gerard Stith of the Typographical Society [189]

[180] *Jeffersonian,* Jan. 21, 1846.   [181] Greer, *op. cit., L. H. Q.,* XIII, 266.

[182] E. g., *Picayune,* Sept. 13–17, 1854; *Bee,* Nov. 7, 1855.

[183] *Delta,* May 6, 1860.

[184] Greer, *op. cit., L. H. Q.,* XIII, 101–2, 277 *n.,* 458 *n.*   [185] *Ibid.,* 82.

[186] After the General Assembly took charge of the New Orleans polls, and supervisors succeeded vigilantes, "not even a dog fight" occurred at the election of 1859 according to the *Crescent,* Nov. 8. But for the turbulent year before, see J. S. Kendall, "The Municipal Elections of 1858," *L. H. Q.,* V, 357 ff.

[187] Greer, *op. cit., L. H. Q.,* XII, 387 *n.*

[188] *La. Sess. Laws, 1840,* 131–35 [no. 117]; *Jeffersonian,* Feb. 1, 1847. See also the discussion of an employers' liability bill in *La. Sen. Debs., 1853,* 149.

[189] See above, 114.

was elected mayor on the Native American ticket in 1858,[190] and other successful candidates boasted of labor support.[191] John Monroe, the Native American who became mayor in 1860, was a stevedore on the levee and entered politics under the auspices of his fellows. Born in Virginia a relative of President Monroe, he championed the working class and never lost its allegiance.[192] But politicians rarely did anything of benefit to labor. Like John Slidell, the Democratic boss, they were not interested in labor but in votes, which were frequently lined up by a judicious distribution of contracts for public works.[193]

Workingmen did little to help themselves politically. Once they organized as an economic group for the purpose of swinging an election and redressing a special grievance. When taxes were levied upon occupations and crafts, a "Mechanics' & Workingmen's Association" sprang up in the old third municipality,[194] where the Irish were numerous.[195] They tried to be nonpartisan, but also "to support such men as will do justice to the working class of the community." [196] Their votes helped to elect a Democratic mayor in 1854.[197] The majority of working-class voters were Democrats, while conservative property holders were first Whigs, and afterwards Know-Nothings or Native Americans. Because the Democrats seldom captured city elections, it is apparent that the political influence of urban labor was small.[198]

Like city workingmen, the majority of small farmers belonged to the Democratic party. In the northern and Florida

[190] *Picayune*, June 8, 1858.
[191] *Orleanian*, Mar. 24, 1852; Greer, *op. cit.*, L. H. Q., XIII, 274 *n.*
[192] Kendall, *History of New Orleans*, I, 228.
[193] *True Delta*, July 29, 1859. See the charges of fraud and oppression, *Const. Conv. Debs., 1864*, 452–54.
[194] *Orleanian*, Mar. 10, 19, 1852.   [195] A. O. Hall, *op. cit.*, 35–36.
[196] *Orleanian*, Mar. 19, 1852.
[197] *Ibid.*, Mar. 24, 1852; *Weekly Delta*, Apr. 21, 1854.
[198] Cf. Greer, *op. cit.*, L. H. Q., XII, XIII, *passim*.

parishes Jacksonian emigrants from the older states remained true to their earliest allegiance.[199] They enjoyed greater political power than urban workers because they dominated more parishes; and being native-born, they were not barred from the polls like the foreigners of New Orleans. So they became the backbone of General Downs' Red River Democracy, which captured the state from the Whigs in the forties,[200] and of John Slidell's rural machine, which steered Louisiana toward secession.[201]

But not all small farmers were Democrats. Poor Creoles and Cajuns, who lived south of Red River in parishes ruled by the Whig sugar planters, voted the Whig ticket. Until 1860 local party leaders controlled St. James, St. Martin, and Terrebonne, and until 1856, Lafourche and St. Landry.[202] It was not the French sugar planters alone who made these parishes Whig, as may be seen in the case of Lafourche. Of one thousand votes cast in the elections of 1856 and 1860, from one to two in every three were conservative,[203] although there were only 471 slaveholders,[204] of whom but 74 were sugar planters.[205] Yet the neighboring parish of Plaquemines, which resembled Lafourche in having many poor French farmers and a few large planters, was consistently Democratic.[206]

It is therefore not clear how the unequal division of small farmers between Whig and Democratic parties may be explained on economic grounds. These farmers had the same

[199] See Appendix, Table 7, and the official returns of these parishes in the presidential elections of 1844, *Southern Traveller*, Dec. 7, 1844; 1848 and 1852, *True Delta*, Dec. 5, 1852; 1856, *Delta*, Nov. 24, 1856; and 1860, *Crescent*, Dec. 4, 1860.

[200] See above, 123–25. [201] *True Delta*, Apr. 29, 1853; *Crescent*, Oct. 8, 1859.

[202] H. Greeley and J. F. Cleveland, comp., *A Political Text-Book for 1860* (New York, 1860), 232–33; see Appendix, Table 7.

[203] *Delta*, Nov. 24, 1856; *Crescent*, Dec. 4, 1860.

[204] *U. S. Cen., 1860, Agric.*, 230.

[205] Champomier, *Statement of the Sugar Crop Made in La., 1858–59*, 25–27.

[206] *Ibid.*; also see Appendix, Table 7.

material interests but did not vote together. They were too ignorant to recognize this anomaly and lacked leaders of their own to correct it. Excluded from the slave plantation system, they could not expect parties led by planters to serve their special welfare. And so they joined these parties from considerations which were not economic. Where they lived, and how the prominent men in their parish stood, influenced their votes. Nationalism, religion, and political inheritance also weighed heavily. The conservative, French, Catholic tradition of the Creole and Cajun farmers south of Red River made them Whigs; the liberal, American, Protestant heritage of farmers to the north made them Democrats.[207]

In state and parish politics personalities and patronage generally overshadowed all other issues.[208] This was not uncommon everywhere in the United States. But in Louisiana the active electorate revealed a peculiar enthusiasm for the dramatic clash of personalities, the stratagems of politics, and the winning of public offices. It was a recurring complaint that "principles have disappeared for a love of men and spoils." [209] Two significant illustrations may suffice. The northern parishes revolted against Slidell in 1859, not on any issue vital to the needs of farmer or planter, but simply to nominate their own candidate for the national Senate.[210] Disappointed in this office, they were consoled by the selection of a local planter for governor.[211] It was a rebellion of timeservers and place seekers. Pierre Soulé waged an unequal contest with John Slidell for control of the Democratic party throughout the fifties; the

[207] The effect of these social influences upon political sympathies was early observed by the visiting New England lawyer, J. W. Windship. See E. S. Brown, *op. cit.*, *M. V. H. R.*, XI, 570–79, esp. 571, 575.

[208] *Delta*, Sept. 19, 1852.　　　[209] *True Delta*, Aug. 28, 1852.

[210] The revolt may be conveniently followed in the anti-Slidell *Crescent*, with ample quotations from the country press, throughout 1859. See esp. Sept. 13, Oct. 7, 17, 29, Nov. 14, 17, Dec. 22, 1859.

[211] *True Delta*, Apr. 5, 1859; *Crescent*, Oct. 29, 1859.

differences between them were at first personal,[212] and always concerned patronage.[213] The press delighted in this feud, and the followers of each fought it out with passion.[214] Soulé was no match for Slidell. But his personal ascendancy over three parishes, Ascension, Assumption, and Lafourche, was so great that they became his pocket boroughs.[215] These battles between politicians for spoils and power enlisted many votes by other appeals than the economic.

Especially successful was the position assumed by the Democratic party as champion of the common people. It was loudly affirmed in the violent attacks made by their newspapers on Whig candidates and policies. Typical was the characterization of a Whig nominee as a "rich [man], not wanting in ambition, [who] stands well with *his order*, the rich sugar planters of the State." For them "the tariff of '42 was a perfect God-send. . . . What cared they for justice or injustice, equality or inequality, so that their wives dressed in silks and brocades, and they slugged their champagne." [216] Only in the sugar parishes were the Whigs able to defend the tariff as "the best friend of the poor man" because it took the place of direct taxation.[217] Such arguments were always ridiculed by the opposition as a vain "attempt to cajole the 'workies,' " which occurred before elections in "a prodigious fit of fellow-feeling

[212] Cf. Greer, *op. cit., L. H. Q.,* XII, *passim.*

[213] "My understanding of the whole affair is about this," wrote a correspondent to the *Baton Rouge Weekly Advocate,* Apr. 10, 1859: "That one set of miscreants belonging to John Slidell, and who are ever ready 'to do his dirty work' have got possession of the Federal patronage, which another set of miscreants belonging to Peter Soulé . . . are anxious to get possession of." This feud, arising from a dispute over who should be senator, took on the color of principle when Soulé supported Douglas, and Slidell, Buchanan and Breckinridge, in 1856 and 1860.

[214] E. g., *Alexandria* [Rapides] *American,* Oct. 22, quoted in *Crescent,* Oct. 29, 1859.

[215] *Louisiana Democrat,* Mar. 21, 1860.   [216] *Courier,* Oct. 30, 1849.

[217] E. g., *St. Landry Whig,* Oct. 10, 1844.

for mechanics." [218] Whig merchants and planters who supported a tariff, conservative banking, and internal improvements earned the scurrilous invective of Democrats.[219] Their whole political philosophy was indicted for being aristocratic. "The whigs despise the 'poor and ignorant,'" claimed a Democratic organ. "To despise the poor is the first step to the institution of high property qualifications for the right of suffrage. Thus to transform a free government into a wealthy oligarchy . . . is the final and abhorrent triumph of whiggery." [220] Whatever may be thought of the florid language of the day, it is difficult to deny what the Democrats alleged: Whig leaders were aristocratic, and their policies conferred special privileges upon a small coterie of people. The majority of farmers and laborers naturally preferred the Democratic party.

Although their vote was never equal to their number,[221] they helped to swing the state in favor of most Democratic candidates for the presidency from 1812 to 1860. The only exceptions were in 1840, when Harrison defeated Van Buren because of the distress arising from the Panic of 1837, and in 1848, when Zachary Taylor, a favorite son, beat Lewis Cass.[222] Yet the Democrats rarely polled over 52 per cent of the popular vote.[223] The Whigs enlisted overwhelming support for the tariff, central banking, and internal improvements among the sugar planters and merchants around New Orleans.[224] Their strength was exhibited in the way they maintained control of the state from 1812 to 1843. Thereafter, however, except for New Orleans and the sugar parishes, Louisiana

[218] E. g., *Jeffersonian,* Feb. 1, 1847.   [219] *True Delta,* Aug. 3, 1852.
[220] *Jeffersonian,* Apr. 5, 1847.   [221] See Appendix, Table 7.
[222] *Niles' Weekly Register,* XXIV, 398, XXXI, 178; A. R. Spofford, ed., *American Almanac for 1878* (New York, 1878), 154–55.
[223] In 1832, however, Andrew Jackson won three-fifths of the votes, and in 1840, Harrison did likewise.
[224] *Niles' Weekly Register,* XXXVIII, 418–19, XLI, 9–12, LV, 385.

was ruled by Democrats.[225] Recruiting their ranks from Irish immigration to New Orleans and the heavy influx of Jacksonian farmers into the northern parishes, the Democracy under John Slidell drove the Whigs into the futile chauvinism of the Know-Nothing movement.[226]

Certain affirmative policies assisted the Democratic party in winning the allegiance of the common people. In the forties, as we have seen, it liberalized the government, established white manhood suffrage, inaugurated free public education, and for a time paralyzed the banks and railways projected by city merchants. Because the party drew strength from rural regions, it generally defended the country against the city in sectional disputes that were aggravated by differences of religion and nationality.[227] In New Orleans it protected Irish immigrants from Know-Nothing intimidation and courted their votes by posing as the "true sympathiser with the masses—the friend of hard hands and honest hearts." [228] Above all, the Democracy promised aid to rising yeomen farmers everywhere by its campaign for more land and cheaper labor. Not free homesteads, which slaveholding Louisiana opposed,[229] but the annexation of Texas, Cuba, and even Mexico were successively endorsed.[230] Within the state several million acres of swamp lands were obtained from Congress.[231] But the farmer who owned a few Negroes was not troubled by want of land so much as the difficulty of buying more slaves, without whose help he frequently could not cultivate the land already in his possession. To reduce slave prices, the Democrats advocated reopening the African trade under the subterfuge of im-

---

[225] *Crescent*, Sept. 14, 1857. Except for the single session of 1852, when Whigs paved the way for their constitutional convention, the General Assembly was also controlled by Democrats.

[226] Cf. Greer, *op. cit.*, *L. H. Q.*, XII, XIII, *passim*.

[227] Lyell, *A Second Visit to the United States* . . . , II, 124.

[228] *Jeffersonian*, Feb. 2, 1847.   [229] *Picayune*, May 30, 1860.

[230] Greer, *op. cit.*, *L. H. Q.*, XIII, 282–83, 288–97.   [231] See above, 84.

porting apprentices.[232] Not one of these measures to procure more land and cheaper labor was ever adopted, except for the annexation of Texas, but each in turn was agitated by the Democrats to rally the votes of yeomen farmers. Where these panaceas failed, denunciation of Free Soil, Abolitionism, and Black Republicanism took their place. The slavery question was "worn threadbare by party demagogues."[233] National problems gradually overshadowed state politics and covered up the lack of local issues.[234] In 1859 the Louisiana Democracy came no closer to domestic affairs in its platform than Washington and Cuba.[235]

Apparently the most effective snare for the votes of the common people was the strategy of John Slidell. He was hailed as "King John," the "autocrat" of Louisiana, and the government of the state was said to "reside in the Custom-House, instead of the Capitol at Baton Rouge."[236] By the astute manipulation of convention and caucus,[237] and painstaking attention to the distribution of patronage,[238] Senator Slidell ruled the state through the suffrage of the country.[239] Down to the election of parish police juries, court clerks, and sheriffs, he enforced party loyalty and demanded the voting of straight Democratic tickets. Often, but in vain, it was predicted that

[232] *De Bow's Review*, XXV, 491–96; S. Herron, "The African Apprentice Bill," *Mississippi Valley Hist. Assn. Proceedings*, VIII, 135–45.

[233] *Alexandria* [Rapides] *American*, Oct. 22, quoted in *Crescent*, Oct. 29, 1859.

[234] *Const. Conv. Debs., 1845*, 621. "Could politicians who make issues to acquire power by the fever of the public mind, be thrown overboard, and public attention be directed to measures for the extension of the culture of cane and the improvement of . . . cotton—the increase in the value and quantity of grains and fruits and the improvement of stock—a change would be produced which would astonish the honest planters who have regarded politics as the natural element of legislation." *Creole*, July 7, 1857.

[235] *Louisiana Democrat*, Oct. 19, 1859.   [236] *Crescent*, Oct. 17, 1859.

[237] *Ibid.*, Oct. 17, Nov. 19, Dec. 22, 1859.

[238] Cf. Sears, *John Slidell*, 99–100.

[239] Greer, *op. cit.*, *L. H. Q.*, XIII, *passim*.

the people would "awake to the fact that they are being used." [240]

For Louisiana was governed by gentlemen. It made no great difference to the majority of people whether power belonged to Slidell or Benjamin, Democrats or Whigs, the country or the city.[241] Planters might accuse the merchants of cheating them, and their interests appear hopelessly irreconcilable,[242] but neither had any trouble in uniting to crush radical measures or to draw the political claws of farmers and laborers. Together the planter and merchant, black belt and city, ruled the state. While planters held the upper hand, filled many offices, and set the tone of public opinion,[243] city lawyers occupied the larger share of offices, represented the merchants, and withal served their planting clients as well.[244] Judah Benjamin was a symbol of the union of interests which dominated Louisiana: he was a lawyer and planter, first a Whig and finally a Democrat. Parties and sections might quarrel over the location of the Capitol,[245] who should have the franchise, and whether personalty or realty should be taxed the more.[246] But the policies upon which they agreed were far more nu-

[240] *Opelousas* [St. Landry] *Patriot*, May 24, 1856; *Creole*, July 7, 1857; *Louisiana Democrat*, Nov. 1, 1859; *Crescent*, Nov. 17, 1859.

[241] "Two bodies of men, living upon old names, cajole, humbug, and plunder the people," exclaimed the *True Delta*, Aug. 28, 1852. "The people have got sick of politics and politicians, who appear to have taken the whole direction and management of both parties into their hands," admitted the *Delta*, Sept. 19, 1852. "The contest has become almost exclusively one of parties for power, not . . . principles—for spoils, not . . . measures. The shades of distinction between the two great parties . . . are scarcely perceptible."

[242] *La. Sen. Debs., 1853*, 143–44.   [243] *Weekly Delta*, Jan. 21, 1860.

[244] Of the Congressmen from 1840 to 1860, half were lawyers, and a fourth, planters. *Biographical Dictionary of the American Congress* (Washington, 1928), 43–44, 45–61. Although more country than city residents attended the Constitutional Convention of 1852, one-third of its members were lawyers. J. Livingston, *United States Law Register* (New York, 1859), 323–32.

[245] *Const. Conv. Debs., 1845*, 425; *La. Sen. J., 1856*, 26.

[246] *Const. Conv. Debs., 1845*, 882–83, 892–97.

merous and important than those over which they wrangled. Progressive taxation of slaveholdings according to size, for example, was never adopted; [247] and not until 1856 were prime field hands taxed more than female or infant Negroes.[248] Land and slaves were always assessed at a fraction of their real value,[249] and bank shares were entirely exempt.[250] Taxes—"the money paid by property to support the government which gives, and maintains its existence" [251]—were extraordinarily light.[252] There was little need of public revenue in a state committed to a policy of agrarian laissez faire. The bulk of its legislation concerned matters of parish government and taxation.[253] Nothing was ever done to promote agriculture,[254] or to better the lot of farmers and laborers. Louisiana was, truth to tell, a slave state policed by gentlemen; and the masses, having no real voice in the government, received from it no benefit.[255]

[247] Cf. W. K. Boyd, "Ad Valorem Slave Taxation, 1858–1860," *Trinity College* [North Carolina] *Historical Papers*, Series V, 31–38.

[248] *La. Sess. Laws, 1856*, 180 [no. 173].

[249] *Rpt. La. Audit. Pub. Accts., 1864*, 56–57, 61, 83.

[250] *Crescent*, Sept. 22, 1857.   [251] *Ibid.*, Feb. 21, 1850.

[252] The state rate was 11 cents on $100. *La. Revised Statutes, 1852*, 485–87. In New Orleans, realty and personalty were taxed 1½ per cent of a very low assessment. *La. Sess. Laws, 1856*, 68–69 [no. 93].

[253] *La. Sess. Laws, 1846–1861, passim.*

[254] *Creole*, July 7, 1857; *Affleck's Southern Rural Almanac . . . for 1856*, 51–52.

[255] *True Delta*, Aug. 3, 1852, Apr. 10, 1853. See above, *n.* 235.

CHAPTER VI

SECESSION AND WAR

Designing demagogues . . . precipitated the State
of Louisiana into a revolution.
                                  —ALEXANDRIA CONSTITUTIONAL [1]
The Irish population, . . . being without work,
have rushed to arms with enthusiasm to support
Southern institutions.
                                  —W. H. RUSSELL [2]

Planters and merchants, in defiance of their own constitution, removed Louisiana from the Federal Union. This action
brought upon the majority of people four years of suffering
and destitution. The war between the states became a civil war
within Louisiana, which was a house divided against itself,
with armies, classes, and races engaged in mortal combat. What
began as a slaveholders' *coup d'état* ended in social revolution.

Louisiana, unlike South Carolina, was never the protagonist
of Southern and State rights. The strongest economic and social ties bound this state to the nation. The Mississippi Valley
fed its commerce,[3] a tariff protected its sugar industry,[4] and
the North furnished many of its leading citizens.[5] All the com-

---

[1] Apr. 3, 1861.   [2] *My Diary North and South*, I, 334.

[3] *Delta*, Jan. 27, 1861; E. M. Coulter, "Effects of Secession upon the
Commerce of the Mississippi Valley," *M. V. H. R.*, III, 277–79.

[4] "This culture must gradually decline, unless the planters can be secure
of not less than six cents a pound." E. Bunner, *History of Louisiana* (New-
York, 1842), 262. Cf. *Alexandria Constitutional*, Nov. 24, 1860.

[5] For biographical sketches of prominent New England merchants, see
Cohen's New Orleans Directory, 1853, 3–6, 37, 43–48; *1854*, 15–17; *1855*, 13–
14, 22, 25. Many "down-easters" like Daniel Adams or Kendall and Holbrook,
editors of the *Picayune*, at first opposed secession and then became its most
ardent apostles. See *Crescent*, Nov. 24, 26, 1860; D. C. Roberts, *Southern
Sketches* (Jacksonville, 1865), 29.

mercial, and half the agricultural, interests of Louisiana depended upon its connection with the nation.[6] A state that occupied the mouths of the Mississippi River and was the gateway to the Middle West would be in no better position to oppose the United States than were France or Spain when they held this vital region. So it was natural for Louisiana to frown upon agitation of the slavery question and to support every mode of reconciliation between North and South.

"Except an occasional Carolinian, there [was] not a disunionist in Louisiana" ten years before the Civil War.[7] The finality of the Compromise of 1850 was generally and heartily approved.[8] All the Whigs and a majority of Democrats endorsed it.[9] Dissent was expressed by only one faction of the local Democracy, led by Senator Pierre Soulé [10] and recruited in part from Carolina emigrants who still read their native Calhoun press and echoed the sentiments of fire-eaters such as Rhett.[11] The old and new Democratic leaders were not of this temper: Senator Downs was too ardent a Jacksonian to sympathize with Southern extremists,[12] and John Slidell knew their views were so unpopular in Louisiana that to adopt them would be to hand the state over to the Whigs.[13]

---

[6] *Picayune*, Nov. 12, 1860.   [7] *Louisiana Spectator*, Aug. 30, 1850.

[8] M. J. White, "Louisiana and the Secession Movement of the Early Fifties," *Mississippi Valley Hist. Assn. Proceedings*, VIII, 278–88; M. E. W. Prichard, "Louisiana and the Compromise of 1850" (unpublished master's thesis, Louisiana State University, 1929), 95.

[9] John Slidell to Howell Cobb, Jan. 28, 1852. U. B. Phillips, ed., "The Correspondence of Robert Toombs, Alexander H. Stephens, and Howell Cobb," *American Hist. Assn. Rpt., 1911*, II, 276. See also *Delta*, July 24, 1851.

[10] White, *op. cit.*, VIII, 281, 286–87.

[11] *Picayune*, Aug. 9, 1850; *Weekly Delta*, Sept. 30, 1850.

[12] Ruffin and McLure, "General Solomon Weathersbee Downs," *L. H. Q.*, XVII, 22.

[13] "As to the Rhetts, Yanceys, &c., the sooner . . . we get rid of them the better," Slidell wrote Cobb, *loc. cit.* Cf. *Delta*, Nov. 5, 1851.

But it was the irony of local politics and their paradoxical relation to federal parties that the nationalism of Louisiana in 1850 was reduced to sectionalism by 1860.[14] At the beginning of the decade the national affiliations of local politicians contradicted the principles for which they stood. Slidell's conservative following at home was then allied with Buchanan and the radical wing of the national Democracy, while Soulé's ultra-Southern faction in Louisiana supported Douglas and the conservative Democrats in the nation at large.[15] Ten years later the situation was no different in federal politics, but reversed in Louisiana. Soulé, still the advocate of Douglas, had become a nationalist like his chief. Slidell, who played Warwick to President Buchanan, shared his hostility to Douglas, and endorsed his support of Breckinridge, had become a sectionalist.[16] Loyalty to men transcended their fidelity to principles,[17] and the accidents and shifts of party politics helped drag Louisiana toward secession.

The Whigs were without any power to resist the tide of Southern nationalism. They committed suicide as a party in Louisiana in 1852,[18] when they deserted their presidential candidate, General Scott, because of his suspicious association with Northerners like Seward.[19] Then they drifted into Know-Nothingism. But they were soon left without party connections because the national convention antagonized Catholic Creoles by refusing to seat one of their leaders, Gayarré, the

---

[14] This view is elaborately demonstrated by Greer, "Louisiana Politics, 1845–1861," *L. H. Q.*, XII, XIII, *passim*.

[15] *Ibid.*, XII, 381.   [16] *Ibid.*, XIII, 462.

[17] Especially in the case of Slidell, who was an avowed unionist as late as 1856, when he urged Buchanan to "build up & consolidate a sound homogeneous national democracy that can defy the attacks of fanatics north & south." Quoted by Sears, *John Slidell*, 137. See Slidell's advice to vote according to conscience in 1860, *Weekly Delta*, Oct. 6.

[18] *Bee*, Nov. 3, 1852.   [19] *Delta*, Oct. 29, 1852.

Louisiana historian.[20] A local remnant of the party carried on in New Orleans and the sugar parishes as Native Americans.[21] Many former Whigs turned Democratic with Senator Benjamin in 1856 and voted for Buchanan, "to save the South" from Frémont and the Republicans.[22] In 1860 some of these prodigals, together with the Native Americans, resumed a position of moderation and supported Bell against the "demagogueism" of Breckinridge and disunion.[23]

At this fateful election Slidell and the extreme wing of the Democracy carried the state for Breckinridge, but with the suffrage of less than half the people. Almost as many citizens favored Bell, who shared with Douglas the remaining votes. The decision between Breckinridge and Bell, the leading candidates, rested with the Red River country, which could not be captured at this late hour from John Slidell's machine.[24]

Because so many small farmers lived in this region, it might appear that their votes pushed Louisiana toward secession. Indeed, large slaveholders had been conspicuous throughout the South as Whigs and conservative unionists,[25] and notably in Louisiana—ten years before.[26] But this was no longer true in 1860. The richest black belt parishes, Carroll, Concordia, Iberville, St. Mary, and Tensas, engaged in the cultivation of sugar

[20] See his *History of Louisiana* (New York, 1866), IV, 678.
[21] Cf. Overdyke, "History of the American Party in Louisiana," *L. H. Q.*, XV, XVI, *passim*.
[22] Baton Rouge *Weekly Gazette and Comet*, July 24, 1859; *Crescent*, July 10, 1860.
[23] *Picayune*, May 31, 1860.
[24] *Crescent*, Dec. 4, 1860. The state cast 22,687 votes for Breckinridge, 20,205 for Bell, and 7,625 for Douglas.
[25] *Louisiana Courier*, quoted by A. C. Cole, *The Whig Party in the South* (Washington, 1913), 133. Cf. *Delta*, Oct. 9, 1856.
[26] *Louisiana Courier*, Oct. 26, 1849. A Whig House, for example, enjoined a Democratic Senate from sending delegates to the Nashville Convention. *La. H. J., 1850*, 120–77.

as well as cotton, voted for Breckinridge. The farming white belt parishes cast a larger proportion of ballots for Bell and Douglas.[27] Only in New Orleans did men of wealth remain conservative and help to carry the city for Bell; but even here they were greatly assisted, according to Slidell, by the poor Irish and Germans who cast half as many votes for Douglas.[28] Laborers had never been interested in the defense of slavery, and not all the Jacksonian farmers were converted to Southern nationalism by 1860. It was rather the large slaveholders who were the most fervent sectional patriots.

The election of Lincoln frightened them and precipitated desperate actions born of fear.[29] There was little difference from their point of view between "Black Republicans" and Abolitionists.[30] They were not angry at what had happened in the long sectional controversy of the past, but intensely apprehensive of what the North might do in the future.[31] John Slidell, hitherto a moderate who thought the South might rule within the Union, now saw no alternative to secession.[32] The Governor, Thomas Moore, was his puppet, and a large slaveholder from Rapides.[33] He called a special session of the General Assembly and demanded the immediate election of a convention for no other purpose than to divorce Louisiana from the Union.[34] In refusing to submit the question of a convention to popular referendum, as required by the Constitution of

[27] See below, Appendix, Table 8.   [28] See above, 145–46.

[29] Few agreed with the German-born lawyer, Christian Roselius, that it was "not in itself a sufficient cause for the dissolution of this Union. It is true," he went on, "that [Lincoln] is the devil incarnate, and . . . Mr. Buchanan is an imbecile, but they are both powerless for harm to the citizens of the South." *Crescent*, Jan. 28, 1861.

[30] *Ibid.*, Jan. 5, 9, Nov. 28, 1860.   [31] *Bee*, July 27, 1860.

[32] Slidell to Buchanan, Nov. 11, 1860, quoted by Sears, *op. cit.*, 174.

[33] Cf. G. P. Whittington, "Thomas O. Moore," *L. H. Q.*, XIII, 6–8; *Crescent*, Oct. 29, 1859.

[34] *Spec. Msg. Gov. Moore to G. A., 1860*, 6–7.

1852,[35] the legislature took the first illegal and revolutionary step toward secession.[36]

During the three weeks that preceded the choice of delegates, a vigorous campaign was waged between two sets of candidates, self-styled Co-operationists and avowed Secessionists.[37] The latter were extreme Democrats, partisans of Breckinridge, and advocates, emulating South Carolina, of immediate, separate, and unconditional secession.[38] Co-operationists, on the other hand, included the followers of Bell and Douglas who preferred to postpone the question of secession to a convention of Southern states.[39] They believed that such a body, led by Virginia, might win the consent of the North to constitutional amendments which would protect slavery and the position of the South in the Union.[40] While they recognized the right of secession as a remedy of last resort, they deprecated its necessity, without denying that the South had pressing grievances.[41] This dilemma weakened the Co-operationists and earned for them the name of "Submissionists."[42] Their opponents were organized in the political machine operated by John Slidell, and profited by the emotional hysteria of sec-

[35] *Const. 1852*, Art. 141. This procedure was required for amending the constitution, which secession would entail, and had always preceded the convocation of earlier conventions.

[36] See the opinion of Randell Hunt, Baton Rouge *Weekly Gazette and Comet*, Dec. 15, 1860, and the protest of a delegate, James Taliaferro, *Crescent*, Jan. 31, 1861, which the convention refused to record in its journal, reprinted in my study, "A Suppressed Co-operationist Protest Against Secession," *L. H. Q.*, XIX, 201–3.

[37] Greer, *op. cit.*, *L. H. Q.*, XIII, 629–33; L. C. Kendall, "The Interregnum in Louisiana in 1861," *L. H. Q.*, XVI, 179–204.

[38] *Crescent*, Jan. 7, 1861.

[39] *Ibid.*, Jan. 5, 1861.

[40] *Alexandria Constitutional*, Dec. 22, 1860, Mar. 30, 1861. Cf. my study, "A Suppressed Co-operationist Protest Against Secession," *L. H. Q.*, XIX, 200.

[41] Co-operation in Louisiana was more conciliatory toward the Federal Union than in other Southern states. *Crescent*, Jan. 5, 1861.

[42] Greer, *op. cit.*, *L. H. Q.*, XIII, 625.

tional patriotism.[43] Planters, press, and pulpit, with few exceptions, called for secession to vindicate the honor and preserve the property of Louisiana.[44]

The result was the election to the convention of nearly two Secessionists for every Co-operationist.[45] Even the city of New Orleans, upon whose merchants and immigrants the Co-operationists had pinned their hopes, went Secessionist by the slight plurality of 380 out of 8,336 votes.[46] A political rupture, immediate and perhaps irrevocable, was now inevitable.[47]

Strangely enough, however, it is impossible to learn whether a majority of people favored secession. Delegates of this persuasion were declared to be elected, and took their seats without contests or charges of fraud. But the official election returns were suppressed. Gossip was rife that the Co-operationists had actually carried the state by more than three hundred votes;[48] and the convention did not quiet these rumors by refusing to make the returns public.[49] Long and loud were the demands of the *Picayune* for their publication.[50] Not until the convention had finished its business, three months after resolving on secession,[51] was a tabulation of parish votes released through a party organ, the *Delta*.[52] Although people were too preoccupied with the swift rush of events to scrutinize what no longer mattered, these belated returns were not above sus-

[43] *Alexandria Constitutional,* Jan. 12, 1861.

[44] L. C. Kendall, *op. cit., L. H. Q.,* XVI, 179–204.

[45] *Weekly Delta,* Jan. 19, 1861. There were elected to the convention 83 Secessionists and 47 Co-operationists.

[46] *Picayune,* Jan. 8, 1861.   [47] *Ibid.,* Jan. 9, 1861.

[48] *Ibid.,* Feb. 17, 1861; diary note of John Purcell, Feb. 4, quoted by J. R. Ficklen, *History of Reconstruction in Louisiana (through 1868)* (Baltimore, 1910), 22 *n.*

[49] *Ibid.,* Mar. 18, 1861. The vote was 72–23.

[50] *Ibid.,* Mar. 29, 1861.

[51] *La. Conv. J., 1861,* 18. The vote was 113–17.

[52] Mar. 30, 1861. A Democratic newspaper, long in favor of secession, it was not the official organ of the convention.

picion.[53] The vote of New Orleans, for example, was given in round hundreds, which never before happened in that city.[54] The total vote of the state was reported to be 25 per cent less than at the presidential election of 1860. If these figures were juggled, it was done with great discretion; but no grave distortion would have been necessary in a tabulation favorable to the Secessionists by 20,448 to 17,296 votes.[55]

Since these returns were the only popular referendum on secession, a brief analysis is in order.[56]

It is difficult to explain why more than twelve thousand citizens, or a quarter of those who participated in the presidential election, were absent from the polls two months later when the issue was clearer and more exciting. One cannot be sure whether they were Breckinridge voters who hesitated to approve secession, or Bell and Douglas conservatives who could not make up their minds. The proportion of stay-at-homes in Co-operationist parishes was not much larger than in those that went Secessionist. But, since the party which advocates the affirmative of an issue generally votes its full strength, it is reasonable to assume that there were enough absentees of negative or Co-operationist persuasion, particularly in New Orleans, to have reversed the election.[57]

The Co-operationists actually carried nineteen of the forty-eight parishes. Of seven which had previously favored Bell, five contained many small farmers. Three—Ascension, Assumption, and Lafourche—were Soulé strongholds which had

[53] The only historians to use them are Fortier, *History of Louisiana*, IV, 3–4, and Greer, *op. cit.*, *L.H.Q.*, XIII, 640–41. Neither questions their validity; Greer gives them in full.

[54] In the official returns, 4,300 to 3,900, and 4,358 to 3,978 in the *Picayune*, Jan. 8, 1861.

[55] *Delta, loc. cit.*

[56] See Appendix, Table 8. The original records, according to the Secretary of State, have been destroyed.

[57] Cf. Greer, *op. cit.*, *L.H.Q.*, XIII, 643–44.

gone for Douglas and still remained true to their leader. The larger part of their overwhelming Co-operationist vote came from the Creole and Cajun farmers so numerous in this section. The other nine Co-operationist parishes, which had formerly voted for Breckinridge, also contained a large proportion of small farmers who cast their ballots against secession once the issue was clear. Soulé had constantly asserted that "nobody but the slave-holder has an interest in the preservation of slavery." [58] Evidently his belief was partly justified. Never before had so many of these nonslaveholders deserted John Slidell's Democracy, but now at the last hour they revolted against fighting for slavery. For them the crisis lost its "sectional character" and became simply a question "of the maintenance of the peculiar rights of a privileged class." [59]

The wealthiest slaveholding parishes, on the other hand, were strong for secession. Of course, many conservative planters favored Co-operation: some were old Whigs who had voted for Bell; others were Breckinridge Democrats who beat a hasty retreat from the dangers of disunion. But the slaveholding parishes which had voted for Breckinridge returned an even larger majority for secession. The *Delta* boasted that the Secessionist delegates themselves owned more Negroes than any equal number of slaveholders to be found elsewhere in the South.[60] Although neither planters nor farmers were of a single mind, many more slaveholders than nonslaveholders welcomed the immediate secession of Louisiana. The planters of Madison, for example, espoused it wholeheartedly; but the farmers of Winn and other northern parishes dreaded the "calamity of dissolution." [61] The election generally ran against secession wherever slaveholders did not cast half the ballots. The

---

[58] *Delta*, Nov. 1, 1860.   [59] Cf. *ibid.*   [60] Jan. 19, 1861.
[61] *Picayune*, Dec. 15, 26, 1860; *Crescent*, Jan. 14, 15, 1861. The *Crescent* election returns, which were incomplete, differ considerably from the official *Delta* figures used in Table 8, in the Appendix.

few exceptions—St. James, East Feliciana, St. Helena, and Rapides—were parishes where yeomen slaveholders were numerous.[62]

There was practically no debate in the convention over the withdrawal of Louisiana from the Union.[63] Nearly two-thirds of the delegates were Secessionists, and their seats were based on slave representation. Governor Moore had seized all national forts and arsenals on his own initiative.[64] Nothing was "left . . . for [the delegates] to do but to confirm his acts." [65] The Co-operationist program, embodied in Rozier's motion to revive the Nashville convention and amend the Federal Constitution in the interests of the South and "continuance of the Union," was overwhelmingly defeated.[66] Only some delegates from New Orleans and the small farming parishes endorsed it.[67] The Co-operationists made their last stand on Fuqua's resolution to refer the question of secession to a convention of Southern states which would be empowered to declare independence and establish a Confederacy. Again they were rebuffed, but this time by only twenty-six votes.[68] Seeing that their cause was hopeless they took counsel together and cast in their lot with the majority for immediate secession.[69] All but seven of them eventually signed the ordinance of secession. Three of the irreconcilables came from New Orleans; the others from the farming parishes of Caldwell, Catahoula, and

[62] See Appendix, Table 8.

[63] The first test came with the election of a Secessionist president, 81–41. *La. Conv. J., 1861*, 5; *Crescent*, Jan. 26, 1861.

[64] *Alexandria Constitutional*, Jan. 19, 1861. This Soulé organ charged that Slidell had ordered their seizure to commit the convention to immediate secession. But the General Assembly had previously appropriated half a million dollars for the "defence" of Louisiana.

[65] *Ibid.*   [66] *Crescent*, Jan. 26, 1861. The vote was 106–24.

[67] *La. Conv. J., 1861*, 15.

[68] *Ibid.*, 11–12, 16; *Crescent, loc. cit.* The vote on Fuqua's substitute was 73–47.

[69] *Ibid.*, 17–18. The vote was, as stated above, 113–17.

Winn.[70] In "joyous and careless temper," [71] the planters of Louisiana committed what their own historian, Gayarré, later called the "sublime imprudence" of secession.[72]

Long ago the *Picayune* had demanded that the convention submit its work to the people lest it be guilty of a *coup d'état*.[73] But this body deliberately refused to take a plebiscite on the ordinance of secession.[74] This was the second illegal and revolutionary step in its high-handed conduct. Doubtless secession would have been ratified, because the withdrawal of other states and the popular hysteria attending the march of events led even erstwhile Co-operationists and conservatives to confess that they were "drifting into secession ideas." [75] But the convention was either too impatient to await a referendum or afraid of a negative verdict. "The time for argument has passed," it was said. "We were sent here to act. We are in times of revolution, and questions of form must sink into insignificance." [76]

The temper and procedure of the Convention of 1861 were revolutionary.[77] It acted like a slaveholders' junto and rode over all opposition without parliamentary decorum. Everything was done in haste; there was little debate. Co-operationist motions were not printed in the journal,[78] nor were protests against secession spread upon its pages.[79] The convention re-

[70] *Ibid.*, 18, 231–32; cf. facsimile in *Rpt. Secy. State, 1902*, opp. 112.

[71] R. Taylor, *Destruction and Reconstruction*, 13.

[72] *History of Louisiana*, IV, 692.   [73] Dec. 16, 1860.

[74] *La. Conv. J., 1861*, 17. The vote was 84–43, with Co-operationists in the affirmative.

[75] *Crescent*, Jan. 28, 1861; diary note of John Purcell, quoted by Ficklen, *History of Reconstruction in Louisiana (through 1868)*, 23.

[76] *Crescent, loc. cit.*

[77] *Alexandria Constitutional*, Mar. 30, Apr. 13, 1861.

[78] But they were noted in the MS *Journal* and summarized in the *Crescent*, official newspaper of the convention.

[79] See my study, "A Suppressed Co-operationist Protest Against Secession," *L. H. Q.*, XIX, 199.

placed the General Assembly without authority from the people and became the ruling legislative body of Louisiana during its two months of solitary independence.[80] Finally, and again without popular mandate,[81] it united Louisiana to the Confederacy, approved its constitution, and elected representatives and senators to the first congress at Montgomery.[82]

Yet the secession of Louisiana was not a slaveholders' *conspiracy*. This was an accusation voiced by many Northerners. Horace Greeley, for example, confused Co-operationists with "Unionists," and claimed that they were reduced to a fictitious minority by fraudulent manipulation of the convention election returns.[83] Although the returns may have been juggled, as we have shown, there is no conclusive evidence in this matter. Even if fraud was perpetrated, the Co-operationists were not unionists, but a party that desired the South to make united representations, and to secede if no redress was secured. William Watson, a Scotsman who resided in Louisiana and later joined the Confederate army, corroborated Greeley's charge of conspiracy by a circumstantial account of the way in which Governor Moore and other Democratic politicians hastened secession.[84] The evidence advanced by Greeley and Watson apparently embarrassed James Ford Rhodes, because he admitted it to be "most inconsistent" with his circumspect conclusion that secession was not a conspiracy.[85] H. E. von Holst [86] and Schouler [87] also agreed with Rhodes. These his-

---

[80] *Picayune*, Mar. 9, 1861.   [81] *Ibid.*, Mar. 29; *True Delta*, Mar. 19, 1861.
[82] L. C. Kendall, "The Interregnum in Louisiana in 1861," *L. H. Q.*, XVII, 124-38, 524-31.
[83] *The American Conflict* (Hartford, 1864) I, 348.
[84] *Life in the Confederate Army* (New York, 1888), chap. I.
[85] *History of the United States*, III, 272-80.
[86] *Constitutional and Political History of the United States* (Chicago, 1876-92), VII, 275.
[87] J. Schouler, *History of the United States of America under the Constitution* (New York, 1894-1913), V, 509.

torians would have found additional evidence in an account by the New Orleans printer, DeWitt Roberts, of how he and other unionists were banished from the city early in 1861 by popular hysteria. It was this unthinking mood, according to Roberts, which swept the state into secession against the will of the majority.[88]

But coercion and precipitate actions all indicated successful minority pressure rather than a conspiracy.[89] James Schouler, in spite of his Northern bias, observed with great perspicacity that the undemocratic procedure by which secession was accomplished "was in pursuance of class and oligarchical political methods to which the slave section of the country had been well accustomed." [90] Government by gentlemen, as we have seen, had for many years been the oligarchical rule of a planting and commercial plutocracy. It was this minority which led the majority of people out of the Union, not by conspiracy but by the exercise of powers they had always possessed, in behalf of the slaveholding philosophy which had become the creed of the South. The majority of people in Louisiana were either opposed or indifferent to secession, but altogether helpless in any event to resist it. They were removed from the Union and attached to the Confederacy by a slaveholders' convention that subverted its own constitutional precedents as well as every principle of democratic government. "Convened without authority from the people of the State," as James Taliaferro, the delegate from Catahoula, declared in eloquent protest,[91] "and refusing to submit its action to them for their sanction in the grave and vital act of changing their government, this Convention violates the great fundamental principle

[88] *Southern Sketches*, 27–28, 35–38.

[89] A recent historian, D. L. Dumond, *The Secession Movement, 1860–1861* (New York, 1931), 208–9, overlooks the evidence that we have given so briefly. Much to be preferred is L. C. Kendall, "The Interregnum in Louisiana in 1861," *L.H.Q.*, XVII, 530–31.

[90] *Loc. cit.*   [91] *Crescent*, Jan. 31, 1861.

of American government, that the will of the people is supreme." [92] The result was to make Louisiana the keystone of the Confederacy without which the whole arch of Southern independence might have crumbled, and the Civil War been averted or at least measurably shortened. It was now sure to be "no holiday game between the two sections." [93]

The entire manhood of Louisiana appeared to rush to arms in defense of secession and their native state. It was estimated that fifty thousand men marched to war.[94] This amazing number was equal to one-seventh of the total white population,[95] and embraced all white men between the ages of eight-

[92] Well might the *Picayune*, Mar. 19, 1861, declare that "it was a fearful responsibility they have assumed, and one which carries with it the obligation to see that the State receives no harm from the [Confederate] compact . . . , for they have disarmed her of the right to see to it for herself."

Less ponderous, almost scurrilous, was the *True Delta*, Mar. 28, 1861: "The revolutionary farce . . . may be said now to have taken definite proportions. . . . At the end of their thirty-five days of painful travail these revolutionists . . . could not muster . . . a quorum to draw the decent drapery of the tomb over the closing scenes of a body which generations yet unborn . . . will long curse as the . . . most disastrous affliction that poor Louisiana, always a prey to needy adventurers and broken-down office-hunters, has ever had to support. Every member of the wigwam [convention] seemed to have made up his mind that democracy was to be slain."

Wrote a correspondent to the *Alexandria Constitutional*, Mar. 9, 1861: "So eager and determined were the defeated and disappointed office-holders of the Breckinridge party to dissolve the Union—to ruin because they could no longer rule—that everything was cut and dried by the New Orleans Democratic Club. . . . The minority accidentally obtained the control of the Convention, boldly and defiantly repudiated the expressed will of the people at the polls and forced the State into separate secession."

The work of the convention "is without precedent," declared the *Alexandria Constitutional*, Apr. 13, 1861, "and an evidence of the general disposition to assume power in derogation of the will of the people and establish monarchial or oligarchial [sic] rule."

[93] *Bee*, May 1, 1861.

[94] *La. H. Debs., 1864*, 89; *Rpt. Secy. State, 1886–87*, 133.

[95] *U. S. Cen., 1860, Prelim. Rpt.*, 134–35.

een and forty-five.[96] Only half, however, volunteered; the rest enlisted after the enactment of conscription.[97] Half the volunteers, moreover, offered their services for only a year, and so many refused to be mustered for longer service that the Confederate government had to accept them on their own terms.[98] The real patriots were the twelve thousand soldiers who enlisted for the duration of the war, to fight through thick and thin, before the summer of 1861 was over.[99]

But not all these men were true volunteers. Many joined the army as the result of economic necessity. Thousands of laborers in New Orleans were thrown out of work by the complete prostration of trade and shipping that attended secession.[100] Few boats plied the Mississippi River, and the levees were quiet and deserted.[101] Irishmen thronged the British consulate with petitions to be sent North or back home; but no funds were available for their repatriation, and they could do nothing but enlist.[102] A multitude of workingmen, confronted by the dilemma of starving or fighting, naturally preferred to fight.[103] The English correspondent, Russell, heard drunken Irish soldiers at Donaldsonville trying to enlist some equally inebriated Spaniards. "Gomey, my darling, get up," they shouted; "it's eleven dollars a month, and food and everything found. The boys will mind the fishing for you, and we'll come back as rich as Jews." [104] Paupers were released from the New

---

[96] *Rpt. Secy. State, 1859, passim.*

[97] *War of the Rebellion, Official Records* [cited hereafter as O. R.], Ser. IV, i, 752–53, 962.

[98] *Ibid.*, 750–51, 902. "War companies form very slowly," admitted Governor Moore in August, 1861, *ibid.*, 533.

[99] *Ibid.*, 444, 628.

[100] Wm. Mure, British Consul, to the Foreign Office, Dec. 13, 1860, *L. H. Q.*, XIII, 33; *Delta*, Apr. 10, 1861.

[101] Russell, *My Diary North and South*, I, 359–60, 369.   [102] *Ibid.*, 361–62.

[103] See above, *n.* 2.   [104] *Op. cit.*, I, 411.

Orleans workhouse at their own request to join the Confederate army.[105] The famous battalion of Louisiana "Tigers" was "recruited on the levee and in the alleys of New Orleans," and their fierce reputation in battle may be attributed to their character of "villainous" men who went under many aliases.[106] The entire Sixth Louisiana Infantry, with a strength of eight hundred, was made up of Irish laborers.[107] These men had all been notoriously hostile to slavery in the past;[108] and it was not from a sudden change of heart that they fought in its defense.

The economic necessity which compelled them to enlist was indicated by the relief provided for their families. In one district of New Orleans over seven hundred Irish families received from five to seven dollars in weekly benefits.[109] As early as the summer of 1861 a free municipal market was established to feed the families of poor volunteers; planters and merchants contributed $9,000 a month for its supply.[110] In the winter of 1862 more than nineteen hundred families obtained food from this depot three times a week.[111]

Social pressure was more powerful than economic necessity in arousing the countryside to arms. The farmers hardly felt the business depression in New Orleans and were not compelled to enlist for want of bread and butter. They turned easily in the northern parishes from raising cotton to cultivating wheat, corn, oats, rye, barley, and vegetables.[112] But enthusiastic neighbors quickly distinguished the patriotic from the indifferent in every rural community, and persuaded the latter to fall in line or leave the parish.[113] So lax had been the old militia system that it was completely revised late in the

[105] MS *Vagrant Record Book, 1859-61*, 504, 540, 542, 568, 579, 590.
[106] R. Taylor, *op. cit.*, 24.   [107] *Ibid.*, 47.   [108] See above, 120, 145-46.
[109] MS *Account Book, Volunteer Relief Committee*, 2-21.
[110] *Picayune*, Jan. 3, 1862.   [111] *Ibid.*, Mar. 30, 1862.
[112] *Ibid.*, Jan. 28, 1862.   [113] *Era*, May 21, 1863.

summer of 1861. The white man power of the state was organized into five military divisions, which comprehended all
the able-bodied between eighteen and forty-five; they were
required to drill several times a week. Permanent courts-martial
enforced discipline, and only the more prosperous were excused by fines of a dollar. Men who evaded drill were put on
a "black-list" as "suspicious and enemies to the South." [114] Under this regime, which amounted to conscription, the slave
patrol of free white men was soon converted into a squad of
Confederate troops.

Only by such compulsion were thousands of poor Creoles
and Cajuns in southern Louisiana awakened from their leth-
argy. "Talk to them of our constitutional rights and the sires
of the Revolution," complained a recruiting officer, and "they
look upon you with astonishment. Some have never heard the
sound of fife and drum. [All] are very civil and peaceable." [115]
One regiment of Cajuns from the Attakapas prairies went off
to Virginia to join Stonewall Jackson,[116] but the majority of
home-loving Creoles and Cajuns would not fight outside their
native state. "That portion of our citizens that are best able to
endure the hardships of a campaign," protested the recruiting
officer, "are not in the field. Our militia laws are too weak to
force those out that are not disposed to fall in with us." [117]

Coercion prevailed more effectively in New Orleans. "In
consequence of the intimidation of the mob," reported Russell,
"or, as the phrase is here, the 'excitement of the citizens,' "
many people were thrust into jail.[118] Charges of Abolitionism
were leveled against those who were conspicuously indifferent to secession.[119] Even to hazard the opinion that the North

---

[114] O. R., Ser. IV, i, 752–53; Opelousas [St. Landry] Patriot, Oct. 5, 1861.
[115] Ibid., 475.   [116] R. Taylor, op. cit., 47.
[117] O. R., Ser. IV, i, 475. This complaint was made in the summer of 1861,
two months before the militia was reorganized.
[118] Op. cit., I, 333.   [119] Roberts, op. cit., 35–38.

would win was to earn six months in the workhouse. "The accused are generally foreigners," observed Russell, "or belong to the lower orders, who have got no interest in the support of slavery." [120]

It was no longer simply a question of "the support of slavery" after Fort Sumter and Lincoln's call for troops. The press had unanimously condemned the prospect of Northern coercion from the start of the crisis.[121] Now the soil of the South —and of Louisiana—was threatened. To its defense rallied yeomen and nonslaveholders as well as planters and their sons, stirred by the fear of invasion and conquest which never fails to animate martial patriotism. Events had moved fast, popular fever risen high. Within a few months the spirit of belligerent loyalty to Louisiana was transformed into the stern stuff of Southern nationalism.[122] The issue became one of "victory or subjugation, . . . the recognition or total destruction of the institutions of the South." [123]

The peculiar institution, upon which all others rested, was slavery, and the South fought to preserve it. Slavery provided cheap labor for the planters, exempted them from manual work, and afforded a comfortable way of living.[124] All the rhetoric of legal and political debate could not conceal this essential economic fact. But slavery was more than an economic institution; it was also a police system which kept one race in bondage to the other, and assured social and political dom-

[120] Op. cit., I, 346.
[121] Delta, Jan. 12, 1861. While the conservative Bee, Commercial Bulletin, and Picayune deplored Louisiana's military preparations, all roundly condemned any force that the government at Washington might muster to oppose them.
[122] Bee, May 1, 1861.   [123] Alexandria Constitutional, Apr. 20, 1861.
[124] Delta, Sept. 7, 1856. "Abolish slavery to-morrow, . . . and what follows? Our sons—it matters not how delicately they have been raised—would make all the sugar, rice, corn, flour, bacon, &c., necessary for our use, all the cotton for our clothes; and our daughters, with their fair hands, would spin, weave and make such garments as would suit our then hardy forms."

inance to all white people.[125] For nonslaveholders no less than slaveholders, therefore, secession and civil war raised the question of race relations by threatening white supremacy.[126] "The interest felt by the nonslaveholders of the South in this question [was] not prompted by dollars and cents. Their zeal for their social institutions [did] not rest upon a pecuniary calculation," [127] but rather upon sentiments of racial prestige. Since poor whites were on nearly the same economic level as slaves,[128] they were all the more desperately afraid of the complete degradation that would befall them if their social and political advantages were taken away, and the emancipated Negro became their equal.[129] To keep him in bondage, therefore, nonslaveholders fought in defense of the property of slaveholders. Having long served as the slave patrol of the South,[130] they now formed the rank and file of its army, determined to keep it a "white man's country."

These were the considerations, conscious or unconscious, which moved nonslaveholders to volunteer; the rest joined the army under some kind of compulsion, economic, social, or military.

To recruit more soldiers to turn back an attack from the North, as the war entered its second year,[131] planters and merchants increased the bounties to volunteers, then forced men out of civil occupations, and finally resorted to conscription. The police jury of Madison, for example, awarded each volun-

[125] Phillips, "The Central Theme of Southern History," *A. H. R.*, XXXIV, 32–35.

[126] *Ibid.*, 33; cf. Phillips, "The Literary Movement for Secession," *Studies in Southern History and Politics* (New York, 1914), 59.

[127] *The* [Lexington] *Kentucky Statesman*, Oct. 5, 1860, D. L. Dumond, ed., *Southern Editorials on Secession* (New York, 1931), 175.

[128] Craven, "Poor Whites and Negroes in the Ante-Bellum South," *Journal of Negro History*, XV, 14–25.

[129] *De Bow's Review*, XXX, 67–77.   [130] *Ibid.*, XXI, 592.

[131] A new quota of 6 per cent of its white population was set for each state. *O. R.*, Ser. IV, i, 902.

teer eighty dollars and promised his family relief of fifteen dollars monthly.[132] Columns of advertisements in the New Orleans press offered bounties of fifty dollars to recruits for three months' service, and municipal relief of twenty-five dollars a month for their wives, and two or three dollars for each dependent child.[133] Store clerks asked employers in vain to continue their salaries after enlistment. "It seems we have a stronger sense of duty," wrote one, "for the majority of wealthy employers, whose property . . . we are called upon to save, take every possible opportunity to place their precious lives beyond risk, claiming exemption on the plea of their foreign citizenship, &c." [134] When the Confederate Congress called in 1862 for nearly ten thousand additional troops from Louisiana,[135] an increasing number were forced to enlist by being ejected from civil livelihood. Planters in Carroll released their overseers and began to supervise their own plantations.[136] Levee contractors were let go, and their Irish laborers replaced by slaves.[137] The provost marshal ordered all white deck hands and roustabouts to be discharged from steamboats, and their posts filled by free Negroes.[138] Finally, a military census was taken of all houses in New Orleans to enroll men eligible for service,[139] and martial law was declared throughout the city and adjoining parishes.[140]

Conscription, which Louisiana already practiced in everything but name, was at last enacted by the Confederate Congress two weeks before Federal ships passed the forts below

---

[132] *Madison Democrat*, Mar. 6, quoted in *Picayune*, Mar. 9, 1862.

[133] *Picayune*, Mar. 12, 1862. Short-term enlistments, although irregular, were especially authorized to raise more men for the defense of the city. See *O. R.*, Ser. I, iv, 837.

[134] *Ibid.*, Feb. 26, 1862. Many New Orleans merchants were French and English citizens.

[135] *O. R.*, Ser. IV, i, 902–3.

[136] *Picayune*, Mar. 28, 1862.

[137] *Ibid.*, Mar. 9, 1862.

[138] *Ibid.*, Apr. 1, 1862.

[139] *Ibid.*, Feb. 28, 1862.

[140] *Ibid.*, Mar. 16, 1862.

New Orleans and captured the city.[141] The avowed purpose of the draft was to keep all volunteers under arms and to sweep all other able-bodied men into service.[142] White men between the ages of eighteen and forty-five were declared liable to duty, and those under thirty-five, unless belonging to exempted classes, were called immediately to serve for three years or the duration of the war.[143] This drastic act, as President Davis said, was not "popular anywhere out of the Army." [144] Its numerous exemptions, especially of one white man for each plantation of twenty slaves, and the permission to hire substitutes, gave rise to the cry that it was a "rich man's war, and a poor man's fight." [145] Of course, this familiar complaint was unjust to the many planters and their sons who were already in the army. But conscription angered the poor because it fell upon them with peculiar harshness. It forced their families, women and children alike, to shoulder the labor essential to a livelihood, even to raising all the crops alone. And it left no way for the men to escape military service unless they fled from their homes. Hence they bitterly resented conscription.[146]

Doubtless this sentiment prevailed in large parts of Louisiana, as well as the rest of the South, but it can nowhere be found articulate because the Federal army soon occupied New

[141] *O. R.*, Ser. IV, i, 1061–62. The congressmen at Richmond, of course, had their eyes fastened on McClellan, laying siege to Yorktown, rather than on Farragut's ships approaching the Mississippi. See J. F. Rhodes, *op. cit.*, III, 167.

[142] A. B. Moore, *Conscription and Conflict in the Confederacy* (New York, 1924), 13–16.

[143] As applied in Louisiana, *Picayune*, Apr. 16, 1862.

[144] *O. R.*, Ser. IV, ii, 154.

[145] Cf. W. L. Fleming, *Civil War and Reconstruction in Alabama* (New York, 1905), 101–2. The act was amended frequently to satisfy complaints. See Moore, *op. cit.*, chaps. IV, VII.

[146] See the *Era*, May 28, 1863, for the account of a captain from Bragg's army.

Orleans and put a stop to Confederate conscription in the most populous section of the state. In the parishes to which the Confederates withdrew, the countryside was combed for men,[147] and a large training camp was established at Opelousas.[148] Although re-enforcements were desperately needed to meet a prospective Federal advance from New Orleans, re-cruiting lagged.[149] Early in 1863, therefore, Governor Moore warned all able-bodied white men between the ages of seven-teen and fifty to enlist within three months or suffer the death penalty of a deserter.[150] Army details scoured the country. Everywhere men were ordered to report, each with his own blanket, haversack, cooking utensils, and whatever clothes he had. No doubt was left in the minds of recalcitrants that death would follow failure to enlist.[151]

Hundreds of farmers and poor whites nevertheless sought refuge in the swamps, where they lived on fish and game, and grubbed for roots. These "draft-dodgers" were especially nu-merous in Catahoula and along the Pearl River in the Florida parishes. The Confederates were unable to track them down in this wild country, full of swamps; guards were posted near their cabins to capture any who returned at night to visit their families and procure food. Since the swamp refugees were generally armed as well as the military searching parties, they killed each other on sight.[152] Yet conscription must have been well enforced throughout northern and western Louisiana,

---

[147] O. R., Ser. I, xv, 789.   [148] Ibid., Ser. IV, i, 1152.

[149] Most Louisiana soldiers had long ago been detailed to the armies in Virginia, Tennessee, and Mississippi, and General Richard Taylor was left with an average of about seven thousand men in Louisiana. See O. R., Ser. IV, ii, 380. This situation led to many complaints by the war governors, Moore and Allen.

[150] O. R., Ser. I, liii, 843; Ser. IV, ii, 398–99.

[151] From Confederate field orders found at Opelousas and published in the Era, May 7, 1863.

[152] Ibid., Apr. 24, May 21, 1863; Apr. 7, 1864.

because the Confederates occupied nearly every parish in this region during the war.[153] Only in the Florida parishes was it admitted to be a dismal failure:[154] scarcely five hundred men were drafted from these piney woods.[155]

The slow demoralization of Confederate Louisiana began in 1863 after the fall of Vicksburg and Port Hudson. With the Federal army in control of the Mississippi River, New Orleans, and the Gulf, the Confederates were deprived of assistance from the East and reduced to the position of a self-sufficient army beleaguered in the interior. This change of fortune led to serious military disaffection. Winn, Jackson, and the adjoining northern parishes became infested with deserters, draft-dodgers, and bands of jayhawkers.[156] Discontent spread like the army worm through the farming country, and the inhabitants boldly drew up papers of grievances.[157] In Union Parish a number of conscripts and deserters banded together to resist the troops detailed to subdue them.[158] Since Confederate regiments were stationed at near-by towns such as Shreveport, Alexandria, and Monroe, it is not surprising that these rebels were caught and punished. Throughout the war nearly five thousand Louisianians left Confederate armies here and elsewhere in the South.[159] Desertion became most frequent, of course, in the last year of the war, when men grew weary of suffering privations for what seemed to be a hopeless cause.[160]

Jayhawking and guerrilla warfare broke out after the de-

[153] We know little about the enforcement of conscription in Confederate Louisiana because, so far as the records are concerned, the state was largely cut off from the war department at Richmond after the fall of Vicksburg. The last dispatches, dated June, 1863, are in *O.R.*, Ser. IV, ii, 416, 585–86.

[154] *Ibid.*, iii, 349–50.　　[155] *Ibid.*, 1101.　　[156] *O.R.*, Ser. I, xxvi, pt. ii, 194.

[157] *Ibid.*, 195, 240.　　　　　　　[158] *Ibid.*, 215.

[159] E. Lonn, *Desertion during the Civil War* (New York, 1928), 231.

[160] For the demoralizing pressure exerted upon troops by their hungry families, see the letters said to have been found in Confederate mail bags and published in the *Era*, Apr. 3, 1864.

structive campaign of Banks up the Red River in 1864.[161] Conscripts who abandoned the army had to steal and kill in order to live. Hiding in swamps, they would send one of their number to join the army and then desert with guns and powder, with which they could attack and loot plantations.[162] St. Landry was infested with so many armed jayhawkers that General Taylor confessed his cavalry was inadequate to suppress them. Led by one Carriere, who became popular for his promise to end the war, they stole food and horses, and burned houses even in broad daylight. They were not "a few isolated desperadoes [but] the entire community in the western part of the parish." [163] Across the Mississippi, in the piney woods of Washington, it was dangerous to travel. Here jayhawkers defied the army and claimed to have a government of their own in opposition to the Confederacy.[164] Yet desertion, sedition, or guerrilla warfare were never as widespread in Louisiana as in the mountains of Tennessee and the Carolinas, and the sand hills of Alabama and Mississippi. If disaffection had been as rife in Louisiana, it would have been crushed by the Confederate forces which occupied the interior of the state.

The country was quiet during the first two years of war, for economic conditions were tolerable. So long as men stayed on the farms, they could feed their families comfortably, and slaves kept the plantations well supplied. Cotton picked in the autumn of 1861 was either sold to New Orleans factors or stored in the gins; but little was planted thereafter because a surplus remained and all foreign markets were closed by the

[161] Sporadic guerrilla raids first occurred in December, 1862. *Picayune*, Dec. 4.

[162] *Era*, May 4, 1864. A notorious band were "Captain Dudley's Jayhawkers," said to have been led by a Calcasieu physician who evaded the draft.

[163] *O. R.*, Ser. I, xxxiv, pt. ii, 962–66.

[164] *Ibid.*, xxxii, pt. iii, 755. Many unionists from Jones and Perry counties, Mississippi, sought refuge here and in the other Florida parishes.

Federal blockade.[165] Large tracts of cotton land were now given over to grains and vegetables.[166] Since cereals could no longer be imported from the Middle West and flour was particularly scarce, the rich Red River lands were sown with wheat.[167] The Ouachita Valley supplied the Confederate armies with so much grain that it acquired fame as the "Egypt of Louisiana." [168] After the mild winter of 1862, many farmers raised enough corn, wheat, rye, and potatoes to fill their barns for two years.[169] As late as the spring of 1863, the Federal army found parts of the Teche country and Attakapas prairies in central Louisiana abundantly supplied with corn, cattle, and hogs.[170] To the country, therefore, it mattered little at first if food prices in New Orleans rose sky-high, and Confederate money depreciated rapidly.[171] Indeed, the "starving time" in the city was a golden opportunity for farmers, who pursued a lucrative trade with New Orleans—even after its capture by Federal troops.[172] This profitable exchange of foodstuffs for gold and silver was finally cut off in the summer of 1862 by order of Governor Moore, and smugglers were arrested and sometimes shot.[173]

Then the country began to suffer the privations of war. The loss of their city trade threw farmers entirely on their own resources. Indispensable manufactures and medicines could no longer be obtained, nor any gold and silver to support the flood of Confederate paper money.[174] Graver and more oppressive was conscription. It took farmers from their fields, and left the women and children to till what land they could.

[165] *Picayune*, Feb. 1, Mar. 20, 1862.   [166] *Ibid.*, Jan. 28, 1862.

[167] John B. Robertson, *Handbook from the Ohio to the Gulf, etc.* (Memphis, 1871–72), 19.

[168] Dunn, *Morehouse Parish*, 22.   [169] *Picayune*, Feb. 1, 1862.

[170] *Era*, Apr. 19, 29, 1863.

[171] *Picayune*, Mar. 20, 1862. Flour was then selling at $20 the barrel.

[172] *Ibid.*, Mar. 28, May 15, June 27, July 2, 1862.

[173] *Ibid.*, July 1, 1862.   [174] *Ibid.; Era*, Mar. 10, 13, 1863.

State bounties and parish relief were of little help to them because these small sums of paper money became even smaller through depreciation.[175] An increasing burden was the support of the army, which lived on the country. Whatever useful property people had, and the food and livestock which they raised for themselves, were commandeered by the army. In the Attakapas country in 1863, for example, Federal troops found five thousand barrels of corn stored in a Confederate supply depot, although the local inhabitants were hungry and begging for food.[176] The Confederates impressed provisions at prices far below the figures to which inflation had driven them.[177] As their paper money became worthless, country people did not object as much to army prices as to selling anything at all for military "shinplasters." By 1863 the commanding officer at Shreveport declared that the farmers "persistently refuse to receive Confederate money in the sales of supplies and in the payment of debts." [178] Wherever possible, however, they traded cotton through the lines to the enemy,[179] and sold food and horses to Federal troops for the more valuable Northern money.[180] With the people "demoralized by speculation and the love of gain," Confederate authorities found it difficult to obtain provisions, and consequently seized and confiscated the property of all who refused their money.[181]

But the soldiers themselves suffered from depreciation of the currency, for their pay sank to nothing, and the truism that "an unpaid soldiery pays itself" began to operate.[182] The country was ransacked and pillaged by Confederate as well as enemy troops.[183] "Is a large army going to pass here?" anxiously inquired a lady who saw Banks advancing on the heels

---

[175] De Bow's Review, V (October, 1868), 911.   [176] Era, Apr. 29, 1863.
[177] De Bow's Review, V, 913–14; Picayune, July 1, Dec. 20, 1862.
[178] O. R., Ser. I, xxvi, pt. ii, 580.   [179] R. Taylor, op. cit., 235.
[180] Era, May 5, 1863.   [181] O. R., loc. cit.   [182] De Bow's Review, V, 914.
[183] Governor Moore to the Secretary of War, July 8, 1862, L. H. Q., XIII, 17.

of Taylor. "One has almost ruined me, and God knows what will become of me if another passes." [184] Banks' army stripped the Teche country of food and livestock in 1863, when little could be done to prevent looting except to shoot a few soldiers caught red-handed. [185] To keep their slaves, many planters fled to Texas, and their plantations fell into the hands of jayhawkers and guerrillas. [186] The poorer people were so destitute that often they were lucky to obtain daily army rations of a pint of corn meal and half a pound of meat. [187] "The abode of peace and contentment [had] become the theatre of waste and want." [188]

Perhaps nothing can better illustrate conditions in the country than the report of a poor white Mississippian who escaped conscription by paddling down the Pearl River to St. Tammany. Here he found the women and children in rags, unable to obtain the cotton cards from which it had been their custom to spin yarn. Many of the men were living in the swamps to evade the draft. Cracked corn was the universal food—eaten dry for bread, and soaked in hot water for coffee. For want of salt, which sold at a dollar a spoonful, no meat could be preserved, and even guerrillas resorted to curing beef by burning it. Powder and guns were so scarce that game could no longer be killed. Occasional supplies of medicine and hardware were run through the enemy lines and sold at exorbitant prices. Although many people had pockets full of Confederate paper money, traders and stores refused to accept it. Destitute families of volunteers and conscripts went from plantation to

[184] *Era*, Apr. 19, 1863.

[185] *Ibid.*, Apr. 30, May 17, 30, 1863. In a single day there arrived in New Orleans from the Teche a caravan eight miles long, consisting of 600 wagons, 6,000 contraband Negroes, 3,000 mules and horses, 1,500 cattle, and untold quantities of food.

[186] A. J. Fremantle, *Three Months in the Southern States* (New York, 1864), 86–87.

[187] *Era*, May 5, 1863.   [188] *Picayune*, Dec. 4, 1862.

plantation begging food of the owners who had been exempted from service.[189] Since these were the conditions in the winter of 1862–63, what came to pass later beggars description.[190]

Without heaping misery on misery, let us turn from the country to the city, from Confederate to Federal Louisiana. New Orleans was captured by Farragut the last of April, 1862, and garrisoned with troops under Butler the first of May. It then became the base from which the Federal government reconquered and reconstructed Louisiana. By the beginning of the next year, when Lincoln issued his Emancipation Proclamation, twelve parishes in the Sugar Bowl had been added to Federal New Orleans,[191] and after the fall of Vicksburg, seven more parishes on the upper Mississippi were secured.[192]

All these parishes, except Orleans and Jefferson, were in the black belt, and the majority of their inhabitants were slaves whose daily labor was not greatly changed by the war. In New Orleans over ten thousand colored people, most of whom were local slaves, lived on army rations.[193] Their food attracted to the city swarms of field hands from near-by plantations. When the planters petitioned General Banks for the return of these Negroes early in 1863, he complied with their request in order to lighten the growing burden of relief and to increase the local production of foodstuffs.[194] Thousands of slaves, destitute and idle, living throughout the country in roofless huts, were ordered back to their plantations, where they went to

---

[189] *Era*, Mar. 13, 1863. Cf. *O. R.*, Ser. IV, ii, 854–55, for partial corroboration by a local Confederate planter.

[190] See the files of the *Era* and *Picayune*, 1864–65.

[191] *Const. Conv. Debs., 1864*, 152–53. According to the Proclamation, of course, slaves were *not* emancipated in these parishes.

[192] *Rpt. Audit. Pub. Accts., 1864*, 94. At that time the following parishes had been restored to the Union: Ascension, Assumption, Avoyelles, Carroll, Concordia, East Baton Rouge, Iberville, Jefferson, Lafourche, Madison, Orleans, Plaquemines, St. Bernard, St. John the Baptist, St. Charles, St. Mary, St. Martin, St. James, Terrebonne, and Tensas.

[193] *Picayune*, Dec. 19, 1862.   [194] *Bee*, Feb. 20, 1863.

work under military supervision for a share of the crop,[195] and "their labor compensated for all expenses." [196] The lot of the slave remained a sorry one.

When General Butler landed at New Orleans with Federal troops, he found thousands of unemployed people face to face with famine. They had long ago been thrown out of work by the paralysis of commerce and trade.[197] The price of food had risen beyond their slender means, with bread selling at twenty cents a loaf and flour at fourteen dollars a barrel,[198] and hundreds of families were subsisting on Confederate doles.[199] This relief was suspended when Federal troops occupied the city. There ensued what the press called "a starving time." Food was scarce, with little bread or meat, and corn meal and rice flour only to be obtained at prices beyond the reach of the poor.[200] Let it be said of Butler [201] that he immediately imported barrels of beef and flour, and distributed rations to the Irish and Germans who thronged the Custom House.[202] To reduce prices, the commissary offered provisions at half the prevailing rates.[203]

The greatest achievement of General Butler was to keep New Orleans free of yellow fever during the war,[204] and in-

[195] *Era*, Apr. 4, 1863.
[196] *O. R.*, Ser. I, xxvi, pt. i, 736.
[197] See above, 171–72.
[198] *Picayune*, Mar. 28, 1862.
[199] *Ibid.*, Mar. 30, 1862.
[200] *Ibid.*, May 6, 15, 1862.
[201] For a one-sided but important defense of Butler, see James Parton, *General Butler in New Orleans* (New York, 1864). No one has appraised this stormy petrel and his erratic behavior in New Orleans with more wit than Stephen Benét in *John Brown's Body*:

> "But the ladies remember Butler for fifty years
> And make a fabulous devil with pasteboard horns
>
> * * * * *
>
> From a slightly-tarnished, crude-minded, vain politician
> Who loved his wife, and ached to be a great man."

[202] *Picayune*, May 6, 13, 1862.
[203] Parton, *op. cit.*, 306.
[204] *Ibid.*, 308–9.

cidentally to provide work relief for the unemployed. To clean the streets, he called on the city authorities to hire an army of laborers.[205] Exasperated by their inability or reluctance to comply, Butler denounced them in tactless but not altogether demagogic language. He remarked upon "the deplorable state of destitution and hunger of the mechanics and working classes of this city . . . [which] does not pinch the wealthy and influential, the leaders of the rebellion." [206] "Painful necessity compels some action in relation to the unemployed and starving poor of New Orleans," he declared after a month had elapsed without action. "Men willing to labor can not get work by which to support themselves and families, and are suffering for food." So Butler put to work two thousand men at fifty cents a day, to be paid by the city, with rations to be provided by the army. Their labor compelled the Confederates to admit "that the federals could clean the streets." These sanitary measures, together with a strict ship quarantine, released New Orleans from the fear and thrall of yellow fever for the first time in its history.[207]

Since thousands of men still remained unemployed, and the commissary could not feed them forever, Butler reorganized and expanded his system of relief in the middle of summer. Additional men were hired at a daily wage of $1.50, paid out of a poor fund of nearly $350,000, which was raised by a capital levy on Confederate bondholders and an assessment of cotton factors.[208] Butler justified this assessment in words

[205] *Picayune*, May 31, 1862.

[206] Parton, *op. cit.*, 305-7. The more intemperate parts of this general order do not concern us, but relate to Confederate destruction of cotton, seizure of bullion, and the alleged violation of passes of safe conduct.

[207] *Picayune*, May 10, June 20, July 10, Nov. 13, 1862; *Era*, Feb. 11, 1863.

[208] *Picayune*, Aug. 6, 1862. Bondholders were taxed one quarter of their subscription; the largest sum was $85,000, but only twenty-six exceeded $1,000. Nearly 100 cotton brokers were taxed an average of $100 ostensibly because

which revealed his aggressive design to separate the classes and court the good will of the majority. "Those who have brought upon the city this stagnation of business, this desolation of the hearth-stone, this starvation of the poor and helpless, should, as far as they may be able, relieve these distresses. It should not be borne by taxation of the whole municipality, because the middling and working men have never been heard at the ballot-box. . . . There are two classes whom it would seem peculiarly fit should . . . contribute. . . . First, those individuals and corporations who have aided the rebellion with their means: and second, those who have endeavored to destroy the commercial prosperity of the city, upon which the welfare of its inhabitants depend." [209] While an oath of allegiance to the United States had been required of laborers applying for army rations, no restrictions were laid on those employed "at the expense of their rebellious neighbors." Married men had priority, but the sons of Confederate soldiers labored beside Irish and German unionists.[210]

By the end of summer the unemployed were again at work in New Orleans, and their daily wage increased in purchasing power as supplies arrived and prices fell.[211] When Butler left in December, 1862,[212] a quarter of the population—thirty thousand white and ten thousand colored—was eking out its liveli-

---

they had advised planters not to ship cotton to the city in 1861. They were assessed again at the end of the year when the relief fund was exhausted. *Ibid.*, Dec. 11, 1862. These taxes were confirmed and defended as just by Butler's successor, General Banks. *Bee*, Jan. 14, 1863.

[209] *Picayune*, Aug. 6, 1862.   [210] *Ibid.*, Aug. 8, 1862.

[211] *Ibid.*, Aug. 25, 1862. Flour, for example, fell from thirty to nine dollars a barrel, and pork was reported to be plentiful at fair prices.

[212] Butler's administration as a whole does not concern us, and space forbids going into his difficulties with banks and foreign consuls, the fiction of his larceny of silver spoons, or the lucrative trade his brother drove in Texas cattle.

hood through government relief or work.[213] An interesting analysis of this situation shows that 10,541 families, consisting of 34,200 men, women, and children, received food during a typical week. They consumed more than 23,000 pounds of pork, 48,000 pounds of beef, and 92,000 loaves of bread, allowing each family two pounds of pork, five pounds of beef, and nine loaves of bread. Of the families on relief, 1,724 were the kin of Federal soldiers, 979 of Confederates, and 7,838 unrelated to any soldiers but absolutely destitute. Among the nationalities represented were 4,657 Irish, 3,932 German, 1,308 colored, 1,200 American, 723 French, 588 English, and 194 Spanish families.[214] This relief system continued for the duration of the war. General Banks reported in 1863 that the Federal government was supporting 24,000 people and ten orphanages.[215] "The commissary department," it was asserted in 1864, "has kept for nearly three years two-thirds of the people from starvation." [216] Even for several months after Appomattox about thirteen thousand of the poor subsisted on doles from the Federal army.[217]

A gradual reduction of the relief rolls during the war came in part from the revival of business. After the fall of Vicksburg and the restoration of river trade between St. Louis and New Orleans, a period of wartime prosperity set in. New stores opened, the levee was repaired, and wharves which had rotted away were rebuilt.[218] The number of Mississippi steamboats arriving at New Orleans doubled, the value of imports tripled, and the receipts of cotton increased six times over any

[213] *Picayune*, Dec. 19, 1862.   [214] *Ibid.*, Nov. 22, 1862.

[215] *O. R.*, Ser. I, xxvi, pt. i, 735–36.

[216] *Const. Conv. Debs., 1864*, 298. This is a palpable exaggeration the way it is stated, but if all *indirect* trade and employment afforded by the army be considered, it is probably true.

[217] *Crescent*, Oct. 27, 1865; *Annual Cyclopaedia, 1865*, 510.

[218] *Era*, Feb. 28, 1864.

preceding war year.[219] This boom furnished employment to thousands.

The wages of labor were better than before 1861, because of the high level of remuneration set by the army for civilian employees, who made up a considerable part of all those at work. Some idea of the range of jobs and wages afforded by government employment may be gained from the schedule announced in general orders for 1864.[220] There was extra pay

Occupation	Daily Rate	Occupation	* Monthly Rate
1st class mechanics	$3.25	Wagon masters	$50.00
2nd " "	2.50	Teamsters	25.00
3rd " "	2.00	Stable hands	25.00
Locomotive engineers	3.25	Blacksmiths	35–45.00
Stationary "	2–3.00	River boat firemen	35.00
Carpenters	2.00	Ordinary boat hands	30.00
Levee laborers	1.25		
Laborers	1.25–1.50	* includes rations	

for Sunday or night labor, and free hospital service for all who were incapacitated at work. The sole disadvantage in military employment was the fact that whoever deserted could be drafted or punished by court-martial.[221]

Many workingmen volunteered and many were drafted for service in the Federal army. It was estimated that ten thousand soldiers who were natives of New Orleans or recent immigrants from the North fought in Louisiana under the stars and stripes.[222] General Banks raised two regiments in the fall of 1863 by conscription. He justified compulsion as the only way to catch a horde of Northerners who had escaped service at

[219] *De Bow's Review*, I (January, 1866), 48–49. Business turnover in 1864 reached the amazing total of $200,000,000 according to *Rpt. Audit. Pub. Accts.*, 1864, 56.

[220] *Era*, Jan. 3, 31, 1864.　　[221] Cf. *Picayune*, Dec. 27, 1862.

[222] *La. H. Debs.*, 1864, 89.

home, fled to New Orleans, and entered upon profitable specu-lations. Poor natives without employment were also drafted, and not a few Confederate deserters who might have been shot if captured as volunteers.[223] The more common prac-tice, however, was to recruit laborers by generous bounties, handsome uniforms, and comfortable barracks near their fam-ilies. By these inducements two regiments of cavalry and two of infantry were filled with volunteers in New Orleans.[224] Not every soldier was satisfied; advertisements for deserters appeared regularly in the newspapers.[225] So great was the need of the army for skilled labor that companies of carpenters, blacksmiths, and mechanics were raised at the soldier's wage of thirteen dollars a month.[226]

Labor outside the army did not fare badly. Since printers were scarce, the Typographical Union won an increase of rates.[227] The Irish who had once worked on plantation levees for fifty cents a day commanded the government rate of $1.25 even for private employment.[228] Unorganized draymen boosted their charges because of the increased cost of hay.[229] The price of everything had gone up, and speculation was rife in cotton, sugar, and luxuries. But for daily necessities the army posted schedules of reasonable charges. Prices were con-trolled to such an extent that the advance in the wages of many occupations was greater than in the cost of living.[230] Labor nevertheless protested that higher prices reduced the average wage to a subsistence level, and a Workingmen's Union Asso-

[223] *O. R.*, Ser. I, xxvi, pt. i, 766–67.

[224] *Era*, Feb. 3, 4, 1864.

[225] E. g., *ibid.*, Jan. 1, 1864.

[226] *Ibid.*, Feb. 3, 1864.

[227] *Ibid.*, Mar. 24, 1864.

[228] *Ibid.*, Jan. 31, 1864. The influence of high army wages on private employ-ment may be clearly seen here.

[229] *Ibid.*, Jan. 24, 1864.

[230] *Ibid.*, Jan. 31, 1864. Bread sold at five cents for a 12- to 13-ounce loaf, and flour at nine to ten dollars a barrel. Rents soared because the army and a multitude of visitors crowded all living quarters.

ciation was organized by over a hundred men to raise their scales of remuneration.[231] This movement, animated by a sense that the Civil War was a contest between free and slave labor, was political as well as economic. "Free Soil, Free Speech, and Free Labor" became the aims of these avowed unionists.[232]

The conclusion to any chronicle of the Civil War must be the sad task of summing up how much life and property were lost in four years of bloodshed and destruction. No state in the South, unless it be Virginia, South Carolina, or Georgia, suffered more than Louisiana.[233] The number of Louisianians who were killed or wounded cannot be accurately counted. Of fifteen thousand men who went to fight with Lee in Virginia, hardly six hundred were said to have returned. This was beyond doubt a gross exaggeration. But at least one-fifth and probably more of Louisiana's able-bodied white men died on the field of battle or in hospitals.[234] How many were planters, and how many farmers, it would be bootless and profane to guess. In the whole South it was estimated that nearly half the white cotton farmers were killed or crippled.[235] The presence in New Orleans of twelve hundred destitute war orphans, supported by the Catholic Church and Federal army, proved that many poor laborers from Louisiana had died in the service of the Confederacy.[236] Since the rank and file of the Confederate army was composed of "those who had worked for wages, and small farmers, or the sons of small farmers," [237] it

[231] *Times*, Dec. 13, 1863; *Era*, Feb. 4, 1864.

[232] *Times*, Dec. 14, 1863; see below, chap. VII.

[233] See J. L. Sellers, "The Economic Incidence of the Civil War in the South," *M. V. H. R.*, XIV, 179–91.

[234] *Annual Cyclopaedia, 1865*, 513, 516. Where 49,510 votes had been polled in 1860, only 28,966 ballots were cast in 1865, despite a registration directed by conservative Democrats who had just returned from the war.

[235] *Opelousas* [St. Landry] *Courier*, May 5, 1866.

[236] *Commercial Bulletin*, Jan. 3, 1867; *Picayune*, Oct. 5, 1867.

[237] *De Bow's Review*, V (October, 1868), 911.

can hardly be denied that the common people suffered the heaviest casualties of the war. Among all the wounded and crippled, the poor faced the darkest future. "The rich," observed a Louisianian, "have lost some property, but something is left to them. The mechanic has but his arms to save him from hunger and poverty. . . . A maimed laborer has no future." [238]

Louisiana lost by the abolition of slavery over one-third of its assessed wealth. As the acrid Doctor Dostie put it: "$170,-000,000 of property has been stricken from among the objects of taxation and raised to the condition of citizens." [239] However desirable this transformation of the Negro from an economic into a social person, it was a severe blow to the black belt parishes, where slaves had exceeded in value all other kinds of property.[240] Their freedom was the greatest misfortune that befell the planting aristocracy.

Consequently, the planters were temporarily prostrate. Some moved to New Orleans to gain a livelihood in trade; [241] others went to work like poor whites and tilled a patch of land with their own hands.[242] The plantations were ruined. Because of the loss of slaves essential to their cultivation, and the destruction of levees, the land was almost worthless. Everywhere it depreciated so much that mortgages were foreclosed at a third of their value.[243] Parish courts in Tensas sold estates for five dollars an acre which had brought one hundred dollars

---

[238] C. E. Fenner, addressing the Workmen's Benevolent Association, *Crescent*, Dec. 20, 1865.

[239] *Rpt. Audit. Pub. Accts., 1864,* 47.   [240] See Appendix, Table 2.

[241] E. g., J. B. Eustis to Howell Cobb, Jan. 6, 1866, U. B. Phillips, ed., "The Correspondence of . . . Toombs, . . . Stephens, and . . . Cobb," *American Hist. Assn. Rpt.,* 1911, II, 676.

[242] E. g., Samuel H. Lockett, MS *Louisiana As It Is,* 101-2. Cf. S. D. Smedes, *Memorials of a Southern Planter,* 231.

[243] H. Latham, *Black and White* (London, 1867), 166.

in 1860.[244] Real property was worth but 30 per cent of its prewar value, and one-third of the land was no longer in cultivation.[245] Rich man and poor man had lost over half the horses, mules, cattle, sheep, and swine which they owned in 1860;[246] but owing to the rise in prices, their depleted livestock was worth almost as much as before.[247] Two-fifths of the sugarhouse machinery and farm implements, according to value, had been destroyed.[248] Because of its heavy capital investment, sugar had been hit worse than cotton. Of more than 1,200 large estates that harvested the cane of 1861, only 180 were struggling to get along in 1865.[249] Forstall, the best authority, estimated that the sugar plantations had lost just short of $100,000,000, besides the value of all slaves.[250] St. Mary, the wealthiest sugar parish in Louisiana, "was ground to powder between contending armies; corn, sugar, cattle, horses, mules and almost all moveable property were carried off, consumed or destroyed; overflows and cotton worms, rains and politicians have done their worst, still we live and breathe."[251]

Almost everywhere the countryside was a scene of desolation. Many plantation houses had been burned, and all were shabby and in disrepair; weeds choked old fields of cotton and sugar, and the fences had tumbled down; wagons and plows stood rusting in the rain; cattle and hogs roamed wild

[244] *Rpt. U. S. Com. Agric., 1867*, 106.

[245] *Ibid.*, 105–6. In these categories, Louisiana and South Carolina suffered more than any other Southern state.

[246] *Commercial Bulletin*, Oct. 11, 1866. Here Louisiana also lost more than the rest of the South. See *Annual Cyclopaedia, 1866*, 8.

[247] *Rpt. U. S. Com. Agric., 1866*, 69.   [248] *Ibid., 1871*, 49.

[249] *De Bow's Review*, II (September, 1866), 305.

[250] Cf. *Picayune*, Sept. 1, 1866. Quoted by H. Latham, *Black and White*, 170–71. The destruction of machinery and livestock amounted to $70,000,000.

[251] *Franklin* [St. Mary] *Planters' Banner*, quoted in *Picayune*, Aug. 7, 1867. For "politicians," see below, chap. VII.

in the swamps; and the levees had disappeared into the rivers for hundreds of miles, turning the lowlands into marshes. There were villages that no longer had a house or an inhabitant, but had already become the "extinct cities" of which people spoke in the legends of later years.[252] "It is a melancholy sight," remarked a traveler through the Red River country as late as 1869. Plantations, deserted or destroyed, "tell a tale, of which the beginning and the ending are very different from each other. Wealth, prosperity, luxury, are . . . the introduction to this story; war, ruin, desolation, the burden; poverty the conclusion." [253]

New Orleans survived the war without the ruin and waste of the countryside. But its old merchants were nearly wiped out. The banks had sent millions of dollars in bullion to the Confederate government after secession. Their remaining assets in 1865 were reported to "consist of Confederate bonds, good for nothing, cotton in the Confederacy, long since burned, and negroes, who are now all free." [254] New Orleans merchants and factors never wholly recovered from the loss of their fabulous wealth.[255] Real estate remained unharmed, but personal property was greatly diminished.[256] The richest men in the city were the many Northern speculators who had thrived on wartime trade.[257]

Louisiana, to sum up, emerged from the Civil War with less than half its former wealth.[258] The destruction and depreciation of property fell especially on the planters and merchants, in whose hands wealth had once been concentrated. General

---

[252] E. g., *Picayune*, Sept. 3, 1881. Among the towns that vanished were Dallas, on the Tensas River, Richmond, once the seat of that parish, and De Soto, opposite Vicksburg, which was engulfed by the Mississippi River.

[253] Lockett MS, 219.   [254] *La. H. Debs., 1865*, 435.

[255] *Picayune*, Aug. 10, 1873.   [256] *Bee*, Nov. 21, 1863.

[257] W. Reid, *After the War* (New York, 1866), 240–41.

[258] *Rpt. Audit. Pub. Accts., 1866*, 199; *De Bow's Review*, III (April–May, 1867), 474–75.

Hurlbut told officials of the state in 1865: "You have to create almost out of nothing. You have to make revenues where the taxable property of the State is reduced almost two-thirds. [It is] a broken-down country." [259] Poverty weighed heavily upon the people, and its distress was not relieved by the chaos and conflict of the reconstruction to follow.

[259] *La. H. Debs., 1865*, 397.

CHAPTER VII

CLASS AND RACE STRIFE

Thy kingdom is divided among the Yankees and
Abolitionists!

—J. B. BROMLEY [1]

My sympathies are with the white man and not
with the negro. My hand is against the African,
and I am for pushing him off the soil of this
country.

—W. T. STOCKER [2]

I am in favor, first, of the poor whites, secondly,
of the middle classes, and lastly of the rich.

—R. KING CUTLER [3]

The reconstruction of Louisiana [4] prolonged the civil war
between North and South and precipitated within the state
first a social revolution and then a counterrevolution. Each
phase was marked by a new constitution which changed, directly or indirectly, the dispensation of power. White labor

[1] *La. Const. Conv. Debs., 1864,* 181.

[2] *Ibid.* Stocker, as one might guess, was the most violent Negrophobe in
the convention. He had been one of the seven Co-operationist delegates to
the Convention of 1861 who refused to sign the ordinance of secession. See
above, 166.

[3] *Ibid.,* 510. Cutler was a New Orleans lawyer who had lived in Louisiana
over twenty years. *Ibid.,* 554; *Gardner's New Orleans Directory for 1866, s. v.*

[4] It is not our intention to repeat the familiar story of reconstruction. The
political history of this period in Louisiana has been exhaustively described
by J. R. Ficklen, *History of Reconstruction in Louisiana (through 1868)*
(Baltimore, 1910), and Ella Lonn, *Reconstruction in Louisiana after 1868*
(New York, 1918). It only remains for us to analyze the part played by white
farmers and laborers. The permanent and far-reaching changes in education,
religious organization, and other social institutions will be treated later for
the light they throw on Populism, with which they appear to be more closely
connected than with reconstruction.

altered the government with the Charter of 1864; black labor, with that of 1868; and the counterrevolution which restored white supremacy was signified by the Constitution of 1879. The long struggle was a political contest between white and colored people for the exclusive right to rule. This has been the traditional theme of historians of reconstruction. But it should not be forgotten that at first neither race was solidly united against the other, nor were the spoils of office their only concern. Political turmoil obscured but did not conceal the deeper social and economic problems of the period. There was the bitter racial question, whether whites or blacks should gain social ascendancy,[5] and the closely related economic question of which class, whatever its color, should own the soil and manage the commerce of Louisiana. Carpetbaggers fought planters and merchants for the possession of rich natural resources and the control of black and white labor. The carpetbaggers were defeated because they turned from economic to political exploitation, preyed upon whites more than blacks, and arrayed all classes of the former race against the latter. The final triumph of planters and merchants, with the essential support of white farmers and laborers, was a counterrevolution which crushed the bewildered and abortive attempts, first of white, and then of black, labor, to rule the state and mold society in their own images.

The revolution began with the establishment of a government under Northern auspices. On Lincoln's initiative,[6] and with the supervision of the Federal army,[7] a civil administration was set up for the territory redeemed from the Confederates. This area embraced nineteen parishes and over half

[5] Ficklen, *History of Reconstruction* . . . , 179 *n.*

[6] Lincoln to Banks, Aug. 5, 1863, quoted in *Times*, May 7, 1865. To Louisiana the President applied his "ten per cent plan" for restoring seceded states to the Union. See J. D. Richardson, comp., *Messages and Papers of the Presidents* (Washington, 1899), VI, 214, and *Era*, Jan. 1, 1864.

[7] *Era*, Feb. 17, 1864.

the prewar population.[8] To elect two congressmen from New Orleans in 1862, scarcely three thousand voters had taken the oath of allegiance to the Union.[9] But more than ten thousand citizens, exceeding one-tenth of the prewar electorate, cast ballots for state officials in 1864; and three-fifths of this number elected delegates to a constitutional convention.[10]

Two leading parties disputed the main issues of the day. The Free State party contended that Louisiana had committed political suicide by secession and must be created anew through the repudiation of secession and the abolition of slavery. Opposed to them were so-called Conservatives, who agreed that secession should be repealed, but desired to retain the Constitution of 1852 and slavery.[11] Both parties were loyal to the Union. Even their divergent views as to the status of the Negro were not wholly irreconcilable, for the Conservatives were willing to accept compensated emancipation. The fundamental issue between them was whether Louisiana should be restored to the control of planters and merchants under the old constitution, or put in the hands of a majority of loyal white people under a new organic law.[12]

The latter view was championed by the Free State party, and it triumphed at the polls not only through the favor of General Banks and the Federal army, but also by virtue of its revolutionary appeal to New Orleans labor. Naturalized immigrants and native mechanics who voted for Douglas in 1860 and opposed secession, had always been loyal to the Union and inclined to economic radicalism.[13] In 1863, with the inauguration of political reconstruction,[14] they organized the Working Men's Union League. Its platform called for the abolition of slavery, the removal of every Negro from Louisiana by colo-

---

[8] See above, 184, *n.* 192. [9] Ficklen, *History of Reconstruction* . . . , 42.
[10] *Ibid.*, 62, 68. [11] *Ibid.*, 46–47.
[12] Cf. *ibid.*, 45–68. [13] See above, 145–46, 147, 190–91.
[14] Ficklen, *op. cit.*, chap. III.

nization, and the admission of all white men to suffrage without restrictions as to residence.[15] These objects had been secretly cherished by immigrant laborers before secession.[16]

Now their Free State candidate for the governorship was Michael Hahn, a prewar immigrant born in Bavaria, whose bitter hostility to the old slaveholding regime attracted a large following. He attacked the Constitution of 1852 as "more calculated to protect and benefit the slaveholder than . . . other classes," and condemned its representation of slaves as unjust "to the small planters and farmers, the adventurous frontiersmen, the honest mechanics." Previous legislatures, in his opinion, had "confined themselves almost exclusively to legislating for the protection of the interests of slavery." [17] A new constitution was necessary to abolish not only slavery but also "the power of the aristocracy," and to give "the poor man that which he has never had—an equal voice in the State." [18]

Hahn's speeches articulated the class interest of labor in New Orleans and exposed the reactionary danger of pleas by the Conservatives for political laissez faire and restoration of the old order.[19] Other candidates on the Hahn ticket excited racial jealousy by attributing to extremists, who composed a third faction, secret designs for Negro suffrage.[20] These adroit tactics contributed to the victory of the party.[21] Numerous if not preponderant among their supporters at the polls was labor.[22] In the Free State torchlight parade on the eve of elec-

[15] *Era*, May 12, 1863. The abolition of residence qualifications appealed to both naturalized foreigners and Northern immigrants.
[16] See above, n. 13.
[17] *Speech of Hon. Michael Hahn, Nov. 14, 1863*, 8-10.
[18] *Era*, Feb. 18, 1864.   [19] *Ibid.*, Feb. 5, 1864.
[20] *Ibid.*, Feb. 21, 1864. The Flanders faction denied this charge. Cf. *Times*, Feb. 14, 1864.
[21] The vote was 6,171 for Hahn (Free State), 2,959 for Fellows (Conservative), and 2,225 for Flanders. See Ficklen, *History of Reconstruction . . .*, 62.
[22] *Ibid.*, chap. III, neglects this aspect of the campaign, and treats the Free State party as General Banks' administration machine.

tion marched the Workingmen's Association, the German Union, the Mechanics' Association, the Workingmen of Louisiana, and the Crescent City Butchers' Association.[23]

Labor was even more prominent in the Constitutional Convention of 1864. According to a workingmen's petition, it was "the only liberty-loving constitutional body, composed purely of the laboring class, that has ever convened in the State of Louisiana." [24] Not all the members, of course, were laborers. But among those whose occupations may be ascertained were two steamboatmen, a few clerks, a tailor, decorator, fireman, and several mechanics and laborers.[25] All the delegates were mildly class-conscious, and the class to which they were most devoted was labor.[26] "It is the poor laboring men who have worked on the canals and streets, and added millions of dollars to the wealth of the city, [that] deserve the consideration of the Convention," remarked one delegate, and his words struck the keynote of the gathering.[27]

The Convention of 1864 was called by General Banks, with Lincoln's approval,[28] chiefly to abolish slavery.[29] It was a revolutionary body, sitting "in a time of revolution," and representing not "a majority of the people . . . , but . . . the entire loyalty of the State." [30] In determining the basis of representation, Banks followed suggestions of the Free State party, and counted only the white instead of all the people.[31] This was done in order to deprive slaveholding planters of their former influence over legislation and to give New Orleans a

[23] *Era*, Feb. 20, 1864. These were not simply banners carried in the parade, but large and active organizations.

[24] *La. Const. Conv. Debs., 1864*, 418.

[25] *Ibid.*, 4–5, 395, 554, 577. Cf. *Gardner's New Orleans Directory, 1866*, q. v.
[26] See above, n. 3.   [27] *Ibid.*, 360.

[28] See above, n. 6.   [29] *La. Const. Conv. Debs., 1864*, 300.

[30] *Ibid.*, 160, 298, 300.

[31] *Era*, Mar. 9, 1864. An electoral basis would have been adopted if there had been any registration lists for the country parishes.

voice proportionate to its numbers.[32] Colored people could neither vote nor be represented,[33] for the delegates were chosen by a white electorate.[34] Sixty-three came from New Orleans, but only thirty-five from the country, because the larger part of the state was still held by Confederates.[35] Over half the votes were cast in New Orleans,[36] which proved that the convention was to be largely a city affair.[37]

For this and other reasons the convention has been subjected to severe criticism by Ficklen. He thought it "in no sense a representative body." [38] But it represented more citizens than the Confederate legislature of western Louisiana, which was meeting without elections at Shreveport.[39] Almost as many people in New Orleans participated in the choice of convention delegates as in some prewar polls, and many more laborers voted now that Know-Nothings no longer intimidated them. But it was impossible for any legislative body to represent the majority in a state divided by civil war.

The Convention of 1864 has also been characterized as an assembly of Northern unionists, men of Banks' party, and not Louisianians.[40] The proportion of delegates who were recent

[32] Banks later admitted that his action was inspired by these motives, which he held in common with the Free State party. See the Louisiana Election Case, 38 Cong., 2 sess., *H. R. Rpts.*, no. 13, 19.

[33] *La. Const. Conv. Debs., 1864,* 247.

[34] Each delegate was supposed to represent 2,384 white people. *Era,* Mar. 9, 1864.

[35] The country was entitled to eighty-seven delegates, but only parts of the following parishes held elections: Ascension, Avoyelles, Concordia, East and West Baton Rouge, East Feliciana, Iberville, Jefferson, Lafourche, Madison, Plaquemines, Rapides, St. Bernard, St. James, St. John, St. Mary, and Terrebonne. *Ibid.,* 4–5.

[36] *Ibid.,* 408.

[37] Even the adoption of a quorum of seventy-six, which would also have been the number had every parish sent delegates, did not prevent the city from nearly forming a quorum by itself.

[38] Ficklen, *History of Reconstruction . . . ,* 69.

[39] Cf. *ibid.,* 65.   [40] *Ibid.,* 69.

immigrants from the North, and natives of New Orleans, cannot be ascertained. But the fact that all had to take the "iron-clad" oath of loyalty to the Union does not necessarily mean that any considerable number were from the North.[41] There were many unionists among the laborers of New Orleans before secession, and they were doubtless ready to show their true colors when Federal troops protected them.[42] Two members of the convention may serve as examples. One was taunted as the "member from New York": born there, he lived in Louisiana twenty-seven years, left before secession, and returned with Butler's army to supervise public works.[43] Another delegate, who protested that he represented "the poor white people, to which class I have the honor to belong," lived in New Orleans twenty-six years and always voted for Democrats, but was apparently anxious to assist in restoring Louisiana to the Union.[44]

Ficklen also criticized the convention because it was so extravagant. He believed that it cost over $100,000.[45] As a matter of fact, it ran up the amazing bill of $364,000.[46] There was no excuse for this enormous waste of public money by a body in which neither carpetbaggers nor corrupt Negroes were present. If one seeks an explanation, however, it may be found partly in the "get-rich-quick" fever which afflicted wartime New Orleans, and partly in the blunders and peculations of the delegates.[47]

[41] *La. Const. Conv. Debs., 1864,* 12–14.

[42] Butler had declared that only the poor in New Orleans were loyal to the United States. *Ibid.,* 360.

[43] *Ibid.,* 554.   [44] *Ibid.,* 395.

[45] Ficklen, *History of Reconstruction . . . ,* 76–77.

[46] *Rpt. Audit. Pub. Accts., 1864,* 30, 40. Figures reduced above to round thousands.

[47] Analysis of the expenses shows that some of the delegates were personally corrupt. For a session of four months, each member received about $1,130, or a little less than ten dollars a day. This was customary remunera-

The members of the convention were too unaccustomed to politics to be well tutored in the management of public affairs. Among them sat no representatives of the old slaveholding regime, although there were some of conservative temper. The most distinguished delegate was Christian Roselius, a brilliant lawyer and erstwhile opponent of secession, who resigned his seat when colleagues voted to subscribe twice to the ironclad oath.[48] His withdrawal left the convention in the hands of a new order of men with little or no experience in public life. Debates revealed their liberal intentions but not the education of gentility. They came from a social class which had never before been important in Louisiana politics. The fact that they occupied seats of power was of even greater revolutionary significance than the new organic law which they compiled.[49]

The Constitution of 1864, contrary to Ficklen, was not simply "a revised and amended copy of the constitution of 1852,"[50] but an extraordinary document which contained reforms and innovations of great social import. It remedied the chief grievances of which farmers and laborers complained before secession. The franchise was extended to all white men who had lived in Louisiana one year;[51] and the basis of representation in both chambers of the legislature was changed from total population to the qualified electorate, without any restriction on the number of seats to which New Orleans might be entitled.[52] The agrarian measures of the Constitution of 1845 were partially revived by forbidding the legislature to

---

tion. A scandalous contingent expense was the sum of nearly $10,000 for liquors and cigars. Half the entire cost of the convention, or $156,000, was for printing the journal and debates, a common source of rebates, commissions, and graft in the later years of reconstruction. But see *La. Sen. Debs.*, *1864–65*, 24–25, 26–29, 79–82.

[48] *La. Const. Conv. Debs., 1864*, 12, 14, 18–20.
[49] Cf. Ficklen, *op. cit.*, chap. IV.
[50] *Ibid.*, 79.   [51] *Const. 1864*, Art. 14.   [52] *Ibid.*, Arts. 11, 23.

charter banks or create corporations by special act.[53] Internal improvements, on the other hand, were encouraged by continuing the provisions of the Constitution of 1852.[54]

But the convention was not content to reform the old order. Its innovations were revolutionary. It abolished slavery,[55] inaugurated progressive income taxation,[56] opened the public schools to every child, black or white, between the ages of six and eighteen,[57] and established a nine-hour day and minimum wage of two dollars for all laborers engaged in public works.[58] The debate on these provisions revealed a startling change in the political temper of Louisiana.

There was no objection to the abolition of slavery,[59] for even the most reluctant delegate conceded it to be inevitable. But a stormy debate arose over the demand of a dozen conservatives that slaveholders be compensated for emancipating their property. The leader of this group, Edmund Abell, spoke for three days like a ghost from the dead, reciting the arguments which had once justified slavery and invoking the constitutional precedents which had protected it. He was himself no longer a slaveholder, but ardently defended the vested rights of others. Human bondage was approved by the fathers of the Republic and supported by the Constitution, he declared. It was superior to other systems of labor, and essential to keep the black from ruinous competition with the white. If slavery must be abolished, however, it was unjust to rob "the widow

[53] *Ibid.*, Art. 121.   [54] *Ibid.*, Arts. 112–14.

[55] *Ibid.*, Art. 1.   [56] *Ibid.*, Art. 124.

[57] *Ibid.*, Art. 141. It should be observed that while this provision extended the age limit of educable children, it did not adopt discriminatory taxes for the support of Negro schools.

[58] *Ibid.*, Arts. 134–35. Ficklen shows himself typical of many political historians of reconstruction in that he does not even mention these extraordinary articles.

[59] Carried by a final vote of 72–13, with the minority standing for eventual, compensated emancipation. See *La. Const. Conv. Debs., 1864*, 224.

and orphan" of their property. A convention that represented only ten thousand voters, few of whom held slaves, had no right to liberate the slave without compensating his master.

Some delegates jumped to the unwarranted conclusion that Abell was upholding rebellion, which was commonly assumed to be synonymous with slavery, and would have shouted him down. But the majority insisted that he be allowed a freedom of speech never before permitted in Louisiana on the question of slavery. Patient, courteously extending his time, they listened to him extolling Negro bondage with pleas that ranged from the Bible, through the Constitution, to considerations of human nature and political economy.[60] Delegates sat dumfounded, astonished by the unreality of his harangue.

Then one after another rose to denounce in turn compensated emancipation, slavery, and rebellion. They excoriated all planters and the old order of society. The slaveholder had destroyed his property by rebellion, they said, and deserved to suffer expropriation. He had no vested rights because the majority of people had never owned Negroes, and the majority alone could determine what was right. To remunerate slaveholders would necessitate taxing for their benefit the free laborers of New Orleans. The poor had lost more than the planters in this civil war. Why not indemnify them for their lives, their farms, their savings? The demand for compensated emancipation was but a ruse to maintain human bondage, to perpetuate the power and increase the wealth of planters who had ruled Louisiana too long. "The emancipation of the African," concluded a delegate from Rapides, "will prove to be . . . the true liberation and emancipation of the poor white laboring classes of the South." So their representatives in the Convention of 1864 voted to abolish slavery immediately and

[60] *Ibid.*, 140–44, 148–56, 165–67, 184–88, 192–94, 196.

without compensation.[61] They did not heed Abell's warning that because of this reform "a system of peonage would be established, all inducement for white labor over-ridden, and the safety of the State menaced." [62]

These delegates lived too close to the Negro to have any desire to make him politically their equal.[63] They showed the race prejudice characteristic of poor whites rather than the sympathies of radical abolitionists. If more farmers had been present, their aversion to the Negro would doubtless have become articulate.[64] When colored people were attacked, however, some delegates rose to their defense. "Drive the negro population from the State," said one, "and you would . . . remove from it the labor-power that made Louisiana before the rebellion . . . a State of planters and merchant princes." [65] But without debate the convention refused to accord colored labor the right to vote.[66] General Banks and Governor Hahn exerted pressure on enough delegates to authorize the legislature, if it so desired, to enfranchise "such persons" as might be deemed fit because of military service, taxation, or education.[67] Except for taxation, these qualifications for colored suffrage had been originally suggested by President Lincoln.[68] When they were presented to the convention, one delegate shouted, "that's a nigger resolution." [69] He was a man from New Orleans by the name of Sullivan, who had once been a poor white laborer; and like others, his prejudice against the Negro was not confined to suffrage.

[61] *Ibid.*, 167–69, 170–72, 176–79, 184, 189–90. To placate the minority, Congress was asked to reward *loyal* slaveholders. *Ibid.*, 313–14.

[62] *Ibid.*, 98.   [63] *Era*, Mar. 16, 1864.

[64] Cf. above, *n.* 2.   [65] *Ibid.*, 216.

[66] *Ibid.*, 211. The vote was 55–26.

[67] *Ibid.*, 450; *Const. 1864*, Art. 15; Ficklen, *History of Reconstruction* . . . , 71 *n.*

[68] Letter to Governor Hahn, quoted by Ficklen, *op. cit.*, 63.

[69] *Const. Conv. Debs., 1864*, 450.

"I will never tax white men to educate negro children," he declared, when a committee recommended separate colored schools to be supported from public funds.[70] Even conservatives like Abell took this stand, for Louisiana slaveholders had prohibited by law teaching a Negro to read or write.[71] Yet General Banks had already established schools for freedmen in New Orleans, and their education seemed as inevitable as abolition. The convention refused, therefore, to keep learning a white monopoly.[72] A long debate raged over the question of who should pay for colored schools, and it was at first resolved to make each race foot its own bill.[73] But friends of the freedman continued to work in committee, traded votes, and finally reached a compromise whereby taxation was left to the legislature with a guarantee of free public instruction for all children, both colored and white.[74] It was to prove the beginning of Negro education in Louisiana.

Perhaps nothing revealed more clearly the degree to which white labor dominated the Convention of 1864 than its establishment of minimum wages and hours. A petition for a nine-hour day had been circulated among the mechanics and artisans of New Orleans.[75] It was presented to the convention and entered in the journal, where one may read the names of nearly fifteen hundred laborers who had signed it.[76] Their appeal was stilted but earnest: "The past recurs to our vivid memory, when the capitalist could demand and exact from us ten to twelve hours a day devoted to toil, physical or mental, as the case required; that they frequently reserved for the white that which was detrimental to the black. Therefore, your petitioners most respectfully ask of you, your incorporation

[70] *Ibid.*, 474–76.   [71] *Ibid.*, 493–94.
[72] *Ibid.*, 475–76. The vote was 44–33.   [73] *Ibid.*, 523. The vote was 50–19.
[74] *Ibid.*, 601. The vote was 53–27. This seems the only possible conclusion after comparing the roll calls. Cf. *ibid.*, 496–99.
[75] *Ibid.*, 450.   [76] *Ibid.*, 418–24.

of some act into the organic law of the State in token of our recognition, by which we may be relieved of the burden we have heretofore borne, that of working to suit the convenience of men who acquired wealth and position to the injury and oppression of us." [77]

This petition was referred to a committee of delegates who were workingmen themselves. Their favorable report was evidence that a social revolution was incipient in Louisiana. Labor was "the most afflicted portion of our race," in the opinion of the committee, and "most likely to be kept down in the cesspool of poverty, simply by the antagonism between labor and capital." The workingman received small pay and endured long seasons of unemployment, but he had to buy his daily bread in small quantities, at high retail prices, with the addition of interest whenever he relied on credit. A multitude of middlemen were said "to produce nothing, . . . serve as speculative go-betweens," and burden labor with extortionate prices. "This popular speculating, this fashionable subsisting upon the labor of the mechanics and workingmen, is becoming well nigh intolerable." It would appear at first glance that these sentiments expressed nothing but hostility to merchants for wartime profiteering. But there was more. "The homage that capital requires of labor is beginning to be insupportable and detestable." Hence "some efficient plan must soon be instituted to . . . emancipate [the poor man] from the mountainous interests and antagonisms that now oppress and keep him in bondage to poverty." [78]

The practical relief proposed by the committee called for maximum hours and minimum wages on public enterprises. A provision that work of this nature be restricted to nine hours a day was passed with little debate.[79] It scarcely needed to be said, as one delegate charged, that this measure was designed

[77] Ibid., 418.   [78] Ibid., 430.   [79] Ibid., 451. The vote was 56–25.

to win approval of the new constitution. It was significant that labor could only be satisfied by this kind of social legislation. The scheme for minimum wages, which was frankly admitted to be a "laborers' bill," was sponsored by a former steamboat-man, Benjamin Orr. The bill was carried, with reduced rates which were made permissive rather than mandatory, by trading votes with those delegates who also desired to establish a wage schedule for the city police.[80] The legislature was authorized to fix the remuneration of all labor engaged in state or municipal enterprises, provided that minimum daily wages should not be less than $3.50 for foremen and cartmen, $3.00 for mechanics, and $2.00 for laborers.[81]

The debate showed that advocates of this law were on the defensive. They argued that it was not class legislation, because the general public rather than any group would eventually pay for these wages as it did for the tariff. The opposition complained that the measure would violate freedom of contract, interfere with the law of supply and demand, destroy the incentive of the poor to work, reduce all to the same level, and "take from the laborer his right to dictate his own terms." The bill was demagogic: nothing but a bid for votes.[82] Each of these objections was to be repeated against all social legislation proposed in the future, but this was the first time they were heard in Louisiana. "I do not ask you to make these men rich," replied the sponsor of the bill, "but to give them enough to eat, drink and wear." [83] As a result of his plea, instead of

---

[80] Ibid., 312, 362, 431–32, 439, 594–95. The vote was 67–10, but compulsion was defeated 42–40.

[81] Ibid., 640.

[82] Ibid., 434–39, 361–63. "Show me the man who advocates the rights of poor men," grumbled conservatives, "and I will show you a man holding a fat position in the city government. A man who, if he had to pay workmen for services out of his own pocket, would sing an entirely different song."

[83] Ibid., 362.

receiving fifty cents a day, laborers on public works could henceforth expect at least two dollars.

This novel concern for labor showed which way the political winds were blowing in Louisiana as the Civil War drew to a close. The workingmen of New Orleans, backbone of the Free State party, made their first stride toward a more democratic social order in 1864. But it was to be their last step for almost a generation.

The new constitution won the approval of President Lincoln, who pushed its ratification; and it was accepted by the people who lived within Federal lines.[84] But they were too small a minority of the white population, and divided into too many factions, to give life to this law. Typical of the cross-purposes at which unionists worked in Louisiana was Denison, collector of the port and local promoter of the presidential ambitions of the Secretary of the Treasury, Salmon P. Chase.[85] Although Denison approved the constitution, he cordially disliked its military sponsor, General Banks, and called his "whole civil reorganization in Louisiana . . . a cheat and a swindle." [86] In Congress the reconstructed government of the state found but little support, since Lincoln's policy was under fire by Wade, Davis, and the radicals.

Because the new constitution had failed to enfranchise the

[84] Ficklen, *History of Reconstruction* . . . , 80–81. The vote in twenty parishes was 6,836–1,566, with New Orleans casting five-eighths of the total ballots.

[85] "Diary and Correspondence of Salmon P. Chase," *American Hist. Assn. Rpt., 1902*, II, 297–458. Unlike Ficklen, who relies heavily on these letters, I do not find Denison a trustworthy observer. He was a zealous but obsequious agent of Chase, and reported affairs to the end that the interests of himself and his employer might be advanced. He was an ardent admirer of General Butler and never saw any good in the work of his successor, General Banks, whom he suspected of being a Seward man. His prejudice against Banks and Hahn, as well as against the social character of the Convention of 1864, leads us to discount much of what Denison wrote.

[86] *Ibid.*, 445.

Negro, it was buried in a Senate filibuster led by Sumner.[87] In vain Lincoln pleaded in the last speech he was ever to make: "Concede that the new government of Louisiana is only to what it should be as the egg is to the fowl, we shall sooner have the fowl by hatching the egg than by smashing it." [88] But there was no agreement at Washington or New Orleans as to what species of egg was desirable. Lincoln wished states to be quickly restored to the Union with a full measure of home rule; the radical Republicans looked upon the South as conquered territory to be retrieved on a conqueror's terms, which would deprive rebel leaders of suffrage but extend it to their former slaves. The Free State party of New Orleans sought a local government responsive to the majority of loyal white people; the demobilized Confederates, an administration which would restore Louisiana to its ante-bellum condition, except that peonage would replace slavery.[89]

It was almost inevitable that Confederates should resume control of Louisiana, when they returned from the battlefield, because they were preponderant in numbers and influence. They had not been disfranchised by the Free State legislature; [90] and none but Confederate officeholders and the wealthiest planters were excluded from citizenship by President Johnson's proclamation of amnesty.[91] The voting strength of the soldiers was immediately enlisted by Governor Wells, a unionist planter who was moved to reconcile the veterans by a shrewd calculation that they held the balance of power in his re-election.[92] Old Democrats campaigned through the country on a platform hostile to Negro suffrage and Northern radicalism,[93] and persuaded the majority of farmers to vote

[87] J. F. Rhodes, *History*, V, 53–55.
[88] Quoted by Ficklen, *History of Reconstruction . . .* , 82.
[89] *Ibid.*, chap. VI.   [90] *La. H. Debs., 1865*, 394. The vote was 46–15.
[91] Richardson, *Messages and Papers of the Presidents*, VI, 310–12.
[92] Ficklen, *op. cit.*, 104–5.
[93] See their platform, *Annual Cyclopaedia, 1865*, 512.

for white supremacy and home rule.[94] They swept the polls and gained possession of the legislature.[95] So spectacular a triumph crushed the opposition, which was only a remnant of the Free State party, unpopular because it lacked Confederate leadership and laid no claim to compensation for emancipated slaves.[96] Thus the Democracy recaptured Louisiana by a peaceful counterrevolution at the ballot box.

But the old order was not to remain. There followed in swift succession the events at New Orleans and Washington that brought in the Federal army, ousted the Democrats from power, filled their places with radical Republicans of both races, and inaugurated the second phase of social revolution by a grant of civil and political rights to the freedmen.[97]

This train of events was unwittingly set in motion by the Democrats. In order to discipline colored labor and make it profitable, the planters who sat in the legislature and on parish police juries enacted vagrancy and apprenticeship laws that horrified the North.[98] To radical Republicans it seemed as if the stalwart Confederates were determined to restore human bondage and cheat the country of the fruits of war.[99] It is true, of course, that the new black code was milder than the old laws of slavery, and not as harsh in Louisiana as in some other states.[100] It recognized no proprietary rights on the part of white men to own and exchange those who were colored; but it did provide for their management and employment as

[94] *Picayune*, July 2; *Times*, Oct. 3, 1865.   [95] *La. Sen. J., 1865*, 25–27.
[96] Ficklen, *History of Reconstruction . . .*, 111.   [97] *Ibid.*, chaps. VI–XI.
[98] *La. [Extra] Sess. Laws, 1865*, 3 ff. The severest laws were enacted by the police juries, not the legislature. See, e. g., W. L. Fleming, *Documentary History of Reconstruction* (Cleveland, 1906), I, 279–81.

[99] J. G. Blaine, *Twenty Years of Congress* (Norwich, Conn., 1884–86), II, 101–2.

[100] For a judicial explanation of the conditions in the South which led to the adoption of these black codes, and their similarity to previous legislation for free people of color, see J. S. Randall, *The Civil War and Reconstruction* (Boston, 1937), 724–30.

something less than free men. It reduced the Negro to a condition which lay between peonage and serfdom. He was to be forever a field hand, and to owe his services to all white planters rather than to individual masters.

The Louisiana black code abridged the freedom of agricultural labor, limited its mobility, and added legal compulsion to the incentives to work which naturally arose from economic necessity. Negroes could not organize unions, nor strike, for whoever was found guilty of "tampering" with them—a word and an idea associated with slavery—to interrupt or improve their employment, was subject to fine and imprisonment. Planters could not create a free market for labor nor raise the level of its wages by competition, since they were required to give certificates to workers whom they discharged, and to hire none but those who showed evidence of having fulfilled their previous contracts. A supply of compulsory labor was assured for the plantations. Agricultural workers were obliged to undertake service for the year within the first ten days of January, and to include in these agreements all members of their families. Each worker was "free" to choose an employer, but some employer he must find, and once a contract was made with him the worker could not quit without forfeiting all wages. The laborer's hire was a prior lien on whatever he raised, and not over half the produce was to be removed from the fields until his charges had been met; to facilitate crop-sharing, which was clearly anticipated, half the wages could be withheld until completion of the annual indenture. Uniform hours of work, ten in summer and nine in winter, were set for all plantations. To enforce discipline and diminish the costs of inefficiency, labor was subject to so many fines that even the best could hardly avoid a few.[101] Except for damages to tools, livestock

101 For sickness, the daily wage was lost; for idleness or refusal to work, a fine double this amount was levied, with wages to be calculated at twenty-five cents an hour and two dollars a day. Each occasion of "disobedience,"

and crops, however, half of the fines were to be pooled in a bonus fund which would be distributed at harvest as a dividend.

These arrangements for resuming operation of the plantations were nominally quite different from the worst realities of slavery. There were even ingenious devices for putting labor under the trusteeship of justices of the peace, who would witness the signing of indentures, enforce them on both employer and employee, hear complaints from either party, and arbitrate their disputes.[102] But such elaborate safeguards of the Negro's rights could hardly be effective, much less equitable, when planters were justices of the peace. Freedmen who were so bold and intelligent as to appeal to them would be confronted by their employer or his friends in the guise of the state.

As a result of these laws, observed Carl Schurz, "the blacks at large belong to the whites at large." [103] Schurz did not exaggerate the Negro's predicament in spite of his radical predilections and sympathy for the race. It was hard to understand how the freedman could escape serfdom in any circumstances so long as he owned almost no land.[104] The difficulties of his situation were apparent to the South. "Negroes must remain in the worst possible condition of slavery so long as the whites own the land, and that they would soon regain and monopolise, if it were all given to the negroes tomorrow." [105] If the Negro was to depend on the white race for his liveli-

---

which included swearing, fighting, neglect of duty, and absence without leave, was to cost a laborer one dollar. Thefts were to be reimbursed double the value of whatever was stolen.

[102] *La. [Extra] Sess. Laws, 1865*, Acts nos. 10, 11, 16, 20, 58.

[103] *Report on Condition of the South, 1865*, 39 Cong., 1 sess., *Sen. Ex. Docs.*, I, no. 2, 24.

[104] *Tribune*, Mar. 1, 1865.

[105] *De Bow's Review*, III (April–May, 1867), 354. Cf. *Picayune*, Oct. 25, 1867.

hood, thought Northern and colored radicals, it was essential that he should be politically free to vote, in order to assert his rights and improve his future. The necessity of colored suffrage was argued at length by two revolutionary newspapers, the *New Orleans Tribune* [106] and *St. Landry Progress,*[107] which were published in French and English by educated Negroes.[108] A copy of the New Orleans paper was sent to every member of Congress, and radical Republicans were inspired to denounce the policies of President Johnson and Southern Democrats.[109]

The agitation of these local newspapers for colored suffrage and civil rights showed that radical reconstruction was not introduced into Louisiana entirely from the outside. Rather was it advocated with equal zeal from within the state by an active minority of free colored people, who had enjoyed liberty even in the days of slavery when their industry accumulated property worth in the aggregate several millions of dollars.[110] They sought to push the social revolution begun by war to an agrarian conclusion in behalf of the masses of their race who had been slaves, to protect their own status, and to admit to power the majority of both races. "The planters are no longer needed in the character of masters"; with this belief they challenged the old order. "Our basis for labor must now be put on a democratic footing. There is no more room, in the organization of our society, for an oligarchy of slaveholders, or

---

[106] Jan. 17, Feb. 22, 1865.

[107] *Le Progrès de St. Landry,* July 27, 1867, published at Opelousas by Michel Vidal.

[108] The editors of the *Tribune* were refugees from San Domingo. One of them, Dr. J. T. Roudanez, was a physician of some affluence. The principal editor, Paul Trevigne, was the son of a soldier in the War of 1812, and spoke several languages. W. E. B. Du Bois, *Black Reconstruction in America* (New York, 1935), 456.

[109] E. g., *Congressional Globe,* 39 Cong., 1 sess., 39.

[110] *Tribune,* Mar. 31, 1865.

[even of] property holders." [111] If the suffrage should remain in practice exclusively white, "we may expect and prepare also for mobs of white against colored laborers, and white . . . against colored mechanics." [112]

But the attempt of some irresponsible white radicals to transfer the franchise from Confederate veterans to freedmen provoked the famous riot of 1866 in New Orleans.[113] It came about in this way. About forty former members of the Convention of 1864 summoned it to meet again by virtue of an ambiguous resolution which had been enacted by this body for its continuation.[114] The purpose of the radicals in renewing its life was to enfranchise the Negro,[115] and probably to drive the Democrats from power. They were embarked on a desperate *coup d'état,*[116] but with the knowledge and apparent support of such influential Republicans in Congress as Thaddeus Stevens, Boutwell, and Conkling, who as members of the radical Reconstruction Committee were seeking to undermine President Johnson and to undo his settlement of the South.[117]

The significance of the rump convention lay in the reaction of national opinion to the bloodshed with which it opened. A colored procession, which stopped to cheer the assembly, ended

---

[111] *Ibid.,* Mar. 1, 1865.   [112] *Ibid.,* May 31, 1865.

[113] *Report of the Select Committee on the New Orleans Riots,* 39 Cong., 2 sess., *H. R. Rpts.,* no. 16, *passim.* This investigation lacked all semblance of judicial procedure and was conducted chiefly to obtain evidence that would justify radical military reconstruction. The report is consequently unsatisfactory, despite the searching questions of the minority member from Pennsylvania. See the analysis by F. P. Burns, "White Supremacy in the South," *L. H. Q.,* XVIII (July, 1935), 592–94, 603–5.

[114] *Rpt. . . . on the New Orleans Riots,* 46–47, 60.

[115] Burns, *op. cit.,* 597.   [116] *Rpt. . . . on the New Orleans Riots,* 439–40.

[117] *Ibid.,* 40–41, 50, 54–57. Judge Howell and the other leaders conferred with Conkling, Stevens, *et al.* Gideon Wells believed that "the New Orleans riots had their origin with the Radical members of Congress . . . [and were] part of a *deliberate conspiracy . . .* to secure . . . Radical ascendancy." Quoted by Burns, *op. cit.,* 605.

in a race riot. About thirty-four Negroes were killed, and over two hundred were wounded. A leading radical, Dr. A. P. Dostie, who was animated by a fanatical ambition to subdue rebels and elevate slaves, was among the four white men who lost their lives, only one of whom was sympathetic to the South.[118] On the other side, so to speak, only ten policemen were wounded, and no one was arrested or punished.[119] Thus it was reported that a massacre had been plotted and perpetrated in cold blood by the New Orleans Democracy, and this was the verdict of the Congressional radicals who investigated the affair.[120] No historian has endorsed their judgment except Du Bois,[121] and it is impossible to untangle the confused and partisan testimony in the case.[122] Violence had always been common in New Orleans, and was inevitable when racial antagonism became fierce.[123] Whatever the true explanation of the riot, it was widely believed outside the South that a white mob had murdered Negroes, with the connivance of government, in order to intimidate a radical convention which proposed to enfranchise the race to which the dead belonged.

A fearful conviction that the South was restoring slavery, however groundless in fact, spread through the North. The

[118] Burns, *op. cit.*, 614–16.

[119] *Rpt. . . . on the New Orleans Riots*, 12–16, *passim.*

[120] *Ibid.*, 16–20.

[121] Ficklen, *History of Reconstruction . . .* , 174–75; Du Bois, *op. cit.*, 464–65.

[122] Mayor Monroe, who was determined to disperse the convention, employed as marshals some notorious thugs, not unlike the police who committed similar outrages against Irish immigrants during his administration before the war. *Rpt. . . . on the New Orleans Riots*, 139–40, 142–47, 441; Monroe to General Baird, 494, 499.

[123] According to Ficklen, *History of Reconstruction . . .* , 175, it was largely caused by "the natural exasperation felt by the white people of New Orleans when it was found that a handful of men proposed, with the assistance of the Federal government, to establish negro supremacy in their midst by putting the heel of the ex-slave on the neck of his former master." Cf. Burns, *op. cit.*, 614.

black codes indicated that the Negro was not wholly free; the New Orleans massacre appeared to demonstrate that the lives of Republicans were in jeopardy. These conditions were thought by radicals to be a natural result of the amnesty and home rule which President Johnson had granted the South. Whether the Congressional leaders were sincere in converting Northern voters to this view, or simply intent on Johnson's defeat and the establishment of Republican supremacy, the events in Louisiana made good propaganda for their plans of coercion.

Nothing more was needed to discredit the Lincoln-Johnson policy in the eyes of the North, and to put the South at the mercy of men in Congress like Sumner and Stevens, but the rejection of the Fourteenth Amendment. This was done in Louisiana by unanimous vote of the aristocrats who controlled the legislature,[124] for they were resolved to invite repression rather than to disfranchise themselves.[125] There followed, as night the day, military reconstruction. Surely no period or policy in American history has earned a less appropriate name; it was not to be one of reconstruction, but of destruction and depression, of partisan dictatorship by corrupt political machines which exploited both races in the name of one.[126]

There will always be speculation over the causes of this calamitous state of affairs. Perhaps what doomed to failure the peaceable reconstruction undertaken by Lincoln and Johnson, at least in Louisiana, was the traditional identification of class with race, a heritage of slavery, so that men were not united by their common economic interests, but divided despite them by color. Racial animosity was always stronger than class con-

---

[124] *Times*, Feb. 1, 10, 1867.

[125] *Ibid.*, Feb. 8, Mar. 17, 1867. Cf. W. A. Russ, Jr., "Disfranchisement in Louisiana (1862–70)," *L. H. Q.*, XVIII (July, 1935), 572–73.

[126] Nordhoff, *The Cotton States in the Spring and Summer of 1875*, 43 ff. Nordhoff wrote the best contemporary analysis of this political pathology.

sciousness; [127] and white people who differed over secession and war were quickly rallied to oppose the Negro, as slave or freedman. Only a minority of the laboring population, entirely white and urban, had found its voice in 1864; its strength wasted away, instead of being recruited by demobilized Confederates, because those who were poor and white were also divided by the enmity born of civil war. The patriotic restoration to office of conservative Democrats introduced the black code as an economic settlement along racial lines. Local leadership was provided by the old planters and merchants and Confederate officers, who had the confidence of all whites in the face of colored suffrage, and there were none to dispute their power but Northern adventurers and native radicals, who were supported by the Republican chiefs in Congress and the colored masses.[128] The necessities of national politics, especially of Republican supremacy and industrial growth, were to cast the die of local affairs. Since the rule of Southern Democrats was not to be tolerated by the victorious North, the radicals were bound to have their spell of power over Louisiana.

Military reconstruction reduced all the former states of the Confederacy except Tennessee to the status of conquered territory, which could regain their sovereignty only by obedience to the dictates of Congress, enlargement of the suffrage to include Negroes, and ratification of the Fourteenth Amendment.[129] To fulfill these conditions in Louisiana, a constitu-

[127] A furtive example of racial rapprochement occurred in the election of delegates to the Convention of 1868. A candidate from Terrebonne, who was actually a poor Creole, was said to belong "to that class which . . . negroes used to designate as 'low white trash' "; and his colleague was a carpenter who had always been a free man of color. Houma *Civic Guard*, Sept. 21, quoted in *Commercial Bulletin*, Sept. 23, 1867. Cf. *ibid.*, Sept. 2, 1867, for a report from East Feliciana.

[128] Cf. Russ, *op. cit.*, 570.

[129] The three reconstruction acts of 1867 which made this policy law are to be found in *U. S. Statutes at Large*, XIV, 428 ff., XV, 2 ff., 14 ff.

ent assembly was elected by all "loyal" men on a war basis, for loyalty was interpreted by General Sheridan as barring Confederate veterans and Democratic officeholders from the polls.[130] A contemporary newspaper estimated that half the white citizens were disfranchised.[131] Whatever the number who were disqualified, and it must have been large, the registration was heavily colored.[132] No one was surprised that radicals elected to the Convention of 1868 all but two of their candidates.[133]

The local Republicans who thus won control of Louisiana had organized their party in 1865. Thomas Durant, an old Douglas Democrat, presided at its first convention. Henry Clay Warmoth, a poor, white lawyer of Southern ancestry who was more a scalawag than a carpetbagger, became its moving spirit. His program from the start was one of radical reconstruction; he promoted it unofficially on the floor of Congress,[134] and came into power when this body made it law. The original party membership was composed of free men of color, emigrants from the North, demobilized Federal soldiers, and native unionists. Northerners were always influential but never in the majority; as late as 1874 there were only about seven thousand voters who confessed to having been born Yankees.[135] The strength of the party at the polls rested with the colored masses.[136] To carry the Convention of 1868, over fifty thousand freedmen were organized in a Republican Loyal League.[137]

[130] Fleming, *Documentary History of Reconstruction*, I, 433-35.

[131] *Times*, Apr. 21, 1867.

[132] Cf. Lonn, *Reconstruction in Louisiana after 1868*, 5.

[133] Ficklen, *History of Reconstruction . . .* , 193. With the colored registration alone amounting to 82,907, there were 75,083 votes cast in favor of holding the convention.

[134] H. C. Warmoth, *War, Politics and Reconstruction; etc.* (New York, 1930), 43-45.

[135] *Rpt. State Registrar of Voters, 1874*, Table 2.

[136] Nordhoff, *op. cit.*, 41.   [137] *Republican*, Nov. 17, 1867.

With the elevation of this race from slavery to free suffrage, the revolution entered its second stage: black labor was ostensibly in a position to control the state. It might be supposed that the Negro would rule the Republican party, not only by the sheer weight of his numerical preponderance, but also because he was led by educated mulattoes such as Oscar Dunn and P. B. S. Pinchback, a type which was the peculiar product of ante-bellum racial relations in Louisiana. That this was not to be the case became apparent early in the Convention of 1868. The delegates elected to this assembly had been drawn equally from both races by agreement of the party chiefs in order to avoid conflicts of color.[138] The important committee to draft a constitution was nevertheless composed of five white and four colored members, who divided by race and submitted different reports. The document which finally emerged from the convention was the product of many compromises, but followed essentially the recommendations of the white majority.[139]   The Negroes suffered another loss when their gubernatorial candidate was defeated by Warmoth on a ballot polled according to color; their nominee was then satisfied with the Lieutenant-Governorship.[140] The colored delegates sustained additional defeats when they lost their fight for agrarian legislation,[141] and against drastic disfranchisement of their former masters.[142] Henceforth the Negroes who had been "Pure Radicals" failed to take the lead in shaping the policy of their party. In vain they had boasted "we have more than

[138] Ficklen, *loc. cit.*
[139] Du Bois, *Black Reconstruction*, 468.
[140] Warmoth, *op. cit.*, 54–55. The vote was close, 45–43. A mulatto, Oscar Dunn, honest and intelligent, was nominated for Lieutenant-Governor.
[141] See below, chap. VIII.
[142] Russ, *op. cit., L. H. Q.*, XVIII (July, 1935), 575–76. Pinchback declared himself opposed to this measure, Article 99, because he believed "that two-thirds of the colored men of this State do not desire disfranchisement to such a great extent."

the ballot: we compose a majority in the State, and with the help of our Radical white friends . . . the colored masses are the masters of the field." [143] White Republicans led by War-moth, Casey, Carter, Kellogg, and Packard became the masters of reconstruction and ruled the state with the support of colored officeholders and voters, and the protection of Federal troops.

The Constitution of 1868 nevertheless gave the Negro many nominal advantages, several of which actually worked to his disadvantage. Although he had but recently emerged from a servile condition of enforced ignorance, and was on the whole illiterate, he was granted the right to vote and to hold any office in the state.[144] These dubious privileges only made him the tool of others until he became intelligent enough to have a will and understanding of his own.[145] For the convention it was enough to open all public schools to freedmen,[146] though five delegates warned their colleagues that to mix the races in this way and to waive all color discrimination would be to wreck the educational system.[147]

No less disastrous for the immediate future of the Negro was the convention's unqualified declaration of social equality,[148] which aroused greater resentment among white people than colored suffrage. It was adopted largely by colored votes at the insistence of Pinchback.[149] The abolition of civil and social discrimination was difficult to challenge in theory and

[143] *Tribune*, Oct. 30, 1867. [144] *Const. 1868*, Arts. 2, 98.

[145] Cf. R. Taylor's illuminating report of his conversation with Charles Sumner on this subject for a revelation of the *non sequitur* in radical thought, *Destruction and Reconstruction*, 245.

[146] Unfortunately for both races the convention rejected a proposal, 56–8, to restrict suffrage after 1872 to the literate. *Official Journal of the Proceedings of the Convention for Framing a Constitution for the State of Louisiana* (New Orleans, 1867–68), 175.

[147] *Ibid.*, 200–1. [148] *Const. 1868*, Art. 13.

[149] *Const. Conv. J., 1868*, 242–43. It was passed, 58–16, and opened public places to both races. Ficklen, *History of Reconstruction* . . . , 198.

as a principle of abstract right.[150] But the traditions and temper of popular white opinion made all questions relating to the freedman a race problem, not one of philosophical doctrine or politics. It was widely believed, even by sensible people, that if the Negro could ride with them in street cars and sit next to their children at school, there would be nothing to prevent miscegenation.[151] The colored press replied that these apprehensions were unjustified, and that Democrats deliberately inflamed them in order to regain political control. Social equality meant nothing more to the intelligent Negro than the right of any man, whatever his color, to come and go in public places, and to pursue his own happiness, provided he did not infringe the equal right of another. There was no thought of racial intermarriage, even among the uneducated, but only of the admission of freedmen to civil society so that they might be free to walk the streets, frequent public institutions, attend schools, and appear in courts of law like other citizens.[152] But white members of the convention who were sympathetic to the aspirations of colored people protested that there was no use in making laws so far in advance of public opinion.[153] Such doctrines were especially offensive to white farmers and laborers, who saw no good in the Constitution of 1868.

This document was hailed by colored radicals as "the deathblow of the slave oligarchy in Louisiana." [154] Their optimism was justified in so far as the old leaders of the state, the planters and merchants, were temporarily disfranchised and their ballots handed over to those who had formerly been their slaves. The power to make laws was ostensibly reposed with a colored majority, for seats in both houses were allotted according to total population.[155] This revival of the 1852 basis of represen-

[150] *Ibid.*, 291–92.   [151] *Tribune*, Apr. 14; *Times*, May 6, 1867.
[152] *Le Progrès de St. Landry*, Sept. 12, 1868.
[153] *Const. Conv. J.*, *1868*, 275–77.
[154] *St. Landry Progress*, Apr. 11, 1868.   [155] *Const. 1868*, Arts. 21, 30.

tation was bitterly resented by white people, because the colored were no longer merely counted but actually allowed to vote and represent themselves. Although the black belt possessed no more legislative seats than before the war,[156] the majority of Negroes in this region, and not a minority of white planters, were now in a position to control legislation. This obliteration of the color line which had previously determined who should constitute a majority in the state led to a fierce struggle between blacks and whites. Peace was to be restored only with the triumph of white supremacy in 1877.

For nine years previous to this date, however, Louisiana was in the grip of carpetbag government. Its political structure, based on the Constitution of 1868, was strong because it centralized "imperial power in the governor's hands." [157] The degree to which he controlled the state became extraordinary as one law after another augmented his overlordship. It is notable that the only opposition to him within the government arose from the Custom House, because he did not administer Federal patronage.[158] In the state he was supreme. He was able to appoint and remove local registrars of voters, tax collectors, and assessors, besides the board of public works and metropolitan police officers for New Orleans; he could name special constables with power to make summary arrests everywhere, and fill all vacancies of office, even in parish police juries.[159] If a hostile judge should be elected to any court, the legislature would gerrymander his district, as in New Orleans, and create a new one, to which the governor forthwith appointed a friendly judge.[160] Elections "were a farce," since "the governor appointed the registrars, and through them returned his

[156] Cf. *U. S. Cen.*, *1860, Prelim. Rpt.*, 262; *Const. 1868*, Art. 22.

[157] *Affairs in Louisiana*, 42 Cong., 2 sess. [1872], *H. Rpts.*, no. 92, p. 21, minority rpt.

[158] See Lonn, *op. cit.*, IV, 73 ff.   [159] Nordhoff, *op. cit.*, 44.

[160] *Ibid.*, 46–47.

friends to the legislature." [161] The registration never tallied with tax or census figures, and in some places embraced more Negroes than were alive. It was easy for corrupt voters to repeat and stuff the ballot box since a citizen could use any poll in his parish or—in New Orleans—in his ward.[162] Whatever the actual vote, a central returning board, composed of a Republican majority confirmed by the Senate, could change the results to suit its own rules of political arithmetic.[163]

This gubernatorial despotism was the antithesis of democratic government. It gave one man, at first H. C. Warmoth and then W. P. Kellogg, the control of elections, courts, and taxation; and by his leadership of the Republican party, he dominated the legislature and the making of laws. The governor was generally supported in the face of local opposition by President Grant, who maintained a "Federal protectorate" over Louisiana with national troops.[164] The state was policed for a decade by soldiers whose mission was to preserve law and order, especially at elections, but the law was whatever a corrupt legislature ratified, elections were determined by fraudulent returns, and the overseer of Louisiana was the governor.

There were nevertheless said to be permanent benefits which accrued from misrule of this type, especially in South Carolina and Mississippi, but they were overlooked until one historian called attention to them in 1910.[165] He claimed that during this period the South achieved democratic government, free public schools, and important social legislation.[166] If these reforms were introduced into other states,[167] Louisiana was conspicuous for their absence. Government became nominally demo-

[161] See above, n. 157.   [162] Nordhoff, op. cit., 65.
[163] Ibid.   [164] Ibid., 68.
[165] W. E. B. Du Bois, "Reconstruction and Its Benefits," A.H.R., XV (July, 1910), 781–99.
[166] Ibid., 795–96.
[167] Cf. F. B. Simkins and R. H. Woody, South Carolina during Reconstruction, which is a pioneer work on this and other questions.

cratic by the Constitution of 1868, as we have seen, but in practice it proved to be despotic. The free public schools which had been established in 1844, and were now open to both races, suffered almost complete collapse because of racial prejudice, fraud, and inefficiency.[168] Of effective social legislation, there was none. When Nordhoff examined the statutes enacted during reconstruction, he "met with dozens of petty swindles," and reached the conclusion that "a more amusing and preposterous exhibition of wholesale legislative plundering it would be difficult to imagine." [169]

Anyone who goes through the sessional laws of this period will confirm Nordhoff's opinion. The overwhelming bulk of the legislation divided itself into two categories, political and economic, which had the single aim of maintaining in power Republican politicians and rewarding their friends. Whether it was the creation of a new parish like Grant, for exploitation by carpetbaggers as notorious as the Twitchells, or the issue of railway, land, and improvement bonds, the telltale mark of fraud was upon each law. There would be no point in a tedious explanation of these corrupt statutes,[170] especially when the truth of their unsavory negotiation, shrouded in discreet mystery from the start, has been forever lost.

It is more important to realize that no race, class, or party could lay a virtuous claim to clean hands. In each case the majority were honest, of course, if only because they were powerless or indifferent. But politicians bribed legislators for party and parish favors, and business men and corporations bribed the politicians for economic privileges.[171] There was

---

[168] *Rpt. State Supt. Pub. Educ., 1872, passim; 1877, passim.*

[169] *Op. cit.,* 60–62.   [170] Cf. Nordhoff, *loc. cit.*

[171] "The legislative corruption involves both parties. Among the principal movers in legislative jobs were wealthy, influential, and highly respectable democrats." *Affairs in Louisiana,* 42 Cong., 2 sess. [1872], *H. Rpts.,* IV, no. 92, p. 37, separate dissent by H. B. Smith. See Warmoth's testimony on Democratic votes for four railway subsidies, *ibid.,* 38–39.

some truth in Governor Warmoth's speech to the bankers who were lobbying to protect and advance their interests. "I tell you," he said, "these much-abused members of the Louisiana legislature are at all events as good as the people they represent. Why, damn it, everybody is demoralizing down here. Corruption is the fashion." [172] In these circumstances even the honorable business man had to resort to bribery to avoid political reprisals and to pay off legislative blackmail, and prices were high because corruption was rampant. But it should be remembered, as Du Bois observed, that colored men obtained only a small share of the graft, which was designated in legislative accounts as "sundries and incidentals," while white men took the lion's share of state bonds, warrants, charters, and land.[173]

Carpetbag rule was eventually caught in two dilemmas, and its failure to solve them provoked violent opposition which led ultimately to its downfall. First was the fact that its electoral majorities consisted of colored votes: without support of the Negro at the polls, radicals could not obtain office; but to rely on the ballots of one race, and that the weaker, was to unite the other and stronger race in implacable hostility; and the Negro would prove to be unreliable in the face of such enemies, because whatever his political allegiance, his economic necessities bound him to the white planter.

Second was the no less important fact that carpetbag government fed on corruption; since radicals lacked the confidence of business or white citizens, and depended on the protection of the Federal army for their precarious tenure of power, they could not draw their party funds and individual perquisites from the economic development of the state. So they turned to political exploitation and feathered their nests directly from

[172] *Rpt. . . . on . . . Condition of the South,* 43 Cong., 2 sess. [1875], *H. Rpts.,* V, no. 261, pt. iii, 973.
[173] *Op. cit.,* 792.

the public revenue, which raised taxes higher without increasing receipts, further depressed trade and agriculture, and completed the process of alienating the white electorate. Each dilemma was inescapable; the first was of a racial and social character, the second, racial and economic; together they issued in the race strife, apparently more social than economic, which finally put an end to carpetbag rule.

Oppressive taxation was largely responsible for bringing men of property and influence into violent collision with the radicals. The rate for the state jumped from 37½ cents on $100 in 1866 to $2.15 in 1871.[174] Notwithstanding these increased levies, the debt rose from about eleven millions after the war to over fifty millions in 1875. There was also a rapid rise in the local rates for most parishes. In Natchitoches, for example, where $13,475 had been sufficient revenue in 1860, the sum of $82,207 was not enough in 1873 to cover local expenses and peculations.[175] These heavy fiscal demands were made of a people who had not recovered from the losses of war before they were further depressed by the Panic of 1873. The consequences for New Orleans were disastrous. Here the value of residential property was cut in half, and the sheriff made more than 47,000 seizures for taxes from 1871 through 1873.[176] The situation was no better in the country.[177] It was especially hard for "small farmers," according to Nordhoff, because they were "forced to pay the heavy taxes, while in many cases their rich neighbors resist[ed]." [178] The fiscal crisis had become acute by 1872.

It was truly said that "office-holders grow rich, while the people are impoverished." With "capital . . . flying from the State, [and] commerce . . . decreasing," [179] resistance to

[174] *Rpt. . . . on . . . Condition of the South*, 974.
[175] Nordhoff, *op. cit.*, 54.   [176] *Ibid.*, 62–63.
[177] See below, chap. VIII.   [178] *Op. cit.*, 59.
[179] *Affairs in Louisiana*, 21, 29, testimony of J. B. Eustis.

confiscatory taxation spread far and wide. A league was formed in New Orleans and the rural parishes to refuse all payments, and merchants and planters were foremost in this rebellion.[180] Some fifty-five lawyers in New Orleans offered to defend tax suits without charge.[181] The movement coincided with the first vigorous and united election campaign by the whites against carpetbag rule in 1872. It can hardly be doubted that the resistance to taxation inspired a relentless struggle for home rule.[182] The "same old crew of political buzzards and insatiable jackals who have robbed and plundered us to the verge of bankruptcy, and paralyzed all industry in the State," [183] could not be borne for long if agriculture and trade were to survive.

While it was chiefly the propertied citizens who rebelled against the oppressive taxation of reconstruction, the poor and white were stirred no less by pride of race and hatred of any Negro who attempted to rule them. Where parish officials happened to be colored, as in Natchitoches or St. Landry, murders and riots were frequent.[184] It was an unpleasant sight for a poor, white farmer to watch a poor Negro grow prosperous in public office, and galling to him to pay the taxes which were too often the source of his prosperity.[185] The colored men who were corrupt, ignorant, dissolute, and bold, though a very small minority, earned for their race the distrust and contempt of the white man.

[180] Rpt. . . . on . . . Condition of the South, 965.   [181] Ibid., 963.

[182] Natchitoches Vindicator, quoted in ibid., 921–27.

[183] Alexandria Caucasian, quoted in ibid., 767.

[184] This state of affairs continued, even without colored officials to incite them, to 1878. See the partisan but revealing Rpt. . . . into Alleged Frauds and Violence in the Elections of 1878, etc., 45 Cong., 3 sess. [1879], Sen. Rpts., IV, no. 855, pt. i; for Caddo, 3–110, 589–93; Natchitoches, 115–66, 484–558; Tensas, 169–354, 453–83; Concordia, 355–78; St. Mary, 381–96; Pt. Coupee, 411–29.

[185] Interview with H. L. Brian, May 2, 1933.

In the rural parishes the hard-working farmers sometimes lost their patience and carried out with violence or intimidation the desperate threats uttered by propertied men or abusive newspapers.[186] It was the poor, white men, to judge by the comparative poverty of such a large proportion of the people after the war,[187] who made up the forces which struggled under McEnery, Ogden, and Nicholls to restore Democratic home rule. They figured in the savage race riots at Colfax in 1873, and Coushatta in 1874,[188] marched among the five thousand citizens who participated in the New Orleans uprising of September 14, 1874,[189] and filled the ranks of the White League.

It is impossible to estimate the strength or to exaggerate the importance of an organization like the White League. When the New Orleans *Bulletin* put its enrollment at fourteen thousand men, "organized and armed," a North Louisiana paper claimed that there were at least ten thousand men who belonged to it in that region alone.[190] The support of newspapers in every part of the state indicated how widespread and strong the movement was.[191] Its temper was desperate, and grew especially bitter in 1874. Two years before, President Grant had robbed the McEnery-Warmoth coalition of their apparent electoral victory and placed Governor Kellogg in power with national troops.[192] The Louisiana Democrats, encouraged by national party successes in the lower house of Congress, were

[186] The *Shreveport Times*, under the vehement editorship of Leonard, set the tone for the country press in the northern parishes.

[187] See below, chaps. VIII, IX.

[188] See H. O. Lestage, Jr., "The White League in Louisiana and Its Participation in Reconstruction Riots," *L.H.Q.*, XVIII (July, 1935), 619–93.

[189] *Commercial Bulletin*, Sept. 13, 14; *Picayune*, Sept. 14; *Times*, Sept. 14, 1874; quoted in *Rpt. . . . on . . . Condition of the South*, 798–807, 814–34.

[190] *Minden Democrat*, Aug. 29, 1874, quoted in *ibid.*, 792.

[191] See citations from nine newspapers in *ibid.*, 764–68, 770–72.

[192] Randall, *op. cit.*, 869.

resolved to throw off the yoke of carpetbag rule. *"We intend to succeed by intimidation,"* not with guns but with a virtuous cause, declared the New Orleans *Times*.[193] But the Shreveport *Times* gave voice to the force which lay behind this peaceable profession: "If a single gun is fired between the whites and blacks in this and surrounding parishes, *every carpet-bagger and scalawag that can be caught will in twelve hours therefrom be dangling from a limb."* [194]

The local political parties, Democratic or "people's" and Republican, had divided the races and set them against one another.[195] Economic coercion of the Negro on the plantations, to change his allegiance or persuade him to be neutral, was approved and widely practiced.[196] Thus the stage was set for the overthrow of carpetbag government and the restoration of white supremacy.[197] All that was needed was a change in the national government, the succession of Hayes to the Presidency, to withdraw Federal soldiers in 1877, for they were the last mainstay of carpetbag rule.

"To use a modern phrase," remarks a recent historian, "government under Radical Republican rule in the South had become a kind of 'racket.' " [198] Charles Nordhoff, an intelligent observer who was the less prejudiced because he had been brought up to hate slavery and sympathize with the Negro, entered an eloquent judgment on conditions in Louisiana which has not been altered by research. A "small band of white men," he wrote in 1875, "have for more than six years

---

[193] Aug. 5, 1874, quoted in *Rpt. . . . on . . . Condition of the South*, [1875], 765.

[194] July 29, 1874, quoted in *ibid.*

[195] See the Baton Rouge platform of the white coalition "opposed to the Kellogg usurpation," in *Picayune*, Aug. 26, 1874, quoted in *ibid.*, 908–9. The Republican chairman, Packard, told Nordhoff, *op. cit.*, 41, that only about five thousand whites voted this party's ticket by 1874.

[196] E. g., *Shreveport Times*, Oct. 14, 1874.

[197] Randall, *loc. cit.*   [198] Randall, *op. cit.*, 852.

monopolized all political power and preferment in the State. They have laid, collected and spent (and largely misspent) all the taxes, local taxes as well as State; they have not only made all the laws, but they have arbitrarily changed them, and have miserably failed to enforce any which were for the people's good; they have openly and scandalously corrupted the colored men whom they have brought into political life; they have used unjust laws to perpetuate and extend their own power; and they have practiced all the basest arts of ballot-stuffing, false registration, and repeating, at election after election." [199] It was gang rule, the kind of government to which American cities were accustomed, but which had never seized a state with such flagrant impunity and ease until the destruction of reconstruction was visited upon Louisiana by misguided national politics and politicians.

There was no genuine relief to be anticipated for many years. After the withdrawal of Federal troops in 1877, white Democrats assumed power, but their "legislation . . . disappointed the people." [200] In the following year almost half the merchants of New Orleans rose in opposition.[201] "The Democratic party," testified a conservative lawyer who had fought for the overthrow of radical Republicanism, "had fallen into the hands of men who were using it . . . to their own ends for a few profitable local offices, and so arranging the election machinery as to deprive the people of a fair expression of the popular will." [202]

The habits of reconstruction politics were not easily broken; its vices lingered on; and special privileges of an economic and political character, notably the Louisiana Lottery, continued to corrupt the government. Nordhoff had predicted

[199] *Op. cit.,* 43.
[200] *Rpt.* . . . *into Alleged Frauds and Violence in the Elections of 1878, etc.,* 446.
[201] *Ibid.,* 435.   [202] *Ibid.,* 433, testimony of Clement L. Walker.

that after Federal interference ceased and white supremacy
had been assured, the Democratic party would split into two
factions, "and each will try, with the help of the negroes, to
beat the other." [203] This was to be the nemesis of Populism in
the nineties. It would then appear to all men that the evils of
reconstruction were not peculiar to carpetbag government or
to any race, but were rather of the nature of economic and
social conditions.

[203] *Op. cit.*, 42.

Chapter VIII

SURVIVAL OF THE PLANTATION SYSTEM

> Small farms and white labor or large farms and
> coolie labor may save the land.
>
> —Daniel Dennett [1]
>
> There is no sale for large tracts of land, and the
> multitude who want small tracts have no money
> to pay for them.
>
> —Picayune [2]
>
> Association is the only means of redeeming the
> working man from slavery.
>
> —C. E. Fenner [3]

Upon the economic reconstruction of Louisiana depended
the immediate livelihood of every family in the state. The
most pressing problem was who could work the land, not who
should rule it. "Cotton and corn," observed a country editor,
"will go further in solving the problem than talk about how we
are to get into the Union and stay in it when we get in." [4] But
economic reconstruction involved more than feeding, clothing, and sheltering a war-weary and nearly destitute people.
Whatever ways and means were contrived to supply these
necessities would determine the character of society in Louisiana for at least a generation. Economic rather than political
reform was required to ameliorate the condition of the majority of people.

[1] [St. Mary] *Planters' Banner*, quoted in *Commercial Bulletin*, Jan. 16, 1867.

[2] July 24, 1873.

[3] Speech before the Workmen's Benevolent Association, quoted in *Crescent*,
Dec. 20, 1865.

[4] *Pointe Coupee Echo*, Dec. 22, quoted in *Commercial Bulletin*, Dec. 27,
1866.

Neither planters nor merchants were interested in theories of political economy. They set to work to repair their buildings and equipment, plant the land, and start the wheels of commerce. Yet it was impossible to plant and trade in the old way, for the times had changed. The land lay in waste, the slaves were free but disorganized, and there was imperative need for credit to replace the capital destroyed by the ravages of war.[5] What was to be done with the land and labor? Where was capital to be obtained? Who would own the land, and who would rent it? Who would hire labor, and who would be hired? These were the vital problems that demanded immediate solution.

It has long been thought that after the Civil War plantations all over the South broke up into small farms.[6] Between 1860 and 1880, according to census reports, the number of Southern landholdings was doubled, increasing from 549,109 to 1,252,-249, and their average size was cut in half, declining from 365 to 157 acres.[7] Such evidence is still cited in historical textbooks to prove that the old plantation system was destroyed by an agrarian revolution.[8] This exaggerated idea arose from the failure of census marshals to distinguish between tenants and proprietors, leaseholds and freeholds.[9] Because land rented by sharecroppers was put in the same category as farms owned outright, and the several tracts held by a planter were not

[5] *De Bow's Review,* III (March, 1867), 305-6.

[6] The following pages on land tenure have been considerably expanded and rewritten from my study, "Survival of the Plantation System in Louisiana," *Journal of Southern History,* III (August, 1937), 311-25, with the kind permission of the editor, W. H. Stephenson.

[7] *U. S. Cen., 1910,* V, 878.

[8] E. g., Charles and Mary R. Beard, *The Rise of American Civilization* (New York, 1927), II, 269; H. J. Carman, *Social and Economic History of the United States* (Boston, 1934), II, 589-90; S. E. Morison and H. S. Commager, *The Growth of the American Republic* (New York, 1930), 627; (rev. and enl. ed., New York, 1937), II, 23-24.

[9] *Rpt. U. S. Com. Agric., 1886,* 418.

registered as a unit,[10] it appeared that peasants rather than peons had taken the place of slaves.[11] An example of the egregious result may be cited from the parish of Catahoula, where 171 farms of less than twenty acres were reported by a census marshal in 1890,[12] although the local tax assessor could find but nineteen.[13]

While there was beyond doubt considerable redistribution in the ownership of real estate, to an extent which the historian is unable to measure for want of accurate census records, nevertheless the plantation system was not obliterated. Since it "was less dependent upon slavery than slavery was upon it," it might be expected to survive the abolition of Negro bondage.[14] In fertile regions where colored labor was plentiful, the large estate remained the primary basis of agricultural production. Far from there being any agrarian turnover, change was confined to methods of labor and finance. Planters thought it best, like a South Carolinian, "to work *several farms* on the same plantation," allotting parcels of their land to freedmen and controlling them through a form of credit known as the crop-lien.[15] Fields once cultivated by gangs of slaves came to be worked by families who shared the produce with landlords; but the subdivision of these estates did not change their ownership. There was less discipline of labor and consequently

[10] This deficiency makes it impossible to use the separate classification of land and landholders according to tenure, which was inaugurated by the census in 1880, as an index of the plantation system.

[11] There are several excellent studies of the development of peonage, especially in Georgia. See E. M. Banks, *The Economics of Land Tenure in Georgia* (New York, 1905); R. P. Brooks, *The Agrarian Revolution in Georgia, 1865-1912* (Madison, 1914); C. M. Thompson, *Reconstruction in Georgia* (New York, 1915). Only Brooks, however, seems to appreciate the difficulties raised by the old census methods; see *op. cit.*, 41-45.

[12] *U.S. Cen., 1890, Agric. Statistics*, 148.

[13] MS *Assessment Roll, 1891*, Parish of Catahoula.

[14] Phillips, "The Decadence of the Plantation System," *Annals*, XXXV, 37.

[15] Jas. E. Crosland, Barnwell Dist., S. C., Feb. 20, 1867, to T. C. Peters, *A Report upon the Condition of the South, etc.* (Baltimore, 1867), 20-21.

less profit for capital than under the black codes of slavery. But "the planter princes of the old time," as Henry W. Grady observed, did not vanish from the South: they were "still lords of acres, though not of slaves." [16] When this fact was at last recognized by the census officials in 1910, they made a special survey of black belt counties, and for the first time designated as a plantation any continuous tract of land which was controlled by an individual or corporation but subdivided for cultivation among at least five tenants.[17] According to this criterion, over one-third of the landholdings in the black belt were found to be organized in plantations. The average size of these estates was 724 acres, or more than six times the average previously reported for all properties without regard to their consolidated ownership.[18] In Louisiana, where almost half the parishes were canvassed, two-fifths of the cultivated land was found to be organized in plantations, which averaged 904 acres in extent as compared with an average of 95 acres reported under the old census methods in 1900.[19]

Although this survey revealed the preservation of plantations, it came too late to correct the contrary reports of earlier decades or to explain how large estates survived the vicissitudes of reconstruction. Considerable light is shed on these two problems by the hitherto unexamined manuscript assessment rolls of Louisiana,[20] the state which it is most significant to consider because it boasted the greatest plantations in 1910.[21] Unfortunately, these ledgers leave much to be desired: almost all rolls before 1873 have been lost or destroyed; returns during

[16] "Cotton and Its Kingdom," *Harper's New Monthly Magazine*, LXIII. (October, 1881), 722.

[17] *U. S. Cen., 1910*, V, 878.   [18] *Ibid.*, 878, 880, 889.

[19] *Ibid.*, 880, 887, 889; *U. S. Cen., 1900*, V, 88.

[20] Stored in the basement of the new Capitol at Baton Rouge.

[21] Although Mississippi had the largest proportion of land organized into plantations, they were smaller than those of Louisiana. *U. S. Cen., 1910*, V, 886, 889.

reconstruction were grossly defective; until 1891 no distinction was made between the races to which owners and tenants belonged; and the number of tenants on each plantation was never recorded. But these local tax lists are a better index to agrarian tenure than the national census reports because they show the size of properties according to their actual ownership, and do not confuse proprietors with lessees, nor the patch of a sharecropper with a farm held in fee simple.

A typical cross section of the distribution of real estate in the planting regions of Louisiana after the Civil War is to be found in five parishes. Two, Concordia in cotton and Iberville in sugar cane, represent the great plantations and staple crops of the Mississippi River bottoms. Two more, Catahoula and Lafourche, illustrate conditions in the adjoining regions of mixed soil and varied topography, where small properties were interspersed among the large, again in either staple. The last parish, Natchitoches, is divided between the cotton-growing alluvium of the Red River and the farming uplands of the north, where agrarian discontent broke forth in Populism during the nineties.[22] Two of the parishes, Lafourche and Catahoula, contained a majority of white people; the others belonged to the black belt.[23]

The following table presents a statistical description of landholdings in these representative parishes. Furthermore, in another part, to these parishes have been added four others, De Soto, Red River, Sabine, and Winn, to include a greater proportion of small farming districts and thus to make sure that the plantation belt is offset by upland regions where the most striking increase in farms might be expected. These additional parishes were the piney woods home of Populism; only

[22] For topography, soil, and staples, see E. W. Hilgard, "Report on the Cotton Production of the State of Louisiana," *U. S. Cen., 1880,* V, 47–48, 51, 55, 66.

[23] *U. S. Cen., 1890,* I, 489–90.

Red River belonged to the black belt and had many plantations. Because the number of tenants on each estate was never reported, even by local assessors, the size of a property is the only available criterion for distinguishing farms from plantations. Local usage suggests the classification of all properties of more than a hundred acres as plantations,[24] but since larger estates might also be cultivated without tenants, tracts larger than five hundred acres, which were impossible to operate except as tenant plantations, are segregated and compared with those under fifty-one acres, which could not support more than the family of the owner. Whatever doubt remains as to the validity of these somewhat arbitrary distinctions may be resolved by reference to the proportions of ownership and tenancy. The table is divided into a static description of the distribution of landholdings in each decade, and a dynamic analysis of the rate of increase or decrease by decades.

THE AGRARIAN PATTERN, 1860 80

(According to selected parishes) [25]

PART I—STATIC DESCRIPTION IN PERCENTAGES

Five Parishes	1860	1873	1880
All Landholders	100.00	100.00	100.00
Proprietors	.....	56.99	52.92
Tenants	.....	43.01	47.08
All Landholdings	100.00	100.00	100.00
Farms (under 101 acres)	65.74	26.02	29.86
Plantations (over 100 acres)	34.26	73.98	70.14
All Farms	100.00	100.00	100.00
under 51 acres	78.16	48.15	53.21
51–100 acres	21.84	51.85	46.79

[24] It was said in 1890 that a farm in the hills of northern Louisiana did not exceed 15 acres per hand. *Proc. La. State Agric. Soc.*, 1890, 30–31. A family of seven able-bodied men and women, boys and girls, could cultivate 105 acres; additional tillage would require tenants.

[25] All percentages are computed from figures in the MSS *Assessment Rolls* except those for 1860, which are derived from the *U.S. Cen., 1860, Agric.*, 202. For the actual figures, see Appendix, Table 9.

PART I [continued]—STATIC DESCRIPTION IN PERCENTAGES

Five Parishes	1860	1873	1880
All Plantations	100.00	100.00	100.00
101–500 acres	67.63	64.06	69.11
over 500 acres	32.37	35.94	30.89

Nine Parishes	1860	1873	1880
All Landholders	100.00	100.00	100.00
Proprietors	.....	60.08	54.71
Tenants	.....	39.92	45.29
All Landholdings	100.00	100.00	100.00
Farms (under 101 acres)	68.71	28.23	31.79
Plantations (over 100 acres)	31.29	71.77	68.21
All Farms	100.00	100.00	100.00
under 51 acres	75.35	43.27	45.99
51–100 acres	24.65	56.73	54.01
All Plantations	100.00	100.00	100.00
101–500 acres	75.46	67.65	72.49
over 500 acres	24.54	32.35	27.51

PART II—DYNAMIC DESCRIPTION OF CHANGES IN PERCENTAGES

Five Parishes	1860–73	1873–80	1860–80
All Landholdings	+ 49.0	+ 26.6	+ 88.5
All Farms	− 41.0	+ 45.2	− 14.4
All Plantations	+ 221.7	+ 20.0	+ 286.0
Proprietors	....	+ 19.0	....
Tenants	....	+ 40.3	....
Agricultural Valuation	−85.2 *	− 2.4	− 85.6 *
Nonresident Values	....	+ 11.5	....

Nine Parishes	1860–73	1873–80	1860–80
All Landholdings	+ 49.4	+ 19.8	+ 78.9
All Farms	− 38.6	+ 34.9	− 17.2
All Plantations	+ 242.8	+ 13.8	+ 290.1
Proprietors	....	+ 15.0	....
Tenants	....	+ 43.2	....
Agricultural Valuation	− 82.5 *	− 1.7	− 82.8 *
Nonresident Values	....	+ 8.0	....

* Exclusive of slaves in 1860.

From this table it is apparent that the plantation system in Louisiana not only survived but also expanded after the Civil War. Between 1860 and 1880 there was nearly a threefold increase in the number of plantations while the number of farms actually decreased. The tendency of the larger properties to outstrip the smaller was strong between 1860 and 1873, and was only partially counteracted in the later years of reconstruction. The multiplication of plantations was accompanied, as might be expected, by an increase of tenancy and absentee landlordship.

Although there was little difference between the agrarian patterns of five and nine parishes, despite the predominantly farming character of the latter, there was a considerable difference between earlier and later years. Farmers survived the ordeal of reconstruction better than planters and tended to increase after 1873. But tenancy spread faster than proprietorship. To look ahead, lest it might be imagined that the plantation system met its doom in later decades, by the end of the century over half the landholders no longer claimed possession of the soil they tilled, and plantations had multiplied to embrace over half the landholdings in the state.

The increase of great estates throughout the century had such cumulative effect that although Louisiana had contained more farms than plantations in 1860,[26] it was dominated by agrarian monopoly in 1900, when its proportion of absentee ownership and overseer management was the largest in the South, and the highest, except for Wyoming, in the entire United States.[27] The evolution of the agrarian pattern in Louisiana was obviously away from the Jeffersonian ideal of free-

[26] *U.S. Cen., 1860, Agric.,* 202. Cf. Gray, *History of Agriculture in the Southern United States to 1860,* I, 530; II, 903.

[27] J. H. Blodgett, "Wages of Farm Labor in the United States," *U.S. Dept. Agric., Miscel. Ser. Bull. no. 26* (Washington, 1903), 54–55.

hold farming and toward the tenancy and insecurity which burden agriculture today.

But the plantation system did not survive in Louisiana without a struggle, bitter and prolonged. Planters were threatened first with confiscation during reconstruction, then with bankruptcy and foreclosure because of adverse economic conditions, and finally with subdivision of their domains at the behest of agrarian philosophers, whose program seemed to be the only solution for grave difficulties of labor and finance.

First to endanger landed property were the freedmen and their radical sympathizers at Washington, Republicans like Carl Schurz and Thaddeus Stevens. "In the independent possession of landed property," as Schurz observed, many Negroes "saw the consummation of their deliverance"; [28] otherwise they would "be liberated from domestic slavery, only to be remitted to slavery to skill and capital." [29] Rumor ran wild through the South that the Negro might obtain "forty acres and a mule" from the expropriation of his old master,[30] and there was apprehension of a colored uprising at Christmas in 1865.[31] In response to a petition from frightened Louisiana planters, General Fullerton of the local Freedmen's Bureau warned the Negro that he was free—free to work, but not to seize his employer's land. "There is no way for you to live but by hard work," Fullerton advised the colored folk. "There is no possible way by which you can procure houses and land for yourselves but by working hard and saving your wages. . . . The Government will not do more for

---

[28] "Report of Carl Schurz on the States of South Carolina, Georgia, Alabama, Mississippi, and Louisiana," *Sen. Ex. Docs.*, 39 Cong., 1 sess., I, no. 2, 30–31.

[29] *De Bow's Review*, III (A. W. S.), 353.

[30] Fleming, *Documentary History of Reconstruction*, I, 350–60.

[31] *Crescent*, Oct. 20, 1865.

you than for the white laborers who are your neighbors."[32]
The landless poor, whether black or white, were not to receive
title to the fields in which they toiled. Southern planters became confident that the agrarian ambitions of Thaddeus
Stevens, to distribute Confederate domains among the freedmen,[33] would be repulsed by Northern conservatives lest such
a revolutionary example excite their own factory hands to
demand a similar division of industrial property.[34]

The specter of agrarianism appeared next in New Orleans
with the inauguration of military reconstruction. When radical
Negro leaders lost faith in the prospect of Federal confiscation,[35] they advised their race to rent and work plantations in
co-operative associations,[36] and to save enough money to buy
sections of the great estates for individual homesteads.[37] To
break up plantations by forcing the sale of small tracts, some
colored delegates to the Constitutional Convention of 1868
proposed that the purchase of more than 150 acres at distress
sales be prohibited. A representative of the poor whites joined
this agrarian bloc with the suggestion that uncultivated land be
taxed double the rate of land in use.[38] But the steering committee, which had a white majority,[39] defeated such threats to
the plantation system; only land sold by order of the courts
was to be broken up into small tracts.[40] After a brief skirmish,
the more progressive Negro leaders abandoned all dreams of

[32] *Ibid.*, Oct. 21, 1865.
[33] *Nation*, IV (May 2, 1867), 345; J. A. Woodburn, *Life of Thaddeus
Stevens* (Indianapolis, 1913), 521–35.
[34] *De Bow's Review*, IV (December, 1867), 587–88.
[35] Cf. Du Bois, *Black Reconstruction*, 459–67.   [36] *Tribune*, Feb. 24, 1865.
[37] *St. Landry Progress*, Apr. 11, 1868.
[38] *Const. Conv. J.*, *1868*, 110, 266–67, 306.
[39] Cf. Warmoth, *War, Politics and Reconstruction; etc.* 54–55; Du Bois,
op. cit., 468.
[40] *Const. Conv. J.*, 266, 306; *Const. 1868, Art.* 132.

agrarian reform; [41] so ended the freedmen's short-lived and feeble attack on landed property.

Although planters were now secure in legal title to their domains, they sometimes lost them beneath the crushing load of taxes imposed by corrupt and extravagant reconstruction legislatures.[42] From the election of Governor Warmoth in 1868 to the downfall of Governor Packard in 1877, the tax rate doubled, and climbed to a peak of 21½ mills.[43] Property had lost nearly half its value, but individual taxes were increased twofold.[44] To avoid expropriation by an avaricious government, planters often pledged standing crops for money to meet their public obligations.[45] The property of citizens who were hopelessly in arrears, when sold at depreciated auction prices, brought the state over a quarter of a million dollars.[46] Fully as oppressive as this burdensome taxation was the arbitrary and inequitable assessment on which it was based. Radicals complained that river-bottom plantations were never

[41] *St. Landry Progress*, Apr. 11, 1868. This intelligent organ of the progressive colored minority deserves more attention: it shows the different course reconstruction might have taken had it not been corrupted by scalawags, carpetbaggers, and ignorant negroes.

[42] Cf. Lonn, *Reconstruction in Louisiana after 1868*, 344–45.

[43] *Rpt. Audit. Pub. Accts., 1879*, 291. Estimates of the taxation and debt of reconstruction vary; our figures are taken from the final summary of the conservatives when restored to power. But Nordhoff, *The Cotton States*, 57, declared that state taxes rose from 37½ cents per $100 in 1867 to $1.45 in 1874.

[44] *U. S. Cen., 1890, Rpt. on Wealth, Debt, and Taxation*, 14, 61.

[45] *Rpt. Audit. Pub. Accts., 1871*, 181.

[46] *Ibid., 1879*, 290. Hard hit was New Orleans, Nordhoff reports, with 47,491 tax seizures by the sheriff between November of 1871 and of 1873. *The Cotton States*, 62. Lonn, *op. cit.*, 345 *n.*, cites the *New Orleans Times*, Feb. 16, 1875, which advertised sheriff sales that would "deprive one hundred and two families of homes." The situation was almost as bad in the country. See *Opelousas Courier*, Oct. 30, 1869; *Shreveport Times*, May 30, 1873. Nordhoff, *op. cit.*, 59, 62, reports 821 sales for 1871–73, but it is not clear whether they were in St. Landry or St. Martin, since the same figures are cited for both, and whether the number refers to parcels of land or to public sales.

taxed enough,[47] and conservatives objected that taxation was unequal and confiscatory, a weapon of official reprisals.[48] When such injustice could no longer be borne, a Tax Resisting Association was organized in 1873,[49] and its stubborn fight against the exploitation of private property by corrupt public officials contributed to the eventual collapse of reconstruction. The *Shreveport Times* took a conspicuous part in this revolt; its editorial propaganda demonstrated that the power of taxation had become an instrument of destruction to the capital of both planters and merchants.[50] Their desperate situation was revealed by the Constitutional Convention of 1879, whose delegates complained that the landed interests had been nearly taxed out of existence, and cited in proof such parishes as Union, where fourteen hundred people were in arrears; Lafayette, where a considerable proportion of land had been forfeited to the state; and Caddo, where it was claimed that taxes left the planter no margin of profit.[51] The temper of outraged landlords found vent in many economic safeguards of the new constitution. Delinquent taxpayers were granted relief, the legislature was forbidden to contract future debts except to suppress insurrection, and the ordinary tax rate was reduced to six mills.[52] Planters who weathered the storms of reconstruction made the new constitution a bulwark of their agricultural system.

How many cotton plantations had changed hands, and how

[47] *Rpt. Audit. Pub. Accts., 1871*, 158; *Msg. Gov. Kellogg to G. A., 1875*, 5.

[48] *Rpt. Atty. Gen., 1878*, 9–10. On this whole question, especially for New Orleans, see Nordhoff, *loc. cit.*

[49] *Picayune*, Apr. 25, 1873; cf. Nordhoff, *op. cit.*, 59.

[50] *Shreveport Times*, Apr. 29, 1873, *et passim*, 1872–76; Nordhoff, *op. cit.*, 42.

[51] "Report of the Committee on Public Debt," *Proc. Const. Conv., 1879*, App., 89, 60, 65, 80.

[52] *Const. 1879*, reprinted in *Rpt. La. Secy. State, 1902*, 220, 217, 174–75, 205.

often, it is impossible to judge. [53] What evidence is available argues against any sudden or sweeping overturn in ownership, for contemporary newspapers made no mention of wholesale transfers. [54] Distress sales, of course, were ordered by the courts after the war to settle estates and liquidate mortgages; [55] a few properties were sold or leased to emigrants and adventurers from the North and West. [56] The names of several old cotton planters were no longer heard after 1865. A majority of antebellum families survived, but in depressed circumstances. Representative of those who had most to lose and lost the most were the Rouths of Tensas, who owned four plantations worth over $800,000 in 1860, when 2,918 bales of cotton were produced, and retained only one small estate in 1870. Scores of families in Tensas could be mentioned—the Andrews, Buckners, Harrisons, Lynches, Montgomerys, and Penns—who had once operated large plantations with handsome profit but now managed simply to hang on to them for a comfortable livelihood. Estates which remained intact generally suffered drastic reduction in the amount of cotton and land which were cultivated. S. C. Daniels, for example, raised 1,125 bales of cotton on 1,785 acres in 1860; ten years later, his widow produced 339 bales on 1,010 acres. [57] Few were the old planters who enjoyed an increased prosperity. Notable among their number was James Gillespie of Tensas, who raised 385 bales of cotton on property valued at $78,500 in 1860, and during the next

[53] Cotton plantations were never reported in a commercial census such as those of P. A. Champomier and L. Bouchereau for sugar.

[54] Cf. *Picayune* and *Commercial Bulletin*, 1866–76.   [55] See above, 192–93.

[56] J. T. Trowbridge, *The South* (Hartford, 1866), 411; Reid, *After the War*, 454–55; *Rpt. Bur. Immig., 1868*, 8. These transactions had begun during the war. See *La. H. Debs., 1864*, 135. Allan Nevins believes that three out of four emigrants "failed ignominiously," *The Emergence of Modern America 1865–1878*, 22; if so, the fourth succeeded magnificently, as in the case of John S. Dymond. Cf. Nordhoff, *The Cotton States*, 71. See below, *n.* 68.

[57] MS *Returns, U. S. Cen., 1860, 1870, La. Agric.* All names are taken from the enumeration of Tensas plantations.

twenty years almost doubled his production on three times as much land.[58]

By 1880 it became apparent in the black belt that the plantation system had been preserved in the cultivation of cotton. Some estates were larger, others were smaller, and all were generally less productive per acre than before the war. Many properties, especially in East Carroll, had passed into the hands of partnerships or companies which administered them through the agency of managers and overseers. New families with names strange to the region were to be found everywhere. But all these changes in ownership and operation failed to disrupt the plantation system. Its destruction appeared to be complete from the erroneous returns of a census marshal in Tensas who reported the "farms" operated by sharecroppers in one district as separate tracts running from five to twenty-two acres each.[59] On another page of the ledger, however, a marshal was overcome by his sense of reality, and fell into old ways and habits of thinking. Under "Plantations" he listed the following estates in order, which may be regarded as representative plantations: [60]

ACREAGE		VALUE ($1,000's)		PRODUCTION (bales—bu.)	
Cultivated	Woods	Property	Products	Cotton	Corn
1) 400	1,700	$25	$22	503	1,500
2) 330	100	6	20	513	——
3) 260	60	8	10	260	650
4) 120	40	4	5	128	600
5) 120	40	4	5	138	320
6) 200	436	3	8	200	1,000
7) 175	120	2.5	7	190	700
8) 500	——	10	13	300	1,000
9) 715	960	30	30	633	4,500

[58] Cf. ibid., 1880.
[59] Ibid., Ward 5, Tensas, Wm. Shannon to Robinson Page.
[60] Ibid.

His figures for value and production were hardly correct, and those for acreage were probably approximate. His error, according to the census, was to enumerate these properties as "plantations," but actually this was the only respect in which he did not err. The feudal pattern of the surviving plantation system was everywhere in evidence, even on the returns of the census marshals.

This was especially true of the Sugar Bowl, where large estates continued to be more common than in cotton, but with greater changes in ownership. The expensive and speculative nature of sugar cultivation, which combined a highly capitalized manufacture with a none too reliable agriculture,[61] led to a revolution in land titles. The prospect of handsome profits attracted capitalists from East and West.[62] They organized partnerships and corporations, and purchased plantations at one-fifth the ante-bellum prices, sometimes for $10,000 or less.[63] Levees were repaired, sugar mills were equipped with new, improved machinery, and seed cane was bought from estates which maintained production during the war. Although crops were comparatively poor in 1866 and 1867, new planters with capital were better able to survive than the old.[64] Consequently, many estates changed hands. Sales were temporarily diminished by a profitable season in 1868.[65] By the following year, however, almost half the planters bore names that slaveholding families would not have recognized. The

[61] L. Bouchereau, *Statement of the Sugar and Rice Crops Made in La.*, 1870–71, viii–xiv.

[62] *Commercial Bulletin*, Sept. 1, 1870. Twenty per cent was said to be a very conservative return on the capital invested in sugar. See Latham, *White and Black*, 169.

[63] *De Bow's Review*, III (March, 1867), 308; *Commercial Bulletin*, Sept. 20, 1867.

[64] Bouchereau, *op. cit.*, 11–15, 40–44; *Picayune*, July 29, 1873; Nordhoff, *The Cotton States, etc.*, 69.

[65] *Crescent*, Jan. 29, 1869.

new element largely represented corporations.[66] Failures among the older and poorer proprietors mounted higher after the bad seasons from 1869 to 1872.[67] On an increasing scale, plantations fell into the hands of a new, capitalistic sugar aristocracy, organized in corporations and financed by banks. At least half the planters after 1870 were either Northern men or were supported by Northern money.[68]

Representative of the larger sugar estates which survived in the Sugar Bowl were nine properties listed as follows by a census marshal of Iberville in 1880.[69]

| | ACREAGE | | | VALUE | PRODUCTION |
| | | | Old | | (hhds.) |
Cultivated	Meadows	Woods	Fields	Machinery	
1) 900	50	250	200	$20,000	225
2) 1,500	50	250	200	20,000	225
3) 450	100	200	300	35,000	150
4) 400	125	200	75	20,000	242
5) 700	150	1,000	250	50,000	332
6) 287	50	30	257	2,000	———
7) 750	100	400	———	5,000	325
8) 800	45	650	100	35,000	325
9) 800	45	300	200	30,000	265

[66] Bouchereau, op. cit., 1868–69, 1–47.

[67] Picayune, Sept. 1, 1871; July 29, 1873.

[68] Cf. Nordhoff, op. cit., 69; H. L. Abbott, "The Lowlands of the Mississippi," The Galaxy, V (1868), 445. This does not indicate a vast Northern exodus to Louisiana; in 1900 only 3 per cent of the population, or 20,838 men and women, were reported as having been born in a Northern state. U. S. Cen., 1900, I, 690–93. Not their number but their ability made Northerners conspicuous, especially in sugar. John Dymond of New York, for example, became the enterprising leader of the post-bellum sugar industry. The carpet-bag governor, Henry Clay Warmoth, represented another type of Northern planter. See his papers in the University of North Carolina Library.

[69] MS Federal Census Returns, La., 1880, Agric., Iberville, 1st ward. These figures, like those tabulated above for cotton, are only approximate. The first two sugar plantations, (1) and (2), were owned by one man, and the figures for value and production are probably joint totals.

In both cotton and sugar the processes of credit and aliena-
tion preserved the plantation system, if not always the ante-
bellum planters. Factors, merchants, and banks in New Orleans enabled them to resume cultivation of their land at the
end of the war when money was easy to borrow.[70] The cotton
crops of 1866 and 1867 were almost total failures: floods de-
layed planting, army worms stripped the stalks, and drought
alternated with heavy rains.[71] After the disastrous season of
1866, it was reported that not one planter in five could start
the next year without giving a lien on his crop for supplies.[72]
When cotton failed again, many planters faced utter destitution.[73] They suffered more from these setbacks, it was said,
than from all the ravages of war.[74] It is extremely doubtful
if the plantation system could have sustained the ruin of war,
crop failures, and the constant political burden of reconstruction, without the credit extended on the basis of crop liens and
blanket mortgages.

Luckily for the larger landholders, however, sufficient capital was generally available in New Orleans, where it accumulated from Northern and foreign investments and the
profits of commerce.[75] "British and other European houses that
deal in exchange," observed Somers in 1871, brought "great
resources to bear on moving the cotton crop." [76] It is really
extraordinary that after 1865 the local money market suffered
no contraction except the periodic stringency which affected
the entire nation at times of severe depression.[77] It was estimated that in 1871 the New Orleans banks and factors ad-

[70] *Commercial Bulletin*, Dec. 22, 1866.

[71] *Ibid.*, Oct. 17, Dec. 22, 1866; *Picayune*, Sept. 19, 1867; *Southern Sentinel*,
Nov. 30, Dec. 21, 1867. For an excellent description of why cotton failed, see
De Bow's Review, III (A. W. S.), 306.

[72] *Commercial Bulletin*, Dec. 22, 1866.   [73] *Picayune*, Aug. 6, 1867.

[74] Dunn, *Morehouse Parish*, 28–29.   [75] *Picayune*, Sept. 1, 1866.

[76] *The Southern States Since the War*, 210.   [77] *Picayune*, Aug. 6, 1875.

vanced $30,000,000 on the next season's crops.[78] While planters paid interest as high as 25 per cent for financial accommodation and soon found themselves bound hand and foot by the crop lien and blanket mortgage, it was this chain of credit which not only revived plantations after the war but also preserved them intact whenever the burden of debt pushed them into bankruptcy.[79] The title to an estate often changed, but seldom its size, for every acre, with all its equipment and crops, was collateral for the credit necessary to work it. Planters and merchants were therefore unable to subdivide their landholdings with any profit, and transfers of title or equity precluded the disintegration of landed monopoly.

No less than the planter or merchant, the Negro helped to maintain large estates by continuing to supply the necessary labor. Learning how to handle freedmen was the chief vexation suffered by planters. They realized that "land without labor is worthless," [80] and at first despaired of obtaining efficient service from the emancipated Negro. Ex-slaves were too demoralized to give promise of working the land.[81] They flocked by the thousands to New Orleans and Shreveport for a season and left their former masters alone in the fields.[82] Conservative pessimists admonished the planters to become independent of colored labor by tilling the soil with their own hands: "Let the white man go to work as if he were Robinson Crusoe, without a man Friday." [83] When the Freedmen's Bureau sent Negroes

[78] *Ibid.*, Sept. 1, 1871. These credits, of course, were made to planters in the whole lower Mississippi Valley and not only to those in Louisiana. In this year, 1871, there were eleven banks operating in New Orleans with a paid-up capital of $7,497,182, total deposits of $15,039,499 which bore no interest, and aggregate assets of $26,944,732. Dividends ran from 9 to 30 per cent. Somers, *op. cit.*, 210-11.

[79] *Ibid.*, Aug. 13, 1873; *Commercial Bulletin*, Sept. 1, 1869; Sept. 1, 1870; *Proc. La. State Agric. Soc.*, *1890*, 36; *1891*, 71.

[80] *Rpt. U. S. Com. Agric.*, *1867*, 426.

[81] *De Bow's Review*, III (A. W. S.), 332.

[82] *Crescent*, Nov. 14, 17, 1865.   [83] *Picayune*, Dec. 1, 1867.

back to the land, however, contracts were made for their services, first in wages, and then in shares of the crop.[84]

It was a slow and difficult process for planter and freedman alike to develop a new system of labor. Because the free Negro did not work as hard as a slave,[85] had less supervision and discipline, and bargained for better terms or landlords during reconstruction,[86] it was generally believed by white people that "the great study and ambition of the race [was] to avoid labor." [87] Trouble often arose because planters would compete with one another in bidding for hands. This practice almost demoralized Negroes on the sugar plantations, according to Bouchereau,[88] and led to unorganized strikes and much dalliance before signing contracts for a new year.[89]

The right of freedmen to strike was not recognized by planters who had long been accustomed to the absolute control of slaves. When Negroes on the sugar plantations in Terrebonne, for example, objected to the planters setting a uniform maximum wage of thirteen dollars a month, and attacked workingmen who refused to strike, the militia intervened. A Negro sheriff appeared with a posse of colored and white people. Ringleaders were quickly arrested, and the discontented sent back to work. To planters this affair looked like an insurrection rather than a strike. It was, however, an earnest attempt by the Negro to secure better working conditions, for he demanded the right to form unions, rent lands by pledging his crop, and receive wages in money for other tasks.[90] This so-called Terrebonne "riot," in which no one was killed or injured, showed that the planter believed absolute control of colored labor was necessary for the profitable cultivation of his

[84] *Rpt. U. S. Com. Agric., 1867,* 416–17.

[85] *De Bow's Review,* III, 356.   [86] E. g., *Crescent,* Jan. 22, 29, 1869.

[87] [St. Mary] *Planters' Banner,* quoted in *Commercial Bulletin,* Jan. 16, 1867.

[88] *Statement of the Sugar and Rice Crops Made in La., 1869–70,* ix–x.

[89] *Crescent,* Feb. 11, 1869.   [90] *Picayune,* Jan. 10, 14, 16, 17, 18, 20, 1874.

estate. It was notorious that white workingmen would not submit to such discipline. When Germans were imported from New York to work on a sugar plantation, they deserted for higher wages within a day after their arrival at New Orleans.[91] Hence the planter preferred to have inefficient but docile freedmen on his land, and upon their labor hung the value of his estate.

Because the Sugar Bowl was the hothouse of colored Republican politics, and labor was sometimes more preoccupied with electioneering than grinding cane,[92] planters in this section found it hardest to operate their estates. They resented the fact that Negroes were always ready to ask for higher wages at the beginning of each season, and laid this insolent "mischief" to the agitation of Republican politicians.[93] But the passing years brought many painful adjustments. Landholders became merchants to their laborers and "relieved them of surplus funds" at good rates of interest.[94] Sheltered, clothed, and directed by the planter, Negroes tended to revert to the daily routine of slavery, without its severest discipline and restrictions. Constant immigration of colored people from the upper South, hunting lucrative jobs on the delta plantations, provided a fair supply of labor, if never enough.[95]

From the difficulties of adapting ex-slaves to plantation tenantry sprang an agrarian philosophy which championed the subdivision of estates. Its most articulate and untiring advocate was Daniel Dennett, editor of the [St. Mary] *Planters' Banner* in the Sugar Bowl, who later preached his gospel from the agricultural columns of the *Picayune*.[96] He was seconded by Bouchereau, compiler of the sugar annual, who saw in small

[91] Trowbridge, *The South*, 414.
[92] [West Baton Rouge] *Sugar Planter*, Dec. 3, quoted in *Commercial Bulletin*, Dec. 7, 1870.
[93] *Ibid.*, Jan. 9, quoted in *Crescent*, Jan. 12, 1869.
[94] *Tensas Gazette*, quoted in *Commercial Bulletin*, Dec. 27, 1866.
[95] *Rpt. La. Com. Emig., 1870*, 7–8.   [96] Jan. 24, 1873, *et passim*.

freeholds an agrarian system which would replace colored peons with a thrifty white yeomanry.[97] James De Bow, famous political economist of slavery, had earlier declared that "the South must throw her immense cultivated domain into the market at a low price, reduce the quantity of land held by individual proprietors, and . . . induce an influx of population and capital from abroad." [98] The press had expected this change to follow the abolition of slavery. Typical was the confident prophecy of the *Picayune,* looking forward to white immigration: "Farms will multiply and plantations will diminish." [99] When an influx of settlers did not appear, it was realized that efforts must be made to attract them. The inefficiency of the freedmen was difficult to tolerate. "Small farms and white labor," as Dennett said, "or large farms and coolie labor may save the land." [100]

First to be tried was the latter alternative. To preserve the plantation system and discipline the Negro, it was planned to import enough Chinese to force the freedmen to choose between competition and starvation.[101] The prospect of Chinese labor, cheap but contented and industrious,[102] was as attractive to planters as to railway magnates on the Pacific Coast. Arrangements were made by the Louisiana commissioner of immigration with the Chinese embassy in Washington.[103] Freedmen were warned that "the cheapest and best labor must command the market," even if it forced them to retire like the Indian to unwanted land.[104] Competition between Chinese and Negroes, it was claimed, would teach the latter to be industrious and thrifty.[105] Some Orientals were brought from Cuba

[97] *Statement of the Sugar and Rice Crops Made in La.,* 1870–71, xix–xx.
[98] *De Bow's Review,* I (A.W.S.), 8.   [99] July 2, 1865.
[100] *Planters' Banner,* quoted in *Commercial Bulletin,* Jan. 16, 1867.
[101] *Ibid.,* Sept. 1, 1870; *Opelousas Courier,* Aug. 21, 1869.
[102] *De Bow's Review,* IV (A.W.S.), 151–52, 362–63.
[103] *Rpt. La. Bur. Immig., 1869,* 4–5.   [104] *Opelousas Courier,* Aug. 21, 1869.
[105] *Commercial Bulletin,* Sept. 1, 1870.

in 1866,[106] and in the following years, colonies of Catholic Chinese from the Philippines.[107] But they soon deserted the plantations to become independent fishermen and truck farmers for the New Orleans market.[108] The idea of keeping large estates intact by replacing Negroes with coolies proved to be a fantasy, if only because Louisiana planters could not compete with the wages offered Oriental labor in California and on the Pacific railroads.[109]

Dennett's other alternative was "small farms and white labor," which required immigration, because native piney woods farmers lacked the desire as well as the means to buy tracts of plantation land. They raised no cry in the press even for the confiscation and distribution of such property. The lowlands, where it was situated, had never attracted them. This region seemed a deathly place because of its malaria, typhoid, and yellow fever. It was, moreover, the black belt, and poor piney woods people were indifferent if not hostile to having poor Negroes for neighbors. Nor did they wish to undertake the arduous task of cultivating the fertile alluvium, which had to be plowed twice and then grew weeds much faster than cotton. The farmer was accustomed to working a small tract of light, sandy land with the help of his family; he could not suddenly change his habits and become a planter.[110] If he had really wanted river-bottom land, there were scores of plantations, deserted since the war, which he could occupy without paying a cent or risking more than a lawsuit.[111] But he preferred to remain on his farm, because he was relatively better off after the war than many planters.[112] The farmer did not

[106] *Opelousas Courier*, Oct. 23, 1869.
[107] *Rpt. La. Com. Emig., 1870*, 9; *Commercial Bulletin*, Nov. 9, 1870.
[108] *Rpt. La. Com. Emig., 1870*, 10.   [109] *Picayune*, Jan. 9, 30, 1870.
[110] *Democrat*, Sept. 22, 1880; and interviews with H. L. Brian, *et al.*, May 1, 2, 1933. Cf. above, chaps. II, IV.
[111] Lockett MS, 215–17.
[112] *Rpt. La. Com. Emig., 1870*, 11–13; and see below, 272.

have the expense of repairing levees and paying heavy interest charges on loans from New Orleans. He was seldom hampered by the inefficient labor of freedmen, for he did his own work. What little cotton he grew yielded him proportionally more net cash than the planter's large crop. Hiding the money in his log cabin, the piney woods farmer continued to follow self-sufficient ways, making his own clothes, producing all the food for his family except coffee, paying only four or five dollars in taxes, and spending but a few more on dry goods and tools.[113] He remained a backwoodsman and humble tiller of the soil, content with his lot; a planter's lordly acres were not in his dream of Heaven.

To recruit white labor for farms and plantations, all eyes turned to Europe. The Southern Commercial Convention met at New Orleans in 1869 and resolved that "the cheap lands of the Southern States should be brought into competition with the public lands of the Northwest, and . . . offered directly to the immigrant either as individuals or in colonies." [114] To encourage foreign immigration, an official bureau was established by conservative Democrats,[115] and maintained by radical Republicans.[116] Thousands of pamphlets, describing Louisiana as a garden of Eden, were sent to shipping agents in Germany and Ireland and scattered abroad.[117] Steamship lines were asked to divert part of their immigrant traffic from New York to New Orleans, supplying a westbound cargo for cotton vessels which would otherwise return empty.[118]

An appeal was made to the self-interest of planters and merchants. "The settlement of a large number of immigrants in Louisiana," it was asserted, "must necessarily *improve the price of lands generally*, increase the amount of production, and

[113] Lockett MS, 129–30, 223.   [114] *Rpt. La. Com. Emig., 1870*, 42.

[115] *La. Sess. Laws., 1866*, 3, Act no. 105.

[116] *Rpt. La. Com. Emig., 1870, passim.*

[117] *Ibid.*, 24.   [118] *Rpt. La. Bur. Immig., 1868*, 10–11.

open new sources of commerce. Every landholder, mechanic and merchant must be benefited by an increase of the *laboring population*." [119] Planters were therefore requested to inform the state employment bureau of the labor that they needed and the terms upon which they would be willing to sell parcels of their land to white immigrants.[120] Their indifferent response may be summarized as follows: [121]

Acreage Available	Lots of	Terms	Extras	People Wanted	Crop
3,000	40–80	100 lbs., cotton per acre; credit, 2 yrs.	Sell cabins, etc.	German	Cotton
7,000	40	$5 per acre; part free for clearing.	—	Colony	Sugar
1,800	Any	$5–10 per acre on partial credit.	Temporary free cabins	Families	Cotton
1,760	10-up	100 lbs. cotton per acre; credit, 2 yrs.	Part already in tillage	—	Cotton
1,000	40	40 acres for each 20 cleared, tilled.	Neighbors offer shares	—	Timber
540	All	$4,000: 1,500 cash, balance 4 yrs.	Cleared bottoms	—	Cotton
512	All	$10 per acre, mostly prairie.	House	—	Stock
500	Any	$12 per acre; rent for clearing it.	—	—	Cotton
500	—	½ shares.	Furnish food and cabins	10 men	Rice
500	50	Free to settlers!	Free cabins!	Families	Cotton
400	40	Sell, credit 6 yrs.	No shelter	Catholic	Cotton

[119] *Ibid.*, 16 (Author's italics).   [120] *Rpt. La. Com. Emig., 1870,* 14.
[121] *Ibid.*, 19–20, 65–75. Only tracts of more than 400 acres are tabulated; seven offers of less land are omitted.

These offers to immigrants were remarkably few in number, considering the amount of uncultivated land, and scarcely cheap enough to keep settlers from going up the Mississippi to free homesteads in the West.[122]

And so Louisiana failed to attract foreign immigration after the war. The Irish and Germans who had come to New Orleans by the tens of thousands before 1860 no longer thronged the levee. Of those who arrived, the great majority sailed up the river to the Middle West.[123] In the fifteen years following the war only eight thousand German immigrants remained in New Orleans.[124] The foreign-born proportion of the state's population, which had reached 13 per cent in 1850, dwindled to 9 per cent in 1870, and 6 per cent in 1880.[125] It had always been said that slavery kept the immigrant from settling in the South, but now it was claimed that the Negro frightened him away.

There were many reasons, of course, for this marked decline of immigration. Foreigners continued to seek lands in the West and could not be diverted to the unfamiliar latitudes of the South, then an unhappy section devastated by war, afflicted with social and political disorder, suffering economic depression, and already pre-empted by Negro labor.[126] Yellow fever, which broke out again in 1867, frightened many prospective settlers.[127] Louisiana was still thought to be a malarial swamp, lying too far south of the cooler latitudes to which the Germans and Irish were accustomed. They found steamship passage to New York cheaper than to New Orleans, and continued to follow the hordes of Europeans who were going West—not South.[128]

[122] For homestead entries in Louisiana, see below, 262–63.
[123] *Rpt. La. Bur. Immig., 1868*, 11–15.
[124] Deiler, *Germany's Contribution to the Population of New Orleans*, 4–5
[125] *U. S. Cen., 1890*, I, 260–61.   [126] *Rpt. La. Com. Emig., 1870*, 5–6, 9, 21–23.
[127] *Rpt. La. Bur. Immig., 1868*, 7.   [128] See above, *n.* 125.

But the fundamental reason why foreigners did not come pouring into Louisiana was the relative lack of economic opportunity for the common man. Plantations dominated the fertile lowlands, which their proprietors would not subdivide, even to obtain labor superior to the Negro or to enhance the general value of real estate by increased settlement.[129] "You want our Germans to take the place of your former slaves," observed the shrewd president of the German Lloyd Steamship Company to the state commissioner of immigration. In vain the commissioner protested that "almost every one in Louisiana has gone to work since the war." [130] He could not deny that immigrants had little chance of buying sections of the fertile river-bottom estates. Welcomed as a laborer, to work by the side of Negroes, the foreigner had no more hope of acquiring a freehold than had the colored man. All too often, as complaints to state officials revealed, immigrants were treated like freedmen. Their food, shelter, and clothing were no better, their discipline no lighter.[131] "As long as a foreigner is willing to work like a mule or a slave, it is all right." [132] Under these circumstances the immigrants who settled in Louisiana preferred to live in New Orleans or on truck patches close to the city, rather than in the old slave quarters of country plantations.[133] The great majority avoided the state altogether, for it seemed to offer them nothing better than a chance to displace the Negro by working and forever living "like a nigger." The best land was monopolized by a plantation system that appeared to promise as little change as the feudal estates of Europe.

It is not difficult to understand why planters refused to subdivide their estates even to attract white immigration. A sugar planter expressed their attitude when he declared that the ad-

---

[129] Cf. *Baton Rouge Advocate*, July 25, 1874.
[130] *Rpt. La. Com. Emig., 1870*, 22.   [131] *Rpt. La. Bur. Immig., 1867*, 13–16.
[132] *St. Landry Progress*, Nov. 9, 1867.   [133] *Rpt. La. Com. Emig., 1871*, 10–11.

vocates of small farms "ought not to be so liberal with other people's property." [134] It was claimed that "arrogant negrolovers" in the North had first raised the cry for peasant freeholds, only to have unthinking editors in the South take up the refrain like so many parrots. "The thing was easy. Buy; but pay nothing." [135] Yet landowners could hardly afford to sell parcels of real estate to those who could not purchase them. We had money and property before the war, said a sugar planter, and risked our capital in the cane fields, instead of cautiously lending it at 5 per cent in New Orleans. After several poor crops, "we have no more credit with [the banks] than so many penitentiary convicts." The merchants hold us up by charging 25 per cent interest. In spite of all these difficulties, "by sheer force of character," we "have pushed the negro in and forced him to make the cotton and sugar" that has saved the South and enabled the land to support the colored people.[136]

The planter engaged in this patriotic work of reconstruction was outraged to hear radicals say that "there are men owning from two thousand to five thousand acres of good tillable land, though scarcely able to cultivate more than a few hundred acres, while hundreds of poor men are living in the poor pine woods where they can scarce make a living." [137] He also resented the advice of conservative newspapers: "If our large land owners were to divide their tracts into small farms, and give every alternate farm rent free for five years to white immigrants, with the privilege of purchasing [it] at the end of that time at a stipulated price, the residue . . . would, in a few years, be worth three times as much as the whole bodies of land are now." [138] Burdened by debt himself the planter could not compete with government homesteads; he was un-

[134] *Picayune*, Aug. 13, 1873.   [135] *Ibid.*, Aug. 7, 1873.
[136] *Ibid.*, Aug. 13, 1873.   [137] *St. Landry Progress*, July 27, 1867.
[138] *Baton Rouge Advocate*, July 25, 1874 (Author's italics).

able to extend credit to others beyond a season's crop, to which his own borrowings were limited. Without almost endless credit, however, no one could afford to buy sections of a plantation. "In this State," the *Picayune* was forced to admit, "there is no sale for large tracts of land, and the multitude who want small tracts have no money to pay for them." [139] Short of bankruptcy, a planter was unable to subdivide his estate with any profit. With his land under heavy blanket mortgages, and his standing crops pledged to a factor, he was bound financially like a serf to his soil. [140]

But the planter's serfdom was voluntary. He was loath to part with the acres which had yielded him luxury before the war. He was confident that land would soon be worth more than ever before; it was the only capital by which he could hope to regain his wealth, and to own a plantation was still to enjoy social prestige. [141] All his social and economic habits led the planter to hold on to his estate. He had been raised a slaveholder and could not easily change himself into a real estate agent, selling his acres in freeholds, or a country squire, collecting rents from white tenants. [142] The situation was correctly summed up by Nordhoff, who observed that many planters in the Sugar Bowl "hold on to their large estates, even when they have not capital enough to work them; and I have seen some plantations which were not worked at all, but on which the owners paid the taxes, and waited for better times. For my part," he concluded sympathetically, "I do not much blame them. Nobody, except a land-speculator, likes to sell land; especially where it has been his home. And these people are not land-speculators." [143]

<hr/>

[139] July 24, 1873; cf. Nordhoff, *The Cotton States*, 71.

[140] *Picayune*, Sept. 25, 1867; *Proc. La. State Agric. Soc., 1900*, 36.

[141] *Rpt. La. Com. Emig., 1870*, 15.   [142] Cf. *Picayune*, Aug. 13, 1873.

[143] *The Cotton States*, 71. It is doubtless true that though planters often acquired their lands by speculation, they did not hold them for this purpose once they had started the expensive cultivation of sugar and cotton.

Yet the social and economic folly of not having broken up the estates was never forgotten in New Orleans. When the depression that followed the Panic of 1873 threw thousands of laborers out of work, the city looked in vain to the country for relief. "So long as there are wastes of idle and unproductive lands blotting the fair face of Louisiana, and starving workmen thronging the streets of New Orleans," it was said, "there can be no such thing as prosperity for the State." [144] In the city there was "an immense amount of idle muscle," and in the country a vast domain of idle land.[145] What prevented their profitable union was the failure of landholding capitalists to finance settlement of the unemployed in the country. Thousands of poor people in the city desired land, it was remarked, "but they have no money for it, and they cannot get it on credit, nor can they purchase it in fifty-acre lots." Millions of acres of idle land lay in the hands of planters and city speculators.[146] This agrarian monopoly was more harmful to the welfare of Louisiana than all the political evils of reconstruction government. "The land-holder and the capitalist hold the fate of this State in their hands more than the politician," declared a correspondent to the New Orleans *Picayune*. "What we want to settle our political, and financial, and industrial troubles is population. It is extremely doubtful if we ever can . . . make Louisiana prosperous without a considerable increase of the farmers of the State. . . . Politicians and political parties have nothing to do with settling up these lands. The land-holder and capitalist must act, or the State will not be saved." [147]

To the aid of settlers who wanted farms came neither the planter nor the landholding capitalist, but the Federal Government. In 1869 Congress opened the public lands in Louisiana,

---

[144] *Picayune*, Apr. 1, 1875.   [145] *Ibid.*, July 25, 1873.
[146] *Ibid.*, Aug. 10, 1873.   [147] *Ibid.*, July 24, 1873.

which embraced more than six million acres, to free homestead entry in quarter sections of one hundred and sixty acres.[148] During the first year less than five thousand acres were entered.[149] But in the next decade over half a million acres passed into private hands.[150]

Little of this vast domain, however, was transformed into farms, for the larger part fell into the possession of speculators, railway promoters, and lumber magnates. Fraudulent or dummy homestead claims were often entered for the purpose of stripping the land of timber.[151] The area of cultivated soil expanded over a million acres in Louisiana during the seventies, partly in the oak uplands, but mainly by the resumption of tillage on plantations, which was indicated by the diminished proportion of unimproved land that had always been greatest on large estates.[152]

Poor settlers continued as before the war to stake out their farms without going through formalities of law.[153] They came in a migratory tide from Georgia, Alabama, Mississippi, and Arkansas.[154] Deserting barren land in their native states, after several seasons of drought and failing crops, they sought to better their condition in the piney woods of northern Louisiana. Some families traveled overland in long wagon trains, and many went on to Texas.[155] Other families, however, being poor, found themselves stranded in Louisiana. In one case, all their worldly goods had been spent for passage on the steamboats to Shreveport, and when skippers landed them at the mouth of Red River, there was nothing to do but settle in the

[148] *Rpt. U. S. Com. Agric., 1868,* 465–66. [149] *Ibid.,* 471.
[150] Cf. *U. S. Statistical Abstract, 1879,* 148.
[151] *Rpt. U. S. Com. Gen. Land Ofc., 1874,* 74–75; *1877,* 220–21.
[152] *U. S. Cen., 1880, Agric.,* 25. See Appendix, Table 1.
[153] Cf. above, chap. IV.
[154] *Opelousas Courier,* quoted in *Commercial Bulletin,* Dec. 25, 1866.
[155] *Picayune,* Jan. 14, 1870.

backwoods.[156] Their clearings were scattered over the pine hills north of Red River, where the "inhabitants claim that it is a very good home for a poor man." [157] This tide of migration from the South Atlantic states reached its crest between 1868 and 1870, and added several thousand families of yeomen farmers to the population.[158]

From the North came farmers, mechanics, and tradesmen to try their thrifty hands at farming in a warmer climate. More than half the Northerners who migrated to Louisiana were said to have settled in the country.[159] They came in families and colonies from states as far apart as Maine and Missouri.[160] Typical of this movement was the "Hamlin Farm Association" from Ohio. Thirty-five men arrived in Sabine Parish in 1872 to learn how to cultivate cotton by working for a season as tenants on a plantation. When other Ohioans joined them the following year, they planned to clear ten thousand acres which were purchased on thirty years' credit.[161] Had such generous credit been available throughout Louisiana, there is little doubt that thousands of farmers, who lacked capital but not energy, would have flocked to the state and transformed its plantations into small freeholds. Since river-bottom estates were closed to them, however, they took up homesteads or squatted on the uplands of the northern parishes.[162]

The small capital and initiative required to establish these farms were not to be found among the poor whites who joined the Negroes as tenants on the plantations. They were often hired by planters to compete with the freedmen. Poor Creoles

[156] *Shreveport Times*, Dec. 21, 1872. It is not clear from this account whether the emigrants were confused over their proper destination, or defrauded by railway and boat companies. Many families, it is reported, were taken free of charge to Shreveport by kindly boat captains.

[157] Lockett MS, 218, 222.   [158] *Rpt. La. Com. Emig., 1870*, 5.   [159] *Ibid.*, 6.
[160] *De Bow's Review*, I (February, 1866), 213.
[161] *Picayune*, Aug. 2, 1873.
[162] Cf. the increase of farms in De Soto and Natchitoches, Appendix, Table 9.

and Cajuns could always be employed in the rolling season to break a Negro strike.[163] When freedmen became too refractory, white labor was imported to replace them. Seven hundred Portuguese were engaged by sugar planters in the single year of 1880.[164] Ten years earlier, one hundred French-Canadian families had been imported by a St. Landry planter through contract with a wealthy landlord of Quebec. By the terms of their indenture the immigrants were to work ten hours a day, and also at night during the grinding season, for a wage of $400 a year. Three-quarters of this money was not to be paid until after the harvest.

Although these families were to be provided with cabins and vegetable patches, it is plain to be seen that they would be treated as freedmen.[165] Planters did not welcome immigrants unless they could work like Negroes. "The Germans want twenty dollars a month," complained an overseer, "and we can hire the niggers for ten and fifteen. The Germans will die in our swamps. Then as soon as they get money enough to buy a cart and mule, and an acre of land . . . they'll go in for themselves." [166]

In the cotton fields, where there was less trouble with colored labor and insufficient capital to provide for its replacement, white tenants were uncommon but not altogether absent. Thrifty German families in St. Landry were said to have made considerable money by renting land for cash.[167] A model colony was developed by one planter who brought from Mississippi twenty-seven families, "bred up to country life in the South, and all with some means." He furnished them cabins, tools, and supplies without interest, rented tracts of land, cleared and fenced, for either cash or a quarter-share of the crop, and built a church and school for his tenants. Although

[163] *Picayune*, July 20, 1874.
[164] *Ibid.*, Sept. 12, 1880.
[165] *Opelousas Courier*, Oct. 29, 1870.
[166] Trowbridge, *op. cit.*, 387.
[167] *Rpt. La. Com. Emig.*, 1870, 37.

a few Negroes were given equal facilities, this project was intended primarily for poor whites. Such enlightened landlords must have been rare, for this planter attracted hundreds of people, who cultivated his property in the parishes of Avoyelles, Rapides, and St. Landry.[168] All too common, on the other hand, were hard-pressed planters who left their overseers to handle white tenants exactly like freedmen.[169]

Just as the plantation system had survived war and reconstruction, with sharecroppers and tenants instead of slaves to cultivate the fields, so had the economy of small farms also persisted.

Nests of petty landholdings could still be found after the war interspersed among the great estates. A traveler in Ascension, for example, observed that on descending the Mississippi and two miles before reaching Bayou Lafourche, "the large plantations cease, and a thickly settled community of small farms take their place along the river front." [170] In one part of a rich sugar parish like St. Mary the census marshal of 1880 enumerated in order these cultivated acreages: 100, 20, 20, 10, 150, 200, 700, 500, 40, 35, 65, 30, 30, of which only those from 200 to 65 grew any cane.[171] Most farms in the plantation areas of the Sugar Bowl continued, as before, to supply the large proprietors with some cane for their refineries, and with a great deal more foodstuffs for their hands. In Iberville there were many Creoles who tilled from five to twenty acres, of which one to four were seeded in cane and the remainder in corn and sweet potatoes.[172] This economic liaison between plantation and farm was natural to a staple such as sugar, since its agriculture could be separated from its manufacture; but it

[168] *Picayune*, July 16, 1879.   [169] *Ibid.*, Sept. 8, 1867.

[170] Lockett MS, "Louisiana As It Is" [1873], 283. It was known as the "Faubourg Laboucanne," a Creole settlement.

[171] MS *Returns, U. S. Cen., 1880, La. Agric.*, St. Mary, Ward 5.

[172] *Ibid.*, Iberville, Ward 4.

was far less common in cotton, which was raised competitively wherever possible by both the planter and the farmer.[173]

A greater diversity of agriculture remained the rule in southern parishes; it was permitted by the climate and stimulated by the demand of New Orleans for foodstuffs. This variation in crops was best exhibited on farms. Vegetable gardens, large and small, were numerous in the districts around New Orleans and up the Mississippi "Coast" where thrifty Germans lived.[174] In St. Bernard there were six Creoles who tilled from forty to eighty acres each, and produced truck worth between $75 and $1,200. The valuation of their farms ran much higher, and in two instances reached $10,000.[175]

The specially cured perique tobacco of St. James seldom failed to fetch good prices and bring prosperity to its Creole producers. Their farms ranged between six and forty acres, but two or three of these would be sufficient to grow from four to eight hundred pounds of tobacco. A typical farmer was Louis Roussel, whose family had worked the same soil long before the war. Louis—for on either side of him lived Charles and Octave Roussel—owned fourteen acres of improved land and five of meadow in 1880; and his crop of eight hundred pounds of perique, grown on five acres, brought him $500, which was the capital value of his farm. In addition to tobacco, he made two tons of hay, sixty bushels of corn, and two hundred of sweet potatoes. Louis did not spend a penny to hire labor, but $16 for fertilizer, because the soil needed to be nourished for the uninterrupted culture of tobacco.[176]

In the southern and western parishes there were many Creole farmers who specialized in rice for a staple, but never wholly departed from a diversity of crops to make them self-sufficient. In Lafourche, for example, a nest of farms, none

[173] See below, 272.   [174] Rpt. La. Bur. Immig., 1867, 31.
[175] MS Returns, U. S. Cen., 1880, La. Agric., St. Bernard, Ward 1.
[176] Ibid., St. James, Wards 1, 2.

larger than ten acres in their improved parts, nor worth above $800, produced between one and two thousand pounds of rice annually, besides corn, sweet potatoes, poultry, and eggs.[177] However primitive their methods of rice culture,[178] these Creoles were industrious and relatively prosperous; it was said of them that they never depended on "Sambo and Dinah," but rolled up their own sleeves and went to work in the field.[179] In Calcasieu, farther west, farmers of the same family name owned four adjoining tracts, of which the largest was twenty acres. With horses, oxen, a few cattle, more swine, and numerous barnyard fowl, they cultivated patches of rice, corn, sweet potatoes, and sugar cane.[180] These peasants, Creole or Acadian in blood, differed little in agricultural practice from their ante-bellum forebears; and they persisted in the petty but diversified farming which marked the transition of a frontier to a more highly developed arable economy, especially in rice.

Where the soil was less fertile and timber abundant, in the Florida parishes, southwestern pine flats, and northern uplands, the farmer turned to commercial lumbering after the war. He did not stop raising his own food and as much cotton as he could, but he also cut into the forests for a "cash crop." Stands of oak or long-leaf yellow pine, a nuisance to the farmer and tempting to his axe, covered the parishes of Calcasieu, Cameron, Grant, Lincoln, Morehouse, Natchitoches, Union, Vermilion, West Feliciana, and Winn. In Lincoln, farmers cut wood at $15 for 10 cords from lots of 25 and 50 acres; in Union a man made $225 on 150 cords from 400 acres; and in West Feliciana, Lane Brandon, who also raised 150 bales of cotton, trimmed 500 cords for $700 from 1,200 acres of forest.[181] Brandon was an exceptionally large planter and

---

[177] *Ibid.*, Lafourche, Ward 3.   [178] Nordhoff, *op. cit.*, 69.
[179] [Plaquemines] *Empire Parish*, Aug. 25, quoted in *Picayune*, Sept. 1, 1866.
[180] MS *Returns, U. S. Cen., 1880, La. Agric.*, Calcasieu, Ward 3.
[181] *Ibid.*, Lincoln, Union, W. Feliciana, Ward 7, *et passim*.

timber operator. It may well be doubted if all the others were simply farmers who eked out a better livelihood by clearing their lands, for some of them were certainly homesteading employees of the new timber companies.

Northern lumber syndicates entered Louisiana along the railways, late in the seventies, purchased vast domains of private and public lands, and cut a wide swath through the forests from the northeast down to the southwest.[182] It was a common practice for these companies to homestead their employees on public land and then strip it of timber; in this none too honest fashion they obtained lumber worth about $25 an acre for $1.25 to $2.50.[183] Railroads joined in the profitable business. The Texas and Pacific "Back-bone grant" up the Red River, through the heart of Louisiana's oak and long-leaf pine forests, was to arouse local Populism by dispossession of the squatters and farmers.[184] The lumber companies got most of the timber. The extent of their operations may be judged from the situation in Rapides Parish, where there were fifteen mills in 1886; the largest one owned in New York, turned out 250,000 feet a day. Long-leaf yellow pines which stood sixty to eighty feet high, one to four inches in diameter, and as many as a hundred to an acre, went crashing to the ground and into the teeth of noisy saws. Great stands of oak, hickory, and walnut fell. As the best timber was thinned out the sawmills moved on, from Caldwell, Catahoula, Grant, Morehouse, Ouachita, Vernon, and Winn in the north to Rapides and Natchitoches in the center, and thence to De Soto, Sabine, and Calcasieu in the west and south.[185]

These northern upland parishes were inhabited by cotton

182 *Picayune*, Feb. 25, 1878; *Times-Democrat*, Sept. 1, 1883.

183 *Cong. Record, 1892–93*, XXIV, 869–70.

184 *Ibid.; The Louisiana Populist*, 1895, *passim;* interview with H. L. Brian, May 2, 1933.

185 Tompkins, *North Louisiana, Its Soil, Climate, Productions, Health, Schools, etc.* (Cincinnati, 1886), 36–37.

farmers, and it is the more interesting to observe their way of life after the war because they were to lead the Populist revolt in the nineties. In 1880 they appeared to be doing well. There were few tenants or sharecroppers among them, and nearly every family owned its land. The majority cultivated from ten to thirty-five acres and generally possessed in addition above a hundred acres of woods or meadow. They kept cattle, sheep, swine, and poultry, and increased the number of fowl rapidly after the war.[186] Everybody was then caught up in the economy of cotton, for good or ill, and struggled continually to enlarge his production of this cash crop; from one to half a dozen bales were grown on the average farm. But upland agriculture was also diversified and remained relatively self-sufficient. Every family still relied on pork, corn, and sweet potatoes for food; but produced more wool from its sheep, larger supplies of butter and eggs, and new fruits from its orchards.[187]

The farm of B. F. Bailey, who later became a Populist leader, represented the industrious and prosperous yeomen. He lived in Winn Parish, the home of local Populism. In 1879, Bailey owned 425 acres, of which 360 were woods, 35 were improved, and the remainder was old meadow. He had one horse, three mules, two work oxen, twelve milch and twenty-six other cows, forty sheep, forty pigs, and fifty-five hens. These possessions might be thought worthy of a small planter; actually they belonged to a well-to-do farmer. The value of his land amounted to only $500, and of his livestock to $460. He raised twenty bales of cotton on twenty-five acres, and hired Negroes for twelve weeks at $50 to assist in the chopping and picking. Cotton was his main crop, but not his only one, for he owed his success to diversifying his labors. He produced 300 bushels of corn on thirty acres, 150 of sweet

[186] MS *Returns, U.S. Cen., 1880, La. Agric.,* e. g., Claiborne.
[187] *Ibid.,* Sabine, Winn.

potatoes on five, 50 of oats on ten, 15 bushels of cowpeas, and enough sugar cane on one acre to make 80 gallons of molasses. From his cows he made 200 pounds of butter, from his sheep he clipped 75 pounds of wool, and from his poultry obtained 150 dozen eggs. Fifty peach trees yielded as many bushels of fruit. During the course of the year he sold one cow and six sheep. This rich and diversified production brought Bailey, besides most of his own supplies, about $1,000: that was its total value.[188]

His farm may be compared with another in Winn which also belonged to a future Populist leader. In 1879 this man owned 560 acres, of which all but 60 were woods. He had a horse, seven milch and twenty-five other cows, eight sheep, twenty pigs, and thirty hens. He raised eight bales of cotton on 12 acres, 300 bushels of corn on 20 acres, and made 260 pounds of butter and 18 pounds of wool. It was extravagantly estimated that the value of all his produce, whether sold or consumed, was $600; but he had spent half this amount to hire colored labor for thirty-two weeks of cotton-growing.[189] It is plain to see that he was a poor farmer for all his apparent wealth.

Innumerable examples of the husbandry of other upland yeomen could be detailed to show that they were dividing themselves into two kinds, the cotton farmer and the self-sufficient farmer. Both raised some foodstuffs, but the former less and less. The majority were poor, but the poorest were those who failed to diversify their crops. In Grant, to cite one parish, there were farmers who cultivated from ten to twenty-five acres, worth between $600 and $900, on which they raised one to five bales of cotton, valued at $50 to $230, and from sixty to two hundred bushels of corn.[190] Since they produced nothing else, it is obvious that they were specializing

188 *Ibid.*, Winn, Enumerator's District 53.
189 *Ibid.*, Winn, Ward 1.   190 *Ibid.*, Grant.

in cotton without the planter's resources to stem adversity and supply every need in cash or kind. Farmers were said to be more prosperous than planters in the years that followed the war,[191] if only because thrifty whites worked harder than colored sharecroppers,[192] but their prosperity depended on the efficiency as well as the zeal of their labor—on the degree to which they remained self-sufficient.

To an increasing extent, however, upland farmers became badly involved in the unremunerative plantation economy of "cotton 'n cawn." Probably half the cotton raised in this region was the product of white yeomen or tenants, not of colored sharecroppers; and the number of bales shipped down Red River grew larger and larger in the seventies.[193] The acreage planted in cotton was greater than that devoted to corn, and the cultivation of both occupied more land than any other crop. Self-sufficiency vanished with the passing of the frontier. This may be seen from the contemporary estimate that supplies had to be imported into any region which gave over one-third of its tillage to cotton. In 1879 the fleecy staple occupied 70 per cent of the cultivated river bottoms, 36 per cent of the long-leaf pine parishes, and 35 per cent of the oak uplands.[194] This specialization in cotton was accompanied by the growth of white tenancy. White workers made up the bulk of the agricultural labor in 1879 in the parishes of Catahoula, Sabine, St. Tammany, Vernon, and Winn, and were nearly as conspicuous as Negroes in Bossier, Claiborne, De Soto, Franklin, Red River, St. Helena, and Union.[195]

As the farmer, like the planter, devoted more of his land and labor to cotton, the crop lien became universal. It could

---

[191] *Picayune*, Jan. 30, 1873; June 11, 1879.   [192] *Ibid.*, Mar. 6, 1870.

[193] Hilgard *Rpt.* [E. W. Hilgard, "Report on the Cotton Production of the State of Louisiana, with a Discussion of the General Agricultural Features of the State," *U. S. Cen.*, *1880*, V, *Rpt. on Cotton Production*, pt. i], 67.

[194] *Ibid.*, 38–39.   [195] *Ibid.*, 83.

be observed throughout the state, as in De Soto, that "very few planters pay cash for everything, and almost no laborers do." [196] The extortion and risk of this system of credit, which plunged a majority of the rural population into debt from which there was little hope of escape, was generally deplored but nevertheless accepted as a necessity to the cultivation of cotton. The crop lien and the staple went hand in hand: to make cotton at all, the poor man must go into debt for seed and supplies; and the larger the debt grew, the more cotton must be planted for quick and easy sale. A bad season checked the spread of the crop lien, but one good season was enough for it to flourish, and it grew faster than the staple it helped to produce.[197]

Thus the plantation triumphed over the farm and assimilated it to specialization in cotton on the basis of tenant labor and the crop lien. "To plant cotton as a money crop, after subsistence is provided for, and to cultivate smaller areas well," was the exhortation of an agricultural expert whom no one heard in the seventies.[198] For the plantation system not only survived, with modifications of labor and finance, but extended to the upland farms to make trouble for the future.

[196] *Ibid.*, 84.   [197] *Ibid.*   [198] *Ibid.*, 39.

CHAPTER IX

RISE OF THE POOR WHITES

Rejoice in a nobler emancipation, which has
stricken the fetters from millions of our own race,
and given an earnest of a better destiny to a class
which has suffered fatally and long.

—E. B. SEABROOK [1]

The grandsons and granddaughters of the Crackers of antebellum days form the mass of what
might be called the "middle class" of the South
to-day.

—S. A. HAMILTON [2]

When at the close of the last century a new class of men appeared as candidates for public office in many Southern states,
and were followed in the present century by men of the same
order, such as Vardaman, Bilbo, Heflin, Blease, Long, and
others who succeeded in reaching the United States Senate,
their political emergence was popularly assumed to be a sign
of the "rise of the poor whites." [3] One of the earliest writers
to voice this opinion dismissed Southern Populism, the agrarian
revolt in the nineties, as "really a Cracker movement." [4] His
view was utterly false,[5] being compounded in equal parts of
snobbery and conservatism, but it carried conviction because

---

[1] "The Poor Whites of the South," *The Galaxy*, IV, 690.

[2] "The New Race Question in the South," *The Arena*, XXVII, 356.

[3] Cf. Den Hollander, *op. cit.*, 422–25.

[4] Hamilton, *op. cit.*, 357.

[5] It may suffice to point out here that in South Carolina over half the
members of the Farmers' Alliance were landowners. *New Economist*, May 25,
1889.

of the increasing host of governors, congressmen, and minor officials who came from humble stock,[6] and owed their elevation largely to the suffrage of people as poor as themselves. Except as individuals, however, they failed to demonstrate the rise of their kind. Their policies were too often but a demagogic snare for votes, or if sincere and thoroughgoing, too rarely enacted into law to help the masses. Save where these politicians won power by fomenting race prejudice, they were brought to the top not by the rise but the uprising of poor white people against intolerable economic and social conditions.[7]

Yet it was commonly believed that in these respects their lot in life had been remarkably improved since the Civil War.[8] Their social and economic progress was taken for granted rather than investigated, and assumed to be further evidence of their "rise." Few thought to ask why, if life had become easier and better for them, they should manifest so much political unrest and economic discontent. Their agitation was never to preserve the *status quo*, except to keep the Negro in his place, but always to enlarge their area of economic opportunity.

This popular but uncritical term, "rise of the poor whites," should be abandoned. It reduces to a paradox the problem it was coined to describe. The phrase developed from the false prewar notion that all nonslaveholders were "poor whites," and that slavery was the only institution which depressed them. With the abolition of human bondage, it appeared that the

[6] This was not always true, as in the well-known case of "Pitchfork Ben" Tillman. See F. B. Simkins, *The Tillman Movement in South Carolina* (Durham, 1926), chaps. II–IV.

[7] Den Hollander, *op. cit.*, 424. For the last century, see J. D. Hicks, *The Populist Revolt, etc.* (Minneapolis, 1931), esp. chap. II. For the present century there is nothing definitive, but a great plenty of periodical literature and journalistic biography.

[8] Cf. above, *n.* 2.

poor whites had been emancipated as well as the Negroes.[9]

But the condition of the majority of white people in Louisiana showed little improvement in 1890 over 1860, and they rose up at the polls because they had failed to rise in field, factory, or shop.[10] To this general truth, which will be elaborated in the following pages, there are two important qualifications.

It cannot be denied, first of all, that an untold number climbed within a generation after the war from poverty to comfort or even opulence, leaving the masses behind them and rising as individuals rather than as a class.[11] In this prosperous group were to be found the most competent sons of planters and merchants whose fortunes had been lost in the war. They were able to redeem their heritage not only by following the virtuous tradition of hard work, but also by starting with important advantages and having good luck. Possessed of paternal land, with a corps of freedmen to furnish cheap labor and produce valuable staples, on which money could be easily borrowed for tools and repairs, their lack of funds was only a passing hardship.[12] Whenever planting families failed to prosper under these favorable circumstances, as many did, their estates were bought by former overseers with enough experience, or Northerners with sufficient capital to operate them successfully.[13] Of the planters who were completely ruined by the war and reduced to the abject condition of poor whites, some remained in hopeless penury,[14] while others regained a fair measure of comfort by the proverbial sweat of their

---

[9] Den Hollander, *op. cit.,* 423. Cf. above, *n. 1.*

[10] B. B. Kendrick, "Agrarian Discontent in the South, 1880–1900," *American Hist. Assn. Rpt., 1920,* I, 267–69. See also G. K. Holmes, "The Peons of the South," *Annals,* IV, 265–74.

[11] E. g., MSS *Assessment Rolls, 1873, 1893,* Parishes of Caddo, Rapides, and Tensas, *passim.*

[12] See above, chap. VIII.

[13] W. H. Harris, *Louisiana* (New Orleans, 1885), 10.

[14] Lockett MS, 101–2.

brows.[15] With "their sons and grandsons following the plow and wielding the hoe," it soon came to be noticed that "in many of the descendants of the old planters a yeomanry is springing up as honorable as our planting aristocracy of yore." [16]

The ranks of yeomen farmers were swelled to a lesser extent by people who had always been poor. Not a few tenants on the sugar plantations eventually acquired farms of their own.[17] In the cotton and piney woods parishes there were also families who prospered.[18] "I have known men," wrote one observer, "who had barely money enough to pay the land office fees for 160 acres of land, and started with only an axe and a pair of oxen; in five years they had comfortable homes and well-tilled farms. . . ." [19] The number and success of these families were exaggerated in pamphlets designed to attract immigration,[20] or in subscription books of local history and biography that were a fashion of the day; [21] but they served to feed the American spirit of optimism with the inference that anyone who worked as hard could do as well.[22] Not until agricultural depression threatened or destroyed the independence of these yeomen farmers in the nineties were they disillusioned. Then they joined their poorer neighbors in the Populist crusade.[23]

[15] "It comes hard for a young man to walk behind a plow who once rode behind a fast trotter . . . [but] in the long run it will be all the better for the rising generation of the South—a generation which is to follow one notoriously brought up in ignorance of work and indolence as to any useful occupation." *Picayune*, Sept. 3, 1867.

[16] *Ibid.*, Sept. 5, 1873.   [17] *Proc. La. State Agric. Soc., 1891*, 41.

[18] *Picayune*, Jan. 30, 1873.   [19] W. H. Harris, *op. cit.*, 25.

[20] E. g., *Rpt. Com. Emig., 1870*, 36–37; H. T. Brown, *Ascension Parish*, 17; W. H. Harris, *loc. cit.*

[21] *Biographical and Historical Memoirs of Louisiana*, I, II; *Biog. and Hist. Mem. of Northwest La., passim; Biog. and Hist. Mem. of Southwest La., passim.*

[22] *Picayune*, Jan. 30, 1873.

[23] B. B. Kendrick, "Agrarian Discontent in the South: 1880–1900," *American Hist. Assn. Rpt., 1920*, I, 267–72.

Not only in agriculture, but also in commerce and industry, men frequently fared well after the war. A noticeable change in their occupations attended the drift of population from country to city.[24] Sons formerly trained to follow their fathers in planting or the professions were apprenticed to trades in the hope of developing manufactures, or articled as clerks with the intention of becoming merchants.[25] Among those who made the most of their straitened circumstances were the Creoles. Their sons often took clerkships in New Orleans to help support large families, and a few rose within twenty years to be the heads of insurance, oil, supply, and brokerage houses.[26] How many Americans shared in the expansion of the city's business as the years went by, it would be impossible to tell, but their number was large and their proportion the greatest.[27] Some foreigners, especially the Germans who had arrived before the war, enjoyed considerable prosperity. Among them were to be found small manufacturers, shopkeepers, and an occasional minister or lawyer.[28] In the country towns, as in New Orleans, many a merchant grew rich by trading on the necessities of planters and taking advantage of liens on their crops.[29] But the man who rose from nothing was always the exception, not the rule; and for every poor family that prospered, there was generally another to take its place either by falling in rank or standing still among the majority of poor, white people.[30]

The grim struggle of impoverished planting and mercantile families to replenish their fortunes, and of needy farmers and

---

[24] The urban proportion of population increased from 27 per cent in 1860 to 31 per cent in 1890. *Rpt. U. S. Dept. Agric., 1894*, New Ser., no. 119, 574–75.

[25] *Picayune*, Aug. 2, 1873.   [26] *Item*, Sept. 10, 1890.

[27] Andrew Morrison, *The Industries of New Orleans* (New Orleans, 1885), 55–181.

[28] Voss, *History of the German Society of New Orleans*, 14, 18, 24, 28, 30, 32, 36, 38, 42, 44, 46, 48, 50, 52, 56, 62, 68, 70.

[29] *Weekly Picayune*, Apr. 25, 1895.   [30] See below, 290–91.

laborers to improve their livelihood, was reflected in the social attitude of the postwar generation. In 1865 the whole South went to work: the only escape from the privations which afflicted all to a greater or lesser extent was toil. Work of some kind became the common lot, and its necessity enhanced the dignity and popular esteem of labor. If the hardest tasks were still reserved for the Negro, there was no longer a belief that white men should avoid drudgery.[31] Observed one writer: "Our people are becoming 'Yankeeized;' our sons and daughters are brought up to depend upon self, to work and to place a value upon the wages of work of every kind. The dignity of labor is admitted and asserted by all. The children of our oldest and best families do manual labor in field or shop, and do not lose caste." [32]

It was a generation of "self-made" men whose individualistic philosophy was colored by the materialism that came of so much concentration on the means of existence.[33] Work was almost a religion, and its rewards, especially if sufficient to banish the necessity of work, were the most desirable of earthly blessings. Push and hustle became the order of the day. As long as all were engaged as families or individuals in a severely competitive and compulsory struggle for comfort, everyone was an individualist.[34] Whoever surpassed his fellows in accumulating "a fair amount of this world's goods" attributed his success to "business integrity" and "financial shrewdness," without being aware of their possible inconsistency. So rare and new were the fortunes won that they became a subject for boasting. Published biographies, paid for by subscribers, would generally include the gross amount of one's business, if

[31] *Picayune*, Dec. 1, 1867, Aug. 19, 1871.   [32] W. H. Harris, *Louisiana*, 10.
[33] "The future for sugar and money overshadows all ideas of education, religion, [and] the moral training of children," was a typical complaint. [St. Mary] *Planters' Banner*, quoted in *Crescent*, Jan. 13, 1869.
[34] *Picayune*, July 13, 1875.

a merchant, or the acreage of one's estate, if a planter.[35] A self-made sugar planter was proud to have it known that he carried insurance worth $20,000 and sent his family North for the summer.[36] To be able to "educate their children and drive in carriages" was the ambition of all parents.[37] One who achieved this distinction by his own exertions was prone to look down on those who had failed, as if they had only themselves to blame.[38] But when a majority of people failed to secure the rewards of the minority, in spite of efforts often as strenuous and persevering, they became disillusioned with the false promise of individualism and combined in unions, both agricultural and industrial, to alter the political and economic system which apparently thwarted their ambition to rise.

Any statement of the inability of the masses in Louisiana to rise after the Civil War must be further qualified. It is not enough to admit that a certain proportion enjoyed prosperity, or to show that all ardently desired to elevate themselves. It should also be remembered that there were few people, poor or rich, black or white, in the North or South, who did not experience some amelioration in their ways of living during the nineteenth century. Such universal benefits as better transportation, communication, medicine, mechanical conveniences, and agricultural improvements were the cumulative result of the technological progress that distinguished this century, and are too well known to need recapitulation here.[39] The life of poor white people everywhere was made easier in so far as they profited indirectly from the increase of knowledge and multiplication of inventions. But the extent to which they shared such progress with people who were not so poor and who

[35] *Biog. and Hist. Mem. of Northwest La., passim.*   [36] *Ibid.*, 599.
[37] *Proc. La. State Agric. Soc., 1891*, 41.   [38] *Picayune*, Aug. 23, 1871.
[39] See D. L. Wells, *Recent Economic Changes* [1886]; E. W. Byrn, *Progress of Invention in the Nineteenth Century;* W. Kaempffert, *A Popular History of American Invention;* C. Singer, *A Short History of Medicine;* and esp. L. Mumford, *Technics and Civilization.*

lived in cities was very small, for of all social groups the chief beneficiary of nineteenth-century science was the urban middle class. A superior income enabled it to enjoy mechanical and scientific advantages which were beyond the reach of the farmer and city laborer.[40]

Public improvements in New Orleans, such as better streets and sanitation, enlarged parks, and the installation of gas and horsecar railways, did not benefit equally the rich and poor.[41] Gas was supplied by a private corporation at a minimum monthly charge of three dollars, which put this convenience beyond the means of thousands of people because it would cost the average laborer one-tenth of his annual wage.[42] Likewise the horsecar railways,[43] with a five-cent fare, were an expensive luxury to the poor, for it cost a department store salesgirl who used them in commuting to work 8 per cent of her weekly wage.[44] The city parks, enlarged in 1871 by the purchase of a great tract of land for nearly a million dollars, lay

[40] Cf. A. M. Schlesinger, *The Rise of the City, 1878–1898* (New York, 1933), 431–32. A good example was the new ice factory, producing 72 tons a day, which was established in New Orleans in 1871, according to Somers, *The Southern States since the War*, 235. "This marvel," wrote Somers with revealing candor, "has been accomplished by Carre's apparatus, founded on Faraday's discovery of the intense cold produced by the volatilisation of liquified [*sic*] ammoniacal gas; and the commercial agent here has been a company, with half a million of dollars capital, who have reduced the price of ice from 40 and sometimes 60 dollars to 15 dollars per ton, and dividing 25 per cent. of profits, to the utter dismay and confusion of Northern ice importers." But with ice at 75 cents per hundred pounds, it was no wonder that Somers speculated on its fitness for bartenders and not for the homes of the poor.

[41] *U. S. Cen., 1880, Rpt. Cities*, 272–74.

[42] The average wage for all Southern cities in 1880 was $346.28. *Times-Democrat*, Dec. 8, 1892.

[43] The street railways in New Orleans in 1880 were equal to 140 miles of single track, and carried over twenty-three million fares annually. *U. S. Cen., 1880, Rpt. Cities*, 273.

[44] Sales-girls in New Orleans stores received from $7.64 to $8.05 weekly in 1885. *Rpt. U. S. Com. Labor, 1895–96*, 492.

unimproved, and the municipal administration made no appropriations for their maintenance. From the glaring summer sun wealthy families could retreat to their shady gardens, but the poor had no better refuge than the barren parks.[45]

The difference in the streets along which they lived was even more apparent. Sidewalks, known as "banquettes," were of brick or plank board in some districts, but of artificial flagstone in prosperous sections. Four in every five streets remained unpaved, although many miles of cobblestones, stone blocks, and pulverized oyster shells had been laid down in business and residential areas.[46] The unpaved streets in squalid parts of the city were repulsive to the eye and nose: originally graded with refuse from kitchens and stables, so thoroughly mixed with the soil as to form 15 per cent of it, their condition was hardly improved during reconstruction years by the street cleaners' practice of raking filth from the gutters to the center of the road, only to have the rain wash it back again. The gutters were not drains, except in the shopping section, but stagnant reservoirs of garbage and slops.[47] Drainage throughout New Orleans remained notoriously bad,[48] three-fourths of the streets not being cleared of liquid refuse in 1871.[49] Seven years later, when yellow fever took four thousand lives,[50] a steam pump was installed to flush the foul gutters with water drawn from the Mississippi; and it forced the debris of the entire city to flow back on the indigent people who lived in the rear near Lake Pontchartrain.[51] From all these so-called public improvements the poor of New Orleans re-

[45] U.S. Cen., 1880, Rpt. Cities, 274–75.   [46] Ibid., 272.

[47] Rpt. La. Bd. Health, 1871, 41–42, 119–20; 1872, 75.

[48] For general drainage, New Orleans adopted the Polder system of Holland, with dikes or protective levees at its borders, and a series of canals through which excess rain water was pumped into Lake Pontchartrain. U.S. Cen., 1880, Rpt. Cities, 287.

[49] Rpt. La. Bd. Health, 1871, 120.   [50] Ibid., 1880, 9.

[51] Ibid., 1882, 369.

ceived little or no benefit, and less comfort than people who could afford to repair civic deficiencies by private facilities.

Class demarcation of the urban population was most clearly evident in the segregation and character of their dwelling places, which had important effects upon their health.

The commercial center, formerly the old *faubourg Ste. Marie* or American quarter,[52] contained the largest proportion of people in 1882. Of ten thousand premises, there were twice as many wood frame buildings as brick, and three in every five were used as dwellings, the remainder as shops or in combination.[53] Eleven years earlier, with almost the same number of buildings, there were reported to be many old "tenement houses" of one story, the floor resting upon the ground, which were condemned as "unfit for human habitation by reason of decay, leaky roofs, dangerous galleries and stairways." The shanties were "generally owned by wealthy landlords, who only respect the demands of the law," and occupied by "the many, urged by necessity and even the consideration of lesser rents." [54] Because of these slums, the death rate in this district was always high, and in 1882 the highest in the city, averaging 38.31 as compared with 26.45 for all New Orleans.[55] Heavy mortality, according to the Board of Health, was "invariably associated with [a] crowded population, living in badly ventilated houses, built on wet and undrained soil, and in no manner provided with sewerage. . . . There exist in the social economy of man no circumstances or conditions which bear the relation of cause and effect with greater cer-

[52] Known as the First District, and bounded by Canal Street, north; Felicity Street, south; the river, east; and the lake, west. *Soard's New Orleans City Directory, 1882*, 41.

[53] *Rpt. La. Bd. Health, 1882*, 388.   [54] *Ibid., 1871*, 49–50.

[55] Per 1,000 inhabitants. *Ibid., 1882*, vi, viii. In the First District, there were 31.87 deaths per 1,000 white people, and 58.04 per 1,000 colored. Two years before the rate had been lower, 20.40 and 36.10, respectively. *Ibid., 1880*, 229.

tainty than bad hygienic surroundings do to misery, degradation, crime and disease." [56]

Similar conditions and consequences could be found south
of Canal Street in the old French quarter,[57] where the next
largest proportion of people and dwellings in the city were
located. Two-thirds of the premises were family homes, the
remainder housekeeping shops, divided almost equally in construction between wood and brick.[58] Although the average
dwelling was very small, it sheltered seven persons,[59] and many
tenements were crowded with immigrants recently arrived
from Italian and Sicilian ports.[60] Their wretched condition was
revealed in 1871 by seven victims of yellow fever: natives of
Malta, all in their twenties, who had come to New Orleans
from Galveston a year before, these men lived in one room,
fourteen by fifteen feet, with a single window looking out on
an alley; garbed in woolen shirts and pants, shoes and straw
hats, they had earned their livelihood by peddling onions,
lemons, and limes.[61] Mortality among the foreign-born and
poor Creoles was great, amounting to twenty-four deaths for
every thousand inhabitants.[62] Many of these fatalities could be
laid directly to the foul privies, contaminated cisterns, undrained gutters, and malarial swamps of the old quarter.[63]

The other districts of New Orleans also exhibited glaring
differences between the dwellings of rich and poor which bore
a direct relation to their health. In the *faubourg Marigny*,

[56] *Rpt. La. Bd. Health, 1879,* 47.

[57] The Second District, bounded by Canal Street, south; Esplanade Street,
north; the river, east; and the city limits, west. *Soard's . . . Directory, 1882,*
41.

[58] *Rpt. La. Bd. Health, 1872,* 87.   [59] *Ibid., 1869,* 21.

[60] *Ibid., 1880,* 229.   [61] *Ibid., 1871,* 66–67.

[62] *Ibid., 1880,* 229; *1882,* vi.

[63] *Ibid., 1882,* 399–410. In the vicinity of St. Ann Street in 1882 smallpox
took sixty-four lives.

situated in the lower part of the city,[64] lived the majority of Germans and many Creoles. Except for a few shops, their frame dwellings were occupied exclusively as homes.[65] Because of the undrained swamps bordering Lake Pontchartrain, malaria prevailed in this section, and largely accounted for the deaths of twenty-five in every thousand inhabitants.[66] Uptown, in the Fourth District,[67] there was a startling contrast between the mean shelters of cotton screwmen and wharf laborers along the Mississippi River and the pretentious homes of the wealthy a few blocks away. This section was famous as the Garden District of New Orleans. Its streets were clean, the gutters well drained. Many of its richer residents left town in summer to escape any risk of yellow fever. The death rate in their neighborhood was consequently the lowest in New Orleans, averaging but eighteen or nineteen per thousand.[68]

Still farther uptown, in the Sixth District,[69] the city began to give way to open country. There were many dairies, and nearly half the inhabitants kept livestock. The sole drainage here consisted of ditches along the streets running from river to lake, which deprived all crossroads of any outlet. Privies were seldom emptied by the sanitary contractors, who excused their negligence with the plea that they were too busy in more crowded neighborhoods. The death rate was not high, except

[64] The Third District, bounded by the lake and river, north and south; Esplanade Street, west; and the city limits, east. *Soard's . . . Directory, 1882,* 41.

[65] *Rpt. La. Bd. Health, 1882,* 413.   [66] *Ibid., 1880,* 229.

[67] Bounded by the river, Felicity and Toledano Streets. *Soard's . . . Directory, loc. cit.*

[68] *Rpt. La. Bd. Health, 1880,* 229-30; *ibid., 1882,* 421-25. Mortality was almost as light in Algiers, the Fifth District across the river, because the few inhabitants, despite little sanitation, were not confined to tenements.

[69] Embracing Jefferson City and bounded by the river, south and west; Toledano Street, east; Carrollton and Marley Avenue, north. *Soard's . . . Directory, 1882,* 41.

for Negroes, averaging twenty-one per thousand, which may
be attributed to the absence of congestion and tenements.[70]
On the outskirts of the city lay the thinly settled Seventh District,[71] inhabited by more colored than white people. Small
truck farms and dairies were numerous. There was no pretense
of public drainage or sanitation, but some relief was afforded
by the location of privies in back gardens, where their contents were used as fertilizer. The rural character of this section reduced its mortality, despite the absence of sanitary precautions, to a figure no larger than in the Sixth District.[72]

The relation between health, housing, and social classes in
nineteenth-century New Orleans may be summed up in the
statement that the death rate was greatest in slums where the
poor of necessity lived. Since "houses, well built, with all the
necessary conveniences, in respectable neighborhoods, that can
be rented for $12 to $20 per month [were] extremely scarce,"
workingmen were "forced to keep their families in shanties
which were [hardly] thought good enough for housing negroes in the days of slavery." [73] Although New Orleans was
free of the towering dark tenements to be found in Northern
cities, the hovels of one or two floors in "the slums and the
swamp" were no less injurious to the health of their occu-
pants.[74] The location and want of proper sanitation in New
Orleans made it one of the most unhealthful cities in the
world; [75] and sickness and disease always took greater toll of
the poor than of the rich.

Except for the constant discrepancy between the mortality
rates of different classes, conditions of health in New Orleans
were gradually improved during the century. For fifteen

[70] *Rpt. La. Bd. Health, 1882,* vi, 441–48. White mortality was 18.07, colored, 28.20.
[71] Formerly Carrollton. *Soard's . . . Directory, loc. cit.*
[72] *Rpt. La. Bd. Health, 1882,* vi, 449–52.
[73] *Picayune,* Sept. 28, 1891.   [74] *Rpt. La. Bd. Health, 1871,* 57.
[75] Cf. A. Nevins, *The Emergence of Modern America,* 323.

years before the war, the average death rate was 56.7; for fifteen years afterward, it was only 34.9.[76]

Lower mortality was partly the result of a decrease in yellow fever. This plague took 22,595 lives from 1845 to 1860, but only 8,405 from 1860 to 1878, of whom half were carried off in the epidemic of 1878.[77] The plague was still attributed on occasion to a mysterious "poison locally grown." [78] But the Board of Health was aware that yellow fever had subsided with the establishment of a maritime quarantine in 1855, and appeared again only after the shipping interests, led by Charles Morgan and his Louisiana and Texas Railroad and Steamship Company, destroyed this medical safeguard by injunction of a local court. Because it had been the practice to charge seagoing vessels thirty dollars for inspection, and to detain them for ten days in costly idleness, the New Orleans Maritime Association fought vigorously against the restoration of a quarantine. The epidemic of 1878 was their reward. After this disaster, the Board of Health, under the splendid guidance of Dr. Joseph Jones, could argue that sanitary measures were essential to public safety, and less expensive to shipowners than closing the port when an epidemic broke out. The legislature was induced by these considerations to renew the quarantine in 1882.[79]

Perhaps equally responsible for the decrease of yellow fever and the general improvement of health was the fact that although New Orleans remained an unsanitary city, it was relatively cleaner after the war than before. The Federal army, with Butler, Banks, and Shepley using the strong arm of military law, had taught people the value of sanitation.[80] Once the army had cleaned up the streets, they never completely reverted to their prewar condition. Such "gross neglect of [the]

[76] Computed from *Rpt. La. Bd. Health, 1882,* viii.

[77] *Ibid., 1880,* 9. Exclusive of epidemic years, the average mortality declined from 49.0 to 32.0 during this period. *Ibid., 1882,* viii.

[78] *Ibid., 1872,* 22.   [79] *Ibid., 1882,* 10–39, 160–61.   [80] See above, chap. VI.

health and life of the people [had been] shown by the Common Council," that all responsibility was transferred to the medical profession with the creation of a Board of Health. Even private property came within its purview. The city was divided into sanitary districts with police inspectors to report all nuisances, the range of which was gradually extended to include everything from improper hygiene to faulty building construction.[81] In 1871 nearly fifty thousand premises were investigated: over ten thousand were ordered to empty privy vaults, and three thousand to disinfect them.[82] This problem of sewage disposal continued to vex every board of health, because the city lacked underground drainage and depended on contractors to cart away "night soil" in buckets and drays.[83] The first thorough inspection of all premises in New Orleans was undertaken in 1882, and rotten floors and roofs were reported as well as foul privies and filthy streets.[84] These investigations had the value of any census and helped to awaken the public to the existence of intolerable conditions. But no reform was possible because the Board of Health lacked compulsive powers over private property. All that it could do about slaughter houses, which gave rise in another connection to the famous Supreme Court cases, was to complain of their location within the city in direct violation of an ordinance the municipal authorities never chose to enforce.[85]

In taking ordinary medical precautions, the Board of Health was more successful. Specimens of milk from every dairy were examined;[86] filthy dwellings, incoming vessels, and public squares were disinfected.[87] In emergencies the board acted quickly to prevent the outbreak of disease. When eight thou-

---

[81] *Rpt. La. Bd. Health, 1869,* 8 *et passim.* [82] *Ibid., 1871,* 31.
[83] *Ibid., 1869,* 20.   [84] *Ibid., 1882, passim.*   [85] *Ibid., 1869,* 29–30.
[86] *Ibid., 1879,* 51. Gross adulteration and impurity of the milk supply was reported: "the sipage-well and cistern water our people pay for as milk pour a handsome revenue . . . into the pockets of our gentle keepers of kine."
[87] *Ibid., 1871,* 31.

sand houses in the French quarter were flooded by a crevasse in 1871, and drainage canals overflowed with the refuse of cesspools, thousands of gallons of carbolic acid were sprayed upon the streets. Threat of a plague compelled officials to take this drastic step in the face of intense opposition from people who preferred the familiar odor of sewage to the nauseating smell of vaporized carbolic acid.[88] The campaign against smallpox was most persistent. This disease afflicted three times as many colored as white people. It was rare in New Orleans before the war, and its virulence coincided with the twofold increase of urban Negro population during the years of reconstruction.[89] To counteract it, the vaccination of school children was made compulsory in 1870.[90] White adults also submitted to inoculation, but the Negroes put more faith in "direct Providential interference" or a "special dispensation of the Deity." [91] All these measures contributed to the prevention of disease and diminished the death rate in New Orleans after the war. The Board of Health was never satisfied with what it accomplished, and its perennial complaints of improper sanitation and poor housing testify to how much remained to be done.

Though the general health of city people was improved, less can be said of any advance in their material welfare. While no comprehensive investigation of their condition was made, and reliable figures are not always to be had,[92] there is enough partial evidence to indicate the general situation of the masses.

In the absence of contrary evidence, it is reasonable to assume that the proportions of people to be found in major occupations after the war showed less change from ante-bellum

[88] Ibid., 1871, 54–55, 62–64.
[89] Ibid., 1877, 191–201. Over five hundred deaths from smallpox were recorded in New Orleans in 1864, 1870, 1873, and 1874.
[90] Ibid., 1870, 25.   [91] Ibid., 1872, 77.
[92] The detailed report of occupations in 1870, for example, like all returns for the Southern states, was defective. See U. S. Cen., 1870, I, 736, 792.

conditions than might be supposed.[93] Since the Negro was no longer a slave, he was admitted to free contractual relations and made up the bulk of the rural lower class in agriculture. Thousands at their first opportunity left the country for the towns and entered into profitless competition with unskilled whites. But the prevailing scarcity of urban jobs combined with old habits and economic needs to keep the majority of Negroes at work on the plantations. The principal shift in their employment came as they were able to withdraw the female members of their families from toil in the fields.

A less important change in occupations accompanied the postwar growth of population and the construction of railways, which expanded the market for goods and services, and consequently attracted more people to the middle-class functions of distribution and service. Until the last decade of the nineteenth century, however, there were but slight increases in their number.[94] Inventions gave rise to a greater variety of new occupations for skilled and unskilled labor. With the postwar development of manufactures, especially after 1880, came a fivefold increase in the actual number of industrial workers, among whom women and children were conspicuous.[95] The result was that the lower class was enlarged out of all proportion to any increase of the middle class, for whites found industrial employment as ex-slaves gained a free status in agriculture, and these masses belonged to a new proletariat which

[93] See Appendix, Table 10. Unfortunately, it is impossible to ascertain exactly what shifts took place in the economic alignment of classes by occupation during the decade of reconstruction. No estimate of classes can be made for 1870 or any later decennial year which could be compared with the estimates for 1860 in Table 4, Appendix. A progressive refinement of census methods in defining and classifying occupations, as well as the addition of former slaves to free employments, make postwar figures altogether different from prewar figures. U. S. Cen., 1890, Population, II, lxxv-ix, xciv-c.

[94] U. S. Cen., 1900, Occupations, 288, 290.

[95] Ibid., Manufactures, II, 297.

appeared to be more numerous than in 1860.[96] Nothing could more clearly demonstrate the failure of the majority of people to improve their social and economic position after the war.

Although New Orleans, along with the entire state, was slow to regain the wealth lost during years of civil war and reconstruction, the process of recovery was completed by the end of the century.[97] From this gradual revival emerged not so many, but much richer, merchants than in the days of slavery. In 1892 there were said to be thirty-five millionaires in New Orleans.[98] The advertisements of clothes and carriages and the variety and display of social activities, as reported in the newspapers of the nineties, pictured the pleasant prosperity of the well-to-do.[99]

But their new wealth was not generously diffused through all ranks of society. In the absence of official reports on income, it is difficult to judge the money earned by different classes. In the lower range of the middle class, estimated after the war to include all who were able to hire a domestic servant, annual incomes ran from $1,500 to $3,000.[100] If the salesclerks in department stores were representative of the poorer "white-collared" families, it is revealing to find that in the decade following 1885 the maximum weekly salary of men advanced from $11.51 to $16.39, and of women, from $8.05 to $9.86.[101] They worked ten hours a day, with half an hour out for lunch; and many brought a cold sandwich rather than spend a quarter for hot dishes in the restaurants.[102] By organizing unions affiliated with the American Federation of Labor, the clerks in dry goods and grocery stores recognized the fact that their

---

[96] See above, *n.* 93, and Appendix, Table 10.

[97] *Times-Democrat*, Dec. 9, 1892.

[98] *Ibid.*, May 11, 1892. Kentucky boasted but 24, and Georgia, 11.

[99] See the *Item, Picayune*, and *Times-Democrat*.

[100] *Picayune*, Oct. 26, 1867.

[101] *Rpt. U.S. Com. Labor, 1895–96*, 492.

[102] *Times-Democrat*, Feb. 15, 1895.

small salaries left them no real claim to be members of the middle class.[103]

The money wages of the working class were but slightly improved after reconstruction, although great advances were supposed to have been made. From 1880 to 1895 the capital invested in New Orleans manufacturing increased 674 per cent, the value of its output, 252 per cent, and the remuneration of all employees, executive and operative, 302 per cent.[104] The average annual wage in Southern cities was said to have jumped from $346 in 1880 to $467 in 1890, an advance of 36 per cent.[105]

But it is difficult to find any factory or craft in New Orleans where these reputed increases were reflected in individual pay envelopes. From 1885 to 1895, cotton mill spinners were advanced in weekly wages from $3.43 to $3.68, weavers, from $4.96 to $5.76, cigar makers, from a maximum of $5.32 to $6.55, awning makers, from $11.33 to $12.10, and press compositors, from $12.95 to $13.31.[106] In view of the boasted advance of 36 per cent in the Southern wage level, it is significant that none of these working people received an increase of even 25 per cent. In skilled crafts such as the building trades and machine shops, bricklayers gained most during the nineties, advancing from 40 to 45 cents an hour, which was an addition of only 13 per cent.[107] But in no working-class occupation did the original remuneration or the slight increases of the eighties and nineties indicate a general distribution of prosperity.

Wages were actually reduced in many lines of work, and remained low in all trades. Between 1883 and 1888 the daily rate of ordinary labor fell from $1.50 to $1.00.[108] Even the skilled crafts fared poorly during the nineties: eight thousand

[103] Ibid., Nov. 26, 1887; Picayune, July 24, 1892.
[104] Times-Democrat, Sept. 1, 1896.   [105] Ibid., Dec. 8, 1892.
[106] Rpt. U. S. Com. Labor, 1895–96, 49, 128, 146, 201, 390.
[107] Ibid., 1904, 447–68.   [108] Times-Democrat, Sept. 1, 1888.

carpenters suffered a loss of hourly pay, while painters, plumb-
ers, and machinists were barely able to maintain their wage
levels.[109] These scales were low in comparison to what crafts
in other cities received. For an eight-hour day in New York,
carpenters obtained four dollars, and in Philadelphia, three
dollars, but for a nine-hour day in New Orleans they earned
only two dollars.[110] The daily pay of ten thousand factory
workers, employed in boots and shoes, breweries, clothing,
cotton, iron, lumber, sugar, and tobacco establishments, ranged
from twenty-five cents to two dollars.[111]

The real wages of the working class, in terms of purchasing
power, never afforded a progressively rising standard of living. While the urban masses were able to buy more and better
food as the years passed, because of declining postwar prices,[112]
their economic position was not greatly improved. A statistician for the Knights of Labor, after a study of conditions in
New Orleans in 1883, estimated that the cost of living for the
average worker's family varied from $480 to $624 a year, with
monthly expenditures of at least $25 for food, $8 for rent, and
$7 for clothing and fuel.[113] So poor were the masses that the
nickel, which had always been the common currency, was
divided in half by storekeepers, who issued brass tags known
as "quarties" to facilitate purchases as small as two and a half
cents.[114]

Whatever measure of comfort the working class enjoyed
came largely from the family purse, to which at least two
members in the average group of five contributed, for women

[109] *Rpt. U.S. Com. Labor, 1904, loc. cit.*
[110] *Southern Economist and Trade Unionist,* Feb. 3, 1900.
[111] *Picayune,* Sept. 1, 1892.
[112] E.g., the falling prices of foodstuffs at New Orleans in *Sen. Rpts.,*
52 Cong., 2 sess., no. 1394, pt. iv, 1654–1767, 1806–9.
[113] *Times-Democrat,* Sept. 1, 1888.
[114] *Ibid.,* Nov. 8, 1892. Named after the old Spanish "quartie," worth six
and a quarter cents.

went to work in order to supplement the low wages of men. These facts emerge from a census of more than five hundred working women in New Orleans in 1886. The majority were unmarried girls, Creole and Irish Catholics, of an average age of twenty-two, who had received an elementary education in public or parochial schools. They lived at home, assisted in housework, and contributed all earnings to their families. Their annual incomes, from a wide variety of shops and mills, ranged from $117 in a mattress factory to $323 in a dry goods store. Nearly six-tenths of these wages went for food and rent, and three-tenths for clothes. Although their average income was higher than in any Southern city except Savannah, and their expenditures the lowest, the common requirements of a decent life absorbed all earnings except for contributions to the church and an occasional fling at fortune in the form of a lottery ticket.[115]

Another illustration of the necessity of the family purse for any degree of comfort is to be found in a report on five families employed in New Orleans textile mills in 1890. Of eight children in this group, five were at school and three at work. None of the mothers labored outside their homes but three provided boarders with food and lodging. The fathers of the five families earned a total of $640 a year, their children, $332, and boarders brought in $106. In every dollar of aggregate income, forty-one cents was spent for food, fifteen for rent, nine for clothes, three for fuel, and one for light, with thirty-one cents remaining for all the other needs of life.[116]

To help the men meet these demands on the family purse, wives, sons, and daughters went to work in field and factory. Those who were colored had been accustomed to drudgery since the days of slavery, but now it also became necessary for

[115] *Rpt. U.S. Com. Labor, 1888*, 19–20, 119–20, 278–79, 316, 339, 408–9, 464–65, 505.

[116] *Ibid., 1891*, pt. iii, 858, 1737, 1992–93, 2006–7.

a large proportion of the white women and children. Including all occupations and both races, the number of children at work between the ages of ten and fifteen nearly doubled during the nineties, increasing from 31,847 to 61,047. The overwhelming majority, of course, were to be found in agriculture rather than industry.[117] Their employment in factories, shops, or warehouses was forbidden by the legislature, but this law was never enforced.[118]

The growing industrialization of New Orleans was based almost entirely on the toil of women and children. Manufacturers came South because labor was 25 per cent cheaper than in the North, and to New Orleans because of its "vast numbers of poor women, and children over 12 years of age," [119] who could be hired more cheaply than men and with less fear of strikes.[120] By 1888 there were fifteen thousand women and children employed in clothing, cigar, and shoe shops. At the textile factories, according to report, not a "pale millhand" could be found, but only girls with "rosy cheeks" who worked ten hours a day for weekly wages of sixteen dollars.[121] In ten representative establishments, during the decade following 1885, the number of women increased 131 per cent, girls under eighteen, 216 per cent, and boys, 116 per cent.[122] While men generally earned at least ten dollars a week, women and children seldom obtained five.[123] They were caught in a vicious circle: seeking jobs outside the home because one man's

117 *U. S. Cen., 1890, Comp.*, Table 79; *ibid., 1900, Occupations*, clxxiv, cclvii.
118 *La. Sess. Laws, 1886* [no. 43] quoted in *U. S. Cen., 1900, loc. cit.*
119 *Picayune*, Jan. 10, 1875. See Appendix, Table 10. Of the females in New Orleans in 1890 over ten years of age, 25 per cent were employed, as compared with 39 per cent of the total population. *U. S. Cen., 1890, Population*, II, clxviii, clxx.
120 *Rpt. U. S. Com. Labor, 1895–96*, 588.
121 *Times-Democrat*, Sept. 1, 1888.
122 *Bull., U. S. Com. Labor*, no. 10, 242, 244, 255.
123 *Rpt., ibid., 1895–96*, 49, 94, 128–29, 146, 201–2, 390, 492.

296 ORIGINS OF CLASS STRUGGLE IN LOUISIANA

income was insufficient to support them, women and children were hired for cheaper services, and consequently depressed still further the inadequate remuneration of husbands and fathers, without raising the family income to a comfortable level.

Their combined labor seldom earned enough to buy homes. Four in every five families in New Orleans in 1890 were tenants.[124] Of the fortunate minority who owned dwellings, a large proportion were not so prosperous as ownership would imply: nearly half the urban mortgages were written on cheap houses for small sums of $1,000 or less.[125] The masses who rented lodgings paid more for poorer quarters, it was said, than in any other old American city.[126] This widespread and expensive tenancy provoked the alarming reflection that "the man who has only his daily wages, with nothing laid up for emergencies, is fast becoming a slave, with the prospect, if any accident should happen to him, of final beggary."[127]

Periodical unemployment was one of the accidents that swelled the ranks of the destitute.[128] The prolonged depression following the Panic of 1873 threatened five thousand families with starvation.[129] They complained bitterly of lack of work, but were told that enforced idleness was the natural consequence of idle industry.[130] As they became desperate for food, after exhausting the charity of butchers and bakers, unemployed workers petitioned the City Council to share public street work among them, "content with a week or a month" taken in turn with regular laborers at the customary daily pay of $1.75.[131] While a few were relieved in this way by a reduction of the prevailing wage to $1.50,[132] and a hundred homeless women were sheltered at a municipal soup house,[133] the

[124] *U. S. Cen., 1890, Rpt. Farms and Homes*, 32.   [125] *Ibid.*, 60–61.
[126] *Picayune*, Sept. 28, 1891.   [127] *Ibid.*, Mar. 20, 1896.
[128] *Ibid.*, Jan. 14, 1870.   [129] *Ibid.*, Mar. 24, Apr. 28, 1875.
[130] *Ibid.*, July 19, 1874.   [131] *Ibid.*, Mar. 24, 1875.
[132] *Ibid.*, Mar. 26, 27, 1875.   [133] *Ibid.*, Mar. 15, 1875.

plight of the majority went unsolved until actual starvation
became their immediate danger. Then nearly two thousand
men, women, and children were sent into the country to provide plantations with cheap labor, and thirty-five hundred,
too old or too weak to work, were furnished with meager
supplies of flour, meal, and rice.[134] This sad spectacle was re-
hearsed on a smaller scale following the Panic of 1893.[135]

Meantime, pauperism grew apace. A multitude of people,
white and black alike, kept body and soul together on thirteen
cents a day toward the end of the century.[136] Many of the
destitute were to be found, not in almshouses, which admitted
few, but in benevolent institutions, of which Louisiana had
more inmates than other Southern states. The majority were
neither colored nor foreign but native whites.[137] Thousands
of boys and girls, orphaned by the death of parents on battlefield or sickbed, were sheltered in municipal and Catholic
asylums.[138] There were also homeless boys who roamed the
streets, slept in alleyways, subsisted on coffee and "fried river
buffalo," and eked out a precarious livelihood by hawking
newspapers.[139] The number of tramps became so large that
New Orleans rebuilt its workhouse and restored the chain gang
for so-called "voluntary paupers."[140] They were arrested by
the police, subjected to a "labor test," and locked up.[141]

To push back the rising tide of pauperism, the New Orleans
Conference of Charities was organized in 1883. Its avowed objects were to protect the community from the imposture of
mendicants, to prevent the duplication of gifts, to aid the deserving by making "employment the basis of relief," and to
"elevate the home life, health and habits of the poor." Like

[134] *Picayune*, Sept. 2, 1875.   [135] *Ibid.*, Apr. 13, May 14, 1895.
[136] *Times-Democrat*, Nov. 8, 1892.
[137] *U. S. Cen., 1890, Rpt. Crime, Pauperism and Benevolence*, pt. ii, 655, 879.
[138] *U. S. Cen., 1880, Rpt. Cities*, 291.   [139] *Crescent*, Feb. 7, 1869.
[140] *Planters Journal*, Aug. 1881.
[141] *Times-Democrat*, Jan. 10, 18, 29, 1885.

the organized charities of other cities the New Orleans Conference was notable for the rigor of its inspection rather than the bounty of its relief. A pitifully inadequate annual budget of $1,200, obtained from individual membership dues of six dollars, defrayed the expenses of a clerk and two investigators. In the course of eight years the Charities reported some degree of assistance to more than eight thousand families, of whom only sixty-three were able to become self-supporting. It was obviously no fault of the others that they remained indigent. Distress was so widespread and constant, even in prosperous years, that during 1891–92 the Unsectarian Aid Society, a ladies' auxiliary, distributed rations to more than 5,000 people, and served lunches to 3,500 homeless unfortunates.[142] An evangelical "rescue mission," located in the slums of the French quarter, gave shelter every night in 1899 to a total of 23,000 destitute men.[143] By the end of the nineteenth century, like other American cities, New Orleans had its "submerged tenth," a significant fraction of the population sunk in hopeless poverty.

To explain the misery of the unfortunate and the depressed circumstances of a majority of the working class, it is important to remember that New Orleans had never recovered its former prosperity after the war. Traffic in cotton, to a considerable extent, and the bulk of grain shipments were diverted by the railways from the Gulf to Atlantic seaports and interior forwarding points.[144] Competition among the spreading railways reduced freight rates below the costs of transportation on the Mississippi River; and since the long haul to the East was cheapest, the West and upper South turned their backs on New Orleans.[145] Louisville, Cincinnati, St. Louis,

---

[142] *Times-Democrat*, May 10, 1892.   [143] *The Worker*, III, no. 9.

[144] *Commercial Bulletin*, Sept. 1, 1870.

[145] *Crescent*, Jan. 24, 1869. In order to attract cotton to the Mississippi Central and Mississippi and Tennessee Railroads, for example, an agreement

Memphis, Vicksburg, and a host of junction towns along the railroads attracted an increasing share of plantation trade.[146] The railroads completed the division of the Mississippi Valley between North and South that had first taken place in the Civil War. Commerce on the river languished, and New Orleans was stranded for want of railroads to tap the interior.[147] In such a city labor could hardly prosper. During the sixties it shared the distress of a hinterland ravaged by war, and during the seventies, of a country prostrated by the depression that followed the Panic of 1873.

The resulting unemployment was not relieved by industrialization, for manufacturing capital was scarce and afraid to embark on new enterprises in the turmoil of reconstruction. Twenty years after secession the number of industrial establishments had actually decreased, presumably through consolidation, and the proportion of the population engaged in manufactures remained the same—an insignificant 1 per cent.[148] Yet there was constant agitation, as before the war, for factories to employ the poor whites. "It is the duty of State governments and of wealthy men of the South to provide employments for our poor white people. . . . A cotton mill is much better than a poor-house."[149] There was one mill which became a poorhouse. The Arizona Cotton Factory, a brick building with 2,400 spindles, was established after the war among the poor whites of Claiborne Parish.[150] Eighteen cottages, each with two rooms, were built to house the local operatives. Financial difficulties soon beset the factory, however, and in 1880 it was sold to a New Orleans syndicate which planned to

---

was made that rates from country towns to New Orleans should be double the charge for through shipments, New Orleans to Memphis.

[146] *Commercial Bulletin, loc. cit.*   [147] *Picayune*, Sept. 1, 1871.

[148] *U. S. Cen., 1900*, VIII, pt. ii, 297.

[149] *Commercial Bulletin*, Dec. 25, 1866. See *ibid.*, Mar. 5, 1867.

[150] *Picayune*, Apr. 22, 1869.

import its labor from the North.[151] Thus ended in failure the only attempt in Louisiana to employ rural poor whites as mill workers.

A few successful textile factories were nevertheless established in New Orleans, where there was a "vast number of poor women, and children . . . [who] can be procured 25% less than . . . at the North." [152] Typical of these mills was one located in the Third District among people whom its president called "docile, industrious, cheerful and intelligent." "To control better our labor," the operatives were housed in company tenements. If additional quarters were built for a night shift, declared the president, "I am confident that a reduction of wages can be made, almost imperceptibly, sufficient to return a handsome interest upon the cost of the buildings." [153] Shrewd management was perhaps essential for a factory to survive, but it hardly contributed to the welfare of its labor.

The chief gain made by the workingmen of New Orleans after the war was increasing organization. While but two labor unions had been established in the days of slavery,[154] eighteen more associations were flourishing by 1880.[155] They formed the backbone of the trade union movement that was to grow strong enough to challenge the merchants of New Orleans in the general strike of 1892.[156] The postwar years may therefore be called the seedtime of the labor movement in Louisiana. Early in the Civil War, as previously observed, the workingmen of New Orleans came to realize that once slavery was abolished in Louisiana, the way would be open for free labor to organize and advance its interests. And so they joined the Free State party, sent delegates to the Convention of 1864, and not only wiped out slavery but also secured constitutional

[151] *Democrat*, Sept. 1, 1880.   [152] *Picayune*, Jan. 10, 1875.
[153] *Report of the President . . . to the Board of Directors of the Louisiana Cotton Manufactory* (1872), 1–8.
[154] See above, 114–15.   [155] *Times*, Dec. 14, 1880.   [156] See below, *n.* 179.

guarantees of minimum wages and hours on public works.[157] Their short-lived success aroused labor to greater activity as the war ended. For the first time in New Orleans the carpenters organized a union,[158] and unskilled labor formed a benevolent association to insure its members sickness and death benefits.[159] Workingmen united, furthermore, to wage a brief but successful struggle for an eight-hour day. A mass meeting of mechanics and laborers was held under a large banner, on which was lettered their slogan, "Eight Hours the Just Time." Resolutions were passed to co-operate toward this end with labor in the North and West, and to vote only for candidates who would make it law.[160]

One of the strangest sights in a city where animosity between white and colored labor often ran high, was the united strike, in 1865, of longshoremen belonging to both races. Demanding an increase of wages,[161] they stopped all work on the river front, and marched down the levee, black and white together. This spectacle must have shocked many a returning Confederate and caused some anxiety as to what would happen if labor should not remain divided by the color line. Not for long, however, did they have reason to fear this prospect. "For the sake of precedent," the shipmasters rejected the strikers' demands, and the police tried to divide them, black from white, by arresting colored longshoremen on the charge of rioting and interfering with nonstrikers.[162]

How different was the situation of the levee eight years later! Not only had racial animosity increased under carpet-

---

[157] See above, chap. VII.   [158] *Crescent*, Nov. 4, 1865.
[159] *Ibid.*, Oct. 28, Dec. 20, 1865.   [160] *Ibid.*, Nov. 4, 1865.
[161] The amount and prevailing rates were not reported by the contemporary press. Mayor Kennedy's statement to Trowbridge (*The South*, 405), that the strikers were already getting $2.50 to $3.00 a day, and wanted $5.00 to $7.00, is difficult to believe. Even the highly skilled screwmen did not earn that wage.
[162] *Crescent*, Dec. 22, 1865.

bag government, but the Panic of 1873 had diminished employment and aggravated the competition of both races for jobs. White longshoremen appealed to General Badger, of the Federal army, to arrest as vagrants the "low, ignorant negroes, who slept under tarpaulins and in barrel houses, and who . . . could afford to work at lower than regular rates."[163] The General arrested as many as he could, but more Negroes took their places. White and colored longshoremen armed themselves with guns and knives. After months of rising tension a riot broke out; the Negroes tried to drive white longshoremen from the levee, attacked the police, and were finally dispersed with several wounded but no one killed.[164] This struggle between the races, one willing to work at twenty-five cents an hour, the other seeking to preserve its jobs at double that amount, shows that even in the city the white man was confronted with the competition of ex-slaves.[165]

This competition was not unwelcome to merchants, shipmasters, and employers in general, because it tended to reduce the wages of the unskilled, white or black, to the level at which freedmen could subsist. Throughout the city, it was reported in 1874, employers were hiring Negroes when white workingmen were on the verge of starvation. Since merchants and planters needed the votes of these laborers to oust the Republican carpetbag government, they were exhorted to "give preference to white over black labor."[166] This policy was adopted by many employers. The steamboat companies, for instance, had been using cheap Negro crews ever since the white roustabouts were sent to fight for the Confederacy.[167] Now they decided to discharge all Negroes and hire whites

---

[163] *Picayune*, Aug. 24, 1874.   [164] *Ibid.*, Jan. 16, 30, 1875.

[165] Many Negro craftsmen, of course, had never been slaves before the war, but highly respected freemen of color. Cf. Nordhoff, *The Cotton States*, 72.

[166] *Picayune*, Aug. 4, 1874.   [167] Trowbridge, *op. cit.*, 388–89.

instead, but "at the same wages as are now paid to black for like labor."[168] It is hardly necessary to remark upon the irony of raising the cry of "white supremacy" in politics, and at the same time reducing this race to colored wage levels. So common was this practice in New Orleans shipping and trade that at last even the highly skilled screwmen and cotton yardmen were threatened with Negro competition. These unions alone preserved their wage scales by organizing the colored laborers into affiliated associations, bound to supply certain numbers of men at the *same* rates obtained by union workers.[169] In return for a smaller proportion of jobs, perhaps, the Negro enjoyed higher remuneration, while the whites protected their own standard of living. Thus the colored screwmen and cotton yardmen were organized by the whites in the midst of the racial animosity that accompanied reconstruction. But no other craft followed their lead.

The lean years after the Panic of 1873 gave rise to many strikes, which revealed the growing strength of trade unionism in New Orleans. The car drivers, working fourteen to sixteen hours a day, and not much better off than their mules, struck twice.[170] Local railwaymen did not join the nationwide walkout of 1877 because their wage reductions were rescinded.[171] But employees of the oil refineries, and cigar makers, went on strike against pay cuts, the former to lose, and the latter to win.[172] In all these conflicts, employers expressed the philosophy of their times, holding that workingmen could individually leave their jobs, but not combine, and never interfere with those who took their places.[173] Labor could best advance its interests, declared the press, not by strik-

---

[168] *Picayune*, Aug. 1, 1874.
[169] *Times-Democrat*, Nov. 26, 1887; *Picayune*, Nov. 26, 1892.
[170] *Commercial Bulletin*, Dec. 2, 1870; *Picayune*, July 27, 1873.
[171] *Picayune*, July 26, 1877.   [172] *Ibid.*, Nov. 8–17, 1877; Mar. 7, 1878.
[173] *Commercial Bulletin*, Dec. 2, 1870.

304 ORIGINS OF CLASS STRUGGLE IN LOUISIANA

ing for higher wages and shorter hours, but by working and saving to "secure . . . the rewards of capital and capital itself." [174] Labor was still inclined to individualism and timidity. As unemployment increased with the protracted depression of the seventies, workingmen petitioned the City Council to hire more men for less time and pay. "Not having work for all," read their petition, "we believe ourselves entitled to an equal share of the work now going on, and would be content with a week or a month." [175] Nothing could show more clearly the distress and helplessness of unskilled labor.

But skilled craftsmen were better able to weather the depression and organize their trades. By 1880, therefore, the following unions were enumerated by name in the New Orleans press: Bricklayers' Benevolent Association, Cigarmakers' Union, Coopers' Benevolent Union, Cotton Yard Men's Association No. 1, Cotton Yard Men's Association No. 2 (colored), Dairymen's Co-operative and Mutual Aid Assn., Grain Shovelers' Association, Journeymen Bakers' Association, Longshoremen's Benevolent Association, Lower Wharf Levee Laborers' Association, Mechanics' and Laborers' Union, New Orleans Street Railroadmen's Association, Screwmen's Benevolent Association No. 1, Screwmen's Benevolent Association No. 2 (colored), Shoemakers' Union, Slaters' Union, Steamboatmen and Laborers Association, Teamsters' and Loaders' Union, Typographical Union No. 17, Union Laboring Men's Benevolent Association.[176] The majority of these associations, as their names imply, were organized to insure workingmen against sickness and death. Although occasionally striking in protest of wage reductions, these unions found the times too hard for more aggressive action than protection against the common hazards of life. Their aim was security rather than improved working conditions.

[174] *Picayune*, Sept. 12, 1867.   [175] *Picayune*, Mar. 24, 1875.
[176] *Democrat*, Sept. 2, 1880; *Times*, Dec. 14, 1880.

Labor in New Orleans was indeed conservative. In 1880 a group of newly arrived German immigrants, schooled in the doctrines of socialism, tried to organize a united front among the city unions. Their program called for a uniform minimum wage of three dollars, in all kinds of work and for both races, and a maximum working day of eight hours. The press was horrified not only by these immediate demands but also by the gospel of class war. They became the bogey of a short-lived "red scare," much to the discomfort of the Foundry Helpers, who were then on strike. Only two unions, the teamsters and cotton yardmen, seem to have joined the socialist movement; and disputes over the strange theories of the immigrants soon led to their withdrawal. Not until the following year did the trade unions unite, and then in a central assembly that was to become the local organ of the American Federation of Labor.[177] "They did not want communism," protested the striking Foundry Helpers, "but simply an increase of wages that would enable them to keep clear of the landlord and grocerymen." [178] Through organization, undertaken in the years of reconstruction, New Orleans workingmen were getting ready to improve their lot. The great general strike of 1892 was to find nearly half the population arrayed in unions and engaged in a desperate but vain struggle for the closed shop.[179]

But New Orleans was not Louisiana, and so it becomes necessary to inquire into the condition of the country people before concluding that the "rise of the poor whites" was a myth. The rural population was classified somewhat arbitrarily by an intelligent contemporary into "three separate and distinct classes, viz: the [former] slaveholding aristocracy, the colored element, and that class that has always been known

[177] *Picayune*, Nov. 25, 1887.   [178] *Democrat*, Sept. 2–11, 1880.
[179] See my study, "The New Orleans General Strike of 1892," *L. H. Q.*, XXI (April, 1938).

at the South as the 'poor whites.' " The majority of whites were
thought to belong to the last category because they were
poor.[180] The degree of their poverty, not as stark and unre-
lieved in the country as in the city, may best be understood
from a summary description of the standards of life among
typical groups. If one had traveled through the country parishes in the years following the war, as Samuel Lockett did
between 1869 and 1871,[181] the condition of the rural poor
would have been seen to vary greatly according to their region
and occupation, but never to have justified any belief in the
"rise of the poor whites."

Inhabitants of the piney woods were well liked by Lockett,
who gave them the character of being "proverbially poor, honest, moral, virtuous, simple-hearted and hospitable," and of
frequently showing "evidence of thrift, comfort and prosperity." Some communities were so isolated and inbred that
ties of kinship bound them together. A very prosperous settlement of only twenty families was Burdick's Creek in Calcasieu, with a church, schoolhouse, and Masonic lodge. "Each
family had its herd of cattle, flock of sheep, and drove of hogs.
They all made their own cotton, corn, potatoes, rice, sugar,
and tobacco; spun and wove their own clothes for summer
and winter wear, made their own leather, and in fact supplied
nearly all of their necessities by home products, with the exception of coffee and a few articles of dry goods." [182] This was
a striking illustration of the self-sufficient comfort of the more
prosperous farmers. They worked hard for their livelihood:
from April through October, they would rise before the sun
was up, drink a cup of coffee, and go about their tasks in the
field until the noonday sun became oppressive; then they
would return to their cabins for dinner, and wait two or three

[180] *Rpt. State Supt. Pub. Educ., 1871,* 119, 122; E. S. Stoddard, Supt.
Second Division.
[181] See below, Bibliography.   [182] Lockett MS, 129.

hours until the sun was well past its zenith; on resuming their duties in the field, they would labor until dark. By following this routine the men and women were able to accomplish strenuous work in a hot climate, and each one could cultivate as much as five acres of cotton and three of corn.[183]

This was an ideal daily schedule for cotton farmers in the northern parishes, and it differed but little from that of Creoles who raised sugar and rice to the south. The latter would stop their morning work about eight to have a light breakfast and water the mules, and always took a longer siesta because of the more intense heat.[184] The poorer Creoles in the lowlands knew what poverty was. One could find them, as in Lafourche, living in cabins behind the levee along narrow ridges bordered by malarial marshes. They were simple, ignorant, and temperate in their habits, with very large families, all closely related in blood. Rice was their main crop, if not sugar, and it grew up to every cabin door. They grew few vegetables, but subsisted largely on rice, fish, wild ducks, and snipe. Leprosy was not unknown among them.[185] Farther north, along the Cane River in Natchitoches, lived more prosperous Creoles, whose blood was now diluted by mixture with other stocks and even with Negroes. Their small houses were constructed in a style peculiar to the Louisiana Creole. Of "wooden frames, filled in with mud," they had "narrow fronts, high sharp roofs," and were snug enough for a colder climate.[186]

Piney woods farmers had a lean and monotonous diet in spite of the variety of their crops. The universal fare in this region, "three times a day for nearly three hundred and sixty five days of the year," was "coarse corn bread and fried bacon," with the addition of "collards" or some vegetable for

[183] De Bow's Review, III (A. W. S.), 307.
[184] L. Bouchereau, Statement of the Sugar and Rice Crops Made in La., 1870–71, xviii.
[185] Rpt. La. Bd. Health, 1880, 219.   [186] Lockett MS, 210.

dinner. Fresh meat and venison, which could still be had for the shooting, were always fried. "Chickens, eggs, milk and butter, all kinds of vegetables, and fruit they could have, but have not," observed Lockett. It was his opinion that to "smash all the frying pans [would improve] the mental, moral and physical condition" of the backwoods people,[187] and he was doubtless right.

Farmers of the Florida parishes were a "sturdy, honest, intelligent, hospitable people." [188] They were "tall, gaunt old fellows, dressed in copperas-colored jeans and great rough boots." They straggled into town with the last cotton, "striving to out-chew their meek-eyed, patient oxen, contentedly 'making' sixteen miles per day, camping out at night, enjoying coffee in a tin cup, and reveling in practical jokes." They would use the proceeds from the sale of their cotton to "get a little calico for the 'ole 'oman,' a great deal of tobacco for the 'ole man,' some flour and a good deal of whiskey," and then drive back to their cabins to live through the winter on fat-back, corn pone, and potatoes.[189]

Cajuns and Creoles who inhabited the prairies were a proud but humble folk, kind and sociable to their own kind but shy and suspicious of any stranger who did not speak their French jargon. They were inclined to be stupid, for their only schooling was to "learn to ride about as soon as they begin to walk." [190] The Acadian prairie house was a wooden frame filled with a mortar of mud and sand. The interior would be neatly but scantily furnished with an old bed, wooden settee, and low chairs with seats of hide, all of home manufacture; from red rafters under the roof hung herbs and skeins of hand-spun cotton yarn ready for the loom. Here the housewife, in dingy blue dress, made the family clothes, cooked its food at a great hearth of glowing fagots, and tended to a multitude

---

[187] Ibid., 130–31.
[188] Ibid., 225.
[189] Picayune, Jan. 13, 1878.
[190] Lockett MS, 141.

of children.[191] These prairie squatters kept large herds of horses, ponies, and cattle on the open range. The livestock was poor, and good only for its meat and hides; "with thousands of cows roaming on the prairies you never see butter or milk." Cajuns and Creoles had no taste for such dairy products, since "cafe noir [was] their nectar, and perique tobacco their ambrosia." A Negro who settled on the Attakapas prairie after the war enclosed his land, and put horses, sheep, and cattle to pasture in fallow tracts of forty acres. Applying manure to the thin soil, he raised crops of corn for winter fodder. His livestock was reputed to be the best in the country because he corralled and fed the animals in the colder months. But his neighbors would not learn by example. "Their half mud huts," observed Lockett, "generally stand in the open prairie, with hardly a yard and garden under fence, and their cattle runs uncared for on the prairies the year through." [192]

Cajuns who dwelt along the southern bayous were even more conservative, and completely untouched by the changing customs of the world outside.[193] Large communities within seventy-five miles of New Orleans were living in 1870 "as they lived a hundred years ago." They were considerably mixed with Spanish, Portuguese, and Italian settlers, but their language remained a French dialect. "An outcast people, [who] sought an asylum in the quiet depths of the Louisiana swamps," they were often beyond the reach of census marshals and tax collectors. Although their haunts abounded in cypress, the "Maison d'Acadien of a century past" was the kind of shelter they preferred: an adobe cabin with mud walls thatched with palmetto leaves. These people had no use for schools, which would only make children "smart" and defiant of the traditions that constituted their lore of life. One community

[191] *Picayune*, Aug. 12, 1888.   [192] Lockett MS, 71–73, 141–42.
[193] *Picayune*, July 28, 1873.

of twelve hundred, in the region of Lafourche and Terre-bonne, lacked an appointed priest, and not half a dozen could read or write any language; there were no books here, not even a Bible, nor newspapers or pamphlets. Yet these illiterate swamp Cajuns were strangely intelligent for all their apparent ignorance. They were independent and contented. Not a week end went by without simple balls or parties, and during the week there were poker games, target shooting, pirogue races, and wrestling, upon which wagers were freely made. Cheap claret and whisky were served at every gathering, but seldom to excess. It was a curious peasant culture which preserved older ways of existence and made no effort to raise or change the material standards of life.[194]

Along the Bayou Jesse in the Attakapas marsh, a network of lakes and streams accessible only to boats, could be found the lowest examples of the swamp Cajuns, shiftless and ignorant, who were sharply distinguished in character from the honest and industrious inhabitants of the prairie. But they had pride of race, for they never mingled socially with the Negroes among whom they lived. Their food was fish and game; their chief occupation was moss picking, and now and then a little woodcutting.[195] This community is an interesting though unimportant example of the "low-down" or "mean whites" who lived as poorly as the poorest Negroes.[196]

Hunters who were also farmers frequented the southern lakes, bayous, and coastal marshes between the Mississippi and Berwick's Bay. A labyrinth of wooded watercourses through the swamps and lowlands of lower Louisiana afforded them plenty of fish and game. They were atavistic pioneers who

[194] *Ibid.; Rpt. State Supt. Pub. Educ., 1871,* 122–23.

[195] *Picayune,* Aug. 15, 1874.

[196] *Ibid.* This account mentions an English immigrant of ante-bellum days whose daughter married a Negro; the father is said never to have been recognized as better than a plantation Negro.

spent the winter months shooting ducks, snipe, deer, and rab-
bits; and paddled down the bayous and over the lakes in quest
of game, packing a tent, blankets, cooking pots, and ammu-
nition in a pirogue, a frail wooden craft about ten feet long
and two feet wide. When the hunting season was over in the
spring they returned to their little farms, planted such vegetables as tomatoes, okra, and melons, and took them to the New
Orleans market for higher prices a full month earlier than
truck farmers on the Mississippi River. In the fall they planted
sweet potatoes for their own use, and at least once a year en-
riched the soil with phosphates by applying to it the refuse
of fishbones. They added to their diet milk, butter, beef, eggs,
and many vegetables, and kept hogs, cattle, and poultry. Their
log or planked houses were comfortable, and roofed with
shingles or palmetto thatch. Hunting and fishing from November to March, they planted their gardens in the cool spring,
idled away the hot summer, raised sweet potatoes in the mild
fall, and then returned to their hunting. It was all done very
casually in happy-go-lucky fashion, for life in the swamps was
easy, with a great plenty of fish and game, and vegetables
growing almost wild. These hunter-farmers had a peculiar and
well-diversified economy; they were remarkable for fertilizing
their gardens, specializing in fancy market vegetables, and at
the same time satisfying their pioneering instinct for adventure
and hunting.[197]

There were always many fishermen in lower Louisiana. The
fisheries continued to prosper after the war, though the rich
oyster banks had been partly destroyed by the Mississippi
floods. In the year which followed the conclusion of hostilities
it was estimated that 100,000 barrels of oysters were dredged
for the New Orleans market. Several hundred oystermen engaged in this work, and earned $300 to $400 a season besides
attending to their small farms.[198] The trade was expanded

[197] *Ibid.*, July 28, 1873.   [198] *Ibid.*, Sept. 16, 1866.

and transformed after 1880 into an export canning industry by the introduction of capital which eventually reached a total of nearly three million dollars. The result was that in 1892 there were over four hundred vessels and eleven thousand people working either in the fisheries or canneries, and shrimp were as important a product as oysters.[199] Shrimp were then cured in the sun and packed in barrels, for each of which the dryers received from $5 to $6.[200] In earlier years, when the business was less commercialized, fishermen sailed in large luggers or flat-bottomed skiffs of one to four tons burden. They would tow small boats to the fishing grounds on the Gulf of Mexico, where they used both seines and lines. A single trip might earn a man as much as $25 when he sold his catch to a local or city market.[201] Many Chinese and Sicilian families joined the Cajuns and Portuguese in the fishing trade after the war; the Orientals proved to be experts in drying shrimp and salting trout. None of these fishermen led a very comfortable existence. The illiterate inhabitants of Timbalier Island, for example, made their homes in squalid, unpainted houses, went without schools, and lacked even the social amenities of peasants.[202] The fisheries were a watery frontier, on inland bayous and lakes no less than along the Gulf Coast, where people were cut off from civilization, and prospered economically only as the market demand of the city drew them into its net.

The life of rural Louisiana was so richly varied that it would be difficult if not impossible to describe every aspect of it. Differences or peculiarities of race, dialect, tradition, habitation, livelihood, and manners distinguished many communities even when they were situated in the same region or parish. Much of the color and reality of their life is probably forever lost, because no record remains of what then appeared so

[199] *Times-Democrat*, Dec. 12, 1892.   [200] *Ibid.*, Sept. 11, 1892.
[201] *Picayune*, July 28, 1873.   [202] *Ibid.*, Aug. 5, 1888.

trivial, natural, and permanent that it was taken for granted and known to all who were concerned with it. Many other groups and settlements, such as the poor farmers, woodsmen, and cattle-herders along the Pearl River, could be identified.[203] But enough have been mentioned already to show the diversity of the countryside.

It would seem doubtful if the condition of the rural poor was much improved after the war. While some groups, like the fishermen, came into new or greater opportunities of earning their daily food, the lot of the majority appears to have changed remarkably little. Indeed, it was shortly to grow worse in the eighties and nineties, and to give rise to the rural revolt known as Populism, in which farmers joined city laborers in a crusade of discontent.

Populism was to be a political uprising of the poor and white who were finally driven to class-conscious action by their long and weary failure, except occasionally as fortunate individuals, to rise in the economic and social scale of living. For more than a generation, from 1840 to 1875, they endured a succession of disastrous circumstances, the competitive disabilities and oligarchic rule of a wealthy slaveholding society, the holocaust of a war that destroyed chattel slavery but little else, and the racial exploitation and misgovernment of reconstruction. Economic depression spread with the passing years as Louisiana failed to recover from the losses of war and plunged into a protracted period of internal strife. The people who were poor and white had changed neither their color nor their condition in any appreciable sense.

[203] *Ibid.*, Feb. 25, 1878.

APPENDIX: STATISTICAL TABLES *

TABLE I—REGIONAL VARIATIONS IN 1860 AND 1880
1860 [1]

Region [2]	% Population [3]			% Free Families [4] without Slaves	% Slave-holdings [4] with 1-5 Slaves
	Total	Free	Slave		
Alluvial lowland	69	71	67	75	59
outside Orleans	..	..	..	57	71
south of Red R.	..	..	..	61	47
north of Red R.	14	7	23	43	35
south of Red R.	55	64	44	78	61
Bluffs	6	3	8	68	74
Prairies	5	5	5	55	49
Oak upland	15	15	17	52	45
Piney woods	5	6	3	73	55
City (Orleans)	25	42	4	..	..
Country	75	58	96	..	..

* It is unfortunate that the absence of reliable statistical information from either local or national sources makes it useless to tabulate much data for the years of reconstruction.

[1] Computed from *Eighth Census, 1860, Preliminary Report*, 262, *Agriculture*, 67, 69, 230; Auditor of Public Accounts, *Report of 1861*, 3–106.

[2] For the parishes in each region, see Hilgard *Report*, 105, and above, *Simplified Regional Map of Louisiana Parishes*. In almost every case, of course, a parish contains several kinds of soil, but, following Hilgard, it is assigned to the region with which it has most in common.

[3] I. e., in the state.

[4] I. e., in the region.

[5] From Hilgard *Rpt.*, 105–6, 134.

TABLE I [continued]—REGIONAL VARIATIONS
1860 [1]

Region [2]	% Farms [4] 3-50 Acres	% Cotton [3] Production	% Sugar [3] Production	% Assessed Property [3]
Alluvial lowland	41	65	84	77
north of Red R.	31	57	0	17
south of Red R.	50	8	84	60
Bluffs	17	6	2	5
Prairies	11	6	0	4
Oak upland	60	19	0	11
Piney woods	66	2	0	2
City (Orleans)	..	..	..	27
Country	..	..	..	73

1880 [5]

Region [2]	% Population [3] Total	White	Colored	% Tilled Land [4]	% Cotton [3] Production	% Sugar [3] Production
Alluvial lowland	63	63	62	..	55	92
north of Red. R.	13	6	19	10	43	0
south of Red R.	50	57	43	9	12	92
Bluffs	5	3	7	15	6	2
Prairies	8	9	7	10	6	6
Oak upland	17	15	20	13	29	0
Piney woods	7	10	4	3	4	0
City (Orleans)	23	35	12	..	..	..
Country	77	65	88	..	..	..

TABLE 2—CONCENTRATION OF WEALTH IN THE BLACK BELT, 1860 [1]

Parish [2]	% People Slaves	Average [3] Slave-holding	Cotton Produced Millions	Sugar Produced Millions	Assessed Property Millions	Value of Slaves Millions
Ascension	64	22	lbs. 0	lbs. 16	$ 9	$ 3
Assumption	53	15	0	17	8	3
Avoyelles	55	15	8	4	5	3
* Bossier	71	21	16	0	6	3
* Caddo	60	15	3	0	7	3
Carroll	76	25	33	0	11	6
* Catahoula	52	18	9	0	5	2
Concordia	91	51	25	0	14	5
* De Soto	63	15	6	0	5	3
* E. Baton Rouge	53	13	4	5	9	3
* E. Feliciana	72	21	9	1	6	4
Franklin	55	12	3	0	?	?
Iberville	72	24	0	10	14	5
Madison	88	39	17	0	12	6
Morehouse	63	15	8	0	5	2
* Natchitoches	56	15	14	0	7	4
Ouachita	60	18	3	0	4	2
Plaquemines	63	24	0	12	6	2
Pointe Coupee	72	20	11	12	10	5
Rapides	61	28	19	12	13	7
St. Bernard	55	20	0	?	2	1
St. Charles	79	32	0	7	3	2
* St. Helena	52	12	2	0	2	1
St. James	70	17	0	13	8	4
St. John B.	58	13	0	4	4	2
St. Martin	51	13	0	7	6	3
St. Mary	78	33	0	30	14	6
Tensas	91	47	56	0	14	7
Terrebonne	56	28	0	17	7	3
W. Baton Rouge	73	27	0	10	5	2
* W. Feliciana	82	32	8	5	8	5
TOTAL	65	24	264	188	242	121
% OF STATE TOTAL	..	..	85	85	58	77

[1] Computed from *Eighth Census, 1860, Preliminary Report*, 262, *Agriculture*, 230; Auditor of Public Accounts, *Report of 1861*, 3–106.

[2] All parishes are alluvial except those marked with an asterisk (*).

[3] In calculating these averages, the number and holdings of slaveowners have been proportionally weighted.

TABLE 3—ANALYSIS OF NONSLAVEHOLDERS IN 1860 [1]

Region	No. Free Families [2]	No. Slave-holders [3]	No. Free Families without Slaves [4]	% Free without Slaves	People in Popu-lation
THE STATE	74,725	22,033	52,692	71	59
Black Belt [5]	28,212	13,935	14,277	51	35
White Belt	46,513	8,098	38,415	81	68
outside Orleans City	14,014	3,929	10,085	68	60
(Orleans)	32,499	4,169	28,330	87	92
Country	42,226	17,864	24,362	58	41
Five lead-ing cotton parishes [6]	3,888	2,031	1,857	47	17
Five lead-ing sugar parishes [7]	5,263	1,906	3,357	63	41
All cotton parishes [8]	27,085	12,097	14,988	55	42
All sugar parishes [9]	15,141	6,067	9,074	60	38

[1] Unfortunately, there are extant almost no local sources of information by which nonslaveholders could be further classified according to other economic differences. [Cf. W. O. Scroggs, "The Archives of the State of Louisiana," *American Hist. Assn., Rpt. of 1912*, 275–95.]

[2] *Eighth Census, 1860, Mortality and Miscellaneous Statistics*, 344.

[3] *Ibid., Agriculture*, 230.

[4] Assuming that each slaveholder was the head of a family, which of course was not always true, and without making allowance for duplication of slaveholders, their number has been subtracted from the total number of free families, including over 3,000 free colored families [*Eighth Census, 1860, Preliminary Report*, 262]. Cf. *De Bow's Review*, XXX, 67–70; U. B. Phillips, "Origin and Growth of the Southern Black Belts," *A. H. R.*, XI, 813.

[5] Because of the inclusion of free people of color, Lafayette and St. Landry are added here to the parishes listed in Table 2.

[6] Tensas, Carroll, Concordia, Madison, and Rapides. *Eighth Census, 1860, Agriculture*, 67, 69.

[7] St. Mary, Assumption, Terrebonne, Ascension, and Lafourche. *Ibid.*

[8] Of the forty-eight parishes in Louisiana, thirty-one produced more cotton than sugar in 1860. *Ibid.*

[9] From the remaining seventeen parishes, Orleans is omitted.

TABLE 4—ESTIMATES OF CLASSES IN 1860 [1]

A—Rural Slaveholdings [2] *and Urban Occupations* [3]

	Free Families	
Class	%	No.
Upper	3	2,579
rural [4]		1,567
urban [5]		1,012
Middle	14	10,064
rural [6]		5,372
urban [7]		4,692
Yeomanry [8]	15	10,925
Lower	68	51,157
rural [9]		24,362
urban [10]		26,795

B—Representative Occupations [11]

	Free Males	
Class	%	No.
Upper [12]	12	13,513
Middle [13]	28	30,414
Lower	60	66,073
rural [14]	38	24,707
urban [15]	62	41,366
skilled [16]	49	20,382
unskilled [17]	51	20,984

[1] The exact figures in the above table should not be misunderstood; they are at best approximations to the facts. The first estimate (A) is the better analysis of all classes except the lower, which is more carefully defined in the second (B). Notwithstanding the mixed data of rural slaveholdings and urban occupations in the first estimate (A), all city slaveholdings being ignored, the total number and percentage of families in each class equals all the free families in the state. In the proportion of slaves held by each rural class, given in the notes below, there is an error of 2 per cent, because of the method of multiplying all slaveholders in each group by the *median* size of their slaveholdings.

[2] Computed from *Eighth Census, 1860, Agriculture*, 230.

[3] Computed from W. H. Rainey, comp., *A. Mygatt & Company's New Orleans Business Directory, etc.* (New Orleans, 1857), 1–240. While not as comprehensive a canvass of occupations as that of the Federal census, especially for the unskilled pursuits of manual labor, this commercial directory was remarkably precise in designating upper or middle class businesses and professions in New Orleans.

[4] All planters who owned from 50 to 1,000 slaves. Their number exceeded the total of plantations over 500 acres in size by only 35, which would seem to indicate that the range of slaveholdings selected for the upper class included all large planters. They constituted 9 per cent of the rural slaveholders, 2 per cent of the free families, and probably owned 51 per cent, or 169,215, of the slaves.

[5] This class embraced all architects, attorneys and lawyers, bankers, commission merchants, cotton press proprietors, cotton, note, and sugar brokers, cotton and sugar factors, newspaper publishers, and wholesale dry goods importers because of their large capital, economic power, and close affiliation with great slaveholding planters.

[6] All planters who owned from 10 to 49 slaves. They made up 30 per cent of the rural slaveholders and probably owned 38 per cent, or 127,060 of the slaves.

[7] This class embraced more than 70 occupations, including all professions of small capital except architecture and law, and all commercial services of retailing, transportation, and supply in which ownership and management was distinct from hired or manual labor.

[8] Small planters and farmers who owned from one to nine slaves. They constituted 61 per cent of the rural slaveholders and probably owned, besides their land, 13 per cent, or 42,259, of the slaves. In adopting this range of slaveholdings for the yeomanry, I am following Gray, *History of Agriculture in the Southern United States to 1860*, I, 500.

[9] This class embraced all rural nonslaveholders.

[10] This class embraced all nonslaveholders in New Orleans except for 1,535 families who, in addition to the 4,169 urban slaveholders, may be assumed to have followed upper or middle class occupations according to *Mygatt's Directory*.

[11] Computed from *Eighth Census, 1860, Population*, 197, on the basis of all free males between 15 and 70 years of age.

[12] This class embraced all planters, as designated by the census, and professional people of every description.

[13] This middle class was exclusively urban and included all merchants, store and shopkeepers, clerks, and domestic servants.

[14] This class embraced all farmers, as designated by the census, farm laborers, overseers, fishermen, woodcutters, etc.

[15] This class embraced all occupations in which manual labor was the chief function.

[16] The criterion of skill is craft. This class included all carpenters, coopers, painters, shoemakers, tailors, etc.

[17] Of this number, 16,493 were listed by the census simply as laborers, presumably without any special skill.

Table 5—Farm Tenure in 1860 [1]

Parish	Total No. Land-holdings [2]	% Holdings Farms, 3-50 Acres	No. Free Families without Land [3]	% Free Families without Land
Ascension	232	71	591	71
Assumption	475	63	804	62
Avoyelles	541	53	510	48
* Baton Rouge, E.	370	41	1,016	73
Baton Rouge, W.	132	33	362	73
Bossier	405	21	250	38
Caddo	436	26	425	49
Calcasieu	271	84	584	68
Caldwell	270	56	242	47
Carroll	513	36	429	45
Catahoula	577	64	436	43
Claiborne	1,119	38	391	25
Concordia	200	17	125	38
De Soto	609	32	302	33
Feliciana, E.	301	4	421	58
Feliciana, W.	143	6	311	68
Franklin	339	45	151	31
Iberville	276	38	484	63
Jackson	744	48	132	15
* Jefferson	80	20	1,939	96
Lafayette	458	7	432	48
Lafourche	281	66	1,227	81

[1] These figures, like those in the preceding tables, should be taken for what they are worth as estimates and proportions rather than as exact measurements. Especially is this true of the table above, because it was calculated, in the absence of comparable state records, from the Federal census, which failed to enumerate farms of less than three acres or to count the number of squatters, who must have been numerous in the frontier regions of Louisiana. An asterisk (*) indicates urban parishes.

[2] *Eighth Census, 1860, Agriculture,* 201.

[3] *Ibid., Mortality and Miscellaneous Statistics,* 344. From this source has been computed the number and proportion of free families in excess of all landholdings in each parish. Bienville is omitted for want of any report.

[4] Omitting the population of Alexandria, Baton Rouge, New Orleans, and Shreveport.

TABLE 5 [continued]—FARM TENURE IN 1860

Parish	Total No. Land-holdings [2]	% Holdings Farms, 3–50 Acres	No. Free Families without Land [3]	% Free Families without Land
Livingston	297	81	527	63
Madison	215	2	172	44
Morehouse	395	30	357	47
Natchitoches	686	49	928	57
* Orleans	175	93	32,324	99
Ouachita	187	32	194	51
Plaquemines	145	51	821	85
Pointe Coupee	513	39	790	61
Rapides	841	69	952	53
Sabine	518	69	229	31
St. Bernard	142	70	139	49
St. Charles	78	28	180	70
St. Helena	396	42	414	51
St. James	179	47	408	69
St. John B.	189	45	540	74
St. Landry	584	21	1,522	72
St. Martin	384	43	711	64
St. Mary	263	12	464	63
St. Tammany	189	87	546	74
Tensas	207	1	234	53
Terrebonne	322	69	604	65
Union	676	41	440	39
Vermilion	175	5	495	73
Washington	405	62	125	23
Winn	343	60	578	62
RURAL TOTAL [4]	17,281	45	18,270	51
STATE TOTAL	17,281	45	57,444	76

TABLE 6—GROWTH OF THE PLANTATION SYSTEM, 1850–60 [1]

Region	% Slaves in Total Population					
	1810	1820	1830	1840	1850	1860
Seven sugar parishes [2]	31.5	40.5	54.5	56.1	50.6	80.5
Four cotton parishes [3]	54.6	68.1	77.6	79.9	84.0	86.2

TABLE 6 [continued]—GROWTH OF THE PLANTATION SYSTEM

Year	% Slaves Distributed in Holdings of							
	1–9	10–19	20–49	50–99	100–199	200–299	300–499	500–999
1850	20	15	23	21	16	3	0.9	1
1860	16	13	22	22	20	5	2	0.9

Year	No. Land-holdings	Average Acreage	Total Value of Holdings	Average Value
1850	13,422	372	$ 98,543,611	$ 7,342
1860	17,328	537	247,984,827	14,311

[1] The first and second series of figures are from Gray, *History of Agriculture in the Southern United States to 1860*, I, 530; II, 903; and the last series from *Thirteenth Census, 1910, Supplement on Louisiana*, 568, 608–9.

[2] Assumption, Iberville, Jefferson, Lafourche, St. Mary, Terrebonne, and West Baton Rouge.

[3] Carroll, Concordia, Madison, and Tensas.

TABLE 7—POLITICAL POSITION OF SLAVEHOLDERS, 1848–61

Parish [1]	Vote [2] in 1848	Vote [3] in 1860	Vote [4] on Secession	Potential % [5] of 1860 Voters Holding Slaves	% Free [6] People Voting in 1860
Tensas	W	Br	S	84	26
Carroll	"	"	"	61	23
Iberville	"	"	"	51	21
Concordia	"	"	"	75	26
Madison	"	Bell	"	63	31
St. Mary	"	Br	"	45	25
Rapides	D	"	"	29	17

[1] Parishes are listed in the order of their wealth as shown by value of farm property. *U. S. Cen., 1860, Agric.*, 66; *Rpt. Audit. Pub. Accts., 1861*, 3–106.

[2] W—Whig; D—Democrat. Official returns of the presidential election which polled the largest proportion of Whig votes ever cast in Louisiana. *True Delta*, Dec. 5, 1852.

[3] Br—Breckinridge; Doug—Douglas. Official returns of the presidential election. *Crescent*, Dec. 4, 1860.

[4] S—Secession; C—Co-operation. Official returns of the election of delegates to the Convention of 1861. *Weekly Delta*, Mar. 30, 1861.

[5] I. e., proportion of all slaveholders to all voters.

[6] I. e., proportion of all voters to the free population.

TABLE 7 [continued]—POLITICAL POSITION OF SLAVEHOLDERS

Parish [1]	Vote [2] in 1848	Vote [3] in 1860	Vote [4] on Secession	Potential % [5] of 1860 Voters Holding Slaves	% Free [6] People Voting in 1860
Pointe Coupee	D	Br	S	71	18
Terrebonne	W	"	C	25	18
Assumption	"	Doug	"	46	14
Ascension	"	"	"	35	18
Catahoula	D	Br	"	28	21
Morehouse	W	"	S	60	20
Avoyelles	D	"	"	53	17
Natchitoches	"	"	C	44	19
St. Landry	W	"	S	51	16
St. Martin	"	"	"	51	22
Bossier	"	"	"	53	23
Lafourche	"	Doug	C	44	13
Caddo	D	Br	S	39	25
W. Baton Rouge	W	Bell	C	52	19
St. James	"	"	"	83	16
St. Charles	"	Br	S	84	14
Bienville	D	"	"	26	18
Plaquemines	"	"	"	52	14
Claiborne	"	"	C	44	19
Jefferson	W	Bell	"	19	15
St. John B.	"	"	"	91	11
De Soto	D	Br	S	57	20
W. Feliciana	"	"	"	60	23
Ouachita	"	Bell	C	23	42
E. Feliciana	"	Br	"	71	19
St. Bernard	W	"	S	42	15
Caldwell	D	"	C	36	17
Franklin	"	"	S	48	22
St. Helena	"	"	C	52	18
Jackson	"	"	S	41	18
Orleans	W	Bell	"	38	6
Lafayette	D	Br	"	91	12
Union	W	"	C	33	18
Winn	—	"	"	24	15
Sabine	D	"	"	31	16
Vermilion	W	"	S	51	11

TABLE 7 [continued]—POLITICAL POSITION OF SLAVEHOLDERS

Parish [1]	Vote [2] in 1848	Vote [3] in 1860	Vote [4] on Secession	Potential % [5] of 1860 Voters Holding Slaves	% Free [6] People Voting in 1860
Livingston	D	Br	S	21	25
Washington	"	"	"	42	16
Calcasieu	"	"	"	42	8
St. Tammany	W	Bell	C	31	15
THE STATE	W	Br	S	43	13

TABLE 8—SLAVERY AND SECESSION [1]

Parish	Potential % of 1860 Voters Holding Slaves	% Free People Voting in 1860	% Total Vote for Breckinridge	% Total Vote for Secession
Co-operationist Parishes				
Ascension	35	18	18	38
Assumption	46	14	30	12
Catahoula	28	21	59	32
Caldwell	36	17	63	34
Claiborne	44	19	50	42
E. Baton Rouge	54	16	41	29
Jefferson	19	15	12	20
Lafourche	44	13	18	37
Natchitoches	44	19	54	46
Ouachita	23	42	39	43
Sabine	31	16	61	31
St. Helena	52	18	51	40
St. James	83	16	34	13
St. John B.	91	11	32	18
St. Tammany	31	15	30	46
Terrebonne	25	18	45	47
Union	33	18	55	47
W. Baton Rouge	52	19	37	0
Winn	24	15	42	14

[1] Computed from sources in Table 7. East Feliciana and St. Landry are omitted from the list of parishes above, because they divided their votes equally between Secessionist and Co-operationist delegates. Cf. Greer, "Louisiana Politics," *L. H. Q.*, XIII, 634–35, 638–41.

TABLE 9—THE AGRARIAN PATTERN, 1860–80 [1]

A—Number and Value of Properties

1—TOTAL NUMBER

Parish	1860	1873	1880 [2]
Catahoula	577	599	738
Concordia	200	302	354
De Soto	609	694	838
Iberville	276	626	774
Lafourche	281	848	896
Natchitoches	686	634	1,046
Red River		464	564
Sabine	518	362	512
Winn	343	686	523

2—NUMBER OWNED BY NONRESIDENTS

Parish	1860 [3]	1873	1880 [2]
Catahoula		108	148
Concordia		82	56
De Soto		83	122
Iberville		89	116
Lafourche		38	27
Natchitoches		104	184
Red River		88	109
Sabine		14	17
Winn		196	76

3—TOTAL VALUE ($1,000's)

Parish	1860	1873	1880 [2]
Catahoula	11,832	639	495
Concordia	6,160	1,569	1,086

[1] All figures are computed from the MS Assessment Rolls for each parish and year except those in 1860, which are taken from *U. S. Cen., 1860, Agric.,* 202, because there are no State Rolls before 1869.

[2] Except Red River, for which the figures of 1881 are used in default of a Roll for 1880.

[3] Not reported.

TABLE 9 [continued]—THE AGRARIAN PATTERN, 1860–80
3 [continued]—TOTAL VALUE ($1,000's)

Parish	1860	1873	1880 [2]
De Soto	2,853	848	736
Iberville	17,749	2,089	1,730
Lafourche	4,630	1,818	2,122
Natchitoches	7,388	930	1,444
Red River		931	1,120
Sabine	1,680	199	253
Winn	950	282	165

4—VALUE OF NONRESIDENTS' ($1,000's)

Parish	1860 [3]	1873	1880 [2]
Catahoula		151	195
Concordia		71	19
De Soto		121	121
Iberville		71	99
Lafourche		33	18
Natchitoches		127	174
Red River		180	220
Sabine		45	62
Winn		59	19

B—Number and Size of Farms and Plantations

5—FARMS UNDER 50 ACRES

Parish	1860	1873	1880 [2]
Catahoula	373	51	53
Concordia	35	10	38
De Soto	199	109	146
Iberville	105	87	156
Lafourche	188	175	242
Natchitoches	337	54	116
Red River		53	78
Sabine	361	31	31
Winn	209	67	53

[2] Except Red River, for which the figures of 1881 are used in default of a Roll for 1880.

[3] Not reported.

TABLE 9 [continued]—THE AGRARIAN PATTERN, 1860–80

6—FARMS OF 51–100 ACRES

Parish	1860	1873	1880 [2]
Catahoula	81	60	106
Concordia	19	12	16
De Soto	121	209	283
Iberville	41	72	88
Lafourche	25	184	212
Natchitoches	124	78	110
Red River		89	126
Sabine	91	41	65
Winn	89	90	66

7—PLANTATIONS OF 101–500 ACRES

Parish	1860	1873	1880 [2]
Catahoula	92	392	478
Concordia	63	85	115
De Soto	250	291	308
Iberville	81	201	235
Lafourche	38	407	404
Natchitoches	194	341	623
Red River		223	290
Sabine	64	235	360
Winn	42	357	284

8—PLANTATIONS OVER 500 ACRES

Parish	1860	1873	1880 [2]
Catahoula	31	96	101
Concordia	83	195	185
De Soto	39	85	101
Iberville	49	266	295
Lafourche	30	82	47
Natchitoches	31	161	197
Red River		99	70
Sabine	2	55	56
Winn	3	172	120

[2] Except Red River, for which the figures of 1881 are used in default of a Roll for 1880.

TABLE 9 [continued]—THE AGRARIAN PATTERN, 1860–80

9—TOTAL FARMS AND PLANTATIONS [4]

Parish	1860	1873	1880 [2]
Catahoula	454	111	159
	123	488	579
Concordia	54	22	54
	146	280	300
De Soto	320	318	429
	289	376	409
Iberville	146	159	244
	130	467	530
Lafourche	213	359	454
	68	489	451
Natchitoches	461	132	226
	225	502	820
Red River		142	204
		322	360
Sabine	452	72	96
	66	290	416
Winn	298	157	119
	45	529	404

[2] Except Red River, for which the figures of 1881 are used in default of a Roll for 1880.

[4] For each parish, the figures in the first horizontal row represent the total number of farms, those in the second, of plantations.

TABLE 9 [continued]—THE AGRARIAN PATTERN, 1860–80
C—*Ownership and Tenancy*

10—NUMBER OF PROPRIETORS

Parish	1860 [3]	1873	1880 [2]
Catahoula		565	698
Concordia		302	329
De Soto		605	645
Iberville		609	591
Lafourche		623	648
Natchitoches		603	950
Red River		402	498
Sabine		229	415
Winn		667	520

11—NUMBER OF TENANTS

Parish	1860 [3]	1873	1880 [2]
Catahoula		395	483
Concordia		875	645
De Soto		448	572
Iberville		109	760
Lafourche		225	318
Natchitoches		435	655
Red River		193	285
Sabine		187	269
Winn		193	396

[2] Except Red River, for which the figures of 1881 are used in default of a Roll for 1880.

[3] Not reported.

TABLE 10—EMPLOYMENT OF THE POPULATION, 1870–90 [1]

Occupations and Sex	Per Cent of Each Sex [2] of Population Employed in		
	1870	1880	1890
Agriculture, fishing, mining:			
Males	58.47	55.55	58.95
Females	46.22	60.78	50.99
Domestic and personal services:			
Males	16.15	23.14	16.30
Females	47.56	32.04	35.71
Manufacturing and mechanical industries:			
Males	10.75	8.89	10.22
Females	4.37	4.43	8.76
Professional services:			
Males	2.59	2.33	2.29
Females	1.29	1.63	2.61
Trade and transportation:			
Males	12.04	10.09	12.24
Females	0.56	1.12	1.93

[1] U.S. Cen., 1890, Population, II, cxi–cxii.
[2] Over ten years of age.

BIBLIOGRAPHY

I—Manuscripts. II—United States Government Documents: (A) Census; (B) Congress; (C) Department Reports; (D) Executive; (E) Special. *III—Louisiana State Documents:* (A) Constitutions; (B) Department Reports; (C) Laws; (D) Legislative Documents; (E) New Orleans. *IV—Newspapers:* (A) New Orleans; (B) Country; (C) Special. *V—Periodicals. VI—Almanacs and Directories. VII—Pamphlets. VIII—Contemporary Books. IX—Travel Books. X—Secondary Books. XI—Secondary Articles.*

I—Manuscripts

Public papers and private correspondence in the form of original manuscripts are as rare as mountains in Louisiana; but even if a great plenty were available, it is to be doubted if they would be sufficiently representative or inclusive for social history. For example, plantation accounts and correspondence, which can be found in many private hands, are irrelevant to this study. Except for tax and land records, therefore, the following manuscripts are of a fugitive character.

Capell, E. J., *Record and Account Books* (1811–67), Pleasant Hill Plantation, Centreville, Miss. Although located across the river, this cotton plantation was typical of its middle-class neighbors, and enjoyed a much longer history than most. [Louisiana State University Library.]

Confederate Volunteer Relief Committee, Account Book (1862), 1st District, City of New Orleans. [City Hall Archives.]

Gayarré, Charles, *Correspondence and Manuscripts.* The historian and Whig politician, who became a Democrat after being rejected as a delegate to the Philadelphia Know-Nothing convention. Chiefly literary, and of little service. [Louisiana State University Library.]

Lockett, Samuel H., *Louisiana As It Is* (1873). Report of a topographical survey by the Professor of Engineering at Louisiana State University, this unpublished book contains information on social conditions in the backwoods from 1869 to 1871. [Howard Memorial Library.]

332

Marshals' Returns for Louisiana, United States Census of Agriculture, 1850, 1860, 1870, 1880. [Duke University Library.]

Parish Assessment Rolls, 1873, 1880, 1881, 1891, 1900, for Acadia, Catahoula, Concordia, De Soto, Iberville, Lafourche, Natchitoches, Red River, Sabine, and Winn. [State Capitol.]

Vagrant Record Book (1859–61), Recorder's Office, 3rd District, City of New Orleans. [City Hall Archives.]

II–UNITED STATES GOVERNMENT DOCUMENTS

A–*Census*

The reports of the Federal Census, needless to remark, are a mine of information for the social historian. They must be interpreted with caution, however, and scholarly advice towards this end is to be found in *The Federal Census,* critical essays by members of the American Economic Association (New York, 1899).

Census Reports, 1870, compiled from the original returns of the Ninth Census, 3 vols. (Washington, 1872). It is unfortunate that the Southern returns in this critical period should be so defective that no confidence can be placed in them. The marshals underestimated the white population of Louisiana, and failed to make any thorough canvass of the farmers scattered over the pine hills.

[*Census Reports, 1880*] Tenth Census, 22 vols. (Washington, 1883–88). Especially valuable are the much neglected reports by E. W. Hilgard, *Cotton Production in the Mississippi Valley and Southwestern States,* V, pt. I, which is the best account of the geography and post-bellum agriculture of Louisiana, and by G. W. Cable, *New Orleans,* an excellent history in *Report on Cities,* XIX. Also useful are *Statistics of Population,* I; *Manufactures,* II; *Agencies of Transportation,* IV; *Valuation, Taxation, and Public Indebtedness,* VII; *Mortality and Vital Statistics,* XI, XII; and *Social Statistics of Cities,* XIX, pt. II.

[*Census Reports, 1890*] Eleventh Census, 15 vols. (Washington, 1892–97). Invaluable are the reports on *Real Estate Mortgages,* XII, and *Farms and Homes: Proprietorship and Indebtedness,* XIII. Also useful are *Population,* I; *Crime, Pauperism, and Benevolence,* III; *Vital and Social Statistics,* IV; *Statistics of Agriculture,* V; *Manufacturing Industries,* VI; *Statistics of Churches,* IX; and *Wealth, Debt, and Taxation,* XV.

[*Census Reports, 1900*] Twelfth Census, 10 vols. (Washington, 1901–2). Especially helpful are *Population*, I, II; *Agriculture*, V, VI; and *Manufactures*, VIII, pt. II.

A Century of Population Growth. Compiled by the Bureau of the Census (Washington, 1909).

Negroes in the United States, Bulletin no. 8, Bureau of the Census (Washington, 1904).

Preliminary Report of the Eighth Census, under the direction of J. C. Kennedy, *Sen. Docs.*, 37 Cong., 2 sess. (Washington, 1862). *Population of the United States in 1860* (Washington, 1864). *Agriculture in the United States in 1860* (Washington, 1864). *Manufactures in the United States in 1860* (Washington, 1865). *Statistics of the United States in 1860*, cited as *Mortality and Miscellaneous Statistics* (Washington, 1866).

The Seventh Census of the United States . . . , J. D. B. De Bow, supt. (Washington, 1853). J. D. B. De Bow, *Statistical View of the United States, a compendium of the seventh census* (Washington, 1854).

Statistical Abstract, 1879. Compiled from current census returns by the office of the Secretary of the Treasury, *H. R. Docs.*, 46 Cong., 2 sess., XXII, no. 51.

Thirteenth Census of the United States, 1910, 11 vols. (Washington, 1912–14). In *Agriculture*, V–VII, is to be found the special survey of Plantations in the South, V, Chap. XII. Also useful for Louisiana is the *Supplement* issued for that state and bound with the *Abstract*.

B—Congress

Affairs in Louisiana [1873], *H. R. Docs.*, 42 Cong., 3 sess., VII, no. 91. The Attorney General's report, with documents and a message from President Grant.

Congressional Globe, 1840–73 (Washington, 1841–73).

Investigation Relative to the General Depression [1878–79], *H. R. Misc. Docs.*, 45 Cong., 3 sess., III, no. 29. Northern and Southern capital unite to recommend laissez faire.

Papers on Political Affairs in Louisiana [1872], *H. R. Misc. Docs.*, 42 Cong., 2 sess., IV, no. 211. Testimony regarding the difficulties which arose between the army and the radical state government. Ably used by Lonn.

Report of the Select Committee on Condition of the South [1875], *H. R. Rpts.*, 43 Cong., 2 sess., V, no. 261. Devoted entirely to conditions in Louisiana, and as partial to Republicans as any reconstruction investigation, this report brings to light the most important testimony on record concerning the Ku Klux Klan, the White League, the Coushatta and Colfax Riots, and intimidation of the Negro by Democrats and Republicans.

Report of the Select Committee on Mississippi Levees [1871–72], *H. R. Rpts.*, 42 Cong., 2 sess., I, no. 44. Depicts bad conditions and recommends national construction.

Report of the Select Committee on the New Orleans Riots [1866], *H. R. Rpts.*, 39 Cong., 2 sess., no. 16. The Committee shows by its partial methods of cross-examination that it was selected to turn the riots into propaganda for radical reconstruction. The minority report is helpful, however, and the historian can make his own cross-examination of several hundred pages of testimony.

Report on Affairs in Louisiana [1872], *H. R. Rpts.*, 42 Cong., 2 sess., IV, no. 92. A detailed account from the Administration viewpoint of the organization of the contested Legislature of 1872.

Report on Cholera [1875], *H. R. Docs.*, 43 Cong., 2 sess., XIII, no. 95. An excellent history of cholera in this country, and especially of the epidemic in 1873.

Report on Condition of the South [1865], by Carl Schurz, *Sen. Docs.*, 39 Cong., 1 sess., I, no. 2. Valuable opinions colored by Republican predilections.

Report on Elections in Louisiana [1879], *Sen. Rpts.*, 45 Cong., 3 sess., IV, no. 855. Evidence that local Democrats retain power by intimidating the Negroes. Partial.

Report on Federal Officers in Louisiana [1876], *H. R. Rpts.*, 44 Cong., 1 sess., IX, no. 816. Over seven hundred pages of testimony are set forth to prove that Federal supervision of Louisiana is able, honest, and efficient; but see the searching minority report.

Report on the Louisiana Election of 1876, *Sen. Rpts.*, 44 Cong., 2 sess., IV, no. 701, I, II, III. The Republicans testify at great length that the Democrats used intimidation and fraud to carry the elections of 1876. A jealous and self-righteous report by those who were beaten at their own game.

Report on Relief of the Louisiana & Texas R. R. [1879], *Sen. Rpts.*, 45 Cong., 3 sess., II, no. 732.

Report on the New Orleans, Baton Rouge & Vicksburg R. R. [1878], *H. R. Rpts.*, 45 Cong., 2 sess., II, no. 1018. Recommends incorporation of the Texas Pacific system. Here Northern and Southern capital unite to obtain the troublesome Back-bone land grant which provoked so much Populist discontent.

Wholesale Prices, Wages, and Transportation [1893], *Sen. Rpts.*, 52 Cong., 2 sess., III, no. 1394. A valuable statistical review by Senator Aldrich's committee.

C–Department Reports

An Account of Louisiana [1803], *being an Abstract of Documents in the State and Treasury Departments,* by direction of President Jefferson (Washington, 1803). Compiled from travel and official reports.

COMMISSIONER OF AGRICULTURE, *Report of 1865, H. R. Docs.,* 39 Cong., 1 sess., XV, no. 136; *1866, H. R. Docs.,* 39 Cong., 2 sess., XV, no. 107; *1867, H. R. Docs.,* 40 Cong., 2 sess., IX, no. 91; *1868, H. R. Docs.,* 40 Cong., 3 sess., V, no. 3; *1870, H. R. Docs.,* 41 Cong., 3 sess., XIII; *Reports, 1871–79,* issued separately. Invaluable statistics and special surveys.

COMMISSIONER OF LABOR, *Annual Reports, 1884–1904.*

COMMISSIONER OF PATENTS, *Reports on Agriculture, 1850, H. R. Docs.,* 31 Cong., 2 sess., no. 32, pt. ii; *1851, H. R. Docs.,* 32 Cong., 1 sess., no. 102, pt. ii; *1852, Sen. Docs.,* 32 Cong., 2 sess., no. 55, pt. ii; *1858, Sen. Docs.,* 35 Cong., 2 sess., no. 47, pt. ii. The other reports, from 1845 to 1861, were less useful.

COMMISSIONER OF THE GENERAL LAND OFFICE, *Report of 1849–50, Sen. Docs.,* 31 Cong., 2 sess., II, pt. ii, no. 2; *1852, Sen. Docs.,* 32 Cong., 2 sess., no. 4; *1855, H. R. Docs.,* 34 Cong., 1 sess., I, pt. i, no. 1; *1860, Sen. Docs.,* 36 Cong., 2 sess., I, no. 1; and *1868–79,* issued separately.

DEPARTMENT OF AGRICULTURE, *Report of Statistician* [1890], "Farm Wages, 1869–1890," New Series Rpt. no. 73; *Report* [1894], "Urban Population Trends in the South," New Series Rpt. no. 119; "Price and Crop Summaries, 1865–1895," Circular no. 1 [1896]; J. H. Blodgett, "Relations of Population and Food Products in the United States, 1850–1900," Bulletin no. 24 [1903]; Blodgett, "Wages of Farm Labor in the United States," Bulletin no. 26 [1903]; *Annual Reports,* 1901, 1903–5, 1907.

D—*Executive*

J. D. Richardson, *Compilation of the Messages and Papers of the Presidents* [1789–1897], 10 vols. (Washington, 1896–99).

E—*Special*

War of the Rebellion, Official Records of the Union and Confederate Armies, Series i, iii, iv.

III—LOUISIANA STATE DOCUMENTS
A—*Constitutions*

Dart, B. W., editor, *Constitutions of the State of Louisiana, etc.* (Indianapolis, 1932).

Debates in the Convention for the Revision and Amendment of the Constitution (New Orleans, 1864). Although the convention was extravagant to publish these lengthy debates, the historian must count himself lucky in having them.

Journal of the Convention Called for the Purpose of Re-adopting, Amending, or Changing the Constitution of the State of Louisiana (New Orleans, 1845).

Journal of the Convention to Form a New Constitution for the State of Louisiana (New Orleans, 1852). It is unfortunate that the debates of this important convention were never recorded.

Official Journal of the Proceedings of the Constitutional Convention of 1879 (New Orleans, 1879). The liquidation of carpetbag rule.

Official Journal of the Proceedings of the Convention of the State of Louisiana (New Orleans, 1861).

Official Proceedings of the Convention for Framing a Constitution for the State of Louisiana (New Orleans, 1867–68). Journal of the famous radical convention.

Official Report of Debates in the Louisiana Convention (New Orleans, 1845). Nearly one thousand pages of debates provide great insight into the political philosophy of ante-bellum Louisiana.

Ordinances Passed by the Convention of the State of Louisiana (New Orleans, 1861).

SECRETARY OF STATE, *Report of 1902* (Baton Rouge, 1902). A convenient compilation of all the nineteenth-century constitutions.

B—*Department Reports*

ADJUTANT GENERAL, *Report of 1857* (New Orleans, 1857).

AUDITOR OF PUBLIC ACCOUNTS, *Annual Reports, 1847–61, 1864–79,* generally bound with legislative documents of the House or Senate. These reports are more detailed than those of any other department, and usually contain an economic census of each parish. Especially important but much neglected is the controversial *Report of 1864* by Dr. Dostie, who goes out of his way to criticize ante-bellum methods of assessment and taxation.

BOARD OF ADMINISTRATORS OF THE CHARITY HOSPITAL, *Annual Reports, 1850–61.* Index to the health and immigration of New Orleans.

BOARD OF HEALTH, *Annual Reports, 1857–60, 1869–75.* Contains social as well as medical data.

BUREAU OF IMMIGRATION, *Annual Reports, 1867–68.*

COMMISSIONERS OF EMIGRATION, *Annual Reports, 1869–70.* The saga of the failure to attract immigration after the war.

REGISTRAR OF VOTERS, *Reports, 1869, 1875.* Unreliable but revealing figures on reconstruction voting.

SUPERINTENDENT OF PUBLIC EDUCATION, *Annual Reports, 1850–61, 1869–77.* Lengthy and invaluable, containing detailed reports from every parish. Especially important are the *Report of 1857,* for a description of the failure of ante-bellum education, and of *1871* and *1874,* for an analysis of "mixed" schools during reconstruction.

C—*Laws*

Chronological List of Constitutional Provisions, Acts and Joint Resolutions of the State of Louisiana Relating to Her Public Lands from 1817 to 1886 (Baton Rouge, 1889). A convenient compilation of immense value for steering one's way through a mass of land laws. It was prepared by the Register of the State Land Office.

The Consolidation and Revision of the Statutes of the State, of a General Nature, prepared by commissioners appointed by the state (New Orleans, 1852). The revised Civil Code and *Code Noir.*

Morgan, T. G., compiler, *Civil Code of the State of Louisiana* (New Orleans, 1853). Annotated with references to decisions of the State Supreme Court.

Phillips, U. B., compiler, *Revised Statutes of Louisiana* (New Orleans, 1856). Prepared under the direction of a joint committee of the legislature.

Rills, J. H., editor, *A New Digest of the Laws of the Parish of Iberville* (Plaquemine, La., 1859). One of the few extant compilations of parish ordinances, this pamphlet sheds much light on the police jury and ante-bellum local government.

Session Laws, 1839–79, enacted by the General Assembly.

D—Legislative Documents

House Debates, 1864–65, 1870, 1871, 1872. [State Law Library and Howard Memorial Library.]

HOUSE OF REPRESENTATIVES, *Special Committee to Investigate the Frauds Perpetrated in the State During the Late Presidential Election* (New Orleans, 1845).

Journals of the House and Senate, 1870, 1871. [State Law Library.]

Journals of the House of Representatives, 1836–41, 1841–45, 1846–47, 1848, 1850, 1855, 1864–67, 1872–79. Except for the session of 1855, these journals are to be found in the State Law Library at New Orleans.

Journals of the Senate, 1835–45, 1848, 1850–52, 1864–65, 1868, 1869, 1871–79. [State Law Library.]

Legislative Documents, 1853–54, 1857–58, 1867, 1869, 1870–72, 1874, 1876, 1878. Here are to be found the special reports of legislative committees and of minor departmental heads and bureaus.

Report of the Joint Committee of Investigation of the Department of Education (New Orleans, 1878). Democratic revelations of the corruption and inefficiency that attended education during reconstruction.

Report of the Joint Committee to Investigate the Land Office (New Orleans, 1878). Pillage of the public domain during reconstruction.

Report of the Senate Sub-Committee on Charitable Institutions (New Orleans, 1878). The sorry plight of the state's famous charities after eight years of corrupt rule.

Senate Debates, First Session of 1853. The only ante-bellum legislative debates which have survived. [Howard Memorial Library.]

Senate Debates, 1864, 1865, 1866, 1870. Essential to a study of the major controversies of these crucial years. [State Law Library.]

E—New Orleans

Annual Report of the Board of Health (Baton Rouge, 1861). Especially important for cemetery returns.

BOARD OF METROPOLITAN POLICE, *Reports, 1868–71.* Local reconstruction government at work.

Comptroller's Reports, 1857, 1860 (New Orleans, 1856, 1860).

Rules and Regulations of the Police Department of the City of New-Orleans (New Orleans, 1852).

IV—NEWSPAPERS

Fairly complete files of all important New Orleans newspapers are to be found in the City Hall Archives. No city in the United States during the nineteenth century had more or better newspapers, and they are today a rich but neglected storehouse of information on the political, economic, and social history of the whole Southwest. It is to be regretted that few country newspapers are available, the great majority having been lost or scattered to the four winds. Knowledge of conditions in the rural parishes may nevertheless be gleaned from New Orleans newspapers by a meticulous study of their quotations from the country press.

A—New Orleans

Bee [*L'Abeille de la Nouvelle-Orleans*] 1845, 1848, 1851–52, 1854–56, 1859–60. A conservative Anglo-French journal, bilingual, the organ of the Creoles. Like its readers, politically, the *Bee* was Whig; after the collapse of Whiggery, it attacked Democratic immigrants without becoming Native American. It took a Co-operationist stand against secession, and joined the conservative Democrats during reconstruction. Ably edited, with literary style, by S. Harby, a Charlestonian. Established in 1827.

Commercial Bulletin, 1845–63, 1866–67, 1869–71. Organ of the mercantile class, owned by a wealthy emigrant from Georgia, Isaac G. Seymour, and edited by a clever Yankee, Stephen Gay. Publication was suspended and the property confiscated by the Federal Army. Like the merchants who read it, the *Bulletin* was Whig, and opposed the swing toward secession. Resuming publication after the war, it was natural for the *Bulletin* to sympathize with conservative Democrats, but never too violently, and never unfairly. It is an indispensable source of information on the commerce, finance, and agriculture of the lower South.

Creole, 1857. Edited by Latham and Harmon as the official newspaper of the Native American city administration. An unsuccessful competitor of the *Bee* and chiefly valuable for its hostile news of immigrants.

Crescent, 1849–62, 1865–69. Started in 1849 by William "Dog" Adams and J. O. Nixon, who employed Walt Whitman for a few months of precious journalism. This newspaper became the stalking-horse of Know-Nothingism, and after its collapse, swung to the Yancey-Rhett wing of the Democracy, championing secession with great influence because of its wide circulation among the masses. After the war, needless to say, it was conservatively Democratic. The *Crescent* was a "gay and festive" paper, as Roberts observed; its local columns, edited by the hard-drinking, brusque Kentuckian, Israel Gibbon, were greatly feared in New Orleans. It was not, however, a scandalmonger. Attracting wide country correspondence, and printing news which other papers did not consider news, the *Crescent* preserved important sociological information for the historian.

Delta, 1845–62, 1869. Democratic, vehemently opposed to Know-Nothingism, the *Delta* supported Soulé, and finally became a warm advocate of secession. Witty, amusing, almost "Dana-esque" in character, the *Delta* was ably edited by Judge Alexander Walker, whom Roberts called "a very Hessian of the press, writing all things for all men—who paid." Established in 1845.

Democrat, 1875–80. Ultra-conservative organ of the Bourbon Democracy and extremely hostile to labor, black and white.

Era, 1863–64. Established early in 1863 to take the place of the *Delta* as the Federal organ of General Banks and Governor Hahn. Important for its wartime dispatches and occasional correspondence from the country.

Jeffersonian, 1845–47. An animated but short-lived political paper which reflected the coming-of-age of Jacksonian Democracy in New Orleans.

Picayune, 1839–67, 1869–76. Founded by G. W. Kendall of New Hampshire and F. A. Lumsden of North Carolina, the *Picayune* gained an influential circulation and commanded much attention in the North and abroad. Conservative in policy, it was Whiggish, opposed to secession and to radical reconstruction. There is much truth in Roberts' comment that this newspaper was "always seeking the paying side, . . . a follower and never a leader of public opinion." Editorially, it was often stuffy and always cautious. Its unrivaled dispatches from outside Louisiana make it indispensable. After the war, it developed commercial and planting news of as much importance as the *Bulletin*. Especially interesting was its campaign, led by Daniel Dennett, for subdivision of the plantations.

Times, 1863–67, 1869–81. Started by Thomas P. May as a Unionist organ, the *Times* continued to be Republican until 1872. Turning to support the Democrats, it was seized by a radical judge and used as the voice of the Negroes. After 1875, the *Times* passed into conservative Democratic hands, and remained under these auspices until it was united with the *Democrat*. Important not only for its changing viewpoint but also for unusual social and economic news.

Tribune, 1864–70. A weekly.

True Delta, 1849–66. The "Irish organ of the South," owned by John McGinnis, who denounced secession, kept arms at his office for self-defense, and was forced to refrain from criticism of the Confederacy. The *True Delta*, an offshoot of the *Delta*, was Democratic, but in 1859 anti-Slidell and pro-Soulé.

B—*Country*

For a complete list of forty-five ante-bellum parish newspapers, of which few are extant, see the *Louisiana State Register* [1855], 127.

Alexandria [Rapides] *Caucasian*, 1874–75. Organ of the local White League, following the *Shreveport Times* in a war on radical reconstruction and "nigger-rule."

Alexandria Constitutional, 1860–61. Weekly Bell-Everett campaign sheet which became the voice of all rural Co-operationists in their opposition to secession. Strong and independent editorials were written by its editor, C. W. Boyce. No newspaper in Louisiana criticized the Convention of 1861 so trenchantly as the *Constitutional*.

[Alexandria] *Louisiana Democrat*, 1859–60. Weekly Democratic organ of the Slidell machine. A typical party sheet, taking its lead from the city press. Edited by E. W. Halsey.

Baton Rouge Advocate, 1858. A daily Democratic newspaper, interested in national politics. Its parent was the *Baton Rouge Democratic Advocate*.

Baton Rouge Comet, 1852–53. Whig daily, edited by George A. Pike, in support of the Convention of 1852 and internal improvements.

Baton Rouge Democratic Advocate, 1847, 1855, a strong weekly organ of the dominant party.

Baton Rouge Gazette, 1852. Whig weekly, edited by Mayhew G. Bryan, who took his lead from the New Orleans press.

[Baton Rouge] *Weekly Gazette and Comet*, 1858. An interesting American Know-Nothing sheet.

[Franklin, St. Mary] *Weekly Junior Register*, 1863. Two issues printed on wallpaper are preserved in the Princeton University Library. Edited by the White Brothers, in the heart of the Confederate sugar country, it offers little evidence of later hardships.

Opelousas [St. Landry] *Courier* [*Le Courrier des Opelousas*] 1854, 1864, 1865–67, 1869–71. A bilingual Democratic weekly that fought the *Patriot* and filled its columns with the gossip of parish politics.

Opelousas Patriot, 1855–62. A bilingual paper issued every fortnight until 1859, when it became a weekly. Whig and Native American.

[Opelousas] *Southern Sentinel* [*La Sentinelle du Sud*], 1866–67. This bilingual weekly was an important rural organ of Governor J. Madison Wells and the Conservatives.

[Opelousas] *St. Landry Progress* [*Le Progrès de St. Landry*], 1867–68. Owned by the Donato Bros., colored, and edited by Michel Vidal, an intelligent colored radical, this weekly represented the agrarian Negro Republicans. It followed the policies of the *New Orleans Tribune*, but never to the extent of copying it. Until one reads either of these newspapers, it is impossible to form a fair judgment of the radical colored wing of Louisiana Republicanism, which was much more intelligent and progressive than historians have been willing to admit. The *Progress* stopped publication during the election campaign of 1868, when a Democratic mob sacked and destroyed its office. (See the *Crescent*, Jan. 30, 1869.)

[Opelousas] *St. Landry Whig* [*Le Whig de St. Landry*], 1844–46. A forceful Whig paper with considerable local news.

Shreveport Times, 1872–76. Established in 1871 under the editorship of Leonard, a bold politician who was allied with the Kellogg Republicans in the Speakership struggle of 1874. His violent editorials made it the most important daily outside New Orleans and reflected the rising temper of white people in the country. The *Times* was a vigorous sponsor of the White League and waged relentless war against "nigger-rule." Complete files are not available, unfortunately, because the original plant was destroyed by fire; and to search its pages, one must go to the only extant file of any run in the *Times* office at Shreveport.

C—Special

Niles' Weekly Register, 1811–49. This well-known national weekly, established at Baltimore by Hezekiah Niles, contains valuable digests of political and economic news from Louisiana. Its conservative Whiggish policies do not distort the facts it reports.

Southern Economist and Trade Unionist, 1897–1900. Four scattered issues, preserved in the Howard Memorial Library, reflect some light on labor before this period. The official weekly organ of the New Orleans Central Trades and Labor Council, endorsed by Samuel Gompers, and committed to skilled craft unionism and nonpartisan politics.

Southern Industry, Vol. III, no. 38, Dec. 10, 1887. Weekly organ of both the local Knights of Labor and the American Federation of Labor, this single copy, preserved in the Howard Memorial Library, lists many New Orleans unions.

The True Witness and South-Western Presbyterian, 1857–59. Established at Jackson, Miss., in 1854, this old school Presbyterian weekly was removed to New Orleans in 1857. Of little value, devoted to sermons, synodical news, and exchange clippings.

V—Periodicals

A helpful guide to local periodicals is Max L. Griffin, "A Bibliography of New Orleans Magazines," *L. H. Q.*, XVII (July, 1935), 491–556.

The American Agriculturist, 1848 (Vol. VII). A monthly magazine, published in New York by C. M. Saxton and devoted to agronomy in general, with more reference to the North than the South.

The American Farmer, 1820–28. Edited by John S. Skinner, and published at Baltimore, the *Farmer* offers occasional information on Southern agriculture.

L. *Bouchereau's Annual Statement of the Sugar Crop Made in Louisiana*, 1869–1900. Statistical reports with editorial observations. Bouchereau was the postwar successor to the following annual:

P. A. *Champomier's Statement of the Sugar Crop Made in Louisiana, 1845–59*. An annual with less comment but important figures.

De Bow's Review, 1846–60, 1861–62, 1866–70 (After the War Series). Edited by the famous political economist of slavery, J. D. B. De Bow, and published at New Orleans, this quarterly is a priceless repository of opinion and information. Although chiefly concerned with the plantation system and its political and commercial interests, De Bow also published valuable surveys of several Louisiana parishes, which seem to have been generally overlooked.

Hunt's Merchants' Magazine and Commercial Review, LVI and LVII.

New Orleans Medical News and Hospital Gazette, 1854–56. A local monthly magazine, edited by Samuel Choppin *et al.*, with monthly reports of the Charity Hospital.

New Orleans Medical and Surgical Journal, 1850–60. Nationally important bimonthly magazine of the medical profession. Edited by the famous New Orleans physicians, Hester and Dowler.

Proceedings of the Louisiana State Agricultural Society, 1887–1900. Contains the papers read at conventions, often by "dirt" farmers, on social and technical problems of agriculture. Issued by the State Bureau of Agriculture. Invaluable.

Soil of the South, 1853 (Vol. III). A monthly magazine, devoted to practical agriculture, and published at Columbus, Ga. Edited by James M. Chambers.

The Southern Cultivator, 1843–46. Another agricultural monthly, printed at Augusta, Ga., and edited by James Carnak.

The Southern Field and Factory, January, 1871. An attempt by E. G. Wall, the editor, to publish monthly an economic periodical at Jackson, Miss. It apparently failed after the first issue.

Southern Medical Reports, 1849–50. Edited by the famous New Orleans physician, Erasmus D. Fenner, these reports contain valuable articles, opinions, and statistics on conditions of health in the

South. For later years, see the New Orleans *Medical and Surgical Journal.*

The Southern Planter, 1852–54. The well-known agricultural monthly edited by F. G. Ruffin and printed at Richmond, Va. It devoted much space to the gospel of fertilizer and diversification.

VI—ALMANACS AND DIRECTORIES

Affleck's Southern Rural Almanac, 1851–52, 1855–56. A general planters' manual, edited by Thomas Affleck of Adams County, Miss.

The American Almanac and Repository of Useful Knowledge, 1844–57, 1861. A Northern grab bag published at Boston by David H. Williams.

An American Almanac for 1878, A. R. Spofford, editor (New York, 1878). Prices and commercial reports.

American Statistical Annual for . . . 1854, compiled by R. S. Fisher & Chas. Colby (New York, 1854).

Appleton's Annual Cyclopaedia, 1861–75, vols. 1–15 (New York, 1861–75).

Biographical Dictionary of the American Congress, 1774–1927, H. R. Docs., 69 Cong., 2 sess., no. 783.

Cohen's New Orleans Directory, 1853–55.

Commercial and Statistical Almanac for 1879 (New Orleans, 1878).

Crescent City Business Directory for 1858–59 (New Orleans, n. d.). Information on trade and commerce. Excellent engravings.

Dictionary of the United States Congress, Chas. Lanman, editor (Philadelphia, 1859). The original of the revised *Biographical Dictionary.*

Gardner's New Orleans Directory for 1858, 1859, 1860–61. The last issue contains an incomplete but suggestive list of planters residing in Arkansas, Louisiana, Mississippi, and Texas.

Kerr's Crescent City Directory for 1856 (New Orleans, 1856). Advertisements and business listings.

J. *Livingston's United States Law Register,* rev. ed. (New York, 1859). Information on the members of the bar in every state.

Louisiana Biographies, A. Meynier, Jr., editor (New Orleans, 1882).

The Louisiana Almanac for 1867 (New Orleans, 1866). A conservative compilation of political data.

The Louisiana Coast Directory, A. Henry and V. Gerodias, editors (New Orleans, 1857). Gives the name of every planter, his staple crop, and the distance of his plantation from New Orleans, on both the right and left banks of the Mississippi, from its mouth to Baton Rouge, and on the Bayou Lafourche. An invaluable survey, hitherto overlooked.

A. Mygatt & Company's New Orleans Business Directory for 1858, 1859. Classification of residents by business or profession for Algiers, Baton Rouge, Natchez, New Orleans, etc.

A Political Text-Book for 1860. Compiled by Horace Greeley and John F. Cleveland (New York, 1860). Convenient compilation of all party platforms and presidential election returns from 1836.

Soard's New Orleans City Directory, 1882.

The Southern Business Directory and General Commercial Advertiser, Rev. John P. Campbell, editor (Charleston, 1854).

United Labor Council Directory of New Orleans (New Orleans, 1894). A complete list of all local trades unions.

VII—PAMPHLETS

There is a large and extremely valuable collection of pamphlets at the Howard Memorial Library, New Orleans.

Carpenter, W. M., *Sketches from the History of Yellow Fever, etc.* (New Orleans, 1844). Disproves the domestic origin of this disease.

Fenner, E. D., *Report on the Epidemics of Louisiana, etc.* (Philadelphia, 1856). A paper on the yellow fever epidemic of 1854–55.

Hall, S. S., *The Bliss of Marriage; or How to Get a Rich Wife* (New Orleans, 1858).

Journal of the Proceedings of the 21st Convention of the Protestant Episcopal Church, Diocese of Louisiana (New Orleans, 1859).

Morrison, Andrew, *The Industries of New Orleans* (New Orleans, 1885). A "booster's" survey for the current Cotton Exhibition.

RAILWAY PAMPHLETS (courtesy Wm. Pfaff):

Address to the People of the Southern and Western States (n. p., n. d.). Published by the local railroad convention; also to be found in *De Bow's Review*, August, 1851.

Address of the Board of Directors of the New Orleans, Opelousas and Great Western Railroad to the Property Holders of . . . New Orleans (New Orleans, 1852).

[Letters and Speeches of James Robb and others] *On Extending the Commerce of the South, etc.* (New Orleans, 1852). Proceedings of the New Orleans railroad convention of 1852.

List of Stockholders of the New Orleans, Opelousas and Great Western Railroad Company (New Orleans, 1852).

Officers, By-Laws and Charter of the New Orleans, Opelousas and Great Western Rail Road Company (New Orleans, 1852).

Payne, B. H., *Report on the Algiers and Opelousas Railroad* (New Orleans, 1851).

Proceedings of the New Orleans, Algiers, Attakapas and Opelousas Railroad Convention (New Orleans, 1851).

Proceedings of the Adjourned Meeting of the New Orleans, etc., Convention (New Orleans, 1852).

Report of the President and Board of Directors of the New Orleans, Opelousas and Great Western Rail Road Company (New Orleans, 1853).

Southern and Western Rail-Road Convention (n. p., n. d.). Proceedings of the New Orleans meeting, 1852.

Report of the President . . . to the Board of Directors of the Louisiana Cotton Manufactory (New Orleans, 1872).

Speech of Hon. Michael Hahn before the Union Association of New Orleans, Nov. 14, 1863. Origin of the Free State Party.

Stowe, H. B., *Key to Uncle Tom's Cabin* (Boston, 1853).

Weston, G. M., *The Poor Whites of the South* (Washington, 1856). Propaganda; significant for its title.

———, *The Progress of Slavery in the United States* (Washington, 1858). A free labor argument that slavery was not required for the cultivation of cotton. Distributed as campaign literature by the Republican Party, this pamphlet is superior to Helper's larger work in tone and facts.

[Judge Whitaker]. *Sketches of the Life and Character in Louisiana* (New Orleans, 1847). Biographical tributes to legal colleagues, reprinted from the *Bee* and *Jeffersonian.*

Zacharie, J. S., *The New Orleans Guide* (New Orleans, 1885). Official guidebook to the Cotton Exhibition.

VIII—Contemporary Books

From this group we omit books of travel, which are so important as to deserve separate classification.

Barbee, W. J., *The Cotton Question* (New York, 1866). An excellent contemporary treatise on cotton agriculture and manufacture, by a Mississippi physician.

Barnwell, R. G., editor, *The New-Orleans Book* (New Orleans, 1851). An anthology of local literature, sermons, and speeches, excluding the Creole.

Biographical and Historical Memoirs of Northwest Louisiana, compiled by The Southern Publishing Company (Chicago, 1890).

Bunner, E., *History of Louisiana* (New-York, 1842). One of the earliest school histories, an elementary text.

Clapp, Rev. Theo., *Autobiographical Sketches and Recollections* (Boston, 1857). By the well-known Unitarian divine who lived in New Orleans for over thirty-five years. Excellent accounts of the cholera epidemic of 1832–33, and the yellow fever in 1837 and 1857.

Darby, W., *Geographical Description of the State of Louisiana,* 2nd ed. (New York, 1817).

De Bow, J. D. B., *The Industrial Resources, etc., of the Southern and Western States,* 3 vols. (New Orleans, 1853); the English edition entitled *Encyclopaedia of the Trade and Commerce of the United States, more particularly of the Southern and Western States: etc.,* 2nd ed. (London, 1854). It is amazing what fresh and useful facts can still be found in this familiar repository of political economy.

Dennett, Daniel, *Louisiana As It Is* (New Orleans, 1876). An economic survey with numerous figures.

Dunn, T. C., *Morehouse Parish* (New Orleans, 1885).

Fremantle, A. J., *Three Months in the Southern States* (New York, 1864).

French, B. F., editor, *Historical Collections of Louisiana* [title varies], 7 vols. (New York, 1846–75). Invaluable for the colonial period.

Gilmore, J. R. [pseud. Edmund Kirke], *Among the Pines: or, The South in Secession-Time*, 5th ed. (New York, 1862). Travels in the Carolina back country with sympathetic observations on the lot of poor whites. Almost a tract in their defense.

Greeley, Horace, *The American Conflict*, 2 vols. (Hartford, 1864). The Republican version of the war, important for its charges that secession was a slaveholders' conspiracy.

Harris, W. H., *Louisiana* (New Orleans, 1885). The official economic handbook of the State Bureau of Immigration.

Helper, H. R., *The Impending Crisis of the South: How to Meet It* (New York, 1857). The well-known Carolinian's appeal to the poor whites against the "lords of the lash."

———, *Compendium of the Impending Crisis of the South* (New York, 1860). Statistical proofs.

Hundley, D. R., *Social Relations in Our Southern States* (New York, 1860). The best appraisal of the Southern middle class and yeomanry, by an Alabamian, who was prejudiced against poor whites.

Ingle, Edw., *Southern Sidelights: etc.* (New York, 1896). An illuminating retrospect which is sensitive to the realities of society in the South.

Latrobe, C. J., *The Rambler in North America*, 2nd ed., 2 vols. (London, 1836).

Lieber, F., *Slavery, Plantations and the Yeomanry* (New York, 1863).

M'Caleb, Thomas, editor, *The Louisiana Book: Selections from the Literature of the State* (New Orleans, 1894).

Martin, F. X., *History of Louisiana*, rev. ed. (New Orleans, 1882). The earliest history of the state by a Creole jurist, first published in 1827, and almost the only source for important contemporary figures.

Norman, B. M., *Norman's New Orleans and Environs* (New Orleans, 1845). A lively guidebook with interesting maps and engravings.

Parton, James, *General Butler in New Orleans* (New York, 1864). A one-sided but important defense of Butler.

Plantation Diary of the Late Mr. Valcour Aime (New Orleans, 1878). The published MS diary of a progressive St. James sugar planter.

Reid, W., *After the War* (New York, 1866).

Rhodes, James Ford, *History of the United States from the Compromise of 1850*, 7 vols. (New York, 1892).

Roberts, D. C., *Southern Sketches* (Jacksonville, Fla., 1865). Invaluable reminiscences of a unionist printer who worked on several New Orleans dailies before the war.

Russell, R., *North America, Its Agriculture and Climate; etc.* (Edinburgh, 1857). A good geography for its time.

Smedes, S. D. (Mrs.), *Memorials of a Southern Planter* [Thomas Smith Gregory Dabney] (New York, 1887). A classic on the life of a Mississippi planter, and his difficult adjustments to reconstruction.

Taylor, Richard, *Destruction and Reconstruction* (New York, 1879). One of the best books of reminiscences by a Confederate general, with many observations on Louisiana, his home and battlefield.

Tompkins, F. H., *North Louisiana, Its Soil, Climate, Productions, Health, Schools, etc.* (Cincinnati, 1886).

Trowbridge, J. T., *The South* (Hartford, 1866).

Watson, William, *Life in the Confederate Army* (New York, 1888). What happened among politicians at Baton Rouge in 1860–61, and among Louisiana troops sent to Missouri, told by a Scotsman who unwillingly fought with the Confederates. Like Roberts, he believes secession was the conspiracy of a minority in Louisiana.

IX—TRAVEL BOOKS

Ampere, J. J., *Promenade en Amérique*, 2 vols. (Paris, 1855).

Brackenridge, H. M., *Views of Louisiana* (Pittsburgh, 1814).

Buckingham, J. S., *The Slave States of America*, 2 vols. (London, 1842).

Burn, J. D., *Three Years Among the Working Classes in the United States During the War* (London, 1865).

Butler, F. A. (Kemble), *Journal*, 2 vols. (Philadelphia, 1835).

——, *Journal of a Residence on a Georgia Plantation* (New York, 1863).

Campbell, Sir G., *White and Black* (London, 1879).

Coulon, G. A., *350 Miles in a Skiff through the Louisiana Swamps* (New Orleans, 1888).

Creecy, J. R., *Scenes in the South* (Washington, 1860).

Darby, Wm., *A Geographical Description of the State of Louisiana* (New York, 1817).

——, *The Emigrants' Guide* (New York, 1818).

Featherstonhaugh, G. W., *Excursion Through the Slave States*, 2 vols. (London, 1844).

Flint, T., *Recollections of the Last Ten Years, etc.* (Boston, 1826).

Hall, A. O., *The Manhattaner in New Orleans* (New York, 1851).

Hall, B., *Travels in North America in the Years 1827-28*, 3 vols. (Edinburgh and London, 1829).

Ingraham, J. H., *The Sunny South; or, The Southerner at Home* (Philadelphia, 1860).

Kingsford, W., *Impressions of the West and South* (Toronto, 1858).

Latham, H., *White and Black* (London, 1867).

Lyell, Sir C., *Travels in the United States*, 2 vols. (London, 1845).

——, *A Second Visit to the United States of North America*, 2 vols. (New York, 1849).

Mackay, A., *The Western World*, 2 vols. (Philadelphia, 1849).

Martineau, H., *Retrospect of Western Travel*, 3 vols. (London, 1838).

——, *Society in America*, 3 vols. (New York, 1837).

Mereness, N. D., editor, *Travels in the American Colonies* (New York, 1916).

Murray, C. A., *Travels in North America 1834-36*, 2 vols. (New York, 1839).

——, *Travels in North America*, 2 vols. (London, 1854).

Nolte, V., *Fifty Years in Both Hemispheres* (New York, 1854).

Nordhoff, C., *The Cotton States in the spring and summer of 1875* (New York, 1876).

Oldmixon, J. W., *Transatlantic Wanderings* (London, 1855).

Olmsted, F. L., *The Cotton Kingdom*, 2 vols. (New York, 1861).

——, *A Journey in the Back Country* (London, 1860).

——, *A Journey in the Seaboard Slave States* (New York, 1856).

——, *A Journey Through Texas; or, A Saddle-Trip on the Southwestern Frontier* (New York, 1857).

Poussin, G. T., *The United States; Its Power and Progress* (Philadelphia, 1851).

Power, Tyrone, *Impressions of America 1833–35*, 2 vols. (Philadelphia, 1836).

Pulszky, F. and T., *White, Red, Black*, 2 vols. (New York, 1853).

Robertson, John B., *Handbook from the Ohio to the Gulf, etc.* (Memphis, 1871–72).

——, *Memorials and Explorations* (New Orleans, 1867).

Russell, W. H., *My Diary North and South*, 2 vols. (Boston, 1863).

——, *Pictures of Southern Life, Social, Political, and Military* (London, 1861).

Somers, Robert, *The Southern States since the War, 1870–71* (London, 1871).

Sterling, J., *Letters from the Slave States* (London, 1857).

Tasistro, L. F., *Random Shots and Southern Breezes*, 2 vols. (New York, 1842).

Thwaites, R. G., editor, *Early Western Travels, 1748–1846; A Series of Annotated Reprints, etc.*, 32 vols. (Cleveland, 1904–7).

Trollope, F. M. (Mrs.), *Domestic Manners of the Americans*, 2 vols. (London, 1832).

Van Buren, A. deP., *Jottings of a Year's Sojourn in the South* (Battle Creek, 1859).

X—Secondary Books

Arthur, S. C. and Huchet de Kernion, G. C., *Old Families of Louisiana* (New Orleans, 1931).

Bailey, L. H., *Cyclopedia of American Agriculture*, 4 vols. (New York, 1907–9).

Bancroft, F., *Slave-Trading in the Old South* (Baltimore, 1931).

Bassett, J. S., *Slavery in the State of North Carolina* (Baltimore, 1890).

Beard, Charles and Mary R., *The Rise of American Civilization* (New York, 1927).

Belisle, J. G., *History of Sabine Parish* (Many, La., 1912).

Bennett, H. H., *The Soils and Agriculture of the Southern States* (New York, 1921).

Blaine, J. G., *Twenty Years of Congress* (Norwich, Conn., 1884–86).

Bowman, I., *Forest Physiography* (New York, 1911).

Boyd, M. C., *Alabama in the Fifties* (New York, 1931).

Brink, F. R., "Literary Travellers in Louisiana between 1803 and 1860" [unpublished master's thesis] (Louisiana State University, 1929).

Brown, W. G., *The Lower South in American History* (New York, 1902).

Butler, P., *Judah P. Benjamin* (Philadelphia, 1907).

Carman, H. J., *Social and Economic History of the United States* (Boston, 1934).

Chinard, G., *Thomas Jefferson* (Boston, 1933).

Christian, J. T., *A History of the Baptists of Louisiana* (Nashville, 1923).

Cole, A. C., *The Whig Party in the South* (Washington, 1913).

Condon, J. F., *Annals of Louisiana 1815–1861* (New Orleans, 1882).

Dabney, C. W., *Universal Education in the South*, 2 vols. (Chapel Hill, N. C., 1936).

Dodd, W. E., *The Cotton Kingdom: etc.* (New Haven, 1919).

Dondore, D. A., *The Prairie and the Making of Middle America: Four Centuries of Description* (Cedar Rapids, Ia., 1926).

DuBois, W. E. B., *Black Reconstruction in America* (New York, 1935).

———, *The Negro Farmer* (Washington, 1906).

Dumond, D. L., *The Secession Movement, 1860–1861* (New York, 1931).

——, editor, *Southern Editorials on Secession* (New York, 1931).

Dunning, W. A., *Reconstruction, Political and Economic* (New York, 1907).

Dyer, C. W., *Democracy in the South Before the Civil War* (Nashville, 1905).

Evans, M., *A Study in the State Government of Louisiana* (Baton Rouge, 1932).

Fay, E. W., *The History of Education in Louisiana* (Washington, 1898).

Ficklen, J. R., *History of Reconstruction in Louisiana (through 1868)* (Baltimore, 1910).

Fish, C. R., *The Rise of the Common Man, 1830–1850* (New York, 1927).

Fleming, Walter L., *Civil War and Reconstruction in Alabama* (New York, 1905).

——, *Documentary History of Reconstruction*, 2 vols. (Cleveland, 1906).

——, *Louisiana State University, 1860–1896* (Baton Rouge, 1936).

Fortier, Alcée, *A History of Louisiana*, 4 vols. (New York, 1904).

——, *Louisiana Studies* (New Orleans [1894]).

Gaines, F. P., *The Southern Plantation* (New York, 1925).

Gayarré, C. E. A., *History of Louisiana*, 4 vols. (New York, 1866); 4th ed. (New Orleans, 1903).

Gray, L. C., *History of Agriculture in the Southern United States to 1860*, 2 vols. (Washington, 1933).

Hammond, M. B., *The Cotton Industry* (n. p., 1897).

Harris, D. W. and Hulse, B. M., *The History of Claiborne Parish* (New Orleans, 1886).

Hesseltine, W. B., *A History of the South* (New York, 1936).

——, *Ulysses S. Grant, Politician* (New York, 1935).

Hicks, J. D., *The Populist Revolt; a History of the Farmers' Alliance and People's Party* (Minneapolis, 1931).

Holst, H. E. von, *The Constitutional and Political History of the United States*, 8 vols. (Chicago, 1881–92).

Jameson, J. F., editor, *Correspondence of John C. Calhoun* (American Historical Association Report, 1899), II.

Kendall, J. S., *History of New Orleans*, 3 vols. (Chicago and New York, 1922).

King, E., *The Great South* (Hartford, Conn., 1875).

King, G. and Ficklen, J. R., *History of Louisiana* (New York, 1897).

Lewinson, Paul, *Race, Class and Party* (New York, 1932).

Lonn, Ella, *Desertion during the Civil War* (New York, 1928).

———, *Reconstruction in Louisiana after 1868* (New York and London, 1918).

McMaster, J. B., *A History of the People of the United States during Lincoln's Administration* (New York, 1927).

———, *A History of the People of the United States from the Revolution to the Civil War*, 8 vols. (New York, 1910).

McTyeire, H. N., *A History of Methodism* (Nashville, 1884).

Marchand, S. A., *The Story of Ascension Parish, Louisiana* (Baton Rouge, 1931).

Merriam, C. E., *A History of American Political Theories* (New York, 1924).

Mitchell, B., *Frederick Law Olmsted, A Critic of the Old South* (Baltimore, 1924).

Moody, V. A., *Slavery on Louisiana Sugar Plantations* (New Orleans, 1924).

Moore, A. B., *Conscription and Conflict in the Confederacy* (New York, 1924).

Morison, S. E. and Commager, H. S., *The Growth of the American Republic*, rev. ed. (New York, 1937).

Nicholson, J. W., *Stories of Dixie* (New York, 1915).

Osterweis, R., *Judah P. Benjamin* (New York, 1933).

Owsley, F. L., *State Rights in the Confederacy* (New York, 1925).

Parsons, V., "A Study of the Activities of the Board of Health from 1855 to 1896 in Reference to Quarantine" [unpublished master's thesis] (Tulane University, 1932).

Phelps, A., *Louisiana; A Record of Expansion* (Boston, 1905).

Phillips, U. B., *American Negro Slavery* (New York, 1918).

——, *Life and Labor in the Old South* (Boston, 1929).

Polk, W. M¹, *Leonidas Polk, Bishop and General*, 2 vols. (New York, 1915).

Posey, W. B., *The Development of Methodism in the Old Southwest 1783–1824* (Nashville, 1933).

Prentiss, G. L., editor, *A Memoir of S. S. Prentiss* (New York, 1899).

Prichard, M. E. W., "Louisiana and the Compromise of 1850" [unpublished master's thesis] (Louisiana State University, 1929).

Randall, J. S., *The Civil War and Reconstruction* (Boston, 1937).

Redford, A. H., *History of the Organization of the Methodist Episcopal Church, South* (Nashville, 1871).

Rhodes, J. F., *History of the United States from the Compromise of 1850, etc.*, 7 vols. (New York, 1893–1906).

Rice, S. A., *Farmers and Workers in American Politics* (New York, 1924).

Rightor, H., editor, *Standard History of New Orleans, Louisiana* (Chicago, 1900).

Rowland, K. M. and Croxall, M. L., editors, *The Journal of Julia Le Grand* (Richmond, Va., 1911).

Rusk, R. L., *The Literature of the Middle Western Frontier*, 2 vols. (New York, 1926).

Russel, R. R., *Economic Aspects of Southern Sectionalism, 1840–1861* (Urbana, 1924).

Saxon, Lyle, *Old Louisiana* (New York, 1929).

Schlesinger, A. M., *The Rise of the City, 1878–1898* (New York, 1933).

Schouler, James, *History of the United States of America, under the Constitution*, 7 vols. (New York, 1894–1913).

Schwab, J. C., *Confederate States of America, 1861–1865: etc.* (New York, 1901).

Scott, N. and Spratling, W. P., *Old Plantation Houses in Louisiana* (New York, 1927).

Sears, L. M., *John Slidell* (Durham, N. C., 1925).

358 ORIGINS OF CLASS STRUGGLE IN LOUISIANA

Semple, E. C., *American History and Its Geographic Conditions* (Boston, 1903).

Simkins, F. B., *The Tillman Movement in South Carolina* (Durham, 1926).

Simkins, F. B. and Woody, R. H., *South Carolina during Reconstruction* (Chapel Hill, 1932).

The South in the Building of the Nation: a History of the Southern States, etc., 13 vols. (Richmond, 1909–13). Esp. J. C. Ballagh, editor, *Economic History, 1607–1865*, V; *Economic History, 1865–1910*, VI.

Stephenson, G. M., *Political History of the Public Lands from 1840 to 1862, etc.* (Boston, 1917).

Thompson, Holland, *From the Cotton Field to the Cotton Mill; etc.* (New York, 1906).

——, *The New South; a Chronicle of Social and Industrial Evolution* (New Haven, 1920).

Thompson, M., *The Story of Louisiana* (Boston, 1889).

Turner, F. J., *The United States, 1830–1850* (New York, 1935).

Vance, R. B., *Human Factors in Cotton Culture; A Study in the Social Geography of the American South* (Chapel Hill, 1929).

——, *Human Geography of the South* (Chapel Hill, 1932).

Voss, L., *History of the German Society of New Orleans* (New Orleans, 1927).

Warmoth, H. C., *War, Politics and Reconstruction; Stormy Days in Louisiana* (New York, 1930).

Wertenbaker, T. J., *Patrician and Plebeian in Colonial Virginia* (Charlottesville, Va., 1910).

Woodburn, J. A., *Life of Thaddeus Stevens* (Indianapolis, 1913).

XI—Secondary Articles

Abbott, H. L., "The Lowlands of the Mississippi," *The Galaxy*, V (1868).

Abernethy, T. P., "Social Relations and Political Control in the Old Southwest," *Mississippi Valley Historical Review*, XVI (March, 1930), 529–37.

Arnold, B. W., "Virginia Women and the Civil War," *Southern History Association Publications*, II, 256–58.

Barker, E. C., "Notes on the Colonization of Texas," *Mississippi Valley Historical Review*, X (March, 1924), 147, 149.

Boyd, W. K., "Ad Valorem Slave Taxation, 1858–1860," in *Trinity College* [N. C.] *Historical Papers*, Series V (1905), 31–38.

——, "Some Phases of Educational History in the South since 1865," *Studies in Southern History and Politics* (New York, 1914), 259–87.

Brewer, W. M., "Poor Whites and Negroes in the South since the Civil War," *Journal of Negro History*, XV (January, 1930), 26–37.

Brown, E. S., editor, "Letters from Louisiana, 1813–1814," *Mississippi Valley Historical Review*, XI.

Buck, P. H., "The Poor Whites of the Ante-Bellum South," *American Historical Review*, XXXI (October, 1925), 41–54.

Burns, F. P., "White Supremacy in the South," *Louisiana Historical Quarterly*, XVIII (July, 1935), 581–616.

Campbell, E. F., "New Orleans at the Time of the Louisiana Purchase," *Geographical Review*, XI.

Cason, C. E., "Middle Class and Bourbon," *Culture in the South*, W. T. Couch, editor (Chapel Hill, 1934).

Cotterill, R. S., "The Beginnings of Railroads in the Southwest," *Mississippi Valley Historical Review*, VIII (March, 1922), 318–26.

——, "Southern Railroads, 1850–1860," *Mississippi Valley Historical Review*, X (March, 1924), 396–405.

——, "Southern Railroads and Western Trade, 1840–50," *Mississippi Valley Historical Review*, III (March, 1917), 427–41.

Coulter, E. M., "Effects of Secession Upon the Commerce of the Mississippi Valley," *Mississippi Valley Historical Review*, III (December, 1916), 275–300.

Craven, A. O., "The Agricultural Reformers of the Ante-Bellum South," *American Historical Review*, XXXIII (January, 1928), 302–14.

——, "Poor Whites and Negroes in the Ante-Bellum South," *Journal of Negro History*, XV (January, 1930), 14–25.

Curry, J. L. M., "The South in Olden Times," *Southern History Association Publications*, V, 35–48.

Dart, W. K., "Walt Whitman in New Orleans," *Louisiana Historical Society Publications*, VII (1913–14), 97–112.

Deiler, J. H., *Germany's Contribution to the Present Population of New Orleans*, pamphlet reprint from the *Louisiana Journal of Education* (May, 1886).

Den Hollander, A. N. J., "The Tradition of 'Poor Whites,'" *Culture in the South*, W. T. Couch, editor (Chapel Hill, 1934), 403–31.

Dodd, W. E., "Social Philosophy of the Old South," *American Journal of Sociology*, XXIII, 735–46.

DuBois, W. E. B., "Reconstruction and its Benefits," *American Historical Review*, XV (July, 1910), 781–99.

Farmer, H., "Economic Background of Southern Populism," *South Atlantic Quarterly*, XXIX (January, 1930), 77–91.

Ficklen, J. R., "Origin and Development of the Public School System of Louisiana," *Report of United States Commissioner of Education*, Vol. II (1894–95).

Foster, J. H., "Forest Conditions in Louisiana," *United States Department of Agriculture, Forest Service Bulletin No. 114* (Washington, 1912).

Gayarré, C. E. A., "Historical Notes on Commerce and Agriculture of Louisiana," *Louisiana Historical Quarterly*, II (1919), 286–91.

Grady, H. W., "Cotton and Its Kingdom," *Harper's New Monthly Magazine*, LXIII (October, 1881), 719–34.

Gray, L. C., "Economic Efficiency and Competitive Advantages of Slavery under the Plantation System," *Agricultural History*, IV (April, 1930), 31–47.

Greer, J. K., "Louisiana Politics, 1845–1861," *Louisiana Historical Quarterly*, XII, XIII, *passim*.

Griffin, H. L., "The Vigilance Committees of the Attakapas Country; or Early Louisiana Justice (1859)," *Mississippi Valley Historical Association Proceedings*, VIII (1914–15), 146–59.

Hamilton, J. G. deR., "Southern Legislation in Respect to Freedmen, 1865–1866," *Studies in Southern History and Politics* (New York, 1914), 137–58.

Hamilton, S. A., "The New Race Question in the South," *The Arena*, XXVII (April, 1902), 352–58.

Herron, S., "The African Apprentice Bill," *Mississippi Valley Historical Association Proceedings*, VIII (1914–15), 135–45.

Holmes, G. K., "The Peons of the South," *Annals of the American Academy of Political and Social Science*, IV (September, 1893).

Kendall, J. S., "The Municipal Elections of 1858," *Louisiana Historical Quarterly*, V.

Kendall, L. C., "The Interregnum in Louisiana in 1861," *Louisiana Historical Quarterly*, XVI (April, 1933), 175–208; (July, 1933), 374–408; (October, 1933), 639–69; also see (January, 1934).

Kendrick, B. B., "Agrarian Discontent in the South: 1880–1900," *Annual Report of the American Historical Association*, I (1920), 267–72.

Koch, J., "Origins of New England Protestantism in New Orleans," *South Atlantic Quarterly*, XXIX (January, 1930), 60–76.

Lestage, H. O., Jr., "The White League and Its Participation in Reconstruction Riots," *Louisiana Historical Quarterly*, XVIII (July, 1935), 617–95.

Lewinson, P., "The Negro in the White Class and Party Struggle," *Southwestern Political and Social Science Quarterly*, VIII (March, 1928), 358–82.

Looney, L. P., "The Southern Planter of the Fifties," *Southern Historical Association Publications* (July, 1900).

McCutcheon, R. P., "Books and Booksellers in New Orleans, 1730–1830," *Louisiana Historical Quarterly*, XX, 606–18.

Moody, V. A., "Early Religious Efforts in the Lower Mississippi Valley," *Mississippi Valley Historical Review*, XXII.

Moore, F. W., "Louisiana Politics, 1862–1866," *South Atlantic Quarterly*, I, 128.

Newton, L. W., "Creoles and Anglo-Americans in Old Louisiana —A Study in Cultural Conflicts," *The Southwestern Social Science Quarterly*, XIV (1933), 31–48.

Overdyke, W. D., "History of the American Party in Louisiana," *Louisiana Historical Quarterly*, VI (January, 1933), 84–91; (April, 1933), 256–77; (July, 1933), 409–26; (October, 1933), 608–27; also XV (October, 1932), and XVI.

Phillips, U. B., "The Central Theme of Southern History," *American Historical Review*, XXXIV, 33.

——, editor, "The Correspondence of Robert Toombs, Alexander H. Stephens, and Howell Cobb," *American Historical Association Report*, 1911.

——, "The Decadence of the Plantation System," *Annals of the American Academy of Political and Social Science*, XXXV (January, 1910), 37–41.

——, "The Economic Cost of Slave-Holding in the Cotton Belt," *Political Science Quarterly*, XX (June, 1905), 257–75.

——, "The Literary Movement for Secession," *Studies in Southern History and Politics* (New York, 1914), 33–60.

——, "The Origin and Growth of the Southern Black Belts," *American Historical Review*, XI (July, 1906), 798–816.

——, "Plantations with Slave Labor and Free," *American Historical Review*, XXX (July, 1925), 738–53.

——, "The Southern Whigs, 1834–1854," *Essays in American History*, 203–29.

Prichard, W., "Routine on a Louisiana Sugar Plantation under the Slavery Regime," *Mississippi Valley Historical Review*, XIV, 168–78.

Ramsdell, C. W., "The Natural Limits of Slavery Expansion," *Mississippi Valley Historical Review*, XVI, 151–71.

Rhodes, A., "The Louisiana Creoles," *The Galaxy*, XVI, 252–59.

Riley, M. L., "The Development of Education in Louisiana Prior to Statehood," *Louisiana Historical Quarterly*, XIX, 595–634.

Roach, H. G., "Sectionalism in Congress (1870–1890)," *American Political Science Review*, XIX (August, 1925), 500–26.

Ruffin, M. M. and McLure, L., "General Solomon Weathersbee Downs," *Louisiana Historical Quarterly*, XVII.

Russ, W. A., Jr., "Disfranchisement in Louisiana (1862–70)," *Louisiana Historical Quarterly*, XVIII (July, 1935), 557–80.

Scroggs, W. O., "The Archives of the State of Louisiana," *American Historical Association, Report of 1912*, 275–95.

Seabrook, E. A., "The Poor Whites of the South," *The Galaxy*, IV, 681–90.

Sellers, J. L., "The Economic Incidence of the Civil War in the South," *Mississippi Valley Historical Review*, XIV (September, 1927), 179–91.

Shugg, R. W., "Negro Voting in the Ante-Bellum South," *Journal of Negro History*, XXI (October, 1936).

——, "The New Orleans General Strike of 1892," *Louisiana Historical Quarterly*, XXI (April, 1938).

——, "Suffrage and Representation in Ante-Bellum Louisiana," *Louisiana Historical Quarterly*, XIX (April, 1936), 390–406.

——, "Survival of the Plantation System in Louisiana," *Journal of Southern History*, III (August, 1937), 311–25.

Smith, W. R., "Negro Suffrage in the South," *Studies in Southern History and Politics* (New York, 1914), 231–56.

Stephenson, G. M., "Nativism in the Forties and Fifties, with Special Reference to the Mississippi Valley," *Mississippi Valley Historical Review*, IX (December, 1922), 185–202.

Stone, A. H., "The Cotton Factorage System of the Southern States," *American Historical Review*, XX (April, 1915), 557–65.

——, "Some Problems of Southern Economic History," *American Historical Review*, XIII (July, 1908), 779–97.

Taylor, A. A., "The Movement of Negroes from the East to the Gulf States from 1830 to 1850," *Journal of Negro History*, VIII (October, 1923), 367–83.

Thomas, D. Y., "Southern Non-Slaveholders in the Election of 1860," *Political Science Quarterly*, XXVI (June, 1911), 222–37.

——, "Southern Political Theories," *Studies in Southern History and Politics* (New York, 1914), 341–64.

Thompson, C. M., "Southern Food Supply—1859–1860," *Proceedings of the American Economic Association*, Supplement to *American Economic Review*, XVII (March, 1927), 11–12.

White, M. J., "Louisiana and the Secession Movement of the Early Fifties," *Mississippi Valley Historical Association Proceedings*, VIII.

Whittington, G. P., "Thomas O. Moore," *Louisiana Historical Quarterly*, XIII.

Wood, E. O., "Public Education in Louisiana During the Reconstruction Period 1866–1876," *Journal of the Louisiana Teachers Association*," IX (March, 1932), 30–34.

INDEX

Levees, 3, 5, 90, 93, 192, 194, 248; in New Orleans, 41.

Lincoln, President Abraham, 161, 197, 206, 210, 211.

Livestock, 12, 15, 45, 101-2, 309; lost in War, 193.

Lockett, Samuel H., 306, 308, 332.

Lumbering, 12, 15-16, 46-7, 263, 268-9.

Malaria, 6, 55.

Manufactures, & cheap labor, 23, 117, 294-6, 299-300; in New Orleans, 117, 290, 292, 293, 295, 300.

Materialism, 34, 36-8, 278-80.

Mechanics' lien, 147.

Merchants, 25, 110; in New Orleans, 25; in politics, 128, 131, 133, 134-8, 140-41, 147, 152, 155, 157, 161; losses in War, 186-7, 194; newly rich, 278; rural, 43, 44; save plantation system, 250-51.

Methodists, 64-5, 66, 67-8.

Miscegenation, 43, 46, 144, 221, 223, 310.

Moore, Gov. Thomas O., 161, 166, 168, 178, 181.

Mortality rates, ante-bellum, 6 n.27, 51-2, 53, 55, 94; infant, 55; post-bellum, 283, 285-7.

Mortgages, plantation, 32 n.70, 110-11, 192, 246, 250-51, 261; urban, 296.

Natchitoches, La., 42-3, 45, 81.

Native American party, Nativism, 128, 147, 159-60.

Negro, free, civil rights of, 222-3; coercion of, 212-15, 217, 230-31, 242-3, 260, 302; demands suffrage, 215-16; in New Orleans, 118-19; in reconstruction, 197, 206-7, 212-17, 220-24, 227, 229, 242-3; voting by, before War, 144.

New Orleans, 1-2, 8, 16, 17, 24, 27, 35, 36-7, 53-4, 55, 56, 58-9, 72, 111-13; churches, 63-4; in election 1860,

161; in reconstruction, 201, 216-17, 224, 225, 228-9, 230, 232; & secession, 163, 169; sections of, 38-9, 283-6; slums, 53; War boom, 188-9; workhouses, 60, 297.

New Orleans Crescent, 118, 150, 341.

New Orleans Picayune, 163, 167, 170, 253, 254, 261, 262, 341-2.

New Orleans Savings Institution, depositors in, 1859, 26.

New Orleans Tribune, 215.

Newspapers, rural, 44, 54, 142-3, 342-4; urban, 60, 62, 340-42.

Nicholson, J. W., quoted, 72-3.

Nonslaveholders, 22-3, 24-5, 318; accept War, 174-5; distribution of, 24-5; in cotton, 25; in New Orleans, 25-6; in sugar, 24-5; life of, 49-50; oppose secession, 164-6, 325; & poor whites, 20, 22-3; & slavery, 146.

Nordhoff, Charles, quoted, 226, 228, 231-2, 261.

Northerners, in La., 15, 43, 47, 58, 157, 194, 201-2, 220, 248, 249, 264.

Occupations, distribution of, 1850, 16, 113, 330-31; 1860, 319-21; 1870-90, 330-31; post-War shifts in, 289-90, 295.

Olmsted, Frederick Law, 9, 12, 26, 103, 118; quoted, 22, 38, 49-50, 104.

Opelousas, La., 49, 50, 65, 73.

Opera, French, 33, 35.

Orphanages, 57, 63, 191, 297.

Orr, Benjamin, 209.

Overseers, 24, 28, 92, 176, 247, 266.

Panic, of 1837, 124, 126, 134; 1873, 228, 262, 296, 299, 303; 1893, 297.

Parks, urban, 281-2.

Pauperism, see Unemployment, Vagrancy.

Penitentiary, state, 60-61, 66, 115-16.

Phillips, Ulrich B., quoted, 6, 94, 236.

Pinchback, P. B. S., 221, 222.

"Piney woods," 9, 10-11, 44-5.